The Low Countries

Cover:

Marijke van Warmerdam.

Shower. 1995.

Schiphol Station.

Photo courtesy Galerie van

Gelder, Amsterdam

TLC

2006 The Low Countries

ARTS AND SOCIETY IN FLANDERS AND THE NETHERLANDS

14

**Published by
the Flemish-Netherlands
Association**
Ons Erfdeel vzw

Contents

Chronicle

With warm regards
from foreign parts

T.

Printed in Germany

Sort. 17/6

Met Office
Fitzroy Road
Exeter
Devon EX1 3PB
United Kingdom

I hate travelling and explorers. Yet here I am proposing
to tell the story of my expeditions
(Claude Levy-Strauss, Tristes Tropiques)

Why does someone take the trouble to get up and go somewhere, to travel? Out of boredom or curiosity? Or restlessness? Or because he once had to follow his herds or his empty belly? For all these reasons and a good many more beside. In the best case he becomes wiser for his travels. Because he has to hone his prejudices on those of other people, because he discovers different conventions which render his own more fragile and more precious.

The travels in this book go to and from the Low Countries. The travellers are tourists who produce statistics, they are writers and artists who sometimes proclaim the journey itself a work of art. In the thirteenth century a Flemish monk journeys to the Mongols *'with his eyes wide open and a steadfast heart'* to convert the Great Khan. He comes back with a report on his travels for the King of France. In Frankfurt the De Brys publish their monumental collection of voyages from 1590 on; its illustrations will make their way throughout Europe.

But there are pocket-sized journeys too: from Brussels to Antwerp, for example, along the N1, a road running through deepest Flanders which few people take any more. And a book about travellers must also find space for the incorrigible non-traveller, who stays at home because he agrees with Pascal that all the evils that befall mankind spring from the fact that he can't stay put in his own room. Which brings us seamlessly to the travels of the mind which this book still has in store for you. Through the Netherlands, a country in confusion after Fortuyn and Van Gogh where the Dutch have raised their voices. Through Belgium, that weirdly cobbled-together Absurdistan which sometimes makes one wonder whether it will live to see its two hundredth birthday, now that its people are more and more torn between blood and soil.

On top of all this, the Netherlands cherishes its art in public space and does its best to be simply happy to live in Vinex-Land; in Flanders we tour the monuments to the memory of the Great War. Mystery is on the march in literature and photos. Pop groups hitting the road seek audiences abroad. Rembrandt stays hidden at home and Bruegel travels to Italy. Verhaeren treks through Europe and Khnopf plays the dandy, while in the writer Brusselmans' life *'nothing worthwhile ever happens'*. Leeuwenhoek looks through his microscope and sees for the first time the migrations of bacteria and spermatozoa. *'Who would be so besotted as to die without having made at least the round of this, his prison?'*: so says Marguerite Yourcenar's hero Zeno in *The Abyss*, at the moment when he leaves Flanders for the South, to discover himself, the world and life.

I most heartily invite you to explore the prison of the Low Lands by the Sea. It's worth the trip.

From Ypres to Verdun

Not the memory, but the spectacle...

An Extract from Geert Mak's *In Europe*

At the beginning of 1999 Geert Mak left Amsterdam for a trip through Europe that was to last an entire year. It was a sort of final inspection: Mak wanted to see how the continent was faring at the end of the twentieth century. But it was also a journey through history: he literally followed the tracks of time, through the century and through the continent, beginning in January with the remnants of the Paris World Fair and roaring Vienna; and ending in December in the ruins of Sarajevo.

Throughout that year Mak travelled along with the century, in a twisted maze of routes, past London, Volgograd and Madrid, past the bunkers in Berlin, the perfumed armoires of Helena Ceaucescu in Bucharest and the toy cars in a deserted nursery in Chernobyl. And he spoke with the witnesses: with writers and politicians, with dissidents and high-ranking officers, with a farmer in the Pyrenees and with the grandson of the German emperor, with numerous Europeans, all of whom shared their stories.

This report of Mak's travels deals with the past and what the past does with us. It is about disunity and ignorance, history and fear, poverty and hope, about everything that divides and connects our new Europe.

Ypres lives off the past, off its step-gables, its newly constructed Middle Ages, off the graves and the dead. Ever since 1927, two buglers from the local volunteer fire department meet each evening at eight to sound the Last Post. Riek Van den Kerkhove has been doing it for nineteen years now, Antoon Verschoot for almost forty-six. They pull up on their bicycles, snap to attention, wait until two policemen have stopped traffic, then let the notes echo from the walls of the enormous Menin Gate with its names of 54,896 dead soldiers. A dozen people stand around, looking on. Within a matter of moments it's over, they shake hands with the policemen, the traffic races off across the cobblestones again.

Antoon's broad face shines with amiability. He's retired now, but he continues to do this. 'It's hard sometimes, in the winter, when you've been sitting nice and warm in front of the TV.' Riek says: 'It's an obligation of honour.' He missed the call only once, when he was busy pulling someone out of the water. But otherwise the Last Post is always played, even when a house is burning down at the same time. 'It goes before all the rest, you know?' Antoon says.

When will the emotion of the Great War fade? When will it finally become history? When will the Battle of the Somme become something like the Battle of Waterloo? I'll hazard a guess: within the next ten years. Somewhere between the third and fourth generation, somewhere between the grandchildren – who can just barely remember those involved – and the great-grandchildren the feeling will change. In the great charnel house at Verdun, the daily mass recently became a monthly one. To the south of the Somme a huge airport is now planned, right across two war cemeteries. See here the writing on the wall. Not the memory but the spectacle gradually becomes the crux of the matter.

At the Queen Victoria's Rifles Café, the tables still bear long rows of *vues stéréoscopiques* from the 1920s. For three-quarters of a century the landlord has been earning a handful of francs with his selection of the grisliest stereo photos: corpses caught in the barbed wire, decapitated Germans, part of a horse in a tree. Today, this has all been raised to perfection. In the IJzer Tower at Diksmuide you can stick your nose in a machine and smell the gas. Chlorine gas actually does smell a bit like bleach, mustard gas a little like mustard. In the impressive In Flanders Field peace museum at Ypres you can enter a darkened room for a trip through no man's land, complete with snatches of dreams: what was going on in the mind of a German or British soldier as he went 'over the top'? The room is full of noise and death rattles, full of images of running soldiers, phantoms from a peaceful life before the war: 'Why me? Why us?' Using a computer program, you can pick out a soldier at will and trace the course of his life. I adopt Charles Hamilton Sorley, a student of the Classics at Oxford. He was killed at Loos, 'a bullet through the head'.

There are other approaches as well. At the new *Historial de la Grande Guerre* in Péronne, all the glory and illusions have been stripped away. The military uniforms and equipment aren't displayed upright, but on the floor, like fallen men. Of course, that's how it was, almost everything here once belonged to the dead. But I am afraid the *Historial* will remain the lone exception. Today little cars trundle on rails through the old citadel of Verdun, like in an amusement park ride, and I am sure: in twenty years' time they will be trundling everywhere, through cunning replicas of the trenches complete with rats, excrement and the smell of corpses, the whinnying of dying horses and the cries of the mortally wounded. Slowly the feeling shifts from one of solidarity to one of curiosity.

Along the toll road from Lille to Paris, the Battle of the Somme is only a tap on the accelerator. In the late summer of 1916, 1.2 million people died here, between two exits. The highway runs at a slight distance along the eastern boundary of the battlefield. Drivers are kept informed of that as well, on big brown signs along the road, LA GRANDE GUERRE, the way a famous chateau or a pleasant vintage might be pointed out elsewhere. Then they flash by, back into the serenity of present-day Picardy.

Here the war has already entered the next phase, that of a popular tourist attraction, a mainstay of the region's commercial infrastructure. Everywhere one finds folders promoting these centres of infernal attraction; staying at my hotel – it is February 15, the heart of winter – there are at least three couples who are touring the front lines, the museums compete by offering even more audio and visual effects. For the first time in ages, I can receive Dutch channels on the TV in my room. On the news they're interviewing tourists who were stranded for a few days in a snowbound Swiss village. 'What we've been through!' one tanned woman says. 'We felt just like refugees.' Another one cries: 'Everything, we've lost everything!' – She's talking about a suitcase full of ski outfits and make-up.

From *In Europe* (In Europa. Reizen door de twintigste eeuw).
Amsterdam: Atlas, 2004. pp. 146-148.
Translated by Sam Garrett

In Europe by Geert Mak, translated by Sam Garrett, to be published by Harvill Press.

Arrival & Departure

Travelling to and from the Low Countries

[RAF DE BRUYN]

Over the last 50 years tourist activity has increased considerably all over the world. More people are travelling, more people are travelling more frequently, more people are earning their living from tourism, whole regions have been able to build their prosperity on the development of tourism. In 1950 the World Tourism Organisation (WTO) recorded 25 million international tourists. In 2004 that figure stood at 763 million.

This explosive increase in international tourism depends on a number of factors such as the economic revival after World War II, the introduction of paid holidays for employees, the increasing use of jet aircraft for scheduled and charter flights and the development of a tourist industry. This strong growth could lead one to suppose that the tourist sector is fairly insensitive to external factors. However, this is not so: economic recession and unemployment dampen the urge to travel in afflicted areas, and war, crime and/or terrorism cause affected destinations to lose favour with the average tourist.

Continental Europe has a privileged position in world tourism. On the one hand our continent contains the most important areas of origin from which inhabitants travel internationally. On the other, European countries are among the most heavily visited in the world. Globalisation is ensuring that more and more countries are becoming travel destinations and that the world tourists are coming from more and more countries. For Europe as destination this means that at present just over half of all international tourists are travelling to or within Europe. In the 1950s this was still true of two thirds of all international tourists.

This article looks at how the Low Countries behave as destination, at the holiday pattern of inhabitants and how the authorities act to promote the Low Countries as effectively as possible as a potential travel destination.

Going to the Low Countries: who can resist it?

Although their surface area is limited, the Low Countries offer a rich and diverse palette as far as opportunities for travel are concerned. A coastline of more than 400 kilometres gives you a constantly changing perspective: from the live-

De Panne, Belgian coast.

The Hague.

ly bustle of the Flemish coast to oases of peace and quiet on the Wadden Islands. A varied coastline with a very extensive tourist offering: a whiff of iodine (at the seaside you can get a breath of healthy fresh air as well as a cold nose), but also a taste of culture (just look at all the activities such as *2003 Beaufort*, *Literaal*, *Theater aan Zee* and *Uitblazen* on the Flemish coast). The historic towns of Antwerp, Bruges, Ghent, Leuven and Mechelen in Flanders, and Amsterdam, Rotterdam, Utrecht and The Hague in the Netherlands, all renowned for the arts, provide a second strong offering. From trendy to romantic, each with a rich and unique past, very central, easily accessible and all close together, bursting with life and activities. These beautiful cities offer, individually and in combination, an intense experience of an authentic past and 'cool' novelties.

And let's not forget the Flemish and Dutch green areas where you can walk through wide, flat polders, cycle through beautiful orchards and poetic landscapes, stroll through country villages, or visit picturesque little towns and enjoy delicious regional dishes: Variety is trumps! And what makes the Low Countries so special is the fact that all these things are concentrated within striking distance of each other.

At present the Low Countries attract about 15 million international tourists a year. This is significantly less than the world leader, France (75 million arrivals) but still more than popular holiday countries such as Turkey (13 million arrivals) or Portugal (12 million arrivals). Germany receives 18 million tourists.

Brussels, Grand' Place.

Veere, the Netherlands.

The global character of present-day tourism to the Low Countries is well illustrated by the statistic that in 2003 tourists from at least 219 different countries, from Afghanistan to Zimbabwe, spent a night in Flanders. Despite this enormous diversity in countries of origin, both the Netherlands and Flanders attract visitors principally from their neighbouring countries. Seven out of ten foreign overnight stays in the Low Countries are by people from Germany, France, the United Kingdom and respectively Belgium (for the Netherlands) or the Netherlands (for Flanders). In the case of the Netherlands the dominance of the German market is striking; almost half the total number of foreign overnight stays there can be attributed to the country's eastern neighbour.

In Flanders foreign tourists prefer to stay in the larger cities, Antwerp, Bruges, Brussels and Ghent. This is partly due to recreational city breaks and partly to business travel. At the same time the cities attract the most international public. Visitors from the USA, Japan or Spain are no exception there. The attraction of the coast and the countryside to foreigners is limited more to the neighbouring countries. A considerable volume of foreign overnight stays results from the creation of a limited number of large-scale holiday villages.

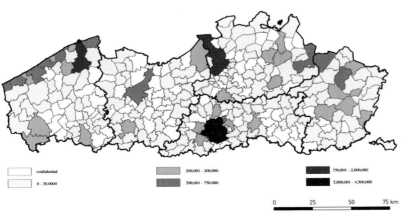

Overnight stays by foreigners in Flanders (2003)

	confidential		200,001 - 200,000		750,001 - 2,000,000
	0 - 20,0000		200,001 - 750,000		2,000,001 - 4,500,000

0   25   50   75 km

Seven out of ten foreign overnight stays in the Netherlands are concentrated in the three western provinces of North Holland, South Holland and Zeeland. North Holland in particular has an exceptional position because of Amsterdam and Haarlem. You are least likely to meet a foreign tourist in the north-eastern provinces of Drenthe and Groningen (Friesland being an exception among these provinces).

Moreover, for the last half century the Low Countries have benefited from a constant increase in foreign interest. If we look at stays in hotels and boarding-houses alone we can see that stays in Belgium are now five times higher, and in the Netherlands six times higher. The greatest increase is in the foreign tourist segment, certainly in Belgium. There we now have at least twelve times as many foreign overnight stays compared to the early fifties, and in the Netherlands eight times as many.

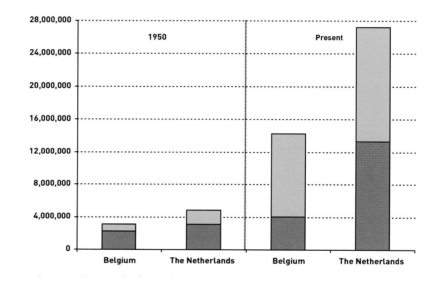

Growth in overnight stays in hotels by country of origin

 home market

foreign market

In the space of fifty years in Belgium the proportion of home (non-foreign) as opposed to foreign stays has completely reversed. At the beginning of the 1950s the proportion of home stays was 70%, in 2003 only 30%. This is another clear indication of the increased international character of tourist travel to the Low Countries.

Travelling in the Low Countries: why do we prefer to stay in our own region?

The Dutch are very loyal to their own country: a good half of all Dutch holidays are taken in the Netherlands. Within the Netherlands, after the coastal region, the province of Gelderland (situated in the centre of the Eastern Netherlands) sees the most home holidaymakers every year. Among other things it has such major attractions as the Veluwe, the Gelderland Rivers Area and the Achterhoek. The second most important province is Zeeland, with a number of attractive North Sea resorts and the Delta Area.

Veluwe, the Netherlands.

The Belgians are more likely to look beyond their borders, with less than a quarter of all Flemish holidays being taken in Flanders. This was not always the case; in the sixties about half of the total of Flemish holidays were taken within their own region.

In those days the coast was, and still is, the most popular holiday location within the home region. Six out of ten Flemings taking a holiday in Flanders do so in one of the ten Flemish seaside resorts. Some forty years ago the Flemish coast accounted for more than seven out of ten Flemish holidays within Flanders. The coast as a traditional seaside and sunshine destination has without a doubt suffered from the rise of mass tourism to the South. At present it continues to compete with destinations with guaranteed sunshine. For this reason, in recent years the way the coast is presented has been adapted to offer more than the beach alone.

The remainder of holidays for Flemish families within Flanders tend towards small-scale accommodation in the country or in one of the large holiday parks (Center Parcs, Sunparks,...). The Flemish towns with an art history, and Brussels, have a great pull for the foreign clientele, but are visited by the home market more on a day-trip basis. The number of Flemings making overnight stays in these towns is rather limited.

In addition to a preference for their own country, the Flemish and the Dutch also have a great liking for ... each other! Seven out of ten Dutch holidaymakers on a short break in Belgium opt for Flanders, the rest for the Walloon area. It may come as a surprise, but you won't find many of them on the Flemish coast. No, the majority of Dutch people in Flanders are to be found in the green areas, where there are a number of large holiday parks that nearly half the Dutch clientele in those areas regard as their own.

At the moment, after France, the Netherlands is the Flemings' favourite travel destination for a short break. Every year we have almost 600,000 Flemish holidays in the Netherlands (in the other direction there are roughly double the number of Dutch holidays in Flanders). The Flemish are to be found principally in the North Sea coastal resorts, the cities (Amsterdam, Rotterdam, The Hague, Haarlem and Utrecht) and West and Central Brabant.

Flemish and Dutch people happily disperse to the most varied and remote corners of the earth. In the Low Countries a great many people go on holiday; at least eight out of ten Dutch people and almost three out of four Flemish people go on holiday at least once a year. These figures are among the highest in the world.

The thirst for travel of people from the Low Countries translates into a series of well-known phenomena such as the great trek south in the summer months. Masses of both the Flemish and the Dutch take their summer holidays in France. The Dutch make over 30 million overnight stays there every year. For the Fleming France is holiday destination number one, be it for a short trip or a long stay.

With Spain as their second most important holiday destination Flemings are making a statement about their hankering for the Mediterranean when it comes to taking a holiday. The Dutch tend to look to Belgium and Germany before thinking about Spain. The neighbouring countries play a leading role as destinations for both short and long stays. For a long time Belgium has been the prime favourite among the Dutch for a short trip, and it still is.

Turkey is the rising star in the holiday firmament for people from the Low Countries. In the space of ten years the number of Dutch holidays in the land of Mustafa Kemal Atatürk increased fourteen-fold, and the number of Flemish holidays in Turkey quadrupled.

Number of Flemish and Dutch holidays abroad

	FLEMINGS			DUTCH	
Destination	Number of holidays (x 1,000)	Number of Percentage (x 1,000)	Destination	holidays	Percentage
France	2,130	29%	France	2,880	17%
Spain	1,133	15%	Germany	2,419	15%
Italy	609	8%	Belgium	2,279	14%
Netherlands	594	8%	Spain	1,648	10%
Germany	509	7%	Austria	1,112	7%
Austria	350	5%	Great Britain	770	5%
Turkey	326	4%	Italy	768	5%
Great Britain	243	3%	Turkey	711	4%
Other	1,535	21%	Other	3,876	24%
Total foreign	**7,429**	**100%**	**Total foreign**	**16,463**	**100%**

Exotic places in other continents can also reckon on a constantly growing interest. In absolute terms these figures remain very low in comparison with foreign holidays in neighbouring countries. An example: the Dutch undertake annually around 160,000 trips to the Far East, as against almost 3 million holidays in France.

The majority of all foreign holidays are still taken in a limited number of countries. About seven out of ten holidays from the Low Countries are in six or so top

destinations. At the end of the 1960s the focus was even more restricted: at that time the six most important destinations still accounted for eight or nine out of ten foreign holidays.

Amsterdam banner on a hotel in Antalya, Turkey.

The increasing desire for travel among people in the Low Countries in recent decades meant that most holiday destinations could profit from an increase in interest. For instance, Dutch people go to France on holiday 11 times more often than 35 years ago, and in the same period Belgium saw an eightfold increase in the number of holidays taken there by Dutch people.

As a result, other countries became less popular with the Belgian holiday-maker. Where at the end of the 1960s Switzerland was the fourth most popular holiday destination, it now has to make do with a twenty-five percent downturn in holiday interest. Italy too, although it can depend on twice as many Flemish holidays as thirty years ago, must concede a share of the market to other sunny destinations such as Greece and Turkey.

What are the Low Countries doing to promote tourism?

In the Netherlands the Netherlands Board of Tourism and Conventions (NBTC) is responsible for the marketing and promotion of that country. In Flanders it is Toerisme Vlaanderen (The Tourist Office for Flanders). Although both organisations face the same challenge, there are a number of differences in their respective briefs and also in their structure and historical background.

The object of the NBTC is the encouragement of tourist and business travel to and within the Netherlands. To this end it develops innovative world-wide marketing and publicity services – including international events and theme years – and so provides added value for partners in the tourist and business travel market, governments and visitors to Holland. The NBTC is active in the area of Holland branding, sales and marketing , PR, market research, data handling, old and new media.

In addition to the same tasks regarding destination marketing Toerisme Vlaanderen also has a brief in the area of physical product development, quality control and social tourism. This means, in concrete terms, that Toerisme Vlaanderen supports local and regional strategic plans and projects, inspects the quality of hotels and camping sites and classifies them in starred categories. Toerisme Vlaanderen develops various programmes for population groups with a low participation rate, aimed on the one hand directly at the population and on the other at intermediary organisations, for example for the building of an adequate supply of accommodation.

Bungee jumping in Scheveningen, Dutch coast.

The broader list of responsibilities for Toerisme Vlaanderen has its roots in history. By the end of the 1930s responsibility for promotion, hotel policy and social tourism had already been brought together in a single national body. When Belgium became federalised a number of social matters were entrusted to the Regions and Communities. 'Leisure and tourism' came under the power of the Communities. The Flemish Community opted to keep the three strands of policy (marketing, quality and participation) within the same organisation, Toerisme Vlaanderen. In this respect Toerisme Vlaanderen holds a unique position; there are few, if any, other examples in Europe of collegiate institutions with the same comprehensive brief.

The NBTC is still a relatively young organisation. It came into being at the beginning of 2004 through the amalgamation of Stichting Toerisme en Recreatie Nederland (TRN) with the Nederlands Congres Bureau (NCB). In the Netherlands the General Association of Tourist Information Offices , Algemene Nederlandse Vereniging voor VVV's (ANVV) was responsible for the promotion of tourism between 1915 and 1968. In 1968 the Nationaal Bureau voor Toerisme (NBT) was established, by the ANVV among others, in order to improve promotion of the Netherlands both at home and abroad. In the 1980s and 1990s there followed a series of mergers of relevant organisations to form the above-mentioned TRN.

Both organisations have undergone the same shifts in accent as far as marketing policy is concerned. Under the influence of new marketing insights promotional activities have focused on PMC's, product-market combinations. The markets are divided between home, neighbouring countries and distant markets. The latest marketing trend in the Netherlands attempts to reflect these divisions in its actions by means of 'proposals', packaging of what is on offer directed at the requirements of specific groups of travellers. Thus the NBTC has the following proposals for the tourist market: Holland City Style, Holland Classics, Holland Beach Fun, Holland Thrills and Holland The Good Life. The business market is tempted with three specific travel products: Let's Meet in Holland, Be Inspired in Holland, and Business With Pleasure. New campaigns stress attractive possible combinations: Vlaanderen-aan-Zee/Flanders by the Sea (Coast and Culture together); Lekker Uit in Nederland/Holidays in Holland; Fietsen en Genieten in Vlaanderen/PedalPLeisure in Flanders ...

Large-scale cultural events have become a 'must' to maintain international attention. Among other things, this 'drive' translates into theme years. Successful campaigns in the past few years have been 2003 Beaufort, Rediscover P.P. Rubens, Fernand Khnopff Retrospective, Corpus Bruges '05,..., Van**Gogh**2003150, Architecture and Design 2004, Rembrandt 400, Water 2005. Finding the occasions to keep on organising large-scale events is a challenge. European collaborative organisations can lend a hand here: Cultural Capital (or

Capitals) of the year (Rotterdam in 2001 and Bruges in 2002), cool**capitals** (the latter is specifically aimed at much-travelled North-Americans), ...

It goes without saying that this sector has also evolved into the e-era. A multi-media approach as the backbone of marketing and advertising campaigns, running personalised marketing campaigns, digital product and image databanks contain all the information needed for making leaflets, following-up mailings, 'shared' image material for journalists (Images of Holland) and so forth. There is a website for every product and every event:

www.vlaanderen-vakantieland.be
www.holland.com
www.lekkerweg.nl
www.water2005.be
www.coolcapitals.com
www.corpusbrugge2005.be
www.vangogh150.nl
www.imagesofholland.nl

One of the posters of the award-winning *'Vlaanderen Vakantieland'* campaign.

On television there are series such as *Vlaanderen Vakantieland* (Flanders Vacation Land), *Bestemming Nederland* (Destination Holland). Joint promotions support worthy causes, e.g. Landelijke Fietsdag (National Bike Day) in collaboration with KWF Kankerbestrijding (Cancer Research).

That these advertising campaigns are also very much appreciated in professional circles is evidenced by the nominations and prizes that the marketing departments walk away with every year. The 2003 advertising campaign 'Vlaanderen Vakantieland blijft je verbazen' ('Flanders Vacation Land never ceases to amaze'), for instance, took four prizes at the Best of Direct Marketing & DRTV Awards; in 2005, winning 'the Gold PAMPA-Award (the absolute top for Flanders) meant that the 'Vlaanderenvakantielandcampagne 2004' could compete at the prestigious Press and Poster Festival in Cannes.

It is not only the private consumer who is showered with attractive leaflets closely tailored to his/her area of interest: the business world is also kept well informed by the newspapers *Informatieblad Toerisme Vlaanderen* and *TRN matchmaker*.

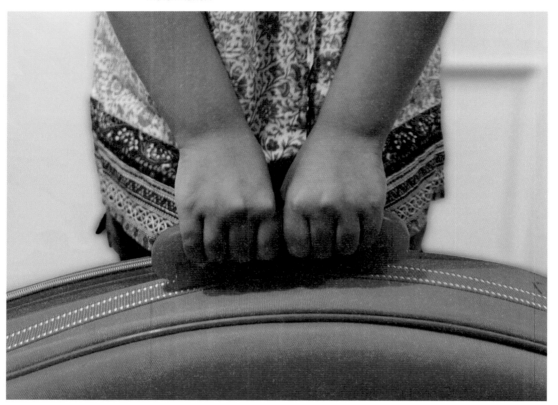

Co-operation?

Do Toerisme Vlaanderen and NBTC work together to promote tourism in the Low Countries? Despite the good understanding between the two NTOs we can't speak of any real structural co-operation as regards promotion policy. There are certainly loose co-operative ventures between Flanders and the Netherlands, such as:

The Coastal Campaign: 'A whole year of the Coast – Enjoyment from De Panne to the Wadden Islands', Belgian and Dutch coastal partners working together to show the 'neighbours' what the coast has to offer.

Benelux Road Show: because the German travel industry presents Belgium, the Netherlands and Luxembourg to the tourist and business market as a BeNe-

Lux-combination, the foreign establishments in Cologne have co-operated; they intend to hold a 2-day workshop every two years.

Inter-regional projects: to encourage co-operation between bordering regions in neighbouring countries the EU provides support for innovative projects; in the recreational tourism field monies from this source provided hikers' huts for cyclists, improved provision for individual boat tours, and so forth.

ETC – European Travel Commission: co-operation in a wider context in the area of marketing and market research. Together with 30 other European NTOs Europe as a tourist destination is being promoted to the long-haul markets and in particular North America.

In Prague the Netherlands and Flanders worked hand in hand to promote the Low Countries. Sadly, a carefully-considered decision to rationalise obliged the NBTC to shed locations such as Prague. In their place come new, very promising markets such as China (an office in Beijing has been opened).

Could the two NTOs cooperate more closely? Clearly, Flanders and the Netherlands each have their own culture and background. The concentration of provision for tourism in this relatively small area is, moreover, so high that retaining separate, independently working organisations is clearly justifiable. Will more extreme globalisation – very palpable in other sectors and in some subsectors of tourism (accommodation, transport, travel industry) – maybe force the public sector to follow suit? For the time being co-operation is confined to a rapprochement on individual projects. ∎

Translated by Sheila M. Dale

SOURCES

ContinuVakantieOnderzoek, CVO 2003

Informatieblad, Toerisme Vlaanderen

Matchmaker, NBTC

NBTC *Jaaroverzicht*, Beleef 2003

NBTC *Jaaroverzicht*, Keuzes 2004

Reisgedrag van de Belgen in 2002, WES Onderzoek & Advies 2003

Structuur en ontwikkeling van het vakantiepatroon van de Belgische bevolking 1967-72, WES 1975

Toerisme in Cijfers 2003, Toerisme Vlaanderen 2004

Toerisme in Nederland, Het gebruik van logiesaccommodaties 2003, CBS 2004

Toerisme Vlaanderen, Annual reports

Toerismestatistieken, NIS

The Adventurous Endeavours of Joost Conijn

Potentialities of Autonomous Travel through Life

[JELLICHJE REIJNDERS]

OK-KUL 09

Spring 2005. On a small airfield in the Czech Republic, Joost Conijn is putting the finishing touches to the aeroplane in which he will soon be setting out on a journey. Holding a can of oil paint in one hand and a brush in the other, he's putting the plane's registration number on the tail. At the O of *OK-KUL 09* the film starts. This opening shot encapsulates months of welding, tuning and testing in one simple, meaningful act. On paper the aeroplane can now fly, but one can't foretell whether it will in fact fly for real. As Conijn suspends two full tanks of fuel under the plane and practises calling the control tower with a Czech airman, the first test flight is coming ever nearer.

At full throttle, he drives the aeroplane down the runway. Just before the end of the airstrip, the plane roars into the sky. Holding his breath, Conijn tempts fate and takes to the air. The plane has no roof. From the open cockpit the artist looks directly down over the edge, the pressure of the air squeezing his features. People, trees and roads are swallowed up in the landscape. The change in perspective gives an overview. Zooming out as he climbs, zooming in as he lands – the aeroplane is an extension of his body and the camera a continuation of his gaze. In a week he will set off on his journey and, on the spur of the moment, he will land on a flat piece of land in a valley, in a field next to a house, just like that. But his plan takes an unforeseen turn and the shots of flying won't actually make the film.

Conijn's work is prompted by his desire to transport himself autonomously from one unknown place to another. With an independent attitude he moves through life, through the world, through the air. Driven by his urge for freedom and drawn by adventure, he heads for the unexpected. Joost Conijn (1971-) makes films in which he undertakes journeys, travelling by vehicles he has constructed himself to go beyond the big road and run into novel encounters, or in which he follows seven feral children on their daily explorations in an area between a city and a free state. Travel as a sequence of unprecedented events, sparked off by his fascination with people and cultures that do not pursue dominant self-complacent doctrines.

Car on roof and *Aeroplane*

Stills from *Aeroplane*
(Vliegtuig, 2000, DVD, 25'):
Courtesy Joost Conijn/
Lisson Gallery.

When he was young, Conijn would set off on his homemade bike as soon as he got a chance. His first long journey took him to India on a reclining bicycle. A few years later Conijn tore round the roof of the Sandberg Instituut, where he went to study after completing his course at the Gerrit Rietveld Academie. In a car consisting basically of four wheels, a small motor and with his own body serving as axle, chassis and bodywork, he was driving in circles, crossing a site of chimney-stack. His feet fastened to the suspension of the rear wheels, his arms jammed between the front wheels, his hands on the controls, he grazed the edges of the tall building. Experimenting with the relationship between the human body and the machine, he was testing his ability to move along under his own steam – in a particularly physical and immediate way. He was taking a risk and took the responsibility for any consequences that the experiment might generate. Anyone watching *Car on roof* (Auto op dak, 1996, DVD, 2.5') in the knowledge that this man-car has no brakes worries that every turn might end in a fall. But for the artist, falling is not an option. Body and soul are fully focused on the plan that for weeks has been his life. There's no holding back; nothing will distract him. Not the danger of the precipice, and certainly not the thought that other people will assume his plan is not feasible. Conijn does not gear his plans to assumptions about what is and what is not possible.

Conijn investigates boundaries of human ability and focuses on possibilities – starting with his own. In 1999, when he was straining every nerve to carry out a test flight in his first self-built aeroplane, he took himself off to the Moroccan desert: the Netherlands is a small country with a lot of rules. *Aeroplane* (Vlieg-tuig, 2000, DVD, 25') was prompted by Conijn's desire to fly independently. For a year he worked on building the aeroplane at De Fabriek in Eindhoven. Onlookers were impressed by his dedication and by his welding skills; the art crowd was particularly taken by the neat metaphor. But the artist really did want to fly.

Stills from *Aeroplane* (Vliegtuig, 2000, DVD, 25'). Courtesy Joost Conijn/ Lisson Gallery.

He transported the aeroplane to a large hangar belonging to the former Amsterdamse Droogdok Maatschappij (ADM, Amsterdam Dry-Dock Company). This hangar was next to his caravan, in the western dock area in Amsterdam, on a disused site occupied by artists, urban nomads, anarchists, non-conformists. It was a fantastic place to work. Lots of space, no restrictions. This is where he prepared the one-man plane for flight, tuned the engine, tested the controls, reinforced the orange canvas around the tail and wings, varnished the propeller, taxied a little way across the field. Some engineers thought his plan was great, but most of the experts he asked for advice preferred to stick to the book. Conijn, however, doesn't want to waste time on formal rules.

At the end of 1999 he left for the Moroccan desert, towing the plane behind his Citroën DS. His efforts were plagued by setbacks. The conditions in the Sahara were difficult. It took time to find a suitable location – a long, level piece of ground to serve as a runway, in a remote area where he could test the plane without being disturbed. A sandstorm blew up and the plane kept breaking down. One morning the engine turned out to have been permanently damaged by overnight frost. But Conijn didn't give in. He called for help from his family and with the new engine block which arrived on a scheduled flight he repaired his aeroplane. The trials were resumed; he raced his plane endlessly over the flattened sand. With that irrepressible willpower as his main motive force, he lifted the aeroplane from the ground and actually flew through the air, against the wind and against all expectations.

C'est une Fence

Three years before *Aeroplane* came out and the level of interest in Conijn's work really took off, he travelled to Morocco to put up a fence. *C'est une Fence* (C'est une Hek, 1997, DVD, 25') begins with his departure. Behind the old Peugeot rolls a trailer full of car parts. The artist is setting off without a script or a definite

destination, allowing himself to be tempted by situations that could take him anywhere. As he travels, he'll find out the course.

After a long journey, Conijn arrives in the Sahara. Sand as far as the eye can see. As far as the horizon and beyond. Not a trail in sight. The bustle of the city and the man from the garage who gestures that he wants to see more money, the last settlements before the desert and the scene with the boy who'd chucked a stone through the Peugeot's rear window are now far away. An immense plain stretches before him. The rules of civilisation have no force in this place; here, the elements rule. The backdrop is impressive. It seems that anything that is installed there just becomes covered in sand and disappears into the greater whole. But then, as the artist is looking for an unknown spot, a figure appears from nowhere. With the timing of a *deus ex machina* in a movie, a man approaches – it's a shot of inconceivable beauty. The man pulls up his motorbike next to the car. Black leather jacket and sunglasses. '*A beautiful place?*' The man laughs in surprise, looks around, points in one direction, points in another direction, waves and disappears from sight. An unlikely encounter. How would one indicate a place in an infinite space?

A beautiful place. Conijn fetches the load from the trailer. Using the mudguards and car doors that he has towed along behind the Peugeot, he builds a construction. It's a fence. In the middle of the sea of sand. The last scene of the film shows him driving at the fence, cutting his speed and stopping just in front of it. The fence hinges open. Calmly Conijn drives the car through the gate into the space on the other side, the unknown planet. He turns the car and comes to a standstill next to the camera. In his element, he laughs into the lens, a bit shy, as though he realises that the moment will never come again. There's the fence, like a beacon in the desert, like a gateway to freedom. Like the realisation of the thought that unlimited freedom is unattainable. The fence opens up a space and locates a momentum. Just as exploring borders is a way of discerning a space or a concept, so travelling appears to be a modus for Conijn to relate to environment as a possibility. Away with prejudices, into the real.

Wood Car

Wood Car (Hout Auto, 2002, DVD, 30') is a film about a journey in a car that runs on wood. Adapted from a method used in the Second World War, the car uses wood for fuel. The search for brushwood is what keeps the car moving. Conijn travels to wooded areas in Central and Eastern Europe. He can pass petrol stations and does not go out of his way to travel on the well-beaten track. He ends up in desolate places, and spends two days in Chernobyl. Rugged mountains, thick forests, little villages, a farm in the fog. The further he penetrates into remote parts of Romania, Moldavia and the Ukraine, the more hospitably he is welcomed. People direct him to a sawmill or give him a little of their winter supplies. A gypsy family helps with the ignition; children run alongside the wood car for as long as they can. Peasant women picking fruit, resting in the grass amongst colourful trees laden with plums, bypass the language barrier by inviting him to share their bread and fresh cheese.

The wood car cheerfully counters expectations, moving at its own speed from event to event, encountering archaic forms of existence. With its friendly appearance – warm varnished skin and flowing lines, looking like a drawing of an archetypal car sketched in one movement – it becomes a most direct intermediary, making friends and prompting spontaneous reactions and bizarre situations. Unlike a deliberate attempt to achieve an invented scenario, the motif of travel comes from curiosity about the unexpected – the unexpected as a road to authenticity.

Siddieqa, Firdaus, Abdallah, Soelayman, Moestafa, Hawwa and Dzoel-kifl

If the focus of his early films is mainly on vehicles and the notion of moving, gradually the camera zooms out to people and cultures who are close to the very basics of life. *Siddieqa, Firdaus, Abdallah, Soelayman, Moestafa, Hawwa and*

Dzoel-kifl (Siddieqa, Firdaus, Abdallah, Soelayman, Moestafa, Hawwa en Dzoel-kifl, 2004, DVD, 40') are seven children in a Dutch family that lives according to Islamic principles. The youngest is three years old; the eldest fourteen. The boys have blonde Mohawks; the girls wear headscarves. They live on the edge of the ADM. Every day the children undertake a voyage of discovery and explore the rough area around the fenced-off sanctuary and the industrial sites ripe for development under the smoke of Amsterdam. They build huts, strip a caravan, find a tree. They make little omelettes, do up bikes, cycle to the Shell shop, try to read together, swim fully clothed in a sun-baked quagmire. They are free to do whatever they do and they make fantastic discoveries.

As they don't go to school and some of the sanctuary squatters won't put up with them, their stamping ground is limited to the corridor between the free state of ADM and the public highway. Their material possessions do not extend much further than a heap of shared clothes, two go-karts, a tricycle, a moped and a couple of much-mended bikes. But the children jump at the slightest opportunity to treat the day as an adventure. The camera follows their unspoiled gaze and opens eyes to the inventiveness with which the children see new possibilities in everyday things.

However, this freedom brings with it a very real danger: exclusion from society. Will they be given the freedom to choose between a freebooting life and a more conventional existence? Their unique quest brings a universal theme to the film: developing your own way of life within a prescriptive context. The film implicitly discusses the socio-cultural limitations that various parties impose on the children's autonomy. But first and foremost Conijn sketches a contagious picture of the children's world – lighting fires, frying eggs, mending bikes – a world that he feels a lot of affinity with. *Siddieqa, Firdaus, Abdallah, Soelayman, Moestafa, Hawwa and Dzoel-kifl* is a disarming manifesto, a tribute to playful inimitability, made out of a desire for authenticity and freedom.

Stills from *Siddieqa, Firdaus, Abdallah, Soelayman, Moestafa, Hawwa and Dzoel-kifl* (2004, DVD, 40'). Courtesy Joost Conijn/Lisson Gallery.

The general meeting of a society in miniature

Stills from *Siddieqa, Firdaus,*
Abdallah, Soelayman,
Moestafa, Hawwa and
Dzoel-kifl (2004, DVD, 40').
Courtesy Joost Conijn/Lisson
Gallery.

Seen from the point of view of the people of the free state, the organised out-side world seems to be a society suffering from a fear of contamination, where individuals who go beyond and challenge the norm are marginalised; a system where the manipulation of images and perceptions is used as a demagogic means of exercising power and prevailing conventions are governed by arbitrary interests. Yet, in some respects, the self-regulated free state seems like a society in miniature. From time to time a fight for territory will break out and here the argument may even centre upon issues such as the borders of the individual, social justice and the integration of newcomers. All residents develop a free way of living and perform a community task that best suits them. DIY talents help with site maintenance, installing the water system, repairing buildings, caravans, boats, washing machines or paving the paths. People who like cooking will bake bread for the community or make the evening meal every now and then. The allocation of roles works itself out automatically.

When he's there, Conijn chairs the general meeting, where conflicting interests are considered. As an honest man with natural authority he invites the parties concerned to give an account of their positions. Questions are asked to clarify the nature of the problem. People who know more about the issue are given a chance to speak and to set forth the conflict as they see it. Conijn analyses the points of view and pinpoints the core of the problem. If no agreement is reached during this process, he proposes a solution that is voted on by those present. The majority view prevails. Agreements are then made about how the solution will be implemented. Conijn does not judge. He creates a situation in which justice can be achieved if those involved take responsibility for it, so that everyone can get back to work again.

An anachronistic constructive counterpart to the status quo

In the early morning of 8 November 2005, Joost Conijn is taken from his bed by a large number of police. Fellow residents of the ADM raise the alarm. The raid, referred to as a 'major inspection', has been brewing for months. The local council is putting pressure on the free state. It probably is all part of a larger operation for political prestige. The city's ragged edges are being tidied up. The uncontrollable practices of wayward social groups are being pushed to the outskirts and slowly but surely driven out. The local media come in droves to record the police unit, backed up by a team of firemen and a cordon of officials, combing the site in search of incriminating material. Shortly before the raid a local council official has fired up the press with a statement insinuating that conditions on the ADM site are intolerable, although nothing along those lines has actually been confirmed. No incriminating material is found, but the media are still eager to go for the insinuations.

On the same day, the artist wins a prestigious art prize: the Cobra kunstprijs Amstelveen. 'The establishment came to throw us out, but then I got an art prize from the establishment,' says the artist on the radio programme Met het oog op morgen. In the interview, he compares the award ceremony and the termino-logy of the jury's report with a local council meeting. Yet he is not dissociating himself from the artistic stage. He is pointing out a convention that is part of the reality in which he operates, a reality in which he consciously positions himself as an independent. The ecosystem of the art world does interest him to a cer-tain extent, but the developments of the free state and some of its residents intrigue him more. Because people do their own thing there, living outdoors and not giving in to formalities. And because it's a place where existential questions – how to live, to survive, to coexist – are all part of everyday life. Whilst most of the ins and outs of the art world seem artificial and predictable to him, this society in miniature still keeps on surprising him, even though he recognises himself in it.

Conijn's film about the children who are repudiated by the ADM is shown on the occasion of the award ceremony at the Cobra museum, to universal praise. The established art world takes a ride on the celebrated artist's wings, and vice versa. But the children cannot come and watch. They have been taken from their caravans by municipal agencies, separated and housed at different secret addresses. First they were looked askance at by some of the fiercer free-state residents and now they're being condemned by society because of the behavi-our of their father? Surely children can't be held responsible for their parents' dogmatic misapprehensions? How can the relevant authorities adopt a superior attitude and firmly maintain that it's in the children's best interests, when no one asks the children? What is civilisation? The film doesn't blunder into thinking in terms of 'us against them'. It doesn't add anything unnecessary, but shows the tender rawness of authenticity.

Structure and development, inimitably natural, infectiously wilful

Siddieqa, Firdaus, Abdallah, Soelayman, Moestafa, Hawwa and Dzoel-kifl was filmed like a nature documentary. Patient and alert, the artist waited for something to happen. The children decided when they had said enough about themselves, and this determined the structure and the end of the film.

In filming and editing, Conijn once again chooses to be guided by the course of events that he finds along the way. From the raw material he selects the individual scenes that carry and articulate his experience, images that could stand alone. He strips them of any excess, throws out the anecdotal and allows their intensity to speak. Then he positions these unfailingly accurate observations within the whole of the film, creating a sense of calm coherence, a unity with a natural, unaffected rhythm. Conijn doesn't impose a narrative on the images, but distils the arc of tension from the sifted material. *Aeroplane* has a clear structure. The viewer is irrevocably drawn along towards a spectacular finale. *Wood Car* has no linear structure of cause and effect. The viewer simply gets in the car and joins the ride.

Conijn's visual language is uncomplicated. Everything is witness to his autonomous mentality and his powerful drive – living life to the full, giving everything. The vehicles he makes, the framing of his shots, the people and the sites he films, they all have their own beauty, like a gentle bend in a river, or a nice, firm stretch of road. Like the incongruity of his appearance. Bright-yellow homemade sandals, leather flying helmet, welding goggles or seventies sunglasses with mirrored lenses – combined with his athletic figure, the result is a casual conspicuousness. It's attractively unconventional. Even though this bravura may help to weave a little mystery around his elusiveness, when it comes to the business of building, travelling, filming and editing, he carries out the task at hand with uncompromising concentration.

OK-KUL 09

In the late summer of 2005 Joost Conijn returns from the Czech Republic. With an unbelievable story and unimaginable pictures. But also with butterflies in his stomach: can he edit the material he has shot to put together the real story? A story of an endeavour to travel the sky. A story about a journey through immense space and a disastrous course of events. About challenging the impossible and exploring the possible, and true fate taking over control. About freedom and about responsibility. The film, which has the working title of *OK-KUL 09*, premières mid 2006. Gallery owners, curators, film programmers, journalists, they all know where to find him. Yet Joost Conijn can't wait to go off on another journey. Maybe to Africa. Perhaps by bike. ■

Translated by Laura Watkinson

Barefoot and on horseback to the Mongols, whom we call Tartars

The Mission of a Flemish monk

[LUC DEVOLDERE]

In terram alienigenarum gentium pertransiet, bona enim et mala in hominibus tentabit – He shall go through the land of foreign peoples, and shall try the good and evil in all people. (Ecclesiasticus, xxxix, 5)

'Vous êtes en Flandre', announces the brown sign along the motorway. The Brussels-London Eurostar tears on through the landscape. I am on my way to Rubrouck, a forgotten village in French Flanders, Northern France, near Cassel. In 1566 Protestant marauders murdered both the pastor and the curate there. Their corpses were dumped in a muddy pond – or did they glide downstream along the IJzer to the North Sea? But I haven't come for the Iconoclasm or a river that here is little more than a brook. At the *Syndicat d'Initiative Yser Houck* they are proud of the village's most famous son, the thirteenth-century Franciscan monk Willem, who swapped the IJzer for the Gobi Desert and saw the Great Khan of Mongolia, but did not convert him. Between 1253 and 1255 he covered sixteen thousand kilometres, sometimes on foot, but mainly on horseback. The story he brought back was forgotten for centuries, though it far surpasses that of Marco Polo, who followed in his footsteps (1271-1295).

A new Flemish giant
in Rubrouck:
frater Willelmus de
Rubruc. Photo by Christine
Devulder & Régine
Dumont/courtesy of
Guillaume de Rubrouck
association, France.

On 14 July 1994, in Rubrouck, the town of Bulgan and this French-Flemish village signed the first French-Mongolian twinning agreement. France does nothing by halves – even in its farthest corners. Two years later the President of the Republic of Mongolia inaugurated the village museum, which is dedicated to Willem and Mongolia. The twinning was celebrated – *noblesse oblige* – with the induction of a new Flemish giant: Willem himself, of course. *'Discover Mongolia in Flanders'* promises the leaflet that they push into my hand at the *Syndicat*. The round Mongolian tent, the yurt, keeps fraternal company with the three altar pieces in the church, Rubrouck's other pride and joy. We've had city marketing, is it village marketing now? Every village does what it can.

Hordes that filled the surface of the earth

Willem, Willelmus, Gullielmus, Guillaume, William: this sturdy Fleming was born here around 1210-1215. After joining the Franciscan order he received his training in Paris, as one of the first generation that hadn't known the saint personally. Around 1250 we find this *lector flandricus*, as a contemporary referred

to him, in the Middle East. It is not clear whether he was already part of King Louis IX's party when the latter embarked in Aigues-Mortes for Cyprus in 1248. Yet again Western Europe was raising men, money and energy for another crusade (the seventh so far). Yet again the men would dwindle, the money would be used up and the energy evaporate. Louis himself was taken prisoner in Egypt in 1250 and only released after a ransom was paid. Was Willem with him? In any case, he knew the Nile Delta and mentions the town of Damietta, which the French had captured.

In December 1248, whilst Louis was preparing for the crusade in Cyprus, envoys from the Mongol commander in Persia arrived, and offered the *'Franks'* a perspective of religious freedom and an an alliance with *'Armenia, Persia and Tartary'*. After the death of Genghis Khan in 1227 the Mongol kingdom had become a new and dreaded player on the chess board of world power. In the spring of 1241 Mongol hordes had conquered Hungary and delivered a crushing defeat to a coalition of Poles, Silesians, Moravians and Templars near the Polish town of Liegnitz. In the winter of 1242, Mongol cavalry crossed the frozen Danube and *'filled the surface of the earth'*, penetrating as far as Split on the coast of the Mediterranean. For Christian Europe this was a rude confrontation with Asian brutalities, carried out by a hundred thousand cavalry, each of whom had another five or so horses behind him. And this at a time when tension with the expansionist Islamic world was increasing.

Guyuk's letter to Pope Innocent IV (1246).

In 1245, Pope Innocent IV sent a French Dominican, André de Longjumeau, with a letter to the Mongolian army's advance guard in Greater Armenia. In the same year he also sent the Italian Franciscan Giovanni de Plano Carpini, who had known St Francis personally, to the Great Khan himself. Carpini set off from Hungary, where the Mongols had wreaked such havoc, through Russia to the Kingdom of the Mongols (*'quos nos Tartaros appellamus'*; 'whom we call Tartars') where, in 1246, he witnessed the enthronement of Guyuk, the son of Ogadei.

When Carpini asked the Khan to convert, he retorted that the Pope and the kings of Europe should first come and swear allegiance to him. If they did not, the Khan would count them as enemies. Carpini was the first European since 900 AD to travel east of Baghdad and return to tell his story, *Ystoria Mongalorum quos nos Tartaros appellamus* (The Story of the Mongols whom we call the Tartars).

In Cyprus Louis IX took over the Pope's diplomatic endeavours. The French King was speculating on an alliance with the Mongols against the Saracens and sent André de Longjumeau on a second journey to the Far East. When Longjumeau reached Mongolia, he heard that the Great Khan Guyuk had been dead for two years already. Guyuk's widow gave him a message for his King that he and his subjects would be annihilated unless he paid an annual tribute. By 1251 Longjumeau was back in the Middle East. Given the failure of this embassy, there was no question of an official diplomatic mission when Willem set off in 1253, after a year of preparations in Constantinople. The French King did give him letters for Sartak, the war lord of the Mongol armies that were encamped closest to Europe, in southern Russia. There were rumours that he had converted to Christianity. It is not entirely clear what Willem's exact intentions were. He himself always stressed that he wanted to preach the faith. He met Longjumeau, who may have talked to him about Germans, *'qui sunt lingue nostre'* ('who speak our language'), and who had been deported by the Mongols to the Far East. Perhaps, as a Fleming who spoke a Germanic tongue, he wanted to give moral support to his linguistic brethren.

The King had probably asked him to keep his eyes and ears open, to try to find out what the Mongols' military intentions were. At any rate, he asked him to report on everything he saw. So on 7 May 1253 Willem set off from Constantinople on a journey to the end of the world – to another world, although he did not know it at the time – armed only with faith, inner strength, robust health, common sense, Franciscan ideals, and loyalty to God and his King. He was in the prime of life, between 35 and 45, and sturdily built. There can be no doubt about his faith, but it did not prevent him from observing the world around him and reporting on it candidly.

Hunger and cold as travelling companions

On 7 May 1253, then, Willem set sail from Constantinople across the Black Sea and landed in the Crimea. He went on from there with four carts, which he later regretted as he would have reached Sartak in half the time with only horses. He was accompanied by Bartolomeo, a Franciscan from Cremona; Gosset, a French cleric; Nicolas, a young slave whose freedom had been bought in Constantinople; an interpreter, who was supposed to speak the Mongols' language but who later proved unreliable; and some drivers.

Having crossed the Don, the travellers reached Sartak's encampment in South Russia (now Ukraine), on 30 June 1253. Louis IX's letter was wrongly interpreted as a proposal to form a military alliance against the Saracens, so Sartak sent Willem further east to his father and hierarchical superior Batu. Batu had acted as king-maker for Mangu, Guyuk's successor as Great Khan, and wielded *de facto* power as ruler of the western part of the vast Mongol Empire. Once he had reached Batu, Willem joined the nomads' trek. On 14 September Batu in turn sent the Franciscan to the Great Khan Mangu. Willem left the French cleric and the young slave behind with Batu and continued south-eastwards with Bartolomeo and the interpreter, changing horses constantly. From there on, hunger and cold were their constant companions. Towards the end of 1253 they reached Mangu's yurt encampment. Initially the Khan showed little interest in Willem, who was obliged to follow the nomads eastwards. On 5 April 1254 he and they reached Karakorum, the capital of the Mongol Empire, located to the south of Irkutsk in the Gobi Desert. He discovered it was no bigger than

A Mongolian horseman in a 15th-century miniature.

Saint Denis, which in those days was just a village outside Paris. Nevertheless, during the brief period when it was at its peak (from 1220 to 1260, when Kublai Khan moved the capital to Beijing) it was the diplomatic centre of the world and received embassies from the Byzantine Emperor, the Khalif, sultans and emirs, the King of Delhi and princes from Russia.

'*There are two quarters in it; one of the Saracens in which are the markets, and where a great many merchants gather on account of the court, which is always near this city, and on account of the great number of ambassadors; the other is the quarter of the Cathayans, all of whom are artisans. Besides these quarters there are great palaces, which are for the secretaries of the court. There are there twelve idol temples of different nations, two mosques in which is cried the law of Machomet, and one church of Christians in the extreme end of the city. The city is surrounded by a mud wall and has four gates.*' The 'church of the Christians' is that of the Nestorians, who had been considered heretics since the Council of Ephesus (431) because they believed that Christ had not only two natures but was also two persons, one human and one divine . Nestorianism had penetrated as far as the Far East and many of the princesses, mothers and wives of the Khans, were Nestorians. Willem considered the Nestorian priests in general

poorly trained and organised. He calls them 'corrupti' ('degenerate'), profiteers and drunkards. In his opinion, they had strayed from the true teaching and adapted too much to their environment. He also informs us that they put no figures of Christ on their crosses because they were either ignorant of His Passion or ashamed of it.

A very special shaman

One of the highlights of Willem's stay was a theological discussion with Muslims, Buddhists and Nestorians, organised by the Khan himself. The debate ended in a draw, the chess pieces were put away and the drinking began. As far as religion went, the Mongols were quite pragmatic. Revelation was alien to them. Their credo seemed to be 'anything goes'. They were guided mainly by their soothsayers, as is clear from the last conversation that our Franciscan had with the Khan, at Pentecost, on 31 May 1254: 'one of the most remarkable interviews in history', according to Christopher Dawson (in: The Mission to Asia). Mangu said that, just as God created different fingers on one and the same hand, he also gave peoples different forms of belief and customs ('ways'). Seventeen centuries after Herodotus gave the West the principles of relativism, this barbarian with a monkey face ('homo simus') expressed the idea – his own idea – that convention is the father of all things. But Willem is no relativist. He had received the training of his time, had Peter Lombard's Liber sententiarum in his travelling bag, and the Bible. We should not expect this man to stand outside or above his own times. His faith knew no doubts. On the contrary, it provided him with an instinctive imperturbability and courage which enabled him to withstand all hardships. 'Vexilla regis prodeunt' he sang, undaunted, bearing the cross high in the air through the Mongols' camp. Again and again, he patiently explained the creed: *'Credo in unum Deum'*. He is prudent and steadfast, and for that alone commands the Mongols' respect. They must have seen in him a very special shaman.

At the end of May 1254 Willem finally received Mangu's permission to return to Europe. The Great Khan gave him a letter for the French King, which said, amongst other things: *'Whosoever we are, whether a Mo'al or a Naiman, or a Merkit or a Musteleman, wherever ears can hear, wherever horses can travel, there let it be heard and known. For the moment they hear my order and understand it but place no credence in it and wish to make war against us, you shall see that though they have eyes they shall be without sight; and when they shall want to hold anything they shall be without hands, and when they shall want to walk they shall be without feet: this is the eternal command of God. (...) And when you shall have heard and believed, if you will obey us, send your ambassadors to us; and so we shall have proof whether you want peace or war with us. When, by the virtue of the eternal God, from the rising of the Sun to the setting, all the world shall be in universal joy and peace, then shall be manifested what we are to be. But if you hear the commandment of the eternal God, and understand it, and shall not give heed to it, nor believe it, saying to yourselves: "Our country is far off, our mountains are strong, our sea is wide," and in this belief you make war against us, you shall find out what we can do. He who makes easy what is difficult, and brings close what is far off, the eternal God He knows.'*

Hulagu Khan, third son of Toloui and brother of Mangu Khan, together with his wife in a 14th-century Persian miniature.

Willem had to leave Bartolomeo behind, as he was too weak to travel. On 18 August 1254 Willem took his leave of him *'in tears'* and set off for the West along a more northerly route. The journey was difficult and exhausting. For two months and ten days he saw neither town nor village. Back in Batu's camp on the Volga, he picked up Gosset and Nicolas, who had been treated as slaves by the Mongols. The journey continued. At Christmas 1254 they were near Mount Ararat, in what is now called Azerbaijan. A year later (1255), he reached Cyprus via Turkey. Louis IX had left for France a year earlier. The provincial of the Order directed Willem to a monastery in Acre, and gave him a teaching assignment. In Acre he wrote the story of his travels, in the form of a long letter to the King.

Post iter omne animal triste? – the post-travel blues

So what had he achieved with his travels? In diplomatic terms: nothing. And as a missionary: only six Mongols were eventually baptised. If one is charitable one might say that the good seed of faith had been planted, sacraments had been administered, one Nestorian converted.

If the objective was to preach the gospel to the unbelievers according to the rule of St Francis, then it had been achieved. When it comes to spreading the gospel, intentions always count for more than results. In the presence of the Great Khan, Willem must have felt like St Francis before the sultan. St Francis himself had said of those who go to the Saracens and other unbelievers that they could deal with them in two ways: *'One manner is, that they cause neither arguments nor strife, but be subject "to every human creature for God's sake" (1 Pt 2:13) and confess themselves to be Christians. The other manner is, that, when they have seen that it pleases God, they announce the word of God'*, even when there are dangers involved: *'And let all the friars, wherever they are, remember, that they have given themselves and surrendered their bodies to the Lord Jesus Christ. And on behalf of His love they ought to confront their enemies both visible and invisible; because the Lord says: He who will have lost his life for My sake, shall save it (cf. Lk 9:24) for eternal life (Mt 25:46).'* (Regula Non Bullata, 16)

Willem followed the rule to the letter. Besides, his belief in the faith is so great that he believes that the Khan would have converted, (*'forte humiliasset se'*) if he himself had only had Moses' power to perform signs. *Quod non.* He had not found the deported Germans but, as we know, the journey is always more important than the goal, the experience acquired more important than the quantifiable result. The opening lines of the *Odyssey* tell us that *'Many cities did [Odysseus] visit, and many were the nations with whose manners and customs he was acquainted'* during his enforced wanderings. More or less the same message is in *Ecclesiasticus* (*The Book of Sirach*) (XXXIX, 5), quoted freely at the beginning of Willem's report: *'He shall go through the land of foreign peoples, and shall try the good and evil in all people.'*

We travel, then, to learn and become wiser. That may not be our intention, but every journey brings us new knowledge and increases that we have already.

Willem was the first to realise that the Caspian was an inland sea, the first to identify Cathay (China) as Antiquity's 'Kingdom of the Seres' and to give a detailed description of the capital, Karakorum. Although he never saw China himself, he discovered from a Tibetan lama that the Chinese used paper money and wrote *'with a brush such as painters paint with, and they make in one figure the several letters containing a whole word.'* He provided a wealth of ethnographic information about the Mongols' way of life. He told of kumiss (fermented mare's milk), which *'makes the inner man most joyful and also intoxicates weak heads, and greatly provokes urine'*; women who didn't lie on beds to give birth; clothes and dishes which were never washed; about a man who had to search for his bride, who was hiding, and abduct her to his house by force. He shared their nomadic existence, searching constantly for grazing land for their horses. (Had

they, perhaps, left Europe in 1242 because their hundreds of thousands of horses had denuded the Hungarian plain of grass?) He described how they took their yurts everywhere with them on large carts.

'*Nusquam habent manentem civitatem sed futuram ignorant*' – 'Nowhere have they any lasting city and of the one to come they have no knowledge'. In this he departs noticeably from the epistle to the Hebrews (XIII, 14): '*Non enim habemus hic manentem civitatem, sed futuram inquirimus*' – 'Our city is certainly not lasting, on the contrary we look forward to the city that will come.' He contributed to linguistics (seeing the link between the Slavic languages) and to comparative religion, in which field his descriptions of Buddhist priests and Mongolian shamans and soothsayers are of great value. He understood the importance of language and interpreters. Willem discovered what it meant to be lost in translation, dependent on bad interpreters, which made it impossible and downright dangerous to explain his faith properly.

Was Willem's letter to Louis IX no more than the ashes of a fire that had died, like every travel story? *Post iter omne animal triste* – all creatures are sad when a journey is over? Did this stalwart Fleming, who had seen the almost endless expanse of the Steppes, the crushing skies above and the snow-covered roof of the world in the distance, manage to adapt again to Christianised Europe? Was his life over after Mongolia? Did he see his stream in Rubrouck again, and think back to the Euphrates? Did he make fun of the West European winters, having seen winter in Siberia? Did he not, for the rest of his life, see the poverty in Acre and Paris against the background of the true face of St Francis' poverty that he had seen in the Far East? We don't know.

In Paris he met the *doctor mirabilis* Roger Bacon, also a Franciscan, and discussed his book with him. Bacon quotes him frequently in his *Opus Maius*, he will have liked the Fleming's empiricism. After his discussion with Bacon in Paris, Willem disappears from view. Did he ever see Louis IX again, or the Holy Land? Or Mongolia? He probably only made the one expedition. What else did his superiors have in store for him? Was he able to find his niche again? What was the last image imprinted on his retina before he died?

The story is copied

A century later, a monk in France (Normandy?) copied Willem's *Itinerarium*. Leiden University Library owns the fourteenth-century manuscript. It is a copy of the best manuscript from the thirteenth century, which can be found at Corpus Christi College in Cambridge (181). The Leiden manuscript is part of the library of Paul and his son Alexandre Petau (Petavius), which Isaac Vossius bought in Paris in 1650 for the library of Queen Christina of Sweden. However, Vossius kept a lot of the books for himself and his books eventually ended up in the library in Leiden.

In the Dousa room of the university library (no walkmans, mobile phones, or cameras, only pencils and whispering), they give me a Plexiglas lectern and a soft cushion for the codex that contains a few historical works about Normandy and Giovanni de Plano Carpini's *Ystoria Mongalorum*. The latter finishes at the bottom of folio 160 with '*explicit ystoria mongalorum quos nos tartaros appellamus*', written in slightly larger letters. The address to Louis IX, with which the *Itinerarium* begins, follows without a break. Only the E of '*excellentissimo*', 'to the most venerable (King)', is decorated with curlicues. There is no sign of a title in this manuscript.

The monk whose duty it was to copy the text did so in a firm, beautiful *littera gothica*. The handwriting is firm and regular. A forest of letters in neat lines completely covers the pages. Willem's report on his travels has been reduced to a compact body of 30 recto verso folios of text. To copy the journey is to go over it again. Travelling in spirit. But it also means writing about the cold with the sweltering heat of a July day outside the scriptorium. What did this anonymous copyist think of as he worked? Or didn't he think? Does copying mean turning the mind off? The copyist forgot just one sentence, or at least he added one sentence afterwards, in the margin at the beginning (f. 162). To write is to make mistakes; to travel is too.

Soon I will be back in the world of mobile phones, walkmans, cameras, noise and non-pencils. But in the meantime I read: '*Scriptum est in Ecclesiastico de Sapiente: "in terram alienarum gentium transiet, bona et mala in omnibus temptabit." Hoc opus, domine mi Rex, feci, sed utinam ut sapiens et non ut stultus: multi enim faciunt quod facit sapiens, sed non sapienter, sed magis stulte, de quorum numero timeo me esse*' – 'It is written in Ecclesiasticus of the wise man: "He shall go through the land of foreign peoples, and shall try the good and evil in all things." This, my lord King, have I done, and may it have been as a wise man and not as a fool; for many do what the wise man doth, though not wisely, but most foolishly; of this number I fear I may be.'

Leafing further, I read about two wise men: *'After that he began confiding to me his creed: "We Mo'al," he said, "believe that there is only one God, by whom we live and by whom we die, and for whom we have an upright heart." Then I said: "May it be so, for without His grace this cannot be." He asked what I had said; the interpreter told him. Then he added: "But as God gives us the different fingers of the hand, so he gives to men several paths. God gives you the Scriptures, and you Christians keep them not. You do not find (in them, for example) that one should find fault with another, do you?" "No, my lord," I said; " but I told you from the first that I did not want to wrangle with anyone." "I do not intend to say it," he said, "for I am not referring to you. Likewise you do not find that a man should depart from justice for money." "No, my lord," I said. "And truly I came not to these parts to obtain money; on the contrary I have refused what has been offered me." And there was a secretary present, who bore witness that I refused an iascot (i.e. 120 francs in gold) and silken cloths. "I dare not say it," he said, "for you. God gave you therefore the Scriptures, and you do not keep them; He gave us diviners, we do what they tell us, and we live in peace." He drank four times, I believe, before he finished saying all this.'*

The last lines of his manuscript deal with the bishop whom the Pope might perhaps send to the Great Khan, and prove the Fleming's good sense and level-headedness: *'(...) oporteret quod haberet bonum interpretem, immo plures interpretes et copiosas expensas'* – 'but he must have a good interpreter – nay, several interpreters – abundant travelling funds, etc.'. The November evening descends on Leiden. The manuscript must be returned. I will get no closer to *frater Willelmus de Rubruc in Ordine fratrum Minorum minimus,* ('the meanest in the order of Friars Minor'). But he was a great traveller, with his eyes wide open and a steadfast heart. ■

Translated by Lindsey Edwards

TEXT EDITION

Itinerarium Willelmi de Rubruc. In: *Sinica Franciscana*, vol. I, Itinera et relationes fratrum minorum saeculi XIII et XIV, collegit, ad fidem codicum redegit et adnotavit P. Anastasius Van Den Wyngaert O.F.M., Florence, 1929, pp. 145-332.

FURTHER READING

Ch. Dawson, *The Journey of William of Rubruck.* In: *Narratives and Letters of the Franciscan Missionaries in Mongolia and China in the thirteenth and fourteenth Centuries. Translated by a Nun of Stanbrook Abbey.* London/New York, 1955.

The Journey of William of Rubruck to the Eastern Parts of the World, 1253-55 as narrated by himself. With two accounts of the earlier Journey of John of Pian de Carpine. Translated from the Latin by W.W. Rockhill. Reprint. First Published in 1900. 1998, 304 p.

The mission of Friar William of Rubruck: his journey to the court of the Great Khan Möngke, 1253-1255, translated by Peter Jackson; introduction, notes and appendices by Peter Jackson with David Morgan, London, 1990.

The translation used is that of W. W. Rockhill. At times, however, Peter Jackson's version has been adopted within that translation.

See also: depts.washington.edu/uwch/silkroad/texts/rubruck.html

From Turpan to Kashgar

The bus is not suitable for foreigners

An Extract from Adriaan van Dis' *A Barbarian in China*

A Barbarian in China is Van Dis' travel report about his journey along the silk route. The title of the book, which became a bestseller in the Netherlands, recalls Henri Michaux' *Un barbare en Asie* (published in 1933, revised in 1945 and translated by Sylvia Beach as *A Barbarian in Asia* in 1949), a pithy, incisive and cutting look at 1930s Asia through this Belgian's eyes.

The driver has only got one eye. I'm not particularly surprised. We've been waiting for four hours already in the chill morning air. I have flapped myself warm like a penguin and am fed up with all the moaning. Just let him start driving soon. Minoroo says that we won't arrive in Kashgar (Kashi) until four days from now, a day later than we were assured yesterday. I'm in a hurry. Winter is approaching, and the more we time we waste, the more snow there'll be in the Khunjerab pass.

The Chinese don't like the idea of quick. They believe a tortoise sees more during a journey than a hare.

One-eye is to take us one thousand two hundred and fifty kilometres through Xinjiang; with on our right-hand side the mountains, behind them the Russian border, and on our left the Taklamakan desert, a world of sand where it's freezing cold in the morning and the midday sun heats up the buckle on your belt so much you burn your stomach on it. We are leaving from Daheyon, the railway station where passengers have to get out for Turpan, an hour's journey into the sand. Not a place to stay long in: two streets of jerry-built shacks, some cooks behind cooking fires, children, women and men in uniform – not a tree, plant or even a banner that exhorts you to lead an industrious and responsible life. Nobody lives here for personal pleasure. Only the children have fun. They lay sheep-bones on the rails, push ramshackle buses and laugh at a couple of idiotic Westerners standing round their rucksacks stamping themselves warm. On this particular morning, they are gaping at Minoroo. Minoroo is a Japanese in a threadbare Mao jacket – only his beard makes him look different. He gets people's attention even so, as everything he asks the Chinese he writes on his hand. Since the Japanese got their written characters from China one thousand five hundred years ago, both peoples can read each other's characters – though without understanding each other. Minoroo's left hand is already blue with ink on both sides.

Valérie tells the driver to hurry up. She is French, is studying Chinese at the Sorbonne and above all is good at swearing. To begin with, I thought she was a man, when I saw her a couple of days ago, muttering beneath a fur hat, standing in front of the ticket office. She was beside herself with rage, as she had already implored them for three days for a seat on the bus to Kashgar. But the answer was always: *Mei you... mei you...* not possible, we don't have. While the Chinese had no problem buying their tickets. 'Why don't you fly to Ürümqi?' a woman behind the ticket-window asked. 'The bus is not suitable for foreigners. You will get cold, get dirty, ill, there are wolves in the desert.'

There is only one asphalted road to Kashgar. The stops where the bus calls are not 'open' to foreigners. Only a non-stop ride has recently been permitted. Official bodies do not encourage the trip. The official authorities are not keen on foreigners straying outside the approved paths. That is why I too am standing in the queue for a ticket. Minoroo's hand has finally helped us get a seat. Minoroo knows the art of smiling. He shows an understanding of things we have little understanding of: that a half-empty bus is called full whenever we want to sit in it and that driver One-eye can only leave when the sun has sufficiently warmed up the engine.

The sun is up, the engine throbbing.

From *A Barbarian in China. A Journey through Central Asia* (Een barbaar in China. Een reis door Centraal-Azië). Amsterdam: Meulenhoff, 1987. pp. 11-12.

Translated by John Irons

Portrait of the Traveller with Burin and Printing Press

The Representation of Dutch Maritime Expansion
in the De Bry Collection of Voyages

[MICHIEL VAN GROESEN]

When the Dutch Republic first embarked on overseas expansion, its impact was immediate. After the meagre profits of the first Dutch expedition to Asia in the late 1590s, the second voyage provided a clear indication of the lucrative possibilities of the trade in pepper and spices. Before the Dutch East India Company was founded in 1602 and given a monopoly of trade outside Europe many smaller companies had tried their luck, and by 1599 eight different companies from various towns and provinces of the Dutch Republic were participating in the East India traffic. While most of these early expeditions opted to follow the 'Portuguese' route around the Cape of Good Hope, several adventurers tried to find alternative avenues to the riches of the Orient: among them were explorers like Willem Barentsz and Jacob van Heemskerck, attempting to find a north-eastern passage, and Jacques Mahu and Simon de Cordes, who sailed westward aiming to emulate Magellan's circumnavigation. Both expeditions ended in disaster.

In the realm of early modern paradoxes that was the Dutch Republic, however, disaster of this type also meant success. Success, in particular, for the Amsterdam booksellers Cornelis Claesz and Zacharias Heyns, whose investments in bringing news of the overwintering in Novaya Zemlya and the tempestuous conditions in the Strait of Magellan provided quick and ample returns. Both narratives, written by Gerrit de Veer and Barent Jansz Potgieter respectively, were avidly read by the Dutch public, and were later included in all the important Dutch compilations of overseas journeys. The appeal of the accounts was also confirmed by the almost instant translations into German and Latin, which appeared within a year of the original publications. These translations were made for the monumental De Bry collection of voyages, published in Frankfurt between 1590 and 1634. This series comprised twenty-five folio volumes containing the cream of early modern European travel accounts. All the journals included were translated into German and Latin, and thus made available to a wider international readership.

Theodore de Bry (who died in 1598; ill. 1) and his sons Johan Theodore and Johan Israel, a Reformed dynasty of publishers and copper engravers, had lived in Strasbourg, Antwerp, and London before moving to the centre of the European book trade, Frankfurt, to set up their own publishing firm in 1590. They introduced the technique of including copper engravings in printed works to Germany, and their beautiful illustrations quickly became the trademark of the firm's publications. The collection of voyages was indisputably the officina's magnum opus, consisting of reports of European expeditions to Africa, Asia, and the New World. Inspired in the late 1580s by the Oxford geographer Richard Hakluyt, a strong proponent of English colonisation of the Americas, the De Brys generated publicity throughout Europe for overseas expansion. To enhance the reputation of this collection they often added new illustrations to the translated accounts, even when the original editions had already included iconographic material. Further modifications were made to the contents of some of the narratives, perhaps less conspicuous but not necessarily less influential. The resulting, newly constructed representation of the overseas world, in both texts and images, persisted well into the seventeenth and eighteenth centuries.

De Bry and De Veer: the crew who came in from the cold

Gerrit de Veer's *Waerachtighe beschryvinghe van drie seylagien ...* (1598) was a classic example of an early modern best-seller. With most of the crew miraculously returning from Novaya Zemlya after having been given up for dead by almost everyone in Amsterdam, many eagerly awaited the details of so much misfortune. Cornelis Claesz, the leading publisher in the field of travel accounts, maximised the report's commercial potential, incorporating more than thirty copper engravings depicting encounters with polar bears and the construction of the Behouden Huys. This 'House of Refuge', a log cabin made from the wood of one of the two Dutch ships, enabled most of the crew to survive in the Arctic region for nine bitterly cold months.

The De Brys gratefully included copies of the original plates in their versions, published as part of Volume III of the *India Orientalis* series in 1599 (German) and 1601 (Latin). Several pictures were omitted from their set of illustrations, or had their most exciting features combined into a single composition. With so much iconographic material available, the urge to add new engravings was predictably limited, yet the one plate that the publishers did decide to add is all the more intriguing. Generations of Dutch schoolchildren have been told the story of the heroic overwintering at Novaya Zemlya, and the interior of the Behouden Huys from the De Bry collection has become one of the staple illustrations of that tale (ill. 2). The plate depicts the small crew sitting around a cauldron of soup and a roasted arctic fox with the bedridden, gravely ill ship's captain Willem Barentsz the only blemish on the otherwise pleasant, homely atmosphere.

The engraving is remarkably accurate, as archaeological studies at Novaya Zemlya in the 1990s have demonstrated. The ground plan of the cabin, with the bench-type beds along the perimeter walls, closely matches recent finds in the Arctic region. The clock, when compared to the original piece now in the collection of the Rijksmuseum (ill. 3), is depicted with stunning precision. This illustration, then, was not invented in the De Bry workshop in Frankfurt, like so many other pictures newly inserted into the collection. It must instead have been designed by one of the travellers, or by someone who had direct access to one of the survivors in Amsterdam. Why, then, did Cornelis Claesz, who had a nationwide circle of friends including geographers, travellers and engravers, and who must surely have been able to lay his hands on this picture, decide against including this revealing view of life in the log cabin?

2

The answer can probably be found by looking at the publisher's editorial strategy. After the belated, unexpected return of the surviving crew members to Amsterdam, the excited Dutch readership was eager to learn of the inconceivable hardships their countrymen had endured. A shrewd publisher like Cornelis Claesz was unlikely to pass up such an opportunity, and as the engraving of the seemingly comfortable Behouden Huys may not have fitted the bill, it was sacrificed as a result. The De Brys, in Frankfurt, had other concerns. Their broad, international readership did not share the immense anticipation of the Dutch customers. In order to reach all of their potential readers, moreover, another poignant problem had to be adressed: the confessional conflict ravaging the Old World automatically extended to distant shores when European overseas expansion gained momentum. Although a large segment of the readership of the De Bry collection may well have been Protestants, a significant group of customers were either Catholics, or irenics hopeful of a possible reconciliation of the Christian confessions. The De Brys, in order not to alienate a large share of their potential readership, opted in their collection to emphasise the guile of the European explorers, and even their superiority abroad, often at the expense of the indigenous peoples they encountered. Hence the plate of the expertly-built, comfortable log cabin, constructed to successfully conquer the almost unbearable conditions, was readily included in the De Bry volumes.

De Bry and Barent Jansz: naked natives and fearful giants

The first Dutch attempt at circumnavigation was as much a failure as the voyage to Novaya Zemlya. Only one of the five ships that left Rotterdam in 1598, and a fraction of their crews, returned safely to the Dutch Republic. The account of this unfortunate voyage, *Wijdtloopigh verhael*, appeared in Amsterdam in 1600; it was composed by the publisher Zacharias Heyns and based on the journal of the ship's physician Barent Jansz. Heyns' intentions were probably twofold: firstly, he sought to deflect the blame for the mission's failure from the only surviving captain of the fleet, Sebald de Weert, whom he had known for a long time. Secondly, he strove to ensure that the account would achieve the same best-seller status as Gerrit de Veer's narrative. Both objectives were served by emphasising the suffering of the crew. Illness, thunderstorms, and a hostile reception by the indigenous people of the southernmost part of the American continent therefore epitomised the Dutch interpretation of the expedition. The original work included eight illustrations, all woodcuts, three of which depicted the mythical 'Patagonian Giants' as fearsome individuals with a menacing attitude.

The De Bry family, in their collection, included eleven plates. All of these were, as usual, accompanied by captions which were written for this specific purpose – usually paraphrased excerpts of the main text – and assembled at the end of the volume concerned, *India Occidentalis* IX (German 1601, Latin 1602). Besides including information on the Dutch experiences in Patagonia, the De Brys also concentrated on the brief sojourn in West Africa, on the way to the Strait of Magellan. Whereas Barent Jansz and Zacharias Heyns had devoted only one of their eight illustrations to this meeting, the De Brys added a second engraving. The encounter between the Dutch captain De Weert and an indige-

4

nous woman near Cabo Lopez on the West African coast, in the modern-day country of Gabon, had clearly caught their eye. Barent Jansz, in his journal, had introduced this unexpected meeting as follows: '*When in the morning, the captain stood in his doorway, he was approached by an old woman.*' The De Brys translated this sentence, but they also modified it slightly. They reported in both Latin and German that: '*... when in the morning, the captain stood in his doorway, he was approached by an old woman*, who was entirely naked.'

Not only is this reference to the woman's nudity not found in the original account, but the Dutch text contains no reference whatsoever to any presumed nudity of the West Africans. The single Amsterdam woodcut devoted to West Africa in fact showed all the locals wearing at least some sort of garment to cover their genitals (ill. 4). The textual addition of the De Brys, however, was not an isolated revision. In their adapted version of the original Dutch illustration,

QVOMODO HOLLANDI RE-
GVLVM QVENDAM LITTORALIS
tractus Guineæ inuiferint.
IV.

OSTQVAM *Hollandi, cum maxima vndæ potabilis, rerumq, neceſſariarum aliarum inopia côflictati, multis ſuorum infirmatis & decumbentibus littus Guineæ attigiſſent, legatos ſuos cum interprete, ad loci eius Regulum amandarunt. Rex itaque de Hollandorum appulſu edoctus, habitu ſuo ſuperbiſſimo ad illos prodiit. Induerat enim ſe palla Gallica, & caligis ex purpureo panno ſartis, & tæniis ex auro ſpurio conſtratis, cæteroquin nec induſio, nec tibialibus, nec calceis amicitus. Caput illius longa, eaque in apicem deſinente vitta, ex panno croceo, aut rubro cæruleoq, texta, opertum erat. Hoc habitu ante Hollandos preſſa humilique ſella deſidebat, pedibus eius ovina pelle ſubſtratis. Poſt ipſum omnes eius nobiles, in totum nudi conſederant. Hollandico itaque præfecto ad Regulum ingreſſo, rex illum in conſimili ſella ſtorea inſtrata conſidere iuſſit. Quo facto, quod opus erat, per interpretem tractabatur. Interea vero Almirans omnes infirmos ex nauibus in terram exponi, ibidemq, probè curari iuſſerat, dum plerique rurſus convaleſcerent. Illic mortuos, terræ mandabant. Iſti homines, ad Hollandorum quidem aſpectum primum valdè agreſtes & formidoloſi erant. Poſtea autem aſſueſcentes magis, ita miteſcebant, vt cum illis de omnibus probè tractari poſſet.*

ee 3

5

the West Africans had been carefully undressed, leaving the international readership with a more disturbing image of the West Africans than the Dutch audience had received (ill. 5). In the caption to this illustration, the De Brys once more confirmed the nudity of the West Africans. Whereas the original Dutch account had stated of the local chief that: '*he had been surrounded by his nobility*', the De Brys made sure that their texts and images correlated, declaring instead that: '*he had been surrounded by his nobility, who were entirely naked.*'

The efforts by the De Brys to have texts and images support each other, indicate the systematic nature of these alterations. The second De Bry engraving of the Dutch visit to West Africa, one without a counterpart in the original, further affirmed the nakedness of the indigenous people. On the right of the new illustration, the meeting was depicted between captain De Weert and the woman who, according to the textual additions of the De Brys mentioned before, approached him on his doorstep, *while entirely naked.'* Again, the illustration corresponded with the statement in the modified text. Yet what is even more apparent is the selectiveness of the Frankfurt publishers. The woman, hidden away in the original edition, had clearly been chosen by the De Brys to represent disquieting qualities of the West African people which, in their opinion, had not received enough attention in the Dutch version.

The heightened contrast between the cultured Dutch and the primitive indigenous people they encountered was even more emphatic in the three De Bry engravings depicting the 'Patagonian Giants'. The first of three Amsterdam woodcuts of the giants portrayed them in the impressive manner that the usually well-informed Dutch readership would have expected. The large man in the foreground had been depicted with his weapon raised, seemingly ready at all times to provide a hot reception for unwanted visitors (ill. 6). The corresponding De Bry illustration showed not a trace of such an exhibition of indigenous power. In marked contrast, the Patagonians, despite their presence in numbers, were represented as fearful instead of fearsome (ill. 7). The armed giant who most closely resembled the Dutch prototype was unmistakably on the run. The arrival of one small boat with European sailors, introduced by the De Brys, had led to

6

disarray among the supposedly fearsome Patagonians, with smoke rising from the barrel of one of the rifles.

The second Dutch illustration of the Patagonians showed a woman and her two children. Three immaculately dressed and well-armed Dutchmen, added to the illustration in the De Bry collection, provided an obvious civilised contrast to the three Patagonians. The third and final woodcut of Patagonia in the Amsterdam edition represented a typical indigenous couple. Barent Jansz's rather sterile illustration, strongly reminiscent of those often used in contemporary European costume books, showed a woman who looked like the Patagonian woman in the previous plate, flanked by a man with feathers on his head and around his waist (ill. 8).

HOLLANDI IN FRETO MAGEL-

LANICO IVXTA INSVLAM QVAN-
dam grandes & portentofos homines in-
ueniunt.

VIII.

V M aliquando Hollandi in freto Magellanico vna aut altera fcapha verfus infulam quandam remos agerent, infperato ipfis feptem lintres, vaftis horrendifq, & illis nudis hominibus plenis occurrerunt, quorum longitudo decem vel vndecim pedum erat. Cutis horum fubfufca vifebatur : ipfi vero toti nudi capillos è capite longos promiſsoſq, fundebant. Hi ad Hollandos inuadendos, cum feſe auidè inſtruerent, animo eorum percepto, Hollandi in eos Mufquettis ſtrenuè defulminarunt, & ex omni numero tres derepente morti dederunt. Quod videntes Barbari, remis incitatis, feſtinò in terram ſe receperunt, euulfiſq, è terra arboribus, contra Hollandos aduenturos feſe obuallarunt, cum ſpiculis, tum ſaxis interim minitabundi. Attamen Hollandi, cum perfequi hos Gigantes & fruſtraneum & nimis periculofum putarent, eos miſſos fecerunt. Barbari autem, cum tempore quodam tres ex Hollandis fortuitò comprehendiſſent, inuſitata & miſerabili lanicna eos commaclarunt. Hæc figura quoque ſcapharum, quas illi vſurpant, formam exprimit.

ff **3**

7

In the third De Bry engraving, the evocation of costume books had disappeared, as the Patagonian man in the foreground was depicted lying on the ground, with his hands bound together (ill. 9). Although the man had already been dead when the Dutchmen found him, the overriding impression of this engraving, and indeed of the complete set of three De Bry engravings, was nevertheless one of defeat for the indigenes. Whereas the original sequence of Dutch illustrations had presented readers with an image of the 'Patagonian Giants' as a ferocious community, essentially a confirmation of the existing views of the Patagonians in sixteenth-century Europe, the De Brys, in their own sequence, had replaced solid strength with blind panic, so that readers would be left not with an idea of savage power, but with the comfortable impression of European supremacy overseas. The concluding engraving of the set of three in the De Bry collection irrefutably confirmed the predictable outcome of a clash between well-armed Europeans and an unsophisticated indigenous populace, regardless of their impressive size.

The two accounts, and the modifications to these accounts, show two different sides of the editorial strategy of the De Bry family. When given the oppor-

tunity to include accurate pictorial material of European adventures abroad, they did. The engraving of the interior of the Behouden Huys was in all likelihood designed in Amsterdam, but it was nevertheless eagerly included by the De Brys in their version of De Veer's tragic narrative. When, on the other hand, the existing iconography was considered insufficient, the family reverted to their own skills of design and engraving, which frequently resulted in a significant alteration of the representation of the overseas world. The undressing of Barent Jansz's West Africans at Cape Lopez and the transformation of the Patagonian Giants into a group which easily succumbed to European firearms are cases in point. These examples reveal a deeper purpose behind the modifications made in Frankfurt. In order to meet the demands of their heterogeneous, international group of readers, the De Brys stressed the otherness of the natives encountered on distant shores, juxtaposed by European technical expertise and civility. The early Dutch maritime expeditions, by Gerrit de Veer and Barent Jansz, but also by other early icons of adventure like Jan Huygen van Linschoten, Willem Lodewijcksz, and Pieter de Marees, were made to fit this pattern. ∎

FURTHER READING

Ch. T. Beke (ed.), *The Three Voyages of Willem Barents to the Arctic Regions (1594, 1595 and 1596)* [Works issued by the Hakluyt Society, vol. 54] (photomech. Reprint). New York, 1964.

J. Braat, J. Gawronsky, J. B. Kist, *et al.* (eds.), *Behouden uit het Behouden Huys: catalogus van de voorwerpen van de Barentsexpeditie (1596), gevonden op Nova Zembla.* Amsterdam, 1998.

S. Burghartz (ed.), *Inszenierte Welten. Die west- und ostindischen Reisen der Verleger De Bry, 1590-1630. Staging New Worlds. De Bry`s illustrated travel reports, 1590-1630.* Basle, 2004.

M. van Groesen, 'Barent Jansz. en de familie De Bry. Twee visies op de eerste Hollandse expeditie "om de West" rond 1600'. In: *De zeventiende eeuw* 21-1 (2005), pp. 29-48.

F. C. Wieder (ed.), *De reis van Mahu en De Cordes door de Straat van Magalhães naar Zuid-Amerika en Japan 1598-1600* [Werken van de Linschoten-Vereeniging, vols. 21, 22, 24]. The Hague, 1923-25.

From Africa to Africa

The Return of a Dead Traveller

An Extract from Frank Westerman's *El Negro and Me*

December 1983. In a Spanish museum of natural history, nineteen-year-old Frank Westerman finds himself standing face to face with a stuffed African – El Negro. Who is this man? Who stuffed his body? Twenty years later, the author follows El Negro's journey from Paris (1831), via Barcelona (1888) to the Pyrenees, where he was on display until 1997.

Along the way he brings El Negro to life as a commentator on his time: an unknown black man who – nailed to a pedestal – casts a disturbing perspective on European views of slavery, colonialism and racism.

But what does he say about us, here and now? Through the probing account of his own experiences in development-aid, Frank Westerman also reveals how the historical views on race which El Negro embodies still survive in modern guises.

These two threads in *El Negro and Me* inevitably lead to post-apartheid South Africa, where the author prepares for a final confrontation with El Negro. The following extract is Westerman's epilogue.

On 5 October 2000 El Negro was given a Christian burial in Botswana. 'In the spirit of Jesus Christ,' the priest said with his hand on the Bible, 'who also suffered, amen.'

Sitting next to the stage that had been erected to hold the remarkably small casket were dignitaries from Botswana (the first lady, the foreign affairs minister, the parliamentary speaker) and Spain (the ambassador, a dozen or so lesser diplomats and, from Madrid, the curator of the anthropology museum). An awning, supported by two rows of tent poles, protected the guests of honour from the heat of the sun. From the funeral procession's arrival in Tsholofelo Park (in an outer suburb of the capital Gaborone) to the final salute by white-gloved buglers, the ceremony lasted exactly two hours.

After each speech, Setswana songs played over the speakers and the rows of mourners swayed in time. Their parasols swayed along with them and that produced what was possibly the day's most enchanting scene. In any case, the singing helped to dispel the sense of horror that had taken charge of the crowd: all those who had walked past the bier (four feet long) the previous evening had felt cheated: this couldn't possibly be El Negro. Only a skull had been visible under the glass window, that was all, and that sight was hard to reconcile with the pictures of El Negro in his museum getup that had appeared in the *Botswana Gazette* and *The Reporter*. The few journalists who were familiar with the autopsy report were just as stunned: the skull on show in the casket had an almost full set of teeth; these hadn't been visible on the X-rays. People clapped their hands over their mouths, but no one dared to protest out loud.

In Tsholofelo Park a groundsman told me the details of the burial: who stood where (from Alphonse Arcelin and the military band to the 'special reporter' Miquel Molina) and the subjects of the speeches ('the desecration of El Negro's body' and 're-establishing the dignity of a shared African ancestor'). To prepare for the ceremony they had mowed the grass and pulled a rusty climbing frame out like a rotten molar. The only thing that survived was the rocket that justified the name 'Luna Park'.

The curator of Spain's National Anthropology Museum, under whose supervision El Negro had been stripped back to the bone, wore a black cocktail dress, knee-length or maybe shorter. This dress did not make her decision to deliver El Negro in a dismantled state any more palatable; it was black enough, her dress, but way too revealing – people were still muttering about it long after.

In 2004 the grave looks neglected and battered. Twelve pickets in the national colours of black, white and blue (meaning: racial harmony plus the promise of water) mark a small patch of ground. The posts are crooked and someone has stolen the decorative chain that once linked them. A scratched sign in English and Setswana announces:

'El Negro'
Died c. 1830
Son of Africa
Carried to Europe in Death
Returned Home to
African Soil
October 2000

No one ever heard another word about the original plan to declare this place a national monument.

There is no headstone or marble slab, just a hole that has been filled and covered with sand.

From *El Negro and Me* (El Negro en ik). Amsterdam: Atlas, 2004. pp. 237-239.
Translated by David Colmer

Out and About with Bruegel

[M A N F R E D   S E L L I N K]

Pieter Bruegel the Elder may be seen as one of the few artists who for centuries have played a role in determining the perception and image of Flanders. Whether historically accurate or not, many people – and certainly not only foreigners – still associate the southern Low Countries with the stereotype of 'Boeren-bruegel', or 'Peasant Bruegel': the world seen as one great gluttonous feast, complete with food, drink and dance, in picturesque, slightly chaotic villages in the countryside. However interesting it may be to speculate about the extent to which the image and the self-image of 'the' Fleming flow into each other, in this article I would like to draw attention to a completely different aspect of Bruegel's work, one that is closer to the historical reality of his time, which can perhaps bring us closer to the figure of the artist, who is often difficult to get a handle on, and which at the same time can also provide us with the necessary information about the artistic and intellectual climate that he lived in. 'Out and about with Bruegel' follows the artist on his journeys and excursions in Flanders and far beyond.

New horizons

Little is known for certain about Bruegel's life. A great deal has to be inferred from indirect evidence and a posthumous biography. He was born in an unknown location (possibly Antwerp) at some point between 1525 and 1530 and it appears fairly certain that he was apprenticed to his later father-in-law Pieter Coecke van Aelst in Antwerp. It must have been in the workshop of the widely travelled and erudite Coecke van Aelst, familiar as he was with the Italian Renaissance, that the young artist was encouraged to see more of the world and to visit Italy in particular. Although there is no absolutely indisputable documentary proof of this, all kinds of indirect evidence make it almost certain that he made a journey to that Mediterranean peninsula in the years 1552 to 1554. One of these sources is the biography written by Karel van Mander, the artist and biographer of artists, who published the first comprehensive account of Bruegel's life in his *Schilder-Boeck* or 'Book of Painting' in 1604. Van Mander, who was able to rely on informants from circles close to Bruegel and his family,

Pieter Bruegel (after Domenico Campagnola), *Italian Landscape*. 1554. Drawing, red-brown ink, 33.3 x 46.6 cm. Kupferstichkabinett. Staatliche Museen zu Berlin.

recounts that the young artist travelled via the South of France (Lyons) through the Alps to Italy. Drawings and paintings that are more or less topographically reliable show that he certainly visited Rome, where he drew the banks of the Tiber, and possibly Naples, as there exists a painting of a Neapolitan harbour scene that is usually ascribed to Bruegel, and also Reggio Calabria, where he captured the Strait of Messina. Given the demonstrably significant influence of Venetian art (Titian and Domenico Campagnola) on his landscape drawings, it is tempting to assume that he also visited Venice and then set off northwards via the Alps on his way back to Flanders.

The young Bruegel's Italian journey may have taken two to three years. In 1555 landscape prints based on his designs were published by the Antwerp publisher Hieronymus Cock, which makes it likely that he had returned by then. The artist was clearly overwhelmed by the mountain landscapes that he must have travelled through on the journey to Italy and back. In the words of Karel van Mander: *'On his travels he drew many views from life so that it is said that when he was in the Alps he swallowed all those mountains and rocks which, upon returning home, he spat out again onto canvases and panels, so faithfully was he able, in this respect and others, to follow Nature.'* It should not be forgotten that Pieter Bruegel, whose renown nowadays is primarily due to his painting, initially concentrated on drawing and on preparing designs for prints, with a strong emphasis on landscapes. This long journey will certainly not only have broadened his visual horizons. During such trips contact with artists, humanists, scholars and art lovers from far and wide was just as important to many artists. In Bruegel's case, we know, for example, that he was in close contact with the then renowned Croatian miniaturist Giulio Clovio, who had arrived in Rome in 1553 as part of the retinue of Cardinal Alessandro Farnese. As well as providing an entrée into the world of potential patrons, this was evidently a close artistic friendship. The inventory of Clovio's estate describes, in addition to three other works by Bruegel, a (no longer extant) miniature *'of which one half is by his [Clovio's] hand, the other by Pieter Bruegel'*. Perhaps, as occasionally happened elsewhere, the two painted a picture together to seal their friendship. It is also tempting to

Pieter Bruegel,
*View of the Ripa Grande
in Rome*. c.1553.
Drawing, brown ink,
20.7 x 28.3 cm.
Collection of the Duke of
Devonshire, Chatsworth.

imagine that Bruegel's astounding ability in his later works to keep his painting recognisable right down to the smallest details was influenced by Clovio's skill in the genre of the miniature and so goes back to experiences gained during his Italian journey. It was also during this period that the painter spent time with the sculptor Jacob Jonghelinck, brother of the merchant and court dignitary Nicolaus, who ten years later would become his most important patron in Brussels. In that respect as well, Bruegel's journey, seen in retrospect of course, was a crucial step in his artistic career. Then as now, when people spent a lengthy period of time together in foreign parts networks would often develop almost of themselves.

When he returned from Italy with a head full of impressions and folders full of sketches and drawings, he had enough material to supply him for his whole artistic career. For artists of the sixteenth and seventeenth centuries the importance of collecting landscape motifs can scarcely be overestimated. They would carefully construct each painting from their imagination in the safe environment of the workshop, making use of their own visual impressions and, even more often, of prints and drawings that others had made. The influences that Bruegel had absorbed on his long journey were rapidly '*spat out*', in the words of Van Mander, and left a deep impression on the landscape art of his time and long afterwards. Around 1555–1556, In de Vier Winden, the print shop belonging to the aforementioned Hieronymus Cock, published a series of twelve etched and engraved mountain landscapes in a large format. The compositions have a typical structure: a combination of mountain views in the background, a river landscape reminiscent of Southern Italy in the middle, and typical Flemish hamlets and farmhouses in the foreground. The most spectacular sketch is simply known as *The Large Alpine Landscape*. The breadth of the landscape, the overwhelming beauty and grandeur of nature and the insignificance of the human – pictured upper right, looking down into the valley along with the viewer – are combined in a striking way.

This alpine landscape from 1555–1556 is incidentally one of the few prints from a Bruegel design that can be labelled as a 'pure' landscape. A narrative

element, sometimes secular, sometimes religious in nature, was introduced to other landscape prints, presumably on the initiative of the publisher Cock. There was as yet no tradition of publishing landscapes without a subject and perhaps Cock did not yet have the courage to start such a tradition. Scarcely three years later the situation was completely different – the work of Pieter Bruegel had played a key role in this – and in 1559–1560 Cock brought out a spectacular series of Brabant village scenes and Flemish landscapes, drawn by a still-unidentified artist from Bruegel's immediate circle who is known only as the 'Master of the Small Landscapes'. A new genre was born. It should also be noted that the concept of the 'pure' landscape must be understood in a specifically sixteenth-century context. No matter how capable people were, since the verses that Petrarch had dedicated to this subject, of enjoying the beauty of the landscape and depicting it on paper and panel, in the mid-sixteenth century this would certainly have been seen in a Christian-humanist light. Although not every artist, let alone everyone who looked at the pictures, will have had the same degree of sensitivity, for many people at the time the creative power of God was manifest in the landscape, whether directly or in somewhat veiled layers of meaning. The literal and the figurative discovery and decoding of the world were still very much interconnected at that time; in an academic sense, geography, cosmography and theology were closely related.

Joannes and Lucas van Doetecum (after a design by Pieter Bruegel), *The Large Alpine Landscape*. c.1555-1556. Etching and engraving, 36.8 x 46.8 cm. Museum Boijmans Van Beuningen, Rotterdam.

Seascapes and excursions to the countryside

Bruegel's desire for travel certainly did not disappear after his return to Flanders. It may have been less exotic, but when he was living in Antwerp, and in Brussels from 1562–1563 until his death in 1569, nature and landscapes very clearly continued to fascinate him. Perhaps his longing for distant shores played a part in the wonderful and meticulously recorded 'ship portraits' published in 1561–1562 as a series of prints after designs by Bruegel. You can almost see Bruegel wandering around the harbour in Antwerp, capturing all kinds of boats in his sketch-

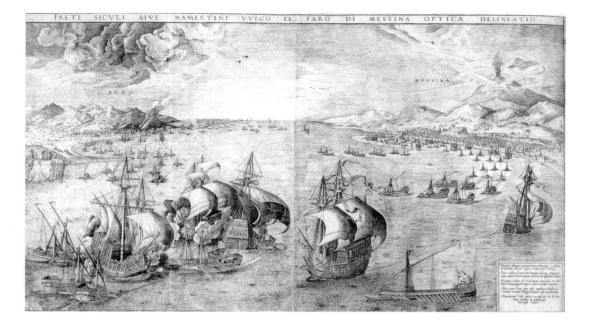

Frans Huys (after a design
by Pieter Bruegel),
*Battle in the Strait of
Messina*. 1561.
Etching and engraving,
42.8 x 71.7 cm.
Museum Boijmans Van
Beuningen, Rotterdam

books and returning to his workshop to develop them into a seascape, which in turn could enter the imagination of those who saw the picture and transport them to distant shores. Bruegel himself did not embark on any other long journeys. He did, however, undertake many excursions to the areas around Antwerp and Brussels. Tangible proof of this is provided by a marvellous drawing of a bend in the river Scheldt with the village of Baasrode in the background. Baasrode, near Dendermonde, was an important stopping place for boats at the time, because large and heavily laden vessels could just reach this village upstream from Antwerp on one tide. It is an attractive thought to picture the artist taking a trip on the forward deck of some sloop or other – the drawing has clearly been made from some height above the water – and depicting the peacefully rippling Scheldt.

The fact that Bruegel regularly went on (day?) trips after his return from Italy is confirmed (once again) by Karel van Mander. The biographer stresses how much the artist enjoyed visiting villages and hamlets in the countryside, using *'a very pure and subtle technique with the pen with which he drew many small views from life'*. Although this passage is almost always quoted to illustrate Bruegel's interest in peasants and country people, it can also be understood in the context of his fascination with the landscape of his immediate surroundings. It is not difficult to find clearly identifiable reflections of the Brabant landscape in Bruegel's paintings, particularly the area known as 'pajottenland'. Unfortunately, no sketches made on site or drawings of the Flemish and Brabant landscape developed in the workshop have been preserved, with the exception of the view of Baasrode and two other river views. With only a paltry sixty or so surviving drawings by his own hand, we can only speculate that most of the hundreds of drawings he must have made on his travels have been lost for ever. What remains, however, is more than impressive and testifies to an artist who enjoyed travelling and had a keen eye for the beauty of nature. Whether it was a wild alpine landscape, a charming Italian valley or a wide river view in Flanders, Bruegel

Frans Huys (after a design
by Pieter Bruegel),
Three Caravels in a Storm.
c.1561-1562.
Etching and engraving,
22 x 28.6 cm.
Museum Boijmans Van
Beuningen, Rotterdam

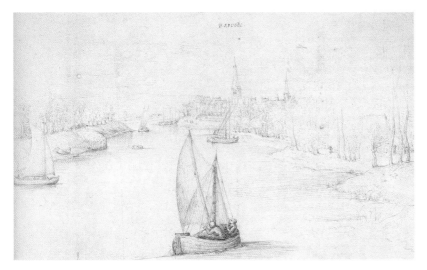

Pieter Bruegel,
*View of the River Scheldt
near Baasrode.* c.1555.
Drawing, grey-brown ink,
24.9 x 42.1 cm.
Kupferstichkabinett,
Staatliche Museen zu
Berlin.

knew how to capture the characteristic features of a landscape without lapsing into dry topographical precision, thus ensuring that his work would always continue to captivate the viewer. Even without knowing where Bruegel drew what, with his landscape drawings in our hands we can allow ourselves to be carried away and make a journey in our minds. This is perhaps typical of an artist who elsewhere in his oeuvre was uniquely successful in putting a distance between himself and reality, visually summing up the bitter and complex spirit of his time in grotesque masterpieces such as Mad Meg and *The Triumph of Death*. To end on a speculative and psychological note, maybe Pieter Bruegel was so good at capturing the landscape for the very reason that, more than any other artist, he was so skilled at distancing himself mentally from the visual reality. ■

Translated by Laura Watkinson

Pieter Bruegel,
Hunters in the Snow.
c.1565.
Panel, 117 x 162 cm.
Kunsthistorisches
Museum, Vienna.

FURTHER READING

Roger Marijnissen, *Bruegel, het volledige oeuvre* (Antwerp, 1988) is a beautifully illustrated book on Bruegel's work that is still up-to-date. In his book *Bruegel* (1st edition, London, 1977), Walter Gibson skilfully places the artist and his work in the context of his time. For recent research and further literature and source references, see Manfred Sellink, *Pieter Bruegel de Oude, meestertekenaar* (Rotterdam, 2001) and particularly the catalogue *Pieter Bruegel the Elder: Drawings and Prints* (Museum Boijmans Van Beuningen, Rotterdam, 2001). For the landscape in Flemish art of the sixteenth and seventeenth centuries, see the catalogue *De uitvinding van het landschap: Van Patinir tot Rubens 1520–1650* (Koninklijk Museum voor Schone Kunsten, Antwerp, 2004).

See also www.bruegel06.be for Bruegel exhibitions in Belgium (12 May-3 September 2006)

NOTE

The English quotations from Karel van Mander are taken from: Karel van Mander, *The Lives of the Illustrious Netherlandish and German Painters ....,* with an introduction and translation, edited by Hessel Miedema, vol. 1, Doornspijk, 1994.

Christoph Fink's Travel Accounts

Aesthetics of the Contemporary Worldview

[FILIP LUYCKX]

Amongst modern Flemish artists who have an original approach to the theme of travel, Christoph Fink (1963-) is a name that cannot go unrecorded. Recent exhibitions in Cleveland, Ohio, and at The Drawing Center in New York confirm the international interest in his work.

Travel has a great deal to do with abandoning our familiar categorisation of time and space and going in search of new horizons, with the aim of accelerating our experiences or slowing them down. A number of phases can be distinguished in the works of Christoph Fink. As spectators we have access only to the final installation, which does, however, document the preceding elements meticulously. Fink first maps out a journey between a point of departure and a final destination, by way of a number of checkpoints such as large roads, towns or mountain peaks. This already serves to establish a narrative thread, along which he can structure all his observations. As he cycles or walks along

Atlas of Movements. Studies of Continental Europe (bicycle), a selection: movements #6 (Ghent-Faro), #7 (Ghent-Geneva-Zurich-Ghent), #8 (Ghent-The Hague-Ghent), #12 ((Ghent-Venice-Ghent), #28 (Ghent-tour du Mt Blanc-Ghent), #35 (Ghent-Etna(-Ghent)), #37 (Ghent-Pointe de corsen-Grenoble-Geneva-Ghent). Blue and black ink on paper cut-out (210 x 165 mm), 2003. © Christoph Fink.

this route, his path is certainly subject to the varying nature of the terrain and the circumstances. The precise route to be followed between the checkpoints depends partly on chance. This makes the course of the journey unpredictable, but also fascinating.

Time and space

The traveller's home base indicates the nature of the biotope with which he is familiar. It is inevitable that a resident of the Low Countries will have a different view of the world from, for example, a Tibetan. The artist sets off alone on the journey, on foot, by bicycle, by car, in a plane or by train, making use both of the

Preparatory study for
horizonline drawing.
ø 1000 mm, acrylic paint
on paper cut-out, studio-
view, 2004.
© Christoph Fink.

most elementary form of movement and of the most technologically advanced forms. The manner in which we move from one place to another has a profound effect on our way of life and on our view of the world. Although this is not so explicitly obvious from the artist's notes and graphic representations, political and economic reality are constantly lurking in the background, because they change the landscape so fundamentally. Not only commercial transport, but also holiday travel, involves making social choices and gives rise to all kinds of other effects. The experience of travelling, the time that we invest in it and the areas that we pass through all help to determine our vision of our destination. Every form of movement from A to B results in a specific experience of time and offers the opportunity to absorb other aspects of the surroundings. Along the way, the artist makes irregular stops at note-taking points where, in addition to the time and the distance travelled, he records a variety of impressions in short sentences: the weather, cloud formations, the landscape and buildings, the amount of traffic, sensory perceptions, animals and flowers, the food, practical travel details, the state of the road, emotional reactions. Impressions of this kind are expressed in notes that depend on chance and on the artist's attention. In the evolution of Fink's work, we can see how the subjective contribution steadily declines in importance in favour of a search for the significance of his projects within developments in society. More than ever, the autobiographical aspect is giving way to conclusions that could have been reached by anyone in that place at that time. Even the emotions that he notes down have a general character. The most accurate account possible of the perception of time and space is gaining the upper hand over a strictly personal agenda. The artist has an eye for the wealth and intensity of details, no matter what kind of landscape is involved. Even though the configuration of such observations constantly varies from one moment to another, we can experience such intensity of experiences for ourselves anywhere in the world. The facts observed do not represent any economic value. Equivalent experience of the landscape is freely available to all of us at every moment and in every place.

An original kind of geography

Numerical data referring to time and space make up a considerable part of Fink's information. His own experience of the place and the point in time in which he is situated always forms the central point of his documentation. Using this as a starting point, he plots an original form of geography that spans countries and continents. The horizon moves as we stride through the landscape. However close the central point is to us, the horizon always remains just as far away.

Upon returning home, Fink spends weeks and months processing the details of different journeys with no less intensity. Using graphic representations, sculptures and sound montages, he reconstructs his experiences and looks for new connections between the various journeys and with the wider geographical context. His perception does not stop with that one experience during the journey: it is expanded, drawing both on his notes and on his memory. The accumulation of details creates abstract lines with their own aesthetic. The abstraction into notes, figures and methods develops into an autonomous system that leads

Atlas of Movements, Movement #59 (The Clevelandwalks). Detail, ink and pencil on paper cut-out + printed text on paper, (10000 x 1365 mm) + preparatory studies for horizonline drawing (ø 1000mm). Installation view nadjaVilenne galerie, Liège, Belgium, 2004. © Christoph Fink.

a life of its own on top of the observations made on location. However, concrete experiences still lie behind every line and every word of the text. As the graphic and auditory processing takes up considerably more time than the journey itself, it adds a significant amount of both impressions and interpretation. This phase too, which takes place in the seclusion of the studio, occurs away from the public eye. Many artists in the 1990s created performances from which the audience was excluded, though they did get to see documentary evidence of the event. What is remarkable about Fink's work is the way the private journey actually occurs out in the open, in a space that is always accessible. The key element for the artist is not the idea of the presence of the public, but a silent invitation to experience our movements through the landscape in a more conscious way.

Transferring the aforementioned processing to the exhibition site adds fur-

Atlas of Movements,
Movement #31,
Eindhoven - Meerhoven
(The Netherlands), three
walks. Ballpoint ink on paper,
detail of travel notes, 1997.
© Christoph Fink.

ther impressions and systematisation. The act of processing now gains a spatial and public dimension. Everything is adapted to fit both the architecture and the geographical position of the new location. Fink combines the distance travelled and the time spent to form one total installation. All the connections, systems, measurements and calculations start from this point. Charts cover tabletops that have been designed according to the distance travelled or the amount of time that has passed. A whole range of abstract data and actual memories is brought together for physical confrontation with each other. He often draws horizons on the walls in order to chart the position of the exhibition space in relation to the wide world outside. Sound fragments and slides also allow the exhibition visitor to reconstruct the journey audiovisually. During our visit we can sense for ourselves different sorts of time coming together.

Earth Time Model,
4.55 billion years. Ceramic
disc, 'periodically' engraved,
ø 249 mm, 1660 g, 2005.
© Christoph Fink.

The wealth of time

Different concepts of time intersect in Fink's artistic activity. Objective systems of measurement go hand in hand with the way in which we experience time. There are many nameless experienced times that constantly influence each other. There are moments when we perceive the progress of time, or indeed the infinity of time, more sharply, for example when we are covering a distance and keeping an open eye to our surroundings. Relating to external processes of time in the landscape allows us to move from a functional level of time to a feeling of endless time, in which we let ourselves be carried along on the stream of life with no set time or destination. Surrendering to so-called emptiness can in fact open us to an intense experience of the wealth of time. As far as the memory is concerned, this experience of time with no schedule is perceived as very lengthy. Whilst memory reconstructs the journey, all kinds of things happen along the way. Even during the journey, it is impossible to record all the events and connections. Fink's observations seem vast in comparison with the capacity of our memories. But even his documentation falls short in the face of the unrelenting onwards march of temporal and spatial impressions. His minute reconstruction in the studio or the museum requires more time than the actual journey. When we visit the exhibition we too can step outside the functional perception of time for a moment, but time still carries on just the same.

Many measurement systems come together in Fink's installations to form one single point in time and space. They all exert a simultaneous influence, yet it is impossible to form an idea of all those systems in a single moment. They cover a wide range both of objective standards for mapping the world and of subjective position-finding. All of us are our own central point somewhere in the world. On the other hand, a lot of objective systems have come about through cultural conventions. In Fink's work, we ascertain how these systems of measurement gradually shift from the objective to the subjective level. The interface between objective time and experienced time is particularly blurred.

The average moment

The alert traveller has an intense experience of the totality of the landscape at a particular moment in time. His immersion in his wide surroundings calls

to mind the sixteenth-century inventers of the Flemish landscape. Just like now, that was a time when the worldview was rapidly changing and people were also developing an eye for other aspects of their geographical surroundings. Humanists and artists were seeking new ways of depicting the evolving concept of the world. With such figures as Abraham Ortelius and Gerard Mercator scientific cartography, globes and atlases were extremely popular in the Low Countries. The paintings of Joachim Patinir, Pieter Bruegel and Joost de Momper depict a handful of nondescript figures striding through immense panoramas, where, regardless of their personal story, normal life is carrying on as usual on different levels. In a similar way, the perception of time in Fink's journey intersects with numerous other perceptions of time, both in the artist himself and in the surrounding landscape. At first sight Fink's notebook appears to have sprouted from the brain of a geographer, a surveyor or a town planner. His descriptions fall outside the realms of economics and tourism. The meticulous attention that Fink pays to plain and simple facts stimulates our interest in the average moment in the standard landscape. His choice suggests a totality with no practical use but great experiential value. The artist never loses sight of the geographical context in which he is situated, such as its position with regard to the latitude, the height, the position of the rivers, the time zone and so on. This is a place where objective and subjective systems intersect.

Whilst the point of departure may be subjective, the meticulous nature of the artist's self-imposed system speaks of a serious methodology. Although his work does not follow scientific criteria, it does bear witness to a comparable precision and discipline. His research does not aim for completeness. It is his own personal system, but it does not refer to his own person. A comparison with historical cartography makes Fink's position even more credible. Both are systematic investigations of the world. Pioneers such as Mercator and Ortelius worked according to the scientific norms of their time, whilst Fink's form of precision falls outside the scientific community, but could possibly influence it. In both cases, an attempt is being made to find a suitable visual language to express a changing view of the world. The cartography of the Renaissance could not rely to any great extent on scientific consensus. Its findings have long been superseded and today its significance is primarily cultural-historical and aesthetic. The same may also be said of Fink's work, of course, but in addition it does also contain an important research component. In this sense, his work is in line with the international tendency to recognise art as an entirely valid form of independent research. Another characteristic of historical cartography is the way it filled Terra Incognita with legendary figures and names. This magical aspect is completely lacking in Fink's work. He does not speculate about the mystery, but he certainly makes us sense that it exists. His codification system for the world contains no secrets. Each of his works comes with a brief manual. The degree of complexity tallies with our modern conception of time and distance, but never lapses into deliberate obscurity. As in any scientific system, all elements of the symbolism can be unravelled.

First and foremost, Fink is looking for a spirituality that is in harmony with the evolving view of the world. This endeavour does not conflict with the material world, but actually stems from it. Unlike in objective science, the artist enters into the territory of perceptual values and providing sense and meaning. As well

Atlas of Movements, Movement #61 (The Leuvenwalks), Detail. Ink and pencil on paper cut-out, nadjaVilenne galerie, Liège, Belgium, 2004. © Christoph Fink.

Atlas of Movements, Movement #52 (The Frankfurtwalks), Ink and pencil on paper cut-out + printed text on paper. (540 cm x 136 cm + extention 45 cm x 237 cm). Detail, exhibition view, Manifesta, Kunstverein Frankfurt, Frankfurt, Germany, 2002. © Christoph Fink.

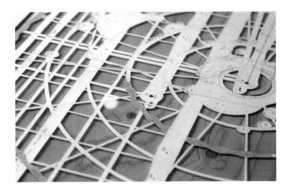

as awareness, experience and the expression of experience play a leading role in a system of aesthetics that is all his own. Through his research we experience how the world is in a constant state of flux. The number of possible experiences appears to be infinite and each of these experiences is in some way unique. Most facts can never be reconstructed or verified. We ourselves undergo no more than a minute fraction of all possible experiences and are no more than insignificant fragments in the overall structure of space and time. ∎

Translated by Laura Watkinson

Notices to Travellers

W.J. van Zeggelen (1811-1879)

Kees the Traveller

[SELECTED BY ANTON KORTEWEG]

Kees buys a passport, stuffs his purse,
and wants to see the world;
hurtles through space and shrinks, by train,
a hundred hours to – ten.

Kees looks around, with reeling head,
and wipes his spectacles;
the whole world seems to lurch and spin
to plague him as he drowses.

Kees gives a moan and rubs his nose,
smells only stench and steam;
and mutters: if I had the choice,
I'd rather take it slow.

Kees plucks up courage, straightens up,
speaks to a passenger,
who glances at him, stiff and proud,
and doesn't grasp a word.

Kees weighs his purse and heaves a sigh,
yearns for his trusty pipe;
and each red-collared customs man
makes Kees shake in his shoes!

Kees roams great cities, gawping round,
missing now this now that,
he's shoved aside and trampled on
along the crowded path.

Kees runs with sweat, wears out his legs,
eats food he doesn't like,
crawls into bed stiff as a board,
and – if only he could sleep!

Kees turns back and longs for home,
curses the alien land,
modestly praises his own wee house,
his own fire on the hearth.

Kees insists folk marvel at his trip;
they grant him all the new
and splendid things he's ... visited? ...
No, that he's passed by.

From *The Poems* (De dichtwerken). Rotterdam: Uitgeversmaatschappij Elsevier, 1876. 1846[1]
Translated by Tanis Guest

Kees op reis

Kees spekt zijn beurs en koopt een pas,
en wil de wereld zien;
en vliegt door 't ruim en maakt, per as,
van honderd uren – tien.

Kees kijkt in 't rond en suizebolt
en veegt zijn bril eens af:
't is of de wereld draait en tolt,
de dommelaar tot straf.

Kees klaagt zijn nood en wrijft zijn neus;
en ruikt slechts stank en stoom;
en 't woord ontvalt hem: had ik keus,
dan liever log en loom!

Kees krijgt wat moed en schikt zich wat
en spreekt zijn reisbuur aan;
deez' gluurt hem toe, vrij stroef en prat,
en kan hem niet verstaan.

Kees wikt zijn beurs en zucht ervan
en derft zijn lange pijp;
en ieder rood-gekraagde man
brengt Kees wat in de knijp!

Kees tuurt in 't rond door grote steên
en mist nu dit dan dat,
en wordt verdrongen en vertreên
op 't druk belopen pad.

Kees zweet zich dood en loopt zich lam
en eet wat hij niet lust,
en kruipt naar bed verstijfd en stram,
en – vond hij dan nog rust!

Kees keert terug en snakt naar huis,
verwenst het vreemde land,
roemt zedig eigen haard en kluis,
waar 't eigen vuurtje brandt.

Kees eist bewond'ring voor zijn tocht;
Men ziet het Kees wel aan,
dat hij veel nieuws, veel schoons,... bezocht?...
Neen, is voorbijgegaan.

Nicolaas Beets (1814-1903)

Steaming

Steaming, steaming, steaming!
  Clear across the world!
I've got myself a seat on
  The longest line there is.
Just seven days I'm taking
  For a quick trip to Japan,
In that wooden wagon,
  Driver! How's your steam?

Steaming, steaming, steaming!
  Flying down the track!
Who wants to just sit dreaming
  Can go by horse and cart,
Huns and Poles and Russians
  I'll see within a week,
In the time it takes you
  To sail to Sneek and back.

Wife! don't sit there moping!
  Please don't be so daft!
Before you've done with weeping
  I'll be heading back.
Before those socks are finished
  That you're knitting now
I'll be back home already
  With my dearest heart.

Steaming, steaming, steaming,
  Fast through field and wood,
Over deep wide rivers,
  And straight through the rock!
Filled in are the valleys!
  Mountains felled like trees!
I'm off to buy a tea-tray
  Of Chinese lacquer-work.

Is the fire burning nicely?
  Is your water boiling, chum?
Get that loco moving
  Which will give me wings!
Steaming, steaming, steaming!
  Are you crazy, man?
I've arrived already,
  Before I've even gone.

From *Poems* (Gedichten). Leiden: A.W. Sijthoff, no date. 1876[1]
Translated by Tanis Guest

Stoomen

Stoomen, stoomen, stoomen!
   Heel de wereld door!
'k Heb een plaats genomen
   Op het langste spoor.
'k Wil in zeven dagen
   Even naar Japan,
Met dien houten wagen
   Voerman! Kookt je span?

Stoomen, stoomen, stoomen,
   Vliegen langs de baan!
Die wil zitten droomen,
   Mag met paarden gaan,
Moffen, Polen, Russen,
   Zie ik in een week;
Zeil jij ondertusschen
   Heen en weer naar Sneek.

Wijf! zit niet te pruilen!
   Wees toch niet zoo dom!
Voordat je uit kunt huilen,
   Ben ik al weerom,
Eer de kousen klaar zijn,
   Daar je nu aan breit,
Zal ik al weer daar zijn
   Met mijn dierbaarheid.

Stoomen, stoomen, stoomen,
   Snel door veld en bosch,
Over diepe stroomen,
   Midden door de rots!
Aangevuld de dalen!
   Bergen omgehakt!
'k Ga een theeblad halen
   Van Chineesch verlakt.

Gloeit het vuurtje lekker?
   Raast je water, maat?
Voort maar met den trekker,
   Die me vliegen laat!
Stoomen, stoomen, stoomen!
   Kerel! ben je gek?
'k Ben al aangekomen,
   Eer ik nog vertrek.

Jopie Breemer (1875-1957)

The Traveller

The traveller travels to and fro
From Amsterdam to Hengelo
And sometimes too to Krommenie,
To Beetserzwaag and Middellie.
He reads his paper on the train
And always takes his case with him
He has a high white collar on
Speaks not a word to anyone
Sits there in silence by the window
The traveller travels to and fro.

De reiziger

De reiziger reist heen en weer
Van Amsterdam naar Wormerveer
En ook wel eens naar Krommenie
Naar Beetsterzwaag en Middellie.
Hij leest zijn krant in de coupé
En neemt altijd zijn koffer mee
Hij draagt een witte hoge boord
En als hij zit zegt hij geen woord
Hij praat nooit met een ander heer
De reiziger reist heen en weer.

From *Jopie Breemer's Volume of Outpouring* (De ontboezemingsbundel van Jopie Breemer).
Amsterdam: Bert Bakker, 1998. 1913[1]
Translated by Tanis Guest

Richard Minne (1891-1965)

International Trains

Clear the track and make way for the international trains:
they restored self-confidence to a generation
that once crawled along in ox-carts and palanquins
and now rushes through the night at 90 mph.

In these international trains there is born
the brotherhood that's measured in dollars and pounds,
Armstrong and Vickers, the grain cartel,
the new nationalities that nobody's ever heard of.

Clear the track and make way for the international trains:
they open up the future like drawing back curtains,
and bring us perfumery, guano and shoes,
the League of Nations and all kinds of swindles.

Internationale treinen

Laat vrije baan aan de internationale treinen:
zij schonken 't zelf-vertrouwen weer aan een geslacht,
dat kroop in ossewagens en in palankijnen,
en nu aan 140 ijlt doorheen den nacht.

In de internationale treinen wordt geboren
de broederschap, die men bij pond en dollar meet,
Armstrong en Vickers, de trust van 't koren,
de nieuwe nationaliteiten waar niemand van weet.

Laat vrije baan aan de internationale treinen:
zij schuiven de toekomst open als gordijnen,
en brengen ons reukwerk, guano en schoenen,
den Volkenbond en appels voor citroenen.

From *Open House and Other Poems* (In den zoeten inval en andere gedichten).
Amsterdam: G.A. van Oorschot, 1955. 1927[1]
Translated by Tanis Guest

Jacqueline E. van der Waals (1868-1922)

The Train

One day when I was travelling
Out of town, and sitting in the train,
And there in silent resignation
Patiently waited till the time
– By the slow progress of the clock –
Should come for my train to depart,
It happened that a train was switched
Into the platform next to mine
And passed my window. I well knew
The strange effect that this could have,
But to my wayward eye it seemed
That my train was moving forward
Past that other, alien train,
Which didn't seem to move at all.

When I just kept moving onward
– But knew I hadn't moved at all –
It grieved me that my sense of sight
Deceived me so in broad daylight,
And that my knowledge could not counter
My eyes' stupid trickery.
And in despair at that illusion
I shut my eyes tight as I could
And I pleaded: 'Train, stand still!'
With all the passion I could muster. . .
But for all my efforts, all my pleas,
I couldn't get that train to stop.

When someone is so sure of something
He almost feels it in his hands,
Sees it happen before his eyes,
And then thinks: it isn't so,
He feels so weary and so low,
He doubts the whether and the how,
Despairs of everything he sees
Whether it be real or no,
In the end he's lost all certainty
Of what is and what is not.

That morning as I journeyed I
Addressed my soul after this wise:
'The foolish thing I did just now
Was, that by a fleeting thing,
Which had no rest or permanence,
I judged the rest and permanence of things.
So, my soul, if you should doubt
Your own permanence or being
Amid a fluid, fleeting world,
Seek your certainty in God,
The one forever stable point
On which you can fix your gaze.'

From *Fractured Colours* (Gebroken kleuren). Nijkerk: G.F. Callenbach n.v., no date. 1924[1]
Translated by Tanis Guest

De spoortrein

Eens op een dag, toen ik de stad
Verliet en in den spoortrein zat,
En daar in stille lijdzaamheid
Geduldig wachtte tot de tijd
– Bij 't langzaam voortgaan van de klok –
Zou komen, dat mijn trein vertrok,
Geschiedde 't, dat in 't naaste spoor
Een trein rangeren ging en voor
Mijn venster schoof. Ik kende wel
De vreemde werking van dit spel,
Maar 't scheen mijn onbetrouwbaar oog,
Alsof mijn trein zich voortbewoog
Voorbij dien andren, vreemden trein,
Die onbeweeglijk bleef in schijn.

Toen ik nu al maar verder reed,
– Ik wist toch, dat ik dat niet deed –
Werd ik bedroefd, dat mijn gezicht
Mij dus bedroog in 't volle licht,
En, dat mijn inzicht niets vermocht
Tegen dit dom gezichtsbedrog.
En in mijn wanhoop om dien waan
Heb ik mijn ogen dichtgedaan,
Heb ik gebeden: 'Trein, sta stil!'
Met al de hartstocht van mijn wil…
Maar, wat ik smeekte, deed of dacht,
Ik heb hem niet tot staan gebracht.

Wie iets zo zeker weet en vast,
Dat hij het haast met handen tast,
Het voor zijn oog gebeuren ziet,
En dan bedenkt: het is zo niet,
Die voelt zich zeer bedroefd en moe,
Die twijfelt aan het of en hoe,
Die wanhoopt aan het al of niet
Van alle dingen, die hij ziet,
Die is op 't eind de zekerheid
Van alle zijn en niet zijn kwijt.

Dien morgen sprak ik op mijn reis
Tot mijne ziel op deze wijs:
'De domheid, die ik straks beging,
Was, dat ik aan een vlottend ding,
Dat zelf geen rust of vastheid had,
Der dingen rust en vastheid mat,
Dus zoek, indien gij twijfelt aan
Uw eigen vastheid of bestaan,
Te midden van wat vloeit en vlot,
Mijn ziel, uw zekerheid in God.
Het enig, eeuwig vaste punt,
Waar gij den blik op richten kunt.'

Jan van Nijlen (1884-1965)

Notice to Travellers

Never get on the train without dreams in your luggage,
then you'll find decent lodging in any town or village.

Calmly and patiently sit by the open window;
you are a traveller and safely incognito.

Dredge from your past the fresh eyes of a child,
both cool and keen, excited and beguiled.

All you see growing in the dark spring fields you view,
you can be sure, was planted just for you.

Let the commercial travellers have their say
about the latest films; God smiles and waits his day.

Give every station-master a polite 'Hello';
without their signal not one train would ever go.

And if the train won't move, much to the detriment
of your desire and hopes, the hard-won cash you spent,

keep calm and open up your bag; draw on its store
and you will find you've wasted not an hour.

And if the train pulls in to some peculiar place
you'd never even heard of, not once in all your days,

then you have reached your goal; then you learn with surprise
what travel means for wanderers and the truly wise...

Above all, be not amazed when, past trees just like home,
a quite ordinary train transports you straight to Rome.

Bericht aan de reizigers

Bestijg den trein nooit zonder uw valies met dromen,
dan vindt ge in elke stad behoorlijk onderkomen.

Zit rustig en geduldig naast het open raam:
gij zijt een reiziger en niemand kent uw naam.

Zoek in 't verleden weer uw frisse kinderogen,
kijk nonchalant en scherp, droomrig en opgetogen.

Al wat ge groeien ziet op 't zwarte voorjaarsland,
wees overtuigd: het werd alleen voor u geplant.

Laat handelsreizigers over de filmcensuur
hun woordje zeggen: God glimlacht en kiest zijn uur.

Groet minzaam de stationschefs achter hun groen hekken,
want zonder hun signaal zou nooit één trein vertrekken.

En als de trein niet voort wil, zeer ten detrimente
van uwe lust en hoop en zuurbetaalde centen,

blijf kalm en open uw valies; put uit zijn voorraad
en ge ondervindt dat nooit een enkel uur te loor gaat.

En arriveert de trein in een vreemdsoortig oord,
waarvan ge in uw bestaan den naam nooit hebt gehoord,

dan is het doel bereikt, dan leert gij eerst wat reizen
betekent voor de dolaards en de ware wijzen...

Wees vooral niet verbaasd dat, langs gewone bomen,
een doodgewone trein u voert naar 't hart van Rome.

From *Collected Poems* (Verzamelde gedichten). Amsterdam: G.A. van Oorschot, 2003. 1943[1]
Translated by Tanis Guest

M. Vasalis (1909-1998)

The Sea Dike

The bus rides like a room across the night.
The road is straight, the dike is without end.
At left the sea, tamed but recalcitrant.
A little moon distils a delicate light.

In front of me the young, close-shaven necks
Of a couple of sailor boys. They do their best
To stifle yawns, they stretch their arms and legs,
And on each other's shoulders drop to rest.

Then dreamily there drifts into my ken
The ghost of this bus, transparent glass
Riveted to ours, now clear, and then again
Half drowned in the misty sea. The grass
Cuts straight through the sailors. Then I see pass
Myself as well. Only my face
Is drifting on top of the surface swell
And moves its mouth as if it would tell
A story and could not, a mermaid distressed.
There is to this journey, I feel somehow,
Neither start nor finish, only at best
This strangely split unending Now.

Afsluitdijk

De bus rijdt als een kamer door de nacht
de weg is recht, de dijk is eindeloos
links ligt de zee, getemd maar rusteloos,
wij kijken uit, een kleine maan schijnt zacht.

Voor mij de jonge pas geschoren nekken
van twee matrozen, die bedwongen gapen
en later, na een kort en lenig rekken
onschuldig op elkanders schouder slapen.

Dan zie ik plots, als waar 't een droom, in 't glas
ijl en doorzichtig aan de onze vastgeklonken
soms duidelijk als wij, dan weer in zee verdronken
de geest van deze bus; het gras
snijdt dwars door de matrozen heen.
Daar zie ik ook mezelf. Alleen
mijn hoofd deint boven het watervlak.
beweegt de mond als sprak
Er is geen einde en begin
aan deze tocht, geen toekomst, geen verleden,
alleen dit wonderlijke gespleten lange heden.

From *Parkland and Deserts* (Parken en woestijnen). The Hague: A.A.M. Stols, 1941. 1940[1]
Translated by A.J. Barnouw

Bergman (1921-)

Travel Letter

dear friend how splendid things are here
the cows in calf call forth a tear

the railway track winds through the dale
a woman runs the waterfall

a meadow rings each house or farm
that all beguile with postcard charm

folk shuffle past at measured pace
and not a step do they retrace

it's said god made us humans small
though fashioned us to stand up tall

the whole scene's here before my eyes
it almost could be paradise

and everything's so splendid here
at times it's quite too much I fear

Reisbrief

waarde vriend het is hier prachtig
de koeien zijn ontroerend drachtig

de spoorlijn loopt dwars door het dal
een vrouw beheert de waterval

elk huis of hok met beemd en gaard
verkoopt men op een ansichtkaart

de mensen lopen traag en stug
en komen op geen stap terug

men zegt god heeft ons klein gebouwd
maar sneed ons uit behoorlijk hout

dit alles sta ik aan te zien
zo is het paradijs misschien

en verder is hier alles prachtig
het wordt me soms wel eens te machtig

From *The Contents of the Surface* (De inhoud van het oppervlak).
Amsterdam: Em. Querido's Uitgeverij b.v., 1975.
Translated by John Irons

Miriam Van hee (1952-)

Fear of Flying

my father doesn't want to fly
he says statistics prove
the risks too clearly he wants
solid ground beneath his feet
or at least water, my father is
his own yardstick, he
commands respect

each year my sister books
journeys overseas she wants
to go to places where I
haven't been but
then falls ill and cancels
so she fights against
something that dwells within
a pain that's an abyss

and gains our confidence because
we believe her when she asks us
where we're off to for a holiday,
waits for no answer
and says, america for me

Angst voor vliegen

mijn vader wil niet vliegen
hij zegt dat statistieken
overduidelijk de risico s bewijzen
hij wil grond onder de voeten
of minstens water, mijn. vader
meet zich niet, hij wordt
gerespecteerd

mijn zus boekt elk jaar
overzeese reizen ze wil
op plaatsen zijn waar ik
niet ben geweest maar
ze wordt ziek en annuleert
zo vecht ze tegen iets
dat binnen in haar woont
een bodemloze pijn

en wint vertrouwen want
wij geloven haar als ze ons vraagt
waarheen wij op vakantie gaan,
niet op het antwoord wacht
en zegt, ik naar amerika

From *The Relation between the Days. Poems 1978-1996* (De band tussen de dagen, gedichten 1978-1996).
Amsterdam: De Bezige Bij, 1998. 1992[1].
Translated by John Irons

Ingmar Heijtze (1971-)

Notice to Travellers

They open and close you
then they talk like they know you
they don't know you
Joni Mitchell

Within me there's a sea and that is me.
It's ten years now since I last saw myself.
Each time I journey to me, half-way there
I turn around and come back empty-handed.
Somebody says it really is enough
to make me weep, but where
can a sea shed tears? Somebody else
is jealous. He says: 'You at least
have got a story.' Foam floats
through his field of vision. I repeat:
the sea has got no story.

Within me there's a distant city. That's
where I must go. But everything is long
ago and maybe, when I'm there,
I'll walk around, see nothing, fail to recognise
a soul and homesickness will wrack me
just as much. Within me there's a country
I could travel to, before it
got too small, it lies in green tiles
between asphalt roads, each square beneath
the sky so empty, I keep on
getting blown back home.

Time, sea, city, country,
sky and squares are there
both day and night, some day I'll sail
away inside my head but always
I travel with myself and I refuse
to whine point-blank: not in the train,
not on the bus, my sole trip's plain –
to Halfway-There, to Empty-Handed
and return – no one can perish
so imposingly as me. There is a sea
in me in which I drown.

Bericht aan de reizigers

They open and close you
then they talk like they know you
they don 't know you
Joni Mitchell

Er zit een zee in mij en dat ben ik.
Ik heb mezelf al tien jaar niet gezien.
Wanneer ik naar mij toe reis, keer ik
halverwege onverrichter zake terug.
Iemand zegt dat ik er eindelijk eens
om zou moeten huilen, maar waar
laat een zee zijn tranen? Iemand
anders is jaloers. Hij zegt: 'Jij hebt
tenminste een verhaal.' Schuim
drijft door zijn blikveld. Ik herhaal:
de zee heeft geen verhaal.

Er zit een verre stad in mij. Daar
moet ik heen. Maar alles is zo lang
geleden en misschien, als ik er ben,
loop ik wat rond, zie niets, herken
geen mens en huilt mijn heimwee
even hard. Er ligt een land in mij,
daar kon ik vroeger reizen maar het
werd te klein, het ligt in groene tegels
tussen asfaltwegen, ieder plein onder
de hemel is zo leeg, ik waai steeds
weer terug naar huis.

De tijd, de zee, de stad, het land,
de hemel en de pleinen zijn er
dag en nacht, ik moet eens lekker
weg in eigen hoofd maar altijd reis
ik met mezelf mee en ik ben klaar
met het gedrein: niet in de trein,
niet met de bus, alleen naar
Halverwege Onverrichter Zake
en terug – niemand kan zo groots
vergaan als ik. Er zit een zee
in mij en ik verdrink.

From *Shadow Accounting* (Schaduwboekhouding). Amsterdam: Podium, 2005.
Translated by John Irons

Menno Wigman (1966-)

Night Train

This then, all told. An alien and threadbare gaze
   in misted window-pane. That severed head,
that Hitler minus the moustache: that's me?
   Can ever a fond mother have believed
in that conceited stuck-up grouch? My god,

where is the pillager who slept with Valkyries,
   the poet who rode his birds and violins?
I am so tired, so frozen fast within a curse
   and in the filthy pane that gives the game away
I see my vacant gaze just one more time

framed there by fear and smoke and self-reproach.
   Too late. No passion urged me to the edge,
no Donne or Whitman seized my pen. Too late.
   And just like everything encumbered with this life
      I'm on my way and will arrive.

Nachttrein

Na alles dit. Een vreemde, afgeleefde blik
   in een beslagen ruit. Dat afgehakte hoofd,
die Hitler zonder snor: ben ik dat echt?
   Heeft daar, in die verwaande iezegrim,
heeft daar een moeder in geloofd? Mijn god,

waar is de plunderaar die met Walküren sliep,
   de dichter die op vogels en violen reed?
Ik ben zo moe, zo vastgevroren in een vloek,
   en in de vuile ruit die zich verspreekt
zie ik nog één keer mijn verloren blik,

omlijst door angst en rook en zelfverwijt.
   Te laat. Geen hartstocht dreef mij naar de grens,
geen Gorter of Lodeizen greep mijn pen. Te laat.
   En zoals alles wat met leven is behept
      ben ik op weg en kom ik aan.

From *During Summer All Cities Smell* ('s Zomers stinken alle steden).
Amsterdam: Bert Bakker, 1997.
Translated by John Irons

A Road Less Travelled

The Road to Antwerp Beach – A Journey along the N1

[DEREK BLYTH]

Photo by Derek Blyth.

When I moved to Brussels at the end of the 1980s, I was attracted more than anything by the historic cities of Flanders. I spent all my spare time walking around the streets of these extraordinary cities, simply fascinated by the richness of the architecture, the dark interiors of the churches, the unexpected glimpses of canals. I loved the hidden details, the places the guidebooks don't mention, like the secret course of the River Leie in Ghent, the walled gardens in Bruges and the strange emptiness of the left bank of the Scheldt in Antwerp. It felt as if I was living at the heart of one of the greatest urban civilisations in the world.

So why, I began to wonder, did Belgians not share this opinion? As soon as they could afford it, the people I knew were leaving the city, buying a plot of land on the edge of some little village, picking a house out of a Batibouw catalogue, and then spending ridiculous amounts of time arguing about the colour of artificial stone for the patio terrace. This was not happening in Florence, or Paris, or Prague, or Edinburgh, and I was not sure why it was happening in Flanders.

When I decided to drive from Brussels to Antwerp on the old N1 road, it was partly an attempt to discover the other Flanders, the space between the cities. I imagined that the whole journey would take a day at most. The total distance is 46 kilometres and the speed limit is normally 70 kilometres an hour. Even if I seriously dawdled along the way, I'd be in Antwerp by late afternoon, I thought; but I was wrong, and it took a day to cover the first 18 kilometres and two days to reach the end of the journey.

Willebroek Canal.
Photo by Derek Blyth.

Rubbish and royalty

The N1 used to be the most important road in Belgium. It linked Brussels, the capital, with Mechelen, the cathedral town, and Antwerp, the port. It was like the A1 in Britain, or Route 66 in America, or the Via Appia in Italy, a road that was more than just a means of getting somewhere. But now it is difficult even to find out where the N1 begins. It ceased to be the main road to Antwerp when the A12 was built, and lost any remaining significance when the six-lane E19 motorway was constructed. No one now uses it to drive from Brussels to Antwerp, which is exactly why I wanted to do it.

I picked up the road beside the Willebroek Canal in a fairly grim industrial zone. It runs past railway yards, gravel barges, car dumps and, somewhat unexpectedly, the grounds of the royal palace. I was surprised, and slightly comforted, to discover that the Belgian royal family has, as its next-door neighbour, the Brussels Region's rubbish incinerator plant. Even the Royal Brussels Yacht Club, further along the canal, sits in the middle of the Port of Brussels industrial zone, which is not necessarily the perfect spot to sit on a varnished wood deck sipping cocktails.

Chungking Boiled Bristles

The N1 leaves the city below the elevated section of the Ring motorway, which is normally jammed solid, because it is a real road that goes somewhere, unlike the N1, which is a road to nowhere, or at least to nowhere more important than Vilvoorde.

It was not part of the plan to stop in Vilvoorde, of which I knew very little, apart from a recollection that it was here that William Tyndale was executed as a heretic. This did not seem a good reason to stop, especially as I was feeling slightly heretical myself, travelling to Antwerp on the N1 rather than the motor-

way. But then I happened to glimpse the main church, an appealing Brabant gothic building, and decided that it might be worth taking a quick look around the town. Even then I was not expecting much, and so I put two 50 cent coins in the meter, allowing me an hour of parking, which seemed more than enough.

I was of course wrong about Vilvoorde, which is a fascinating Flemish town, though William Tyndale may not have agreed. I found a little museum devoted to the Protestant martyr, though it was closed that day. It occupies a quite strange chapel at the end of a courtyard where I also noticed two large orange pumpkins sitting on a wooden crate stencilled with the words 'Chungking Boiled Bristles'.

I was still thinking about boiled bristles as I entered the gothic church and discovered one of the most astonishing gravestones I have ever seen. It depicts a medieval Flemish knight who chose to have himself represented on his grave-stone as a decaying corpse. That was not the only surprise. The church, which is kept open by volunteers, is a fascinating place full of odd details, such as an elaborate baroque pulpit which originally stood in a church in Antwerp and a set of baroque choir stalls from the Abbey of Groenendael. I spent a long time look-ing at the stalls, which are carved with plump cherubs, monsters and angels, but the most captivating details were the wooden figures which, I found out later, are carrying symbols of the Passion of Christ.

I was already feeling positive about Vilvoorde when I went inside the library on Grote Markt, and discovered a warren of intimate rooms, stained glass win-dows, iron staircases and a remarkably rich collection of English literature. My brief tour of Vilvoorde ended in a quite grand café located in a converted nine-teenth-century meat market. I could easily have spent longer in this attractive town, but it was getting late and I was still only twelve kilometres from Brussels.

The N1 turns into a four-lane highway on the west side of Vilvoorde, passing houses that were built in the Thirties in an optimistic modern style, using glazed tiles, rounded corners and metal balconies. It struck me that these were the first utopian houses, built by families searching for a new life outside the cities. They now seem a bit depressing, as if Utopia had failed to arrive.

Then I made a little detour. I was looking for Het Steen, the country house that Rubens bought in 1635. I knew it was close to Vilvoorde, but the landscape seemed flat and empty, not at all as it appears in those romantic landscape paintings, such as *A View of Het Steen in the Early Morning* in London's National Gallery. I was about to give up when I noticed a country house hidden in the trees. There was no sign to say that this was Het Steen, but I was convinced by the look of the building and the muddy lane running through the wood. The sun by that time was low in the sky, and as it shone through the green stained-glass windows, casting long shadows on the lawn, I could easily imagine Rubens, a bit stiff with old age, strolling across the lawns, playing the country gentleman.

On the way back to the N1, I drove past a row of new villas in a variety of eclectic styles – Old Flemish, Modernist, Dallas – and it struck me then that the owners were living a romantic myth that went back as far as Rubens. He was one of the first city dwellers to discover the sensual pleasures of the Flemish countryside, and in so doing inspired an urban exodus that has now virtually destroyed the landscape.

It was getting dark and I realised that it was going to take longer than I had imagined to reach Antwerp. So I turned around, took one last look at Het Steen, and drove back to the city. It took no time at all, because all the traffic was coming out of Brussels, returning to Utopia.

Our Lady of the N1.
Photo by Derek Blyth.

Villa near Elewijt.
Photo by Derek Blyth.

Photo by Derek Blyth.

The mystique of the duffel coat

Cornelius Kilianus
Dufflaeus, Duffel.
Photo by Derek Blyth.

Back on the N1 on a bitterly cold February morning, I had driven through Mechelen, and was waiting at traffic lights when I noticed a sign pointing to Duffel, 4 kilometres away. I had always wanted to visit Duffel, mainly because of the name, so I turned down the road and parked near the centre. I was half expecting a small museum of local history that would explain the origin of the duffel coat, but there was nothing. If Duffel had been in Britain, I realised, there would have been a Duffel Heritage Centre and no doubt several shops selling duffel coats and bags. This is partly explained by the romantic mystique of the duffel coat in Britain, where this garment – with its distinctive hood, toggles and rope ties – evokes heroic war films starring the inevitable John Mills, battling the sea in the thick of an Atlantic storm, muffled up in a duffel coat.

I visited the town archives, partly to escape the biting wind, but also in the hope of finding an entire section devoted to the famous coat. The archivist was very helpful and searched through the records, but all he could come up with was one small photocopied monograph on the local cloth industry published about twenty years ago. I found out from this that Duffel was known in the Middle Ages for a distinctive type of cheap, coarse cloth mainly worn by the poor. The cloth was exported to England and Lübeck and even Riga, and ended up in America as one of the cheap items, along with glass beads and nails, that the Dutch gave to the Indians in exchange for Manhattan.

But who invented the duffel coat? I had assumed that it had originated in Duffel, but the archives contain no evidence of this. I did some research later, and came across a source that suggested that the duffel coat was developed in the 1890s as a garment for British naval officers. It was made of thick wool cloth from Flanders, but it can't have come from Duffel, as the local cloth industry had died out by then.

On the way back to the car, I passed a statue to Cornelius Kilianus Dufflaeus, who was born in Duffel in 1530. Cornelius is celebrated as a poet, translator, proof reader and compiler of the first dictionary of the Dutch language. As I admired the statue I wondered idly if he ever wore a duffel coat, but I somehow thought not.

A Bavarian beer hall and Elvis on St Anna Beach

I was soon back on the N1, driving past a more recent strip of utopian architecture, glimpsing white houses, round porthole windows and low industrial buildings. Yet there was a stubborn rustic element here, a bucolic fantasy with its roots in Bruegel, which was at its most whimsical in the various designs of roadside letter boxes at the end of each garden, some in the shape of thatched cottages, others resembling bird houses, but the most enchanting featuring plump cherubs perched on beer barrels. This, I think, may be Flanders' unique contribution to the history of road architecture.

Then I found the Bavarian beer hall, just outside Kontich. I already knew about this relic of the 1958 Brussels World Fair, or I would probably have driven straight past. This immense Bavarian tavern, which could seat 3,000 people, had been one of the highlights of the fair, but it was empty on the morning of my visit and also a bit depressing, at least to someone who had been hoping for a cheerful Bavarian waitress carrying six mugs of beer. A few months later it had been converted into a Chinese restaurant.

Goodbye, Bavarian
beer hall.
Photo by Derek Blyth.

Antwerp.
Photo by Derek Blyth.

I had by now reached the suburbs of Antwerp and was beginning to realise that the journey was near its end, and all that remained was to crawl through city traffic and hunt for a car park. And then I remembered there was a different route, and I moved cautiously into a lane that led to the Ring.

I was heading for the left bank of the Scheldt. I just had to drive through the Kennedy Tunnel and take the first exit. A broad boulevard with hardly any traffic led straight to the river. And there it was, the Cathedral, perfectly positioned at the end of a four-lane highway, separated by the broad river Scheldt, and looking just as it does in the famous view painted by Jan Bonnecroy in 1658.

Yet I did not stop there. I felt that a road trip needed a different ending, like Jack Kerouac sitting on a wrecked pier looking across to New Jersey, and so I followed the road around the bend in the river. It came to a dead end on the edge of a silver birch wood. I parked and walked through the trees. An icy wind was blowing as I reached the St Anna Beach on the Scheldt. This was the ending I had been hoping for, but it was too cold to stand around, so I started walking along the dike.

The far side of the river was lined with oil refineries, chemical plants, burning gas towers. But it was peaceful on the left bank, just mud flats and darting magpies and abandoned caravans. I passed a strange thatched cottage that looked like something in a fairy tale and finally reached the last building on the dike. It was a café, decorated with ship models and nautical maps, and completely empty. I sat down at a window table looking out on the river and then I noticed that they were playing an Elvis song, which seemed somehow the only possible music for such a strange lonely spot, which seemed more like New Jersey, at least to me. ■

Even at Home I am not a Tourist

At home he feels like a tourist
He fills his head with culture
He gives himself an ulcer
(Gang of Four, 1979)

Filthy toilets in Genoa. Turbulence between Brussels and Barcelona. Hairpin bends in the Alps. Rambunctious students on the train from London to Cambridge. Small souvenir shops on Mykonos selling ithyphallic polyester satyrs. Lost luggage at Jomo Kenyatta International. A New York hotel with a view of a blank wall with a fire escape. The second coming as traveller's trots of the scrumptious local sausages in Goa. Mexican guides that lure you into a tourist trap with a broad smile full of pearly whites. Copied credit cards in the back kitchen of a Romanian restaurant. Travel is like life itself: brutal, surprising and full of vexation. The German Paul Hentzer noted in 1598 in his *Travels in England during the Reign of Queen Elizabeth* (translated by Richard Bentley and edited by Horace Walpole in 1797) that travelling means a lot of troubles, but then man is born to trouble.

   Despite this, people often think that by travelling they can briefly step outside their lives. If things aren't really going smoothly at work or at home, they are

'due for a holiday'. The pressure needs to be taken off. The batteries need re-charging. Or topping up. All of these are metaphors that create the impression that mobility can prevent woeful dramas of total stagnation or fatal overpressure. And so, for our mental and physical well-being we must have a quick break. Anyone staying at home is insane. Or will in due course become so.

The forward flight or one's own loo?

In his article 'Holidays are no use whatsoever' (*NRC Handelsblad*, 3-4 July 2004) Arjo Klamer, Professor of Cultural Economics at the Erasmus University of Rotterdam, writes: *'Holidays are so important in this country that they have long since ceased to be considered a luxury. They have become a basic need and thus a right.'* I sometime get the feeling that holidays – by which I mean 'travelling' – have almost become a *duty*. More and more, people live from one holiday to the next. Business shut down during the summer, at Easter or Christmas? Then comes the inevitable asking all your colleagues where they are off to. For you have to travel to really relax. And when it comes to proper diversion, money is no object. Even in the frugal Netherlands, where holiday-makers devote 7% of their income on average to their favourite waste of time.

Correction: of course, travelling isn't a waste of time. Well, no more and no less than a game of Klaberjass with your mates, watching the telly, reading a book or just chasing tail on your own patch. It all depends on what you want to do with your life. So if you want to travel, then travel. No sweat. But count me out. Relaxation is not reason enough to get me moving. Ad Vingerhoets, professor of psychology at Tilburg – and a bit of an official Dutch 'holiday guru' – notes the almost religious nature of holidays: *'In the old days we had to go to church – now we have to go on holiday.'* So just call me a heretic.

Of course, a person can be obliged to travel – once in a while. Sometimes that is called emigrating. At other times: being a fugitive. Yet again: having criminal intent. I cannot deny that as a notorious people-smuggler, internationally wanted terrorist, entrepreneurial drugs trafficker or committed sex-tourist you would do better to keep moving. By the way, people on the move have had a bad reputation ever since the Middle Ages. Hieronymus Bosch even depicted travelling hawkers as sinners, with hell their final destination. Now, though, no one would deny that business people have sufficiently honourable motives for being out on the town. Although the philosopher Thorstein Veblen once claimed that *'no one travelling on a business trip would be missed if he failed to arrive.'*

Who, then, has solid, *bona fide* reasons for travelling? Writers would seem to be worthy of mention. Cees Nooteboom, once mockingly referred to as an up-market tourist (for what serious intellectual writes travel accounts for a glossy like *Avenue*?), defines travelling as his *'way of thinking'* – an apparent *'forward flight'* in which he experiences his *'chameleon-like existence'* in it most intense form. A traveller with ambition then, since *'for me, the whole world is a spot I want to make my own. A maze where I would gladly get lost – and then have to be my own Ariadne.'* Another professional traveller from Dutch literature, Lieve Joris, is above all a woman with a mission. She travels the wide world for her books because *'the Netherlands is a blessed isle in a ravaged world'*. That, of course, is not exactly an ideal slogan for, say, a Dutch travel agency. Something like, *ex absurdo*, well of course, why should we stay at home when it's certainly no better anywhere else?

All right though... we travel in order to learn, don't we? Not so, according to yet another Dutch author, Maarten 't Hart, who remarked with some irritation during an interview that he doesn't believe for a minute that travelling broadens the mind: *'For me, travelling is the worst thing there is. (...) Bach never travelled.*

Mozart did, admittedly, but he should have refrained from doing so, especially as a child.' Herman Brusselmans, the Jupiter of the Flemish post-agrarian 'Heimat' novel, sees things somewhat more concretely: *'I once went to Rome for three days. Already on the second day I was wracked by homesickness. It's just not in me. My four white walls or the desolate expanses of the Hungarian steppe – the choice takes no time at all. (...) To put it another way, I always have to be within easy reach of my own WC.'*

The ideal partner of the squat armchair on the move

Is travelling only glamorous in retrospect? These Holland-America-Line passengers on the Statendam would probably have begged to differ.

And yet there must be a thousand and one reasons for travelling, and it doesn't have to be on the vast scale of military interventions, humanitarian aid or writing a bestseller. In *No Shitting in the Toilet* (1997) Peter Moore, who is evidently not so glued to the loo as Brusselmans is, even compiles a top-ten list of reasons for doing so. By travelling, according to him, you can not only find out a great deal about other peoples, languages and cultures, you can also learn to

develop your own initiative and to handle money. No less important is that you can also travel in order to lose weight, escape your creditors, have something to talk about at dinner parties or bore your friends with photos and videos of your travels. All good reasons as far as I am concerned; as long as you don't come trotting along with what I call the 'India Syndrome'. You know, those people who go off abroad (often India, Nepal or Tibet) in order to *discover themselves*. And they do that by living *with* and *as* the local population. They like to brag that they are practising a kind of alternative eco-tourism, but forget that their flight to Katmandu and their treks through the jungle have a far more negative impact on the environment than a coach-load of senior citizens on their way to Benidorm. And on their return they tell you at every suitable and unsuitable opportunity that although you have everything here, the people over there are much friendlier, more hospitable and – above all – more *spiritual*. And then I ask myself ... if our lives are so much more hectic and geared to financial gain, why do they then advise me to *hurry up* and *buy* a ticket to Nirvana?

And there are also plenty of reasons for *not* travelling. It is often claimed that travelling is in people's blood. They constantly want to break new ground, and exceeding geographical limitations is simply a logical first step to that end. Just think of the Mongols' never-ending search for new grazing land for their horses. But are people travellers by nature? The Dutch writer Gerrit Komrij voices his doubts about this in *Drowned Books* (Verzonken boeken,1986): *'One of the insoluble enigmas that clings to the mammal man – who after all is not short of loose ends and question marks – is his urge to travel. What impels the comfort-loving biped, who has developed in the course of evolution into an ideal partner of the squat armchair – indeed, suited to downy cushions as a nut is to a bolt – to say goodbye to his comfortable environment and to expose himself to too much heat, too much cold, to the company of too many people, to car breakdowns and flaming rows, to conspiracies between airline companies and insurance giants, to dust and headaches, to homesickness and the mindless universal monotony of the souvenir shop? What impels him to abandon his natural state and pitch himself into a nightmare of discomforts and unsuitable behaviour?'* According to Komrij, then, humans are sedentary beings that from time to time allow themselves to be enticed by distant horizons, for *'there is no other reason for travelling than for those moments when everything is born anew. Travelling – I don't like doing it. But the urge for that lyricism can become too great, too great.'* So the backpack is strapped on when the flesh becomes weak and the spirit longs for the sublime.

If one reads some of the travel accounts available, the question is whether it really is worth the trouble to listen to the call of foreign parts. The Groningen humanist Wessel Gansfort travelled from one university to the other in the fifteenth century, but at the end of his life his verdict was that all that travelling was bound to lead to spiritual weakness. Two centuries earlier, the writer Jacob van Maerlant had nothing nice to say about travelling abroad: *"Tis all perfidiousness and vicious crime'*. And Jacob Haafner, who could not settle in the Netherlands and travelled in the eighteenth century through such countries as present-day India, Sri Lanka and Indonesia, castigates himself for his own wanderlust. It is *'an unhappy, incurable craving'* and a *'stupid romantic urge for foreign encounters and adventures'*. It is not absolutely necessary, by the way, to travel abroad in order to moan and groan about travelling. In the summer of 1823, Jacob van Lennep and Dirk van Hogendorp made a sight-seeing walking tour through the Netherlands. In their account of their travels, the two young men had little positive to tell about their experiences. The Frisians were pigheaded and addicted to drink, those from Groningen were haughty, those from Drente behind the times and those from the south unmistakably backward. Paul Theroux's pithy comment *'travel is only glamorous in retrospect'* make a most inelegant belly-landing here.

But it's not all trouble and affliction on the road. As early as the late fourteenth century, Dirc van Delf in his *Tafel van den Kersten Ghelove* exhorts his readers to step out into the world. Anyone who always stays at home is no better than an otter or a mole. Ogier Ghiselin van Boesbeeck (Busbequius to his humanist friends), from 1555 to 1562 the Holy Roman Empire's Flemish emissary to Constantinople, was a compulsive traveller, but he had a keen eye for the beauty of nature and cities and collected a host of facts about old inscriptions and the flora and fauna of what is now Turkey. He noted things down with the surprised curiosity of a fully-fledged tourist, despite the fact that three centuries later the word *'toerisme'* ('tourism') was still not to be found in the first edition of the great Van Dale Dutch dictionary of 1864.

No talent for holidays

As soon as you let slip that you do not go travelling of your own accord, there is always some smartass who has to quote from Blaise Pascal's *Pensées*: *'All man's troubles come from not knowing how to sit still in one room.'* Bookworms from the Low Countries can also come out with something a bit more longwinded: *'It seems to me that I travel the world in greater safety on a geographical map and that I learn more from history books'* (Erasmus) or: *'Oh, travel-eager spirit, you can save yourself the trouble/ and see in this play the world great and wide/described and painted in a brief span of pages'* (Joost van den Vondel on the atlas of his compatriot Blaeu). For the person less fond – or completely unfond – of books and maps, there are now enough travelogues, survival shows and other travel programmes on the television. And the truly modern armchair traveller naturally goes in for virtual travel in cyberspace.

But do we really need culturally justified excuses not to travel? Surely it can't be that problematic to leave our room? Over the course of the twentieth century people got more and more free time, wages increased, roads improved, motorised vehicles made their appearance and finally employees in countries such as Belgium and the Netherlands not only got paid holidays but were even given holiday money. The journey itself became less important than the destination. The Belgian industrialist Georges Nagelmackers, founder of the Compagnie internationale des Wagons-lits (1872) and of the legendary Orient Express (1883) wrote: *'What tourist or businessman (...) would not like to step into a compartment where he can spend the night in a bed, between clean sheets and under a blanket,*

to sleep soundly without fear of being disturbed and wake up in the morning only a few kilometres from his final destination.' Travel in the twenty-first century is really not a tough job at all, if one leaves out of account ever-longer check-in times, shoe bombers, biometric passports and sky marshals. Of course there are also people who moan that travel has lost a great deal of its elegance and style. The Flemish artist Jan de Cock for example, who refers to the Eurostar as *'pure bureaucracy on wheels'* and would rather travel to London by container ship: *'a microcosm of steel, the sea is wide and unpredictable, the route is always different.'* It goes without saying that the democratisation of travel has been inversely proportional to the aesthetic content of the journey. But must that prevent me from travelling to destination X? Possibly, although not in my case, considering I feel no need to set off X-wards anyway. And naturally, mass tourism also has pernicious effects on coral reefs, forests, sea turtles and the increasingly worn floor of Canterbury Cathedral. But if I am not in X, I impact on the home environment instead.

In short: I don't need a reason for not travelling. Just as you don't need one when you decide you *will* go and pack your suitcases. The above is not a diatribe against tourism – and most certainly not against travelling. It's just that I do not feel your restlessness. Let me be as static as Oblomov or even as flabby as Jabba the Hut. Ad Vingerhoets – the 'holiday prof' himself – is a much-travelled

Translated by John Irons

man and now he never goes on holiday any more: '*It has not made me any happier. Maybe I simply have no talent for holidays.*' That is how I feel, too. For me there is no anticipation, no holiday depression or euphoria of the unknown – and absolutely no post-holiday blues or enthusiastic braying that you really should have been there. Some people have a talent for making a simple outing into a real mini-trip. They are able to find every single commemorative plaque and broken-off border post and will promptly come up with some anecdote about it. I feel no such urge. Perhaps you think I'm a bit of a queer fish, a nihilist or even a weirdo. If that's the case, at least you don't have to worry that I will turn up in your neighbourhood. For most of the time I sit at home. ■

Photo by Filip Matthijs,
taken at home, obviously...

Raining cats and dogs.

Food horrible.

Natives unbelievably
rude.

Wish I was home
already...

T.

Printed in Germany

Sort. 17/6

Center for Folklife
and Cultural Heritage
Smithsonian Inst.
750 9th Street, NW, S. 4100
Washington, D.C 20013-7012
USA

The Dutch Raise their Voices

[GERARD VAN WESTERLOO]

If the International Quality Press is to be believed, the entire Netherlands has recently undergone a complete metamorphosis. Until recently it was supposedly inhabited by a collection of decent, tolerant, liberal, open-minded burghers who willingly opened their doors to fugitive French Huguenots, Portuguese Jews, Antwerp Stocking Merchants and other refugees of conscience. But hardly had the twenty-first century made its entrance than these same unbelievably kind-hearted characters could not find words enough to express their abhorrence of the wave of colourful arrivals from places like Somalia, Bosnia and even Pakistan who arrived seeking refuge along the banks of the great rivers. To add insult to injury, they built places of worship not to the glory of the God of the Netherlands but in honour of Allah, who is notoriously intolerant of other Supreme Beings.

This dramatic quasi-romantic representation of events, which by and large is widely believed not just outside but also within the Netherlands, seems too neat to be true. Can a nation's character really change so fundamentally in the space of a couple of years? Amsterdam's motto describes its citizens as *Valorous, Resolute and Merciful'*, but during the five years of the German Occupation, for example, that was only true for a couple of days when they protested at the treatment of Jews during the February Strike. After that, they looked the other way as their Jewish neighbours were dragged from their homes by the lorry load. Nevertheless, praise be to God and Allah, however xenophobic the inhabitants of Holland, Zeeland, Gelderland, Friesland, Groningen and the other provinces might appear to have become, the situation is not entirely bleak. When a hard-bitten government minister decided to repatriate 26,000 immigrants, including numerous schoolchildren, churches across the land filled with people pleading for clemency, as a result of which the minister's stony heart softened to the tune of at least 13,000.

The seven-year fashion virus

Nonetheless, a shift in attitude has manifestly taken place, and may perhaps be explained by another fairly constant factor in the Dutch make-up. There is a universal but erroneous belief that I and my compatriots are level-headed and down-to earth. It's a great pity, but nothing could be further from the truth. How this misunderstanding arose is a mystery to me, but perhaps it stems from the fact that our ancestors regularly had to stand shoulder to shoulder on the dykes, sandbags at the ready, to hold back the water in the millraces, ditches and canals. This preoccupation presumably left them no time to spend slaughtering each other on matters of principle.

Be that as it may, I do not believe that any other country in the world suffers so badly from the seven-year fashion virus as the Netherlands. One only has to turn off the motorway and drive through the new housing estates that have invariably been built in places once perpetually under threat of inundation. With a bit of practice one can accurately date each residential block to within seven years. That is about the length of time that a particular style remains fashionable. Before your very eyes, the fashion for residential zones and railway sleepers makes way for that of living at the water's edge; the period of cute gables follows seamlessly from that of stark walls. The Dutch have a marked tendency to be original all at once and in the same way. And the abruptness of these changes in fashion could never sensibly be described as 'level-headed'. In that respect Dutch behaviour can appear rather hysterical, as astonished visitors to this country during an important football championship will observe. No, I suspect that there is much truth in the judgement of James Kennedy, an American historian with Dutch roots. According to him, a striking characteristic of the Dutch through the ages has been their liking for new dogmas – he observes a centuries-old pattern of *'sudden, radical and mass conversion'*.

Not much historical insight is required to date the most recent change in fashion or 'mass conversion'. It took place during the couple of months before the 2002 elections, the months that saw the stormy rise and the Shakespearean fall of Pim Fortuyn. This charismatic man was, as it were, the very embodiment of the Dutch fashion virus. As a Marxist lecturer when the Left was in vogue, he tried in vain to join the Communist Party. But when the Right became fashionable he courted the smart real estate operators for whom Marx and Lenin were about as attractive as a fishing net to a herring. With his highly developed instinct for the *zeitgeist* this man succeeded more or less single-handedly in reversing the fashion trend of the preceding period, undeservedly remembered for being supremely tolerant, and initiating a period which has acquired an equally unfounded reputation for heartless intolerance. In fact, it is much more the case that '*the tall, bald homo from Rotterdam*' found the words and possessed the eloquence to express something that had long existed in Dutch society but had not been articulated unambiguously for fear of denunciation by the political and media elites. It was a long-simmering dissatisfaction with a world that uncontrolled waves of immigration had changed out of all recognition.

But until very recently, any hint of complaint from those who bore the brunt of this change, the labouring and middle classes, meant that they ran the risk of being branded as fascists or worse by the elite. I myself experienced this when thrown to a seething crowd of professors, lecturers and students at the University of Amsterdam who were furious at a long article of mine in *Vrij Nederland*. In it, I had allowed ordinary Amsterdammers to speak their minds and express their indignation at the facile manner in which the political elite made them shoulder the consequences of the flood of immigrants. It was precisely that incongruence that Pim Fortuyn, in that piercing voice of his, was able to put into words that everyone could understand. Soon after, Paul Scheffer repeated the exercise more intellectually in his famous essay on what he called '*the multi-cultural drama*'. It did not go down at all well in his own social-democratic circles.

Pim Fortuyn was not a man to mince his words. The columns that he wrote for the weekly *Elsevier* magazine were about as peace-loving as a fox in a chicken-run, while in his speeches around the country he compared the behaviour of the average, respectable Dutch politician unfavourably with that of Osama Bin Laden. After his death, the decibel level in political debate and the media subsided to fairly normal levels, persuading some people to believe, wrongly, that the swing to intolerance had been a sudden aberration. But setting aside the tone of that debate, I personally found the most liberating effect of the Fortuyn episode was that the taboo on the slightest hint of intolerance was buried together with Fortuyn himself.

The possibility of self-destruction

Beneath the much vaunted toleration of the past, there lurked something less positive but also very Dutch, namely a lack of any real interest in those of different beliefs. Nowadays of course they tend also to be of a different colour. For centuries Dutch Protestants and Catholics tolerated each other, but only on condition that they stayed well away from each other's churches. They were, in the words of Abraham Kuiper, sovereign on their own patch. In precisely the same way, the Dutch tolerated the newcomers – so long as they kept to them-selves and did not even think of disturbing the peace. As soon as the rucksacks began to explode (figuratively for now in the Netherlands), such neutrality was squeezed out.

Since then the pitch of public debate in the Netherlands has indeed risen by a couple of octaves. After all, Pim himself had said aloud exactly what he thought, hadn't he? So what had been respectable Moslems were now branded as goat-shagging perverts (the exact words of film director Theo van Gogh). While Allah might well have been a great peacemaker once, he was now the bloodthirsty patron of the suicide bomber. The reaction of growing numbers of Moslem youths has been to join secret societies that have declared war on everything that in their eyes is corrupt, rotten, Western and anti-Allah. One of these self-appointed jihadis slit Theo van Gogh's throat with his scimitar in the firm belief that he was doing his God a great service.

In fact, these are morbid excesses and do not touch the heart of the matter, which is that, post Fortuyn, the Dutch have discarded their earlier fashion of bashfully falling silent whenever the elite spoke, and have embraced a new trend of publicly opposing anything that the elite might support. A perfect example was the 'No' vote to the European constitution. The latest fashion dictated that simply because the political elite, from the right-wing VVD to the Greens on the left, argued so strongly for this constitution, that was reason enough to vote against it.

Recently the Social and Cultural Planning Office published its biennial X-ray of what I can only call the state of the State. Even they were surprised to discover that the great majority of the Dutch deeply mistrusted anything to do with The Hague, politics or government departments. In the space of two years this general mistrust had spread like an infectious virus. At the same time, an equally surprising majority expressed a strong desire for real leadership, a strong man as it were. Or perhaps a strong woman.

This deep mistrust of the current elite and the longing for strong leadership and effective action are all too familiar. They are the symptoms of a confused nation. Those in power have little more to offer than, in the person of Prime Minister J.P. Balkenende, a kind of vague nostalgia for a time when schoolmasters were called 'Sir', a Cabinet Minister was 'His Excellency' and people faithfully went to church every Sunday – a church that could now well be a warehouse for second-hand furniture. Plus the message that the social system as such can only be saved by drastic reform, which is a euphemism for stripping it to the bone. What is completely lacking is a vision of where the country is heading and what it might look like in ten years' time. By then, will the larger cities contain no-go areas and be inhabited entirely by the angry, socially frustrated children and grandchildren of immigrants? Will there still be anyone willing to give lessons to pupils who regularly threaten the lives of their teachers? Is it possible that by then the 7.50 train will as a matter of principle never depart before 9.55? Will the managers by then have succeeded in permanently destroying all respect for manual labour? And will the God of the Netherlands be wearing a white smock and a ring beard?

Beneath the vociferous in which the Dutch now communicate with each other, one can detect their anxiety about the future. Numerous financial scandals ranging from building frauds to an untrustworthy Public Prosecutor's Office have seriously undermined Dutch confidence in their institutions. And they want little or nothing to do with their political parties, all of which without exception have their roots in an outdated worldview.

Some time ago, the respected columnist Henk Hofland, a man who could never be described as a pessimist, expressed a fear that a military coup in the Netherlands was no longer an impossibility. Dissatisfaction had taken too deep a hold on the nation for it to be ruled out entirely. Of course, he was laughed out of court. And it is true that the idea of anti-government tanks heading towards

Sand Sculpture Festival,
Thorn, 2003.

Translated by Chris Emery

the heart of government and the television studios is perhaps rather comical. But Hofland's imagery does make a point. There now exists in the Netherlands an almost unbridgeable gulf between us, the ordinary voters, on the one hand, and those who have been placed above us on the other.

I myself am less inclined to think that the next fashion will come about through machine guns at street corners, more that the political system will simply self-destruct. A party like D66 has, it is true, attempted in vain to bring this about for the past fifty years, but it was the Fortuyn elections that revealed once and for all the system's vulnerability. Since then, the chance of newcomers breaking into it has only increased.

If that ever happens, the brand-new Loud Voice of the Dutch will find a secure place in the system and thereby lose much of its reason to exist. I won't say that the Netherlands from then on will again become the supremely tolerant country that it never was. But at least the intensity and pitch of public debate will drop by a couple of octaves. ∎

Perfectly Happy in Vinex-Land

[MARIEKE VAN ROOY]

'What can you achieve as an architect in a typical Vinex location? There is no real context and the plans are already mainly set, and what's left over is an expressive facade. Only there have you the room to do something. Practising the art of architecture under such conditions is no more than decorator's work, at best a clever kind of decorating': so says the architectural critic Piet Vollaard in the Dutch architectural yearbook for 2000-2001. Vollaard was reacting to the Dutch government's most recent large-scale housing scheme, known as 'Vinex'. The Supplement to the Fourth Policy Document on Spatial Planning (in Dutch: 'Vierde Ruimtelijke Nota Extra, hence VINEX) set out a plan for 635,000 new houses to be built between 1995 and 2005 at inner city locations and on the outskirts of cities. These dwellings are needed to accommodate the growing number of families, but particularly also to keep the well-to-do middle classes in the cities. The launch of Vinex provoked immediate and constant criticism, mainly from experts in architecture. 'The ghettos of the future' and 'an avalanche of "doorzonwoningen"' are some of the critical comments made at the beginning of the nineties. (A doorzonwoning is a house or apartment with windows front and back and no intervening walls, so that the sun shines straight through.)

The extension of the city

The Netherlands has a rich tradition of housing projects initiated by the state. A few years ago we celebrated the centenary of the housing law, which enabled the gems of the Amsterdam School to be built. Between 1945 and 1960 around a million new modern homes were built as part of the reconstruction scheme. These reconstruction suburbs were composed mainly of low-rise buildings and long blocks of three or four storeys, situated on the outskirts of the city. In the seventies and eighties the emphasis was on decentralisation; 16 new towns were created on green-field sites, for example the towns of Zoetermeer, Almere and Lelystad. In the nineties, however, the emphasis was again on the concept of 'the compact city'. In order to prevent the fragmentation of the Dutch landscape, the Supplement to the Fourth Planning Document listed locations close to existing cities. Since the need for housing is most urgent in the Randstad

– the Crescent City which comprises the four largest cities in the Netherlands – the majority of Vinex locations are found there.

The idea behind the new suburbs was the provision of sustainable housing and high quality public transport and the preservation of the distinction between city, village and countryside. It was some of these very elements that attracted criticism. Critics pointed out the monotony of the programme, and public transport was in most cases provided too late with the result that in the suburb of Leidsche Rijn, for example, car ownership is proportionately higher than in nearby Utrecht. There was also a great deal of criticism of the houses themselves. They were considered too small and future inhabitants would have too little scope in personalising them. In response to this last criticism the state has made new arrangements with the developers. Future house owners will have more input and more freedom of choice with regard to house type, size, internal layout and price. On a larger scale also, it must be made possible for window arrangement, roof form, annexes and extensions to be added or modified. There is also pressure to reserve some thirty percent of the suburbs for free plots, on which private individuals can build a home of their choice, subject to certain conditions.

The development of Vinex locations is the responsibility of the municipalities. In cooperation with developers, the urban plan is drawn up as a Public Private Partnership and the desired architectonic character formulated. In general, municipalities remain responsible for public space and private companies are responsible for the housing projects. As the municipalities have total freedom in the design of the suburbs, apart from a few government-regulated conditions such as the requirement to build 30% social housing, the new suburbs differ enormously in outward appearance. In some cases the planners are guided by historical references, in others by the local context, while others again seek renewal by means of spectacular architecture. In all these locations the search for identity and the branding of the new suburbs certainly plays an important role.

The new suburb and the importance of an individual look

The Vinex location at IJburg in Amsterdam derives its identity from the fact that it is surrounded by water. IJburg will consist of eight artificial islands constructed in the lake called the IJmeer, with a total area of about 800 hectares. If everything goes according to plan it will eventually provide 18,000 dwellings for around 45,000 inhabitants, as well as around 300,000 m² for companies, offices and shops, fifteen junior schools and two secondary schools.

The residential area by the water, for which various plans have been produced since the sixties – take for example Van den Broek and Bakema's Pampus plan – has not had an easy ride. After a hard-fought but nevertheless 'failed' referendum in 1997 in which the plan's advocates pointed to the severe housing shortage in Amsterdam and its opponents stressed the unique flora and fauna of the IJ, the turnout at the referendum was below the legal minimum required and so work could start on the development of the new suburb. Despite the fact that the environmental activists had lost out in the end, the relationship between the new islands and the surrounding area was a key factor in the development. IJburg is presented as an island realm in which the splendour of the

IJburg. Photos by
Sjoerd Knibbeler.

IJmeer will as far as possible remain intact. The essence of the development is sustainability. The islands will support high-density building, with limited parking space, and will be provided with high quality public transport. IJburg's location in the IJmeer offers the town the possibility of two new facilities: a beach and a marina. Everywhere in those parts of the plan already realised there is a city atmosphere, largely due to the high-density mix of high- and low-rise buildings. Here you feel you are living not so much in suburbia, more in a logical extension of the existing city.

Despite the fact that the construction is completely different to IJburg, this 'new urban' feeling is also present in Ypenburg Garden City. Here there are very few apartment blocks but mainly low-rise buildings, mostly comprising terraced housing. Ypenburg, located on a former airbase, lies between the cities of The Hague and Delft and is surrounded by three important motorways. It is a typical Randstad location, in which the land is owned by the three small municipalities of Pijnacker, Rijswijk and Nootdorp, while the nearest large city, The Hague, is not formally a landowner but urgently needs this urban extension. The 12,000 houses are divided into five urban residential quadrants, known as 'Velden' (Fields), which have been delegated to some thirteen developers. The externally recruited urban planner Frits Palmboom chose water as the theme for the entire location. He also imposed a number of strict conditions with regard to the application and use of materials, density and public space. In this way there is space for a variety of typologies and experiments, but the whole area still exudes a certain harmony.

In Waterwijk (Waterland) there was space for unusual experiments in the field of architecture and the relationship between public and private space. Here there are two impressive projects by MVRDV, the bureau that is famous for its innovative working methods in which traditional parameters relating to housing are called into question. The Hageneiland (Hedge Island) project, which received worldwide publicity and won the Netherlands Architecture Institute prize in 2002, was composed of 119 dwellings for purchase and rent, each with its own garden. The classic terraced housing with pitched roof and garden has

Ypenburg's Patio Island
project (MVRDV). Photo by
Sjoerd Knibbeler.

Ypenburg's Hageneiland
(MVRDV).
Photo by Sjoerd Knibbeler.

been completely revivified by using the same material for the facade and roof. The architects employed materials such as roofing tiles, aluminium, asphalt plates and polyurethane in distinctive colours that could be used both for the roof and the facade. In the urban plan the traditional rows have been more or less maintained, but between every two, four or six houses there are gaps in the rows so that space is created for green areas, playgrounds or storage facilities in the form of greenhouses and mini houses. These features always appear at different points in the overall plan, so that an intriguing street pattern is created and the gardens vary in size. Parking is provided on the outskirts of the project and the public area between houses is reserved entirely for pedestrians.

Across the water is the same firm's Patio Island project, which could not be a greater contrast to the aforementioned Hageneiland. Here the public areas are literally non-existent. A rectangular grid consists of 12 strips, in each of which are four patio dwellings. From the outside, though, only a blank street wall can be seen, in which the sharp-eyed observer will spot a number of entrance doors that lead to the dwellings situated in the middle of the grid. Each dwelling has its own entrance. Above the enclosed housing block some roofs are protruding, which increase the amount of sunlight reaching the inward-facing houses. The south side of each unit is entirely of glass and is oriented towards the patio. The whole project, including roofs, facades and doors, is faced with black slate on the outer side. On a dark day this makes for a rather sombre effect, while on a bright day the sun is reflected in the facades.

Finally, not far from these two projects there are nine blocks of social housing created by the architects Bosch, and called Big House. From outside each block looks like some kind of barn, finished in dark-coloured brick and with an alternating window pattern. Each block is entered through a high gate behind which is an inner courtyard, where most of the entrances to the individual dwellings can be found. The facades of these courtyards are covered with a green facing

Ypenburg's Big House project (MVRDV). Photo by Sjoerd Knibbeler.

on which is mounted a wire framework for ivy to climb. The ground cover is also natural-looking, for the whole courtyard is covered with (reinforced) grass. The hipped roofs and predominantly green colouration create a lively and vital effect, contrasting with the more defensive outer facade. The inner courtyards are semi-public, but as an uninvited guest one tends to feel uncomfortable there, as though intruding upon the privacy of the inhabitants who, consciously or unconsciously, seem to claim the space as their own.

While the designers of both IJburg and Ypenburg aim for a contemporary architectonic style, a more traditionalist approach is becoming increasingly fashionable in Dutch urban planning. Since the end of the nineties there has been a large-scale return to an old-fashioned kind of design, which developers like because it is popular with potential buyers. Houses from the thirties, castles or country retreats, spark the imagination and provide an instant solution to the problem of the new suburbs' lack of identity. According to the architectural critic Hans Ibelings in *Unmodern Architecture* (Onmoderne architectuur. Hedendaags traditionalisme in Nederland, 2004): *'Where local context and architectural history provide no reference point, then one has to think up something new to be fluid and give history a new twist'*. Two outstanding examples of this are Brandevoort in Helmond and Haverleij in Den Bosch.

Brandevoort, containing around 6,000 houses, was designed by Rob Krier. Together with Sjoerd Soeters he is responsible for the most controversial neo-traditionalist residential areas in the Netherlands over recent years. In collabo-

The core of Brandevoort's Veste. Photo by Sjoerd Knibbeler.

ration with the municipality and the developers, Krier devised an urban plan composed of De Veste (The Fort), a compact urban core surrounded by a moat, beyond which are the 'Buitens' (country places), village-like green residential areas with detached and semi-detached dwellings. Entry to De Veste is via a limited number of access roads that bridge the moat. You then enter an intimate network of streets lined with 'canal houses' each of which differs from the others in height and appearance. The experienced observer will discover, however, that each so-called unique building is repeated elsewhere. On the central square, where there is at present an open space with a snack bar and supermarket in a temporary shed, an old-fashioned cast-iron covered market has already appeared.

The municipality talked about the charm of individual homes in a classic setting, and wanted a return to the classic Brabant village. You nevertheless get
the impression that De Veste represents a universal idea of a romantic village
rather than referring specifically to the archetypal Brabant village. The inhabitants do not seem to mind either way; the rather corny name plates, plant pots
and letterboxes they have put up on their houses fit in perfectly with the surroundings.

Another spectacular example is the Vinex location Haverleij near Den Bosch.
Hemmed in between the Maas, the village of Engelen and the Engelermeer,
nine castles and a fort have been erected in a landscape setting with a total
surface area of 220 hectares. The residential buildings will contain around
a thousand apartments and single-family homes that will be concentrated in
the complexes. There is no private outdoor space, but that means that there is
plenty of space for green areas – ranging from public gardens to reed beds and
woodland – and even for an eighteen-metre-long golf course. The nine castles
contain from fifty to ninety dwellings, while the fort is entirely different from the
rest. This complex was designed by seven architects as a small fortress town
on the sluice near Engelen and offers accommodation in the form of 450 apartments and dwellings of six different typologies.

What the municipality originally had in mind for this project was the typical
terraced housing, such as can be seen elsewhere in Vinex-land. But Sjoerd
Soeters, who was one of those invited to submit a design, proposed a concentration of castles so that as much as possible of the original landscape would
remain intact. This, as a counterpart to the ever-expanding sea of housing
in the Dutch landscape. However, a castle is, of course, a metaphor for much
more. It brings to mind monumentality, luxury, romance and, most important-
ly, security – something that is becoming increasingly important in the Netherlands. It is the combination of these aspects that provided the catalyst for the
municipality to forge ahead with what is for the Netherlands a rather radical
concept.

The Vinex location
Haverleij.

Brandevoort's Veste.
Photo by Sjoerd Knibbeler.

113

Ypenburg, IJburg, Brandevoort and Haverleij are just a few examples of the diversity to be found in Vinex-land. A diversity, though, that is mainly confined to the field of urban planning and structure and to the exterior of the houses. At the level of housing typology and plans little seems to have changed in the past forty years. But that is not really surprising, since developers are tending more and more to disregard architects when it comes to the layout of the houses. All that is left for them is the outside. According to the architecture critic Arthur Wortmann in the Dutch architectural yearbook for 2001-2002: *'Architects, it seems, find it difficult to accept their less relevant role. Even if their input is marginal many of them still want to be involved. What scope they are granted is confined almost entirely to the exterior. There are no typological experiments any more. Behind the ingenious and extravagant facades the same ordinary houses are to be found. Ah, but in this context any talk about facades is outdated. We now talk about the entire "skin" of the houses. Facade and roof have now merged into one grand architectonic statement.'* And that corresponds exactly with what the municipality and developers want to achieve, because with this architectonic statement their particular Vinex suburb can be put on the market.

It would be short-sighted, though, to brand these Vinex suburbs as failures solely on the basis of criticism by the professionals. Surely, isn't it just as important to look at the experiences and opinions of the people who actually live there? And here you are faced with a paradox. For it appears from various studies that the Vinex-dwellers are, with a few reservations – such as the lack of facilities and the delay in providing decent public transport – very satisfied with their new biotope (as can be seen in a RIGO Research report published in 1999). They seem totally contented with their own little patch of suburbia. So perhaps after all the average Dutch person is not hankering after all kinds of new features for the interior of his house. And is that really so strange? Isn't it the case that in this age when image is everything we derive our image increasingly from externals such as clothing, cars and mobile phones? That being so, the *'decorated facades'*, as Piet Vollaard calls them, slot smoothly into that list. ∎

Translated by Joy Kearney

FURTHER READING

Baljon, van Rossum, van Wijk, *De stad in uitersten. Verkenningstocht naar Vinex-land.* Rotterdam, 2001.

Blood or Soil

A Stroll through Belgian Absurdistan

[CARL DEVOS]

Johan van Geluwe,
Poster marking 150 years
of Belgium.
Letterpress print, various
dimensions, 1980.

Belgium, a favourite haunt for lovers of the absurd, is hidden away on the edge of a political twilight zone. Belgium is a state that should not really exist. It is an experiment in wish-fulfilment; an artificial synthesis. Belgium is a no man's land between fact and fiction, a 'faction' if you will; a literary figment of the imagination. It is the cold turkey of pragmatism, the sophist's nirvana.

Historically, the importance of the sophists lay not so much in their actual pronouncements as in their being the first of the pre-Socratics to focus attention on Man rather than Nature and make thought itself a subject of thought. They are now best remembered as the peripatetic hirelings of the word, enthusiastic practitioners of argumentative gymnastics, masters of rhetoric capable of talking any twisted proposition straight. According to Plato, they practised pseudo-politics. They were concerned not with truth but with winning arguments and being right.

In Belgium, 'right' is now either Flemish or Walloon, Dutch-speaking or French-speaking. Previous ideological duellists such as Labour and Capital famously made peace through compromise, while the *Kulturkampf* between Liberals and Catholics finally came to an end after the School Wars of the 1950s. Incidentally, Belgium's educational system has since acquired a worldwide reputation for excellence, though it is still unable to guarantee equal opportunities to all. It produces winners of international mathematics competitions, but does little to help those who enter the system already at a disadvantage.

In the past, socio-economic and ideological conflict was kept more or less within bounds by a process of elitist consensual agreement reached behind closed doors. It also kept Belgium compartmentalised in ideological 'pillars', a form of ideological apartheid, in which the social functions of the state were hijacked by Christian, Socialist or Liberal organisations at government expense. Post-modernism may have allowed individualism and a host of other 'isms' to break down these traditional ideological 'pillars', but it has not removed the divisions. Far from it. Although the 'pillars' appear to have been reduced to the status of efficient service providers, they have still been able to obstruct the wholesale privatisation of Belgium's social fabric. For instance, the role of private insurance in health, unemployment and pensions, though expanding, still lags behind Belgium's neighbours. The pillars may have been dismantled, but the erstwhile ideological rivals are still in control of social security. Old practices have struck deep roots in the damp loamy soil of Belgian society.

This 'Belgian approach' is also clearly visible in the gleaming neo-corporatist welfare state. Respect for traditional ideological and socio-economic differences has led to a system of proportionality (based on wealth and population) and distributive justice that can only function through consensus and compromise. But this consultative welfare state is now starting to creak, corroded by its own success. According to some analysts, globalisation and an aging population have turned the welfare state into an anachronism, a meaningless echo of the 1980s. Yet in spite of 100,000 protestors on the streets of Brussels last October and stout-hearted declarations of intent, the tradition of tinkering with the welfare state continues as it always has, calmly and serenely, in wide and courteous consultation with numerous organisations and panels of experts and subject to a host of regulations and checks and balances. The 'Generation Pact' of Guy Verhofstadt's government, standard-bearer for a modernised *Belgium Inc.*, symbolises this ongoing patching up of the welfare state: it is intended to get more people into work and to keep them there for longer. In defiance of all the changes that have taken place and the undeniable challenges and risks that lie in store, there is no observable sense of an impending apocalyptic socio-economic crisis. There is much sound and fury, but nobody really believes that the Belgian consultative model or its associated welfare state is about to collapse.

The final conflict

The breach between the linguistic regions, however, is quite another matter. The linguistic communities are now the last remaining gladiators in the Belgian arena and their conflict might even threaten Belgium's survival. After the Second World War a whole series of issues, which included collaboration with the Nazis, the controversy surrounding King Leopold's role during the German occupation, the splitting of the University of Leuven in 1968 on linguistic grounds, the different community reactions to the so-called 'Unity Law' in 1960-1961, showed that the linguistic divisions were in urgent need of attention. It has often been argued that if the land of the Belgians ever passes away, it will not be because of religious wars or proletarian revolution but, to strike a melancholic note, because there will be no more 'Belgians' left in the country. However, that is nonsense. To anyone who cares to listen: Belgium will survive. It will even survive another 35 years of constitutional reform. Its survival will not be particularly to the credit of the Royal Family or the unmanageable status of *Brussels DC*; it will be due to the simple fact that there is no majority in favour of carving up the country. Neither among the representatives, nor among the represented. To divide up Belgium in a civilised fashion would require both Walloon consent and Flemish unanimity, but the majority of the Flemish do not want to see the end of Belgium. In the multi-layered identity that they enjoy, increased regional powers can easily be combined with pride in being Belgian. Moreover, non-Belgian observers should not be blinded by Vlaams Belang, the Flemish Interest. Although Walloon attention seems fixated on this far right political party, which under its previous name of Vlaams Blok was condemned for its racism, its importance for Belgium's survival is insignificant. Flemish separatism will never win many votes.

Brussels, Belgium's slum

Tensions between centre and periphery are a structural characteristic of state-building, which usually also involves creating a national identity and dealing with the bullyboy tactics of local magnates. But in Belgium there has never been either a centre or a periphery. Belgium is a flat patchwork quilt. There is the regional dividing line, but it runs between centres or, if you prefer, between peripheries. Brussels, once Flemish, was Gallicised by its status as capital but it never became a centre, except for the road and rail network. In the past, and arguably even today, the French language has enjoyed higher status than Dutch. That meant, and sometimes still means, that anyone wanting to pursue a successful career through our bureaucratic institutions would have to abandon the peasant dialect of 'Flemish' and embrace the language of the Enlightenment and the Paris salons.

Even today the Flemish use the French words for 'suburb' and 'slum'. However, for Brussels this is irrelevant. Nowadays, a third of the population of the Brussels Capital Region are non-Belgian by nationality and an even larger number are of non-Belgian origin. This expanding group could not care less about Dutch or French. Only the Belgians have not yet grasped that fact.

Brussels became the capital of the country, but was regarded by many as an alien imposition. Brussels became for many Belgians what it is for many Europeans. That place, over there, where 'they' live: those people who make our lives a misery with their petty regulations. For the Flemish, Brussels is too Francophone; for the Walloons it is too close to Flanders. Indeed, the Walloons have located their headquarters, the Walloon parliament and government, well away from the Flemish border in Namur. Flanders, on the other hand, completely surrounds Brussels and the Flemish have based their parliament and government within the city for its symbolic value. Between 12% and 17% of Brussels' inhabitants are actually Flemish and their links with the rest of

Flanders must be nurtured. The Walloons regard them as little more than an advance guard for the Flemish army of occupation, so for many years battle has been joined in the Flemish Circle around Brussels. It is a struggle that the Flemish have been losing. In 2005, politics lost its credibility and the Flemish their arrogance on the blood-drenched battlefield of BHV.

BHV, or Brussels-Halle-Vilvoorde, is the most recent political prize to be targeted in the trench warfare between the Flemish and French communities. A relic of the distant past, BHV is an electoral constituency where Flemish and Francophone parties can still compete head to head for the people's votes. Halle and Vilvoorde are Flemish while Brussels, though theoretically bilingual, is mainly French-speaking. Together they make up a single electoral battle zone. Politically, it means that French-speaking politicians can win votes on 'Flemish' territory. Or alternatively, voters living on Flemish soil can cast their votes for French speakers. But nowhere, except in Brussels itself, can French speakers vote for a Flemish party. Nowhere can Flemish parties campaign for French votes on French soil. A court of law therefore determined that the very existence of this constituency was illegal. For provincial constituencies have existed throughout the country ever since 2003. But BHV, in defiance of these divisions, overlaps several provinces, and Flemish candidates complain of discrimination. The court demanded that this anomaly should be sorted out before the next federal elections in 2007. However, the decisions of Belgian law courts are never taken very seriously.

From the beginning, Belgium has been ethnically and linguistically artificial and unstable. In fact one might argue that in essence the conflict is actually *ethnic*. Be that as it may, the country is plagued by tensions between two language groups who, locked in their respective regions, differ fundamentally on a wide range of issues. In Belgium, even Truth is either Flemish or Walloon. Which brings us back to the sophists, and Protagoras in particular. He is famous for the claim that '*Man is the measure of all things, of the things that are, that they are, and of things that are not, that they are not*'. He was referring to the individual human being. But if every individual is the measure of everything and individuals disagree, then there is no objective criterion by which one can determine who is right or who is wrong. In Belgium, a 'Belgian' can never be right. Not only because there are no 'Belgians' left, but because in Belgium, truth and reason have been banished.

The union plays a practical joke: Belgica sui generis

The kindest way to reason sensibly about Belgium is to employ the Socratic Discourse; even thinking about Belgium is best done with good-humoured contemplation. After all, language merely obscures the truth. Ludwig Wittgenstein could have written his *Tractatus logico-philosophicus* in Brussels. His seventh proposition is particularly apposite: what we cannot speak about we must pass over in silence.

But there is a great deal that can be said about Belgium, that splendid experiment in exocentric arrangements, that lovable, comfortingly ugly Belgium which celebrated its 175th birthday in 2005. Since 1970 there has been a succession of constitutional reforms, alien operations that have, on several occasions, nevertheless proved useful. They have even officially rebuilt Belgium into a federal state. Not that there was much choice since without such reconstruction, the country would long ago have become ungovernable. Our federalism works even though its interpretation of the federal state is idiosyncratic, complex and without vision. Inevitably, Belgium suffers from construction faults. The lack of nation-wide political parties means that nobody can speak for Belgium as a whole, and politicians cannot be held to account from outside their own region. Belgium no longer holds national elections and soon there will be no more Belgian constituencies. There is not even a national government. Belgium's government is actually a permanent diplomatic conference. It consists of seven Flemish and seven French-speaking ministers with a Community-neutral prime minister. The seven ministers are elected in their own regions or at least in one of its provinces, so national elections amount to what elsewhere would be regarded as regional elections: the election of the Flemish, Brussels, Walloon or German-speaking parliaments. In other words, Belgium's political dynamic is centrifugal and its federalism is not so much one of 'coming together' but of 'holding together'.

Furthermore, the Belgian federation is essentially bipolar. Although there are three regions, three communities and four linguistic areas, it is evident to anyone familiar with Belgium, and probably axiomatic for an understanding of its politics, that it is dominated by the opposition between the Dutch-speaking and French-speaking political communities. The most obvious difference is language but there are also cultural, demographic, socio-economic and other differences. The differences are undeniable but the situation is often deliberately exacerbated further. In Belgium, for every question, for every problem, for every issue there will always be someone who asks mischievously whether there might not be a relevant Flemish or Walloon point of view to be considered. It is the theme for many a café debate. The tensions between Flanders and Wallonia are the spice for every dish. They seldom form the main ingredient but they add piquancy to the whole. And, as so often happens, he who seeks shall find. This bipolarism has been the source of much misery and almost permanent conflict. One's opposite number, whether Walloon or Fleming, can never be an ally against a third party, but must always remain an opponent in what is often a zero sum game.

That is why there is so much mistrust. The jealous defence of regional authority can prevent the federal government from acting, even when reason dictates that it should do so, as in the saga of the night flights over Zaventem, Belgium's national airport. Although it lies in Flanders, the night flights contravene the Brussels Region's environmental regulations for night-time noise pollution. Since the federal government is not allowed to overrule regional decisions, the government of the Brussels region has been able to plunge the airport of the world's most illuminated country into darkness . Because there is no trust, no regional powers can ever be permitted to fall into federal hands. For then others would also become involved in making decisions.

Bipolar, centrifugal, exclusive, lacking federal political parties, unbalanced – it is a wonder that Belgium still works. Perhaps because of, perhaps in spite of the numerous attempts at constitutional reform. Anyway, in 2007 after the next federal battle of the ballot boxes, another round of reform will take place. It is already being trumpeted as 'one of the most definitive ever'. So not yet completely definitive. But still a little bit. Thanks in part to the glorious Pyrrhic victory of the Francophones in the 'Battle of BHV'.

In 2003 federal elections were held, followed in 2004 by regional elections. The purpose of holding separate elections for the first time in Belgian history was to give the regional parliaments a higher profile and make them better known. Since the federal parliament sits for four years while the regional legislative parliament sits for five, the two elections will not coincide again until 2019. The last time was in 1999. The 2003 elections resulted in Guy Verhofstadt's 'Purple' coalition of 'blue' liberals and 'red' socialists, who made substantial gains at the expense of the Greens and the Christian Democrats. But in the regional elections a year later, the Christian Democrats won back much of the ground that they had lost, while in Flanders the Flemish nationalists also did very well. While the Christian Democrat leader Yves Leterme was trying to put together a cabinet that did not include Vlaams Blok, the Flemish parties held forth on the need to break up BHV 'immediately' and 'without compromise'. Halle and Vilvoorde should join the rest of Flemish Brabant; Brussels should remain separate. It was the only way to combat the spreading virus of Gallicisation. However, splitting up BHV happens to be a federal matter and the Francophones had no intention of acceding to Flemish demands. Had this bitter confrontation been allowed to continue it could have threatened the survival of the federal government and so, in the end, nothing happened. In the meantime, however, enormous damage was done.

Died-in-the-wool Flemings adhere to the principle of *ius soli*: citizenship is tied to the soil on which one lives. In their view, French speakers who live on Flemish soil, in this instance the area around Brussels, are Flemish – whether they like it or not. Any facilities extended to this linguistic 'minority' should be temporary, short-lived and minimal; voting for a Francophone party is plain wicked. French speakers counter with *ius sanguinis*: citizenship is not tied to the soil but is a question of blood. Wherever a French speaker lives, he remains a French speaker and should be granted all the usual rights. Such as voting for someone 'of his own kind'. It is ironic that *ius soli* has much in common with the contract nationalism of French republicans, while *ius sanguinis* is more reminiscent of German nationalism. The Flemish follow the territorial principle; the Francophones the principle of personality. The former is a dam against Gallicisation; the latter is a lubricant for it. There is, therefore, far more at stake than the changing number of Flemish or Walloon seats in the parliamentary chamber. It involves fundamentally different conceptions of citizenship, and this in a country that lacks a national identity and has no citizens of its own.

In Belgium one can see the truth of Seneca's observation that '*Nullum est vitium sine patrocinio*', that there is no vice without patronage or influential support. Belgium has ended up in a vicious circle – a spinning, centrifugal vicious circle at the centre of which lies the desire to secure land for one's own kith and kin. With several more decades of constitutional reform in prospect, one can only wonder what will be left of Belgium, or indeed what will be left *for* Belgium, the state with no citizens. ∎

Translated by Chris Emery

The End of a War

National and Private Monuments Commemorating
the Great War in Flanders

[PIET CHIELENS]

In the course of 2005 an inventory of relics of the Great War in the Westhoek region of Flanders became available. This joint initiative by the Province of West Flanders and the Service for Monuments and Landscapes of the Flemish Community contains over 1200 entries: cemeteries, monuments, bunkers, trenches, memorial plaques, stretches of country, mine craters, stained-glass windows, dugouts, thanksgiving chapels, archeological sites, street names... It will be an exceptionally useful and valuable tool for assessing the significance which the Great War once had for this part of the world, and which it still has to this day. Now that the generation of World War I has practically died out, these relics provide the only material evidence of this devastating experience, and the memorial monuments seem to recover their original significance.

Maurice Langaskens,
In Memoriam. 1916.
In Flanders Fields
Museum, Ypres.

The Front

The front in the Westhoek, between the North Sea beaches at Nieuwpoort and the River Leije at Armentières, was the scene of important and violent battles. The front consisted mainly of two major areas: the Ypres Salient and the Yser Front.

The town of Ypres lay at the centre of the so-called Salient, a forward position of the Allied armies jutting into the German front line where some of the fiercest fighting on the Western Front took place. The Ypres Salient was the scene of four major offensives, among them the first act of chemical warfare: the German gas attack of 22 April 1915 which started the Second Battle of Ypres. Also the Battle of Passchendaele, the final stage of the Third Battle of Ypres, which lasted from 31 July to 10 November 1917 and was one of the most costly British offensives of the war.

Just to the south of Ypres was Messines Ridge, the scene of the Mine Battle of 7 June 1917, one of the most successful British attacks on the Western Front, initiated by the explosion of 19 deep mines under the German front line on the ridge.

To the north was the plain of the River Yser, which had been successfully flooded in October 1914 at one of the most critical moments for the allied nations. After that the Belgian Army had held it as best and as safe as they could.

In the four years between October 1914 and October 1918 soldiers of at least 35 different nationalities died here, in all some 600,000 men. Many of them are still there, or their names and deeds are commemorated in a myriad of ways, as the inventory shows. All the relics serve to remind over 300,000 visitors a year, from all over the world, of what happened here.

The land as the last witness

For those visitors who knew the generation that lived through the war, the stories of the survivors were enough to let them understand the shape and the nature of the war. The encounter with the monuments and relics in the land is just a reminder of their vivid memories of the encounter with the people. Those who never had that chance, and their numbers grow annually, only have the material evidence of the land itself. Now that the generation of World War I is almost extinct, it is the land that was marked by the war and its aftermath which is the final witness. It is this war-shaped landscape that will have to pass on the legacy. To explore the landscape, to understand the importance of the water, of the mud, of the contours of the pathetic small ridges and copses, will be the only way to fully understand the authentic story.

Reading the relics of the fighting in the landscape is one thing; equally important are the symbols and the traces of the commemoration, from very small and personal monuments that stand almost forlorn under the high imprisoning skies, to the large national monuments at the centre of the ceremonies. Why and how were these monuments built after the end of the war, and how can they be used and read by visitors today?

The destruction of a generation and a mother's personal grief

Cemeteries like the huge Tyne Cot Cemetery of the Commonwealth armies at Passchendaele, with its 12,000 graves and 35,000 names of the missing, are easily understood for what they are: witnesses to the vastness of the destruction of a generation. Equally devastating are the mass graves of the German concentration cemeteries at Langemark or Menin, with over 40,000 burials each. The sheer numbers evoke a senseless loss of youth and talent and humanity. What each of those graves means individually can only be understood when one looks at the few personal touches to be found on them. Unlike civilian graves, the soldiers' tombstones are designed to show the equality of the life and death of all military personnel. As they stood united in battle, they stand regimented in death. It's only in the small epitaphs that the private individual emerges. 'Never Forgotten. Mother's darling, brave boy, loved by all' is inscribed on the headstone of Pte. C. Owen of the Border Regiment, who died on 27 July 1916 aged 18, and who is buried in Dranoutre Military Cemetery. Personal grief and individual identity are best expressed in Käthe Kollwitz's *Mourning Parents* at the German cemetery in Vladslo. It is another very personal commemoration, by another mother for another 18-

Käthe Kollwitz.
Mourning Parents (1932).
German cemetery, Vladslo.
Photo by Michel Vanneuville.

year-old son. Thinking of the two, the words of Siegfried Sassoon's 1918 poem 'Reconciliation' spring to mind:

When you are standing at your hero's grave,
Or near some homeless village where he died,
Remember through your heart's rekindling pride,
The German soldiers who were loyal and brave.

Men fought like brutes, and hideous things were done;
And you have nourished hatred, harsh and blind.
But in that Golgotha perhaps you'll find
The mothers of the men who killed your son.[1]

Poetry, of course, also works on a very personal level.

Peter Kollwitz died in the opening moves of the Battle of the Yser on 23 October 1914. His mother, the expressionist sculptress Käthe Kollwitz, had been against his volunteering for the war, but couldn't prevent him meeting his fate. It took her 16 years to make two stone statues of (after the words of Flemish singer Willem Vermandere) *'a father rigid with grief and a mother bending down low'*. The figures were placed by Peter's grave in the Roggenveld Friedhof in Esen in July 1932. In 1956, when graves from many smaller cemeteries were brought together in the cemetery in Vladslo, they were moved with Peter Kollwitz's grave to the *Soldatenfriedhof* Praetbos in Vladslo. The monument expresses the very private grief of one couple for their young son. The statues clearly bear the features of the parents. But it is precisely because the monument is so personal that it is so recognisable, and therefore so timeless and universal. Today it is widely considered to be one of the most universal of all the monuments on the Western Front.

National Monuments

But wars are not commemorated first and foremost by private monuments, because the dying was hardly ever personal, the killing and the dying happened on a large, industrial scale (in days like these one is tempted to say: by mass-destruction). Therefore they needed above all a general commemoration. By group, regiment, division, religion or, and especially, by nation. After all it was all the separate nations who had called their citizens to arms, to become soldiers and fight, so after the war it was their obligation to honour the death of their own.

A number of those national monuments appeared in Flanders after the War. They are all 'national' by nature, yet they are all very different. The differences define some general meaning and purpose for such monuments, yesterday but also today and tomorrow.

The most important of these national monuments in the Westhoek are the Yser Tower in Diksmuide, a Flemish nationalistic monument, built twice; The Menin Gate at Ypres, the oldest of the national monuments here and one that serves a double purpose; and the Island of Ireland Peace Park in Mesen, the most recent and maybe the very last of the large national monuments about the Great War ever to be erected.

The Yser Tower, Diksmuide (1930/1967)
National as in Nationalistic (i.e. Flemish, anti-Belgian)
Supranational in terms of Pacifist

The origins of the Yser Tower lie in the war. Also in the way the Belgian nation was organised in the early days of the twentieth century. Belgium was in its population and by law a bilingual country, yet in practice at the outbreak of the War its army – or certainly the Army Command – was using only one language: French. In the war up to 72% of all Belgian soldiers were Flemish speakers, but almost none of their officers were, nor were the orders they gave. This gave rise to emotions of Flemish frustration, and as a result a search for Flemish recognition and Flemish identity developed among the serving soldiers at the front. One of the ways of expressing this was in the commemoration of their dead comrades.

In 1917 a Flemish artist/soldier called Joe English (his father was Irish) had designed a Celtic cross with on it the pre-war motto of the Flemish nationalist Catholic student movement. It read: *AVV – VVK: 'Alles voor Vlaanderen, Vlaanderen voor Kristus'* (All for Flanders, Flanders for Christ). This 'heroes' cross', as it was called, was used to mark the graves of Flemish soldiers. Like all other expressions of Flemish identity-seeking, the Army Command distrusted its use, wrongly assuming that it was a possible act of insubordination or defeatism. Heroes' crosses were prohibited, sometimes destroyed; later again, after strong protest, allowed, reluctantly.

Destroying a grave-marker is a very sensitive matter because it can easily be interpreted as grave-violation, an act of blasphemy against Flemish martyrs. After the war this happened on a large scale, when the Belgian Army decided that it wanted to use the same design for all its tombstones. The Flemish crosses were replaced by Belgian headstones, the crosses destroyed and in some cases, as in the military cemetery of Adinkerke in 1925, the rubble was used as hardcore for road-building.

The VOS, Vlaamse Oud-Strijders, the Flemish veterans' association, reacted vehemently and the annual pilgrimage to the graves of the Yser, which had started in 1920, became more and more a manifestation not just of commemoration, but of formulating radical political and ideological demands. The early calls for 'No More War' were now increasingly replaced by those for autonomy and outright anti-Belgian ideas. But the political agenda was still kept within bounds by the commemoration. The organising committee decided to erect a memorial at Diksmuide, on the spot where some of the heaviest fighting had taken place. It was to be a tower overlooking the river and the former battlefield. The design was easily found: it had to reflect that of Joe English's cross. He had himself died in August 1918; his remains would rest in the crypt of the monument, along with those of some other symbolic Flemish soldiers, martyrs all. Their bodies would be removed from the hostile Belgian cemeteries and reburied under a gigantic heroes' cross: the Yser Tower.

The tower, plump and serious, was finished by 1930 and in the following years some 37 'martyrs' were selected and transferred to the crypt. The annual pilgrimage to it became immensely popular. In the late 1930s the pilgrimages attracted anything up to almost 200.000 people – almost more than there were Flemish veterans.

In the 1930s the Flemish veterans' association and its political party, the VNV,

The Yser Tower.
Diksmuide.
Photo by David Samyn.

Vlaams Nationaal Verbond, had shown solidarity with the Activist movement, the Flemish movement that had collaborated during the war with the German military command in occupied Belgium. This alienated a lot of its ordinary followers and polarised opinions among those who were for or against the movement for self-determination and the ways to achieve this. The slow pace at which language reforms were applied by a reluctant Belgian government had frustrated the Flemish movement further, and soon large sections of the movement drifted off towards New Order ideas and a radical plea for an independent course away from oppressive Belgium.

It was no surprise that when Belgium was invaded and occupied by Nazi Germany in May 1940 the Flemish nationalist parties, as well as the Yser Tower committee, soon started collaborating with the Nazi occupiers, wrongly believing that by doing so they would be able to realise their programme for autonomy.

It is perhaps also not surprising that the tower was seen as one of the great symbols of this collaboration. On 30 May 1940, only two days after Belgium had capitulated, a bomb dropped by a British aeroplane damaged the tower – perhaps on the orders of the Belgian government who had fled to London? It was in any case a clear warning to those who had chosen to side with the occupiers.

During the war the pilgrimages were far less massive than in the 1930s. In later years some people denied that there ever were pilgrimages, or their importance was largely minimised, but the pilgrimages went on as before, with no attempt at secrecy. They were organised with the support and sometimes the help of the collaborating Flemish parties and were also attended by Nazi representatives.[2]

The 1942 pilgrimage paid a lot of attention to the old symbol of the destroyed heroes' crosses. Rubble was found and collected and brought back to the tower, to be stored – like a relic – in the crypt, next to the real bodies of the Flemish heroes. The ceremony was filmed and documented by members of the Nazi propaganda team.

Other symbols of the earlier war were also commemorated. During the 1943 pilgrimage, a Guard of Honour was mounted at the Crucifix of Nieuwpoort, which had miraculously survived the first war, and which was placed in the crypt of the Tower. The guard consisted of a member of the *NSJV – Nationaal Socialistisch Jongerenverbond*, the Flemish Nazi Youth Movement, and by a member of the Black Brigade (propaganda soldiers of the *VNV* which became the *Dietsche Militie*, the collaborating militia). In that year not only the Flemish dead of the Great War were commemorated but also those who were dying with the Flemish SS brigade *Langemarck* on the Russian front.

After the Second World War a savage repression of all things Flemish was organised, first by the mob in the streets, later by Belgian courts, arresting and sometimes also condemning not just the real collaborators but also a number of naïve Flemish idealists and pre-war activists in the Flemish search for self-determination. In that climate of revenge the Yser Tower, that hateful symbol of anti-Belgian-ness, was destroyed in March 1946. The perpetrators of this crime were never found.

It took the Yser Tower committee a few years to recover. But by 1948 a new pilgrimage was organised. Above the now cruelly exposed crypt, with the Crucifix of Newport still untouched, among the ruins of the destroyed tower, a frail Heroes' Cross emerged. It was a brick replica of Joe English' very first 1915 design for the heroes' cross. It was the first sign of a resurrection that would not be stopped.

The following year, with the rubble of the destroyed tower (as in many war stories there's a lot of rubble in this one) a Peace Gate, de *Paxpoort*, was built. With it the new committee went back to its origins, promoting pacifism rather than Flemish nationalism. But soon that nationalism also would re-emerge. Year by year the numbers of those attending the pilgrimage grew, and by the mid-1950s it was decided that the new and rapidly increasing in affluence Flanders would resurrect its tower. The structure would be bigger than the first one had ever been.

The New Yser Tower was completed by 1967 and took its place with the other symbols on the pilgrimage grounds.

In the post-war era the pilgrimage never became as popular as it had been in the 1930s. But it still drew up to 35,000 people, until a steady decline set in during the 1980s. In 2004 only 3,500 people attended. In 1986 official politics, quite against this trend, selected the tower as the national symbol of the – by now largely gained – Flemish autonomy within the Belgian federal state. To this day large factions of the Flemish community are still very unwilling to accept this official status for the monument. For these people the past cannot just be forgotten, and the tower cannot represent them in their own battle for and acceptance of a rightful form of self-determination.

For a number of years the annual pilgrimage was also attended by European skinheads and neo-fascists. But in the last decade a new committee succeeded in ridding it of this unwanted support and attention. The radical tendencies within the Flemish Movement, who by now had found a political outlet in the extreme right-wing Vlaams Blok, (now Vlaams Belang) that owes its popularity not so much to Flemish nationalist issues as to its racist programme and cheap populism, a Flemish pendant of Steiermark's *Heiderism*, were no longer expressed during the pilgrimages to the Yser Tower. Within the tower a museum about WW1 and the Flemish struggle for autonomy was installed, and other activities in addition to the annual pilgrimage were set up to try and make it once again a pacifist monument first and foremost, with a present-day version of the 'no more war' slogan of the old days.

This is all to the good, yet objectivity forces us to add that in the exhibition within the tower very little is to be seen of the days when it all went dramatically wrong for the Tower and its politics. It seems as if only the successful, harmless half of the story can be told. Proclaim the Pacifism, and downplay the radical anti-Belgian frustration that drove the tower's owners into that despicable collaboration – understandably perhaps, but all the same... Nowhere in the museum nor elsewhere in the domain is this entire history explained, even though all the material elements and all the consecutive steps of frustration, arrogance, revenge, resurrection and purification are there and obvious to everyone. By choosing to represent a Selective Memory the committee have missed a unique opportunity to address the full story in all its complexities and paradoxes and by so doing really turn this monument into a prime example and a relic of 90 eventful years of Belgian history, that certainly deserve to be told.

The Menin Gate Memorial to the Missing, Ypres (1927)
National in terms of glorifying the sacrifice for the Nation (British Empire)
Supranational in terms of Memorial to the Missing

That the story is only half told is not what you can say about the Menin Gate in Ypres. Quite the contrary, it seems that two stories are told at once. The Gate is a memorial to the missing of the Commonwealth armies in the battlefields around Ypres, and it is also a national British monument, the first of several on the Western Front.

At the end of the Great War the medieval town of Ypres was a total ruin. A man on horseback could survey the entire city. In defending it the British and Commonwealth Armies had lost almost one third of all their dead (some 240,000 out of 715,000 in total). Rightly had Winston Churchill said, in January 1919, that there was not a place on earth more sacred for the British race than this town. For this reason he wanted to acquire all of its ruins. His suggestion was declined by the inhabitants of Ypres, who wanted their town and their lives back in a vain attempt to undo all the harm done by the war...

For three years proposals went back and forth between Ypres, Brussels and London until finally an agreement was reached: Ypres would be rebuilt (as true to the original as possible was the inhabitants' wish) and the British would be

Last Post at the Menin Gate
Memorial to the Missing, Ypres.
Photo by David Samyn.

given a gap in the old Vauban ramparts where they could build a monument to commemorate the dead of the war and to express the special place Ypres had won in the collective memory of the British Empire.

Between 1922 and 1927 the structure was built that served as a national monument for the victorious British Empire, strongly reflected in the design by Sir Reginald Blomfield, inspired by a Roman triumphal arch, and by inscriptions like '*Pro Patria – Pro Rege*' or '*To the armies of the British Empire who stood here from 1914 to 1918 and to those of their dead who have no known grave*'.

The final part of that main inscription reflects the Monument's other purpose: this was to be the first of 26 memorials to the missing to be placed along the Western Front. With 102,000 missing out of 240,000 dead the Ypres Salient, and indeed the whole world, needed a strong concept to commemorate those who could not even be honoured by a known grave. Rudyard Kipling, the Nobel Prize winner for literature, whose only son was listed among the missing, was a member of the initial Imperial War Graves Commission and came up with the idea of a monument on which the names of the missing of the battles in the neighbourhood of the monument would be listed on stone or bronze tablets. In a letter he wrote how everyone needed some place to go to: '*You see we shall never have any grave to go to. Our boy was missing at Loos. The ground is of course battered and mined past all hope of any trace being recovered. I wish some of the people who are making this trouble realised how more than fortunate they are to have a name on a headstone in a known place.*' Kipling wrote to William Burdett-Coutts, MP for Westminster.[3] '*This trouble*' was the widespread opposition to the choice of a universal headstone rather than a cross as the standard grave marker. With a Memorial to the Missing such '*a place to go to*' was successfully created. The concept would inspire General Plumer at the inauguration of the Menin Gate on 24 July 1927 to say in his speech: '*He is not missing, he is here.*'

The double purpose and meaning of the Gate is strongly expressed in its design. The contrast between the triumphant outside and the grieving interior with the endless lists of names could hardly be more striking. When the British officer and war poet Siegfried Sassoon saw the Gate, later the same day of the inauguration, *en route* for that summer's Bayreuth Festival, he could only see the triumph, not the tragic dead or the missing. He wrote:

'On Passing the New Menin Gate'

Who will remember, passing through this Gate,
the unheroic dead who fed the guns ?
Who shall absolve the foulness of their fate, –
Those doomed, conscripted, unvictorious ones ?
  Crudely renewed, the Salient holds its own.
  Paid are its dim defenders by this pomp;
  Paid, with a pile of peace-complacent stone,
  The armies who endured that sullen swamp.
Here was the world's worst wound. And here with pride
'Their name liveth for ever', the Gateway claims.
Was ever an immolation so belied
as these intolerably nameless names ?
Well might the Dead who struggled in the slime
Rise and deride this sepulchre of crime.[4]

The poem can still not be recited with any degree of comfort in circles close to the Menin Gate.

As a veteran who could not forget his own war experience, and who had begged his fellow comrades *'never to forget'* (*Aftermath*, 1919), Sassoon could not accept that the nation provided the bereaved relatives and comrades of the dead with an easy halo of heroism and grand decorum which in those years of great grief gave sense to the seemingly senseless sacrifice and honour to the foul circumstances of many dead. Sassoon saw it, and no doubt understood it, but could not accept it all the same.

Soon the good burghers of Ypres would add another *double entendre* to the monument. From the summer of 1928 to this day, with the exception of the occupation during WW2, every night at 8 o'clock volunteers from the local Fire Brigade play the Last Post at the Gate.

It's a short ceremony, but it's a live ceremony, carried out day after day by human beings, not by stone or bronze or mechanical reproduction. Each night the sounding of the Last Post animates all the untouchable coolness of the stark Portland stone. The breath of the firemen and the sound it produces, engulfing and soothing, warms and comforts the souls of the 55,000 missing still somewhere out there deep down in the Flemish mud. That's how I stand at the gate. If you ask the president of the Last Post Association what the ceremony means to him, he will say that it was and is and always will be to thank and honour the brave defenders of Ypres, who died for our freedom and for our independence. And his firemen have fitting uniforms to express that solemn sentiment.

If you were to ask those who attend the ceremony (and in recent years they come in ever growing numbers, of all nationalities, although a majority is certainly British) what it means to them you would get equally differing answers: for some the tune is played for all the dead of all the wars, for some it is just a manifestation of one of the particular glorious moments in the glorious history of the British Empire. A lot depends on where you stand: outside with the triumph, or inside by the names. Once you've accepted that someone might be where his name is inscribed on the walls of a solemn monument, all interpretations are equally valid. And by sticking to a tradition like the Last Post ceremony, for more than 25,000 times and more than 75 years already, the fact that this is a military tune played at funerals, or at the end of a day in a soldier's life, becomes of minor importance as well. As in the desperate soldier's song 'We're here, because we're here': it's there, because it's there. The ritual connotes a vague meaning of grief and of a past history but before anything it connotes just itself. The duality of the building and the duality of the ceremony support each other well, but therefore one could also say erase each other. Is it for the defenders of the town, or also for its German attackers? Is it for the dead or indeed just as much for the living, who are left to grow old? As the fourth stanza of Laurence Binyon's 'For the Fallen', recited almost daily at the Gate, have it:

They shall grow not old,
as we that are left grow old.
Age shall not weary them
 nor the years condemn.
At the going down of the sun
and in the morning
we will remember them[5]

The original purposes are hollowed out and disappear in the distance of time, which allows new generations to come and find their own new meanings for the ritual and the monument. The emptier the meaning, it seems, the better for its continuation. The Menin Gate and its Last Post have thus become a universal expression of the commemoration of the Great War and therefore of War itself and how, at least in the Ypres area, the thought of it never really goes away...

The Island of Ireland Peace Park, Mesen (1998)
National in terms of supranational (North and South Ireland)
Supranational in the sense of Peacemaking

It was therefore appropriate that when, after almost 80 years of civil conflict, in the Island of Ireland an ever-growing majority of the population was slowly working towards peace, that an example from the First World War in Flanders was chosen as a symbol of the complexities and contradictions of history. Nobel Prize winner Seamus Heaney introduced and edited, together with fellow-writer Dermot Bolger, the poetry of the Irish soldier-poet Francis Ledwidge, who had died in Flanders on 31 July 1917. In his introduction Heaney explained how an Irish nationalist could still choose to join the British Army without being unfaithful to his cause, and consequently how cruel it was when the new Irish Republic that emerged from the first bout of civil war, blotted out his memory, considering him to be no more than a collaborator with the hated English. Heaney claimed that nothing was as simple as that, that motives to join or not join a war were complex and that all history was much more complex than the easy mythology of a (new) nation would allow. Going into those complexities,

Heaney seemed to claim, all Irish people would recognise how there was much more that bound them than what divided them. Heaney wrote: '*Ledwidge's fate had been more complex and more modern than that. He very deliberately chose not to bury his head in local sand and, as a consequence, faced the choices and moral challenges of his times with solitude, honesty and rare courage. This integrity, and its ultimately gratifying effects upon his poetry, should command the renewed interest and respect of Irish people at the present time: Ledwidge lived through a similar period of historical transition when political, cultural and constitutional crises put into question values which had previously appeared as ratified and immutable as the contours of the land itself.*'[6]

Some time later, a Journey of Reconciliation Trust, a group of people from both the Republic and Northern Ireland, of both Catholic/Nationalist and Protestant/Unionist backgrounds, was founded, to commemorate yet another event from Flanders' history in the War. On 7 June 1917, during the Battle of Messines Ridge, the Irish divisions, the 36th (Ulster) Division and the 16th (Irish) Division had attacked side by side. They had been together in victory and together in death. After the War nothing of this unity remained; the soldiers, at least the survivors, came back only to a divided island, where again the memory of the dead was blotted out or only partially remembered. Certainly the fact that they had all stood together could not survive. After visiting Flanders, and on the momentum of the newly-acquired fragile Peace, the members of the Trust came upon the idea of building a monument that would commemorate all Irish soldiers together for the first time since the end of the war.

They chose the Irish round-tower as a central symbol, a dated form of architecture certainly, much hated by modern architects, but the choice was very deliberate. The Round Tower hailed from the time when the Irish were defending themselves against the Vikings; thus long before the colonisation by Cromwell or the defeat of the Celtic Chieftains, and long before the religious and economic divides that had ultimately led to the civil war.

In a pattern dictated by the position of the sun on the 11th of November at 11 o'clock, a dialogue is established between the symbolic round tower of old and a modern-day peace pledge.

It reads:

'The Peace Pledge'

From the crest of this ridge – which was the scene of horrific carnage in the First World War, on which we have built a peace park and Round Tower to commemorate the thousands of young men from all parts of Ireland who fought a common enemy, defended democracy and the rights of all nations, whose graves are in shockingly uncountable numbers and those who have no graves – we condemn war and the futility of war. We repudiate and denounce violence, aggression, intimidation, threats and unfriendly behaviour.

As Protestants and Catholics, we apologise for the terrible deeds we have done to each other and ask forgiveness. From this sacred shrine of remembrance, where soldiers of all nationalities, creeds and political allegiances were wasted in death, we appeal to all people in Ireland to help build a peaceful and tolerant society. Let us remember the solidarity and trust that developed between Protestant and Catholic Soldiers when they served together in these trenches.

As we jointly mark the armistice of 11 November 1918 – when the guns fell silent along this western front – we affirm that a fitting tribute to the principles for which men and women from the Island of Ireland died in both World Wars would be permanent peace.

Nearer to the Round Tower stand four tall stone slabs naming the four provinces: Connaught, Munster, Leinster and Ulster. By this treatment Ulster is not a part of a separate country, the United Kingdom, but a province of Ireland, standing alongside the other three. And this is technically correct, for only 6 of the 9 counties of the Province of Ulster form the Northern Ireland that is part of the United Kingdom.

In very much the same vein all the 26 counties of Ireland are listed on the back of the stone that holds the Peace Pledge. They are in alphabetical order, but are spelled out without blank space between the names. You have to know the names before you can identify them. A way of expressing that one exists only in relation to the others.

Inside the Round Tower you can look up straight to the top, and beneath it in the centre of the floor is the outline of the Island of Ireland carved into the bluestone. It's the whole Island, without any dividing border.

An arrow on each of three bronze doors points at it. The doors hide the Roll of Honour with all the names of 49,400 Irish-born soldiers who died in the British Army in the Great War. The Roll of Honour is that made up by order of Sir John French, Earl of Ypres and Lord Lieutenant of Ireland in 1922. It includes all Irish-born soldiers serving and dying in the British Army during the 1914-18 war, but it excludes thousands of Irishmen who served and died in the Australian, Canadian, New Zealand and American Armies.

On the doors the ground plan of the Peace Park is drawn, which is the key to understanding the whole symbolic design. When on the 11th hour of the 11th day of the 11th month the sun is out in the sky, it stands right behind the Stone of the Peace Pledge, whose shadow is cast on the path that leads to the tower; the tower's shadow then points along the same axis. If one were to prolong this axis infinitely, one would arrive in the geographical centre of the island of Ireland. Thus is established by the constellations and the park's ground plan a link between the Peace of the Armistice of 1918, for which the soldiers of the First World War fought and died, with the new Peace of the island of Ireland today. It's a peace acquired by mutual understanding and collaboration of both Irish communities, then as now. Critics say that none of this design is actually truthful, but the symbol is pure and radical. And there is more. Referring back to the dichotomy between the personal and the general, the national, the de-signers of this new national monument tried also to add a personal axis to the Park's ground-plan. The first way – the path that leads from the road towards the Round Tower and the Peace Pledge – is personal.

Upright stones give the number of casualties in each of the Irish divisions serving with the B.E.F. : the 10th (Irish – in fact mixed), the 16th (Irish) and the 36th (Ulster), the culmination of all the individual stories, and the link to the Roll of Honour. Nine thick stone slabs lying in the grass have quotes from the writings and sayings of individual Irishmen who fought.

They are quotes from soldiers, one also an Army chaplain, one also an official war artist and one an MP who served and died. The quotes are compassionate, understanding, condemning war, following the individual witness to the limit. Like the one from William Orpen, official war artist: *'I mean the simple soldier man, who, when the Great War first began, just died, stone dead, from lumps of lead, in mire.'*

There is one exception, quite unexpectedly. The first stone upon entering has a quote by Francis Ledwidge, the soldier-poet whom Seamus Heaney and Dermot Bolger brought back to the foreground. The quote is the last verse of Ledwidge's poem 'Soliloquy', wherein he sums up his life: no glory as a poet and only shame as a dead anonymous soldier.
Only it doesn't read like that in the quote carved on the stone:

It is too late now to retrieve
A fallen dream, too late to grieve
A name unmade, but not too late
To thank the gods for what is great;
A keen-edged sword, a soldier's heart,
Is greater than a poet's art.
And greater than a poet's fame
A little grave that has no name.[7]

There is no shame on the dead soldier, but rather ultimate praise for the sacrifice of the soldier. Only, this is not what Ledwidge wrote. This version leaves out his last, very critical line which turns the whole meaning: *'Whence honour turns away in shame.'* – which is to be found, of course, in Bolger's and Heaney's edition.[8]
It is a very bitter statement indeed.

The line may have been considered all too harsh for the whole undertaking. Maybe this wasn't so for either of the two sides of the Journey of Reconciliation, but it was certainly too harsh for the act of commemoration itself. What's the use of remembering the dead soldier if he himself says that there is only shame in the dying? To Ledwidge it meant shame in his whole life's adventure of going out to war thinking to serve his country, and dying a miserable death rather than becoming a great poet. By adding that final, devastating line, Ledwidge proved that he had found the insight to become just that, a great poet.

And by omitting it, the Island of Ireland Peace Park, this brave but perhaps overambitious national modern peacemaking monument, proved that it couldn't go that far in following the individual complexities of history, but had to stick – like the Menin Gate, like the Yser Tower – with the hollowness of the generalisations any nation needs to provide. It's a lie, a big one against Ledwidge, a smaller one against the national purposes it has to serve.

National monuments – nationalistic, glorifying, transcending – will always be confronted with this paradox. If they want to serve the purpose they were built for, they must stick to the lies of the particular national ideology. If they want to survive in time they should try to address the full complexities of history and shifts of meaning in time, even if that is contradictory and seemingly counterproductive. If they fail to do that, they can only hope that they will become empty, so that each time new users will be able to fill in the gap with their own new meanings and understanding. Personal monuments, like the alignment of personal epitaphs on Commonwealth war graves, or like Käthe Kollwitz's *Mourning Parents*, don't suffer from becoming dated and out of touch. Like the ones they honour they shall grow not old, and go on to comfort those that are left. ■

NOTES

1. Siegfried Sassoon, 'Reconciliation', written November 1918, first published in *Picture Show*, London, 1919.

2. See especially: Carlos Van Louwe & Pieter Jan Verstraete, *De Oorlogsbedevaarten. Kroniek van de 'vergeten' IJzerbedevaarten, 1940-1944*. Kortrijk, 2002.

3. Quoted in Philip Longworth, *The Unending Vigil*. London, 1967.

4. Siegfried Sassoon, 'On Passing the New Menin Gate', written Brussels, 25 July 1927, first published in *The Heart's Journey*, London, 1928.

5. Laurence Binyon, fourth stanza of 'For the Fallen', London, 1914.

6. From Introduction to Francis Ledwidge, *Selected Poems*, introduced by Seamus Heaney – edited by Dermot Bolger, Dublin, 1992.

7. Francis Ledwidge, 'Soliloquy', written February 1917, first published in *Songs of Peace*, London, 1918.

8. Francis Ledwidge, *Selected Poems*, introduced by Seamus Heaney – edited by Dermot Bolger, p. 74. Dublin, 1992.

Self-Willed or Superfluous?

Art in Public Space in the Netherlands

[INGEBORG WALINGA]

People driving along the A27 highway near the Dutch town of Almere – to the east of Amsterdam – cannot help but notice five concrete elephants. The animal sculptures have no tusks or tails, and only the rough outlines of their ears and trunks can be seen. With their big round bodies, they look more like huge cuddly toy animals than jungle giants that have somehow lost their way. At this location with lots of roads in the heart of the Netherlands, drivers cannot stop or get out of their cars for a closer look at this monumental yet touching sculpture group. *Elephants* by the artist Tom Claassen is one of the Netherlands' most appreciated and striking works of art to be found in public space. The sculpture group was commissioned by the Dutch Ministry of Public Works, which stipulated in the contract for the construction of the highway that a work of art be created, and also earmarked a percentage of the construction costs for this purpose. The art consultancy Kunst en Bedrijf provided advice on how to go about the project and organised a closed competition for 24 artists. Out of the three artists short-listed the jury picked Claassen and his proposed five elephants, citing the large dimensions of the sculpture group (which fit in well with its surroundings), the eye-pleasing shapes, as well as the comical and mysterious aspects of the work. The jury expected these big jumbos to surprise and intrigue the passing motorists time and again, and so it has turned out.

Public interest and artistic adventure

Half a century ago, it would have been difficult to imagine that the venerable Ministry of Public Works would ever fork out a substantial sum of money for this type of autonomous sculpture, which, except for its size, lacks grandeur and does not in any way refer to the Ministry. Traditionally, many works of art in public areas commemorate historical persons or events – just think of the statues and other memorials to be seen in almost every town and city – or represent a theme chosen by the commissioning party. In this particular case, the theme could have been 'infrastructure in the Netherlands' or something more abstract like 'connections' or 'dynamism'. It appears that, in this assignment, the artist was given a free hand to come up with something inspired by this particular

Tom Claassen, *Elephants*.
2000. Concrete.
Near Almere.
Photo by P. Post / HH.

location. Claassen has created other animal sculptures for public areas: a sturdy horse in Utrecht; in Apeldoorn a drooling dog and, next to an old people's home, three outsize sparrows, one of which is wearing a pearl necklace! In other words, he is the type of artist who should be given free reign to express himself in a three-dimensional manner instead of being put in the client's straightjacket. Over a 50-year period, those who commission works of art have become much bolder and more daring in their choices.

The period following World War II saw a strong demand for monuments from a whole range of clients: central and local government, companies, non-profit organisations and wealthy private individuals who had the necessary financial resources. They wanted to commemorate events and honour people etched in the collective memory, and were supported in their efforts by the general public. As a result, artists trained as sculptors were in great demand. As the general public became increasingly familiar with contemporary sculpture, people demanded higher quality and more originality. All in all, sculpture received a considerable boost and developed to a higher level.

One of the best-known Dutch monuments connected to the Second World War is the War Monument on Dam Square in Amsterdam's historic city centre, where every year on May 4 the National Remembrance Ceremony is held in the presence of the Queen and other prominent citizens. But perhaps an even more impressive war memorial is the sculpture *The Dockworker* (1952) by Mari Andriessen. This powerfully built male figure with his sleeves rolled up and ready for action symbolises the 1941 February Strike by workers in Amsterdam protesting against the Nazi persecution of the city's Jewish population. The ingredients of art in public space can be seen here: the desire to give expression to public sentiment or public interest; a commissioning party that knows what it wants and has sufficient funding; and artists who have developed their full creative potential (the previous generations of sculptors could be better described as artisans). The interaction of forces that comes into play in realising commissioned art in an outdoor public area (client, artist, consultancy, location, budget and the general public) differs sharply from the mechanics of other art-creating processes.

137

With the increase in assignments, artists grew concerned about the commissioning procedures and quality control. The Dutch Sculptors' Association feared that in the wake of the Second World War the Netherlands would become dotted with mediocre war-related sculptures. To prevent this the sculptors proposed using open competitions, with the various designs submitted being put on show to the public and assessed by committees of experts. These committees included not only the client's representatives, but also often artists or professional art critics. Since then, a similar system in which two to three artists are invited to make sketches of their designs to be judged by a broadly based committee has become commonplace. This method aims to ensure that the commissioning process is fair and untainted by cronyism and other forms of favouritism. Also, this method gives the client more choice; there are so many ways of translating an assignment into reality. On top of that, this approach enables an external expert to examine and assess the various proposals, including their feasibility.

Later on, these committees also consulted the future 'users': local residents or employees of the company commissioning the artwork. Some people oppose giving ordinary people a say in the decision process, fearing that 'the common man' will only accept easily recognisable, figurative art. They are also concerned that public consultation is a recipe for mediocre artworks, all much of a muchness. There are plenty of these around; just look at all the small-scale bronze sculptures on pedestals that take centre stage in shopping centres and residential areas. But it is not so much the general public who should be blamed

Mari Andriessen,
The Dockworker. 1952.
Bronze. Amsterdam.
© SABAM Belgium 2006.

Silvia B, *Ultra*. 2004,
Groningen.
Photo by H. Cock.

for these omnipresent bronzes (usually one member on the commissioning committees represents the public). Often the client lacked the courage to go for a more adventurous option. In actual fact, it is possible to use public consultation to drum up broad support for an artwork. After all, it is often the most active and enthusiastic residents or users who volunteer to sit on the art committee. After getting a close-up view of the entire commissioning process, the public representatives often evolve from being detached onlookers into passionate proponents of the artwork and the artist.

Deploying a crane

Sometimes an artwork is commissioned *before* the construction project has been realised. As a result, there are no residents to be consulted. A case in point was the assignment to create *Ultra* – a striking female figure by the Rotterdam artist Silvia B. *Ultra* marks the entrance to a large building complex that comprises offices and an apartment building in the city of Groningen. The companies who were to move into the offices knew about the art project and paid toward its cost, as did the local government. Not until the building complex and the design for the work of art were completed did the focus shift toward the residents. Understandably, the citizens were wary of the plan to install a grotesque female figure in front of their building. The art commission bent over backwards to inform residents and remove any lingering doubts. It even chartered a crane to hold a piece of cardboard at the spot where the head of the *Ultra* figure would appear, to reassure a female resident fearful that the head would block her view. The woman has meanwhile become one of the artwork's biggest admirers. Using a crane to win over a single person may seem an over-the-top and costly thing to do. But it was precisely this tremendous effort and its positive outcome that created confidence among residents. Disaffected locals can create a lot of disruption and even start legal procedures that can slow down or wreck an art project. So there is every reason to involve them in the whole endeavour.

Particularly in the case of government commissions, the process has become increasingly professionalised over time. The government tends to opt for specific battle-tested procedures, with proper contracts and permanent consultants who also provide advice and support to the artists. In 1951, central government decided to make art a permanent feature of building projects carried out at its behest. To that end, central government adopted the so-called *percentage programme*, which stipulates that between 1 and 1.5 percent of the construction costs be allocated to an art feature. Among the construction projects are new schools, ministry buildings and prisons. Central government also intended to set an example and create more support for the visual arts in our society, and many big cities did follow suit. The result was a spectacular growth in art commissions. Buildings were adorned with murals, stained-glass windows or self-contained artworks, as well as architectural or landscaping features. As regards the percentage programme, the need to involve artists in the building process at an early stage remains a topic of debate. Many artists would very much prefer to develop the art feature in close cooperation with the architect as he goes about conceiving the construction project. Unfortunately, the artwork is often added on as an afterthought because the budget is determined very late in the day or the client shows little interest in this particular aspect. Not every construction project is well suited for a work of art. Moreover, the mandatory inclusion of an artwork may stifle spontaneous cooperation and creative choices. Even so, the percentage programme, which is still being used by central government, has greatly increased the number of art commissions in the Netherlands.

In 2001 the percentage programme had been in place for 50 years. To mark its anniversary, many publications dealing with half a century of government-commissioned art appeared. Among them were beautifully designed and richly illustrated books. A great deal of effort and money must have been put into these books – for their promotional value, among other reasons. After all, a city can use public art to raise its cultural profile. At times, municipalities appear to be competing with eachother to realise the largest number of artworks as though quantity trumps quality. Clearly, commissioned art has become a highly developed business and is no longer seen as the bastard offspring of studio art. The commissioned art sector has its own trade publications, subsidy programmes, consultants and specialist artists. Having reached this elevated status, commissioned art is, naturally, subjected to criticism. Critics grumble about clients who have exaggerated expectations for artworks and about politicians who only value art as an 'ornament' and ignore its deeper meaning. The artists, too, come in for criticism. It is said that they merely churn out objects and show little interest in how public space is used. Another criticism being levelled at artists is that they are unable to compete with the existing urban 'visual violence'. The degree to which you share these sentiments very much depends on how much appreciation you have for the modest or striking contributions that artists have made to public areas.

Landscape design

These days there is a great diversity of art commissions. If we look back at previous decades we can discern specific trends, some of which have withstood the test of time while others have been consigned to the dustbins of history or even been literally wiped off the face of the earth. One such development – land-

Marinus Boezem,
The Green Cathedral.
1987-1996. Flevoland.
Photo by G. Schutte.

Marinus Boezem,
The Green Cathedral.
1987-1996. Flevoland.
Photo by J. Linders.

scape design – deserves special mention. It came to the fore in the late 1960s and 1970s and aimed to strengthen the connection between a building or location and the artwork. Artists specialising in this area were sometimes charged with designing pedestrian areas in shopping centres, playgrounds for schools or urban green areas. One example is the *Waves* project in Arnhem, designed by Peter Struycken. Covering almost 260,000 square feet, it consists of an undulating landscape covered with blue-white pavement. Before its metamorphosis, this area beside the River Rhine had become user-unfriendly and inaccessible because of the various roads crisscrossing the location. Using a pattern of waves, Peter Struycken has created a sense of unity and a spatial experience by covering the whole area with a fluid wave-pattern crossed by a system of broad blue and white paths as though the waters of the Rhine were flowing over the land.

Far removed from the urban areas appeared entirely different forms of landscape art, better known as *land art*. Marinus Boezem began to work on his *Green Cathedral* project in 1978, planting 178 Lombardy poplars in the shape of the floor plan of Notre Dame in the city of Reims in France. He used this gothic building as a model, regarding it as an architectural highlight and as a powerful symbol of the human quest for spirituality. Only when the poplars have reached their maximum height of 100 feet will they match the towering French cathedral. The Province of Flevoland – which consists entirely of reclaimed land – is home to *The Green Cathedral* and other large-sized landscape artworks by internationally renowned artists such as Robert Morris, Richard Serra and Daniel Libeskind.

Please, no more forgettable art!

The trends to be seen in the non-commissioned art sector are echoed in the commissioned art business. For example, some new-media artists who earned their spurs in the museum world have also made forays into public-space art. A case in point is Marijke van Warmerdam, whose film clip of a man taking a shower premièred at the prestigious Biennale art festival in Venice. From 1995, *Shower* was then shown for a few years at the underground railway station serving Amsterdam's Schiphol Airport. The absence of daylight in the station facilitated the projection of the film on a wall. It was a beautiful, surreal and also refreshing sight for passengers arriving at Schiphol sweaty and jetlagged after a long flight: an almost motionless man with water streaming down on him uninterruptedly. Various other art projects have meanwhile taken shape at Schiphol, giving an artistic cachet to the Netherlands' international gateway.

Some artworks in public areas are meant to serve a social purpose, as part of the ongoing move by central government and municipalities toward greater democratisation and public involvement. Often this type of 'social art' is very practical and serves a specific target group. Examples are benches where elderly citizens can sit back and relax, as well as sheltered areas where youngsters can hang out without being a nuisance to local residents. In these cases clients sometimes have unrealistic expectations of the projects. Indeed, one 'social artwork' was expected to reduce school truancy! In projects of this kind the artists often work together with municipal departments. At times, their design

Marijke van Warmerdam,
Shower, 1995.
Schiphol Station.
Photo courtesy Galerie
van Gelder, Amsterdam.

even forms the foundation for the whole plan. But it also happens that their designs are simply pushed to the margins.

More recent years have seen the emergence of 'interactive social art,' which seeks to engage the public and reflect 'real life'. In many cases, this art form does not even produce permanent physical structures. Here it is not so much the government who is driving this trend but the artists themselves. Their art often does not fit into museums, galleries and sculpture parks, and is more suitable for outdoor areas. Ida van der Lee, for example, organises projects about events that have a strong impact on society, such as urban renewal or the closure of a neighbourhood bar. In the *Hang Out Your Washing* project, she strengthened social cohesion in an Amsterdam street called Vrolikstraat; she had called on residents to hang colourful (clean) laundry on washing lines strung across the street to give it a Venetian feel.

Interestingly, art in public (outdoor) areas can benefit the artists in many ways: adequate funding, an open space to work in and a much wider audience. It can also be extremely liberating for artists to be no longer confined to museums or hemmed in by museum culture. However, the artist must, of course, still comply with the client's requirements and go through the commissioning process.

It is good that artists now help to give shape to our public space. However, you *can* have too much of a good thing. With the mushrooming of art in public areas over the past 50 years and the related stifling red tape, a lot of forgettable or even downright disastrous art now takes pride of place in public areas. What

Ida van der Lee,
Hang Out Your Washing.
Amsterdam.
Photo courtesy of the artist.

we need is clients who get closely involved in the project, are audacious in their choices, formulate a clear assignment and then give the artists the artistic leeway to do their work. In return, artists need to take into account the social function that public areas have, while retaining their own distinctive artistic approach. Neither side should underestimate the general public. People do want to be part of this artistic adventure, and they are not content with just having an equestrian statue of a prince or a prime minister in bronze. ∎

Translated by Frans Andersson

Borremans' Circus

[PATRICK T. MURPHY]

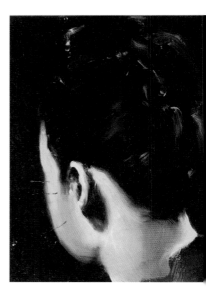

Winter and summer till old age began
My circus animals were all on show,
Those stilted boys, that burnished chariot,
Lion and woman and the Lord knows what.

('The Circus Animals Desertion', W.B.Yeats)

Michaël Borremans,
The Hair. 2002.
Canvas, 30 x 24 cm.
Photo courtesy Zeno x
Gallery, Antwerp.

Michaël Borremans (1963-) has a deft touch with the handling of paint. At a time when painting itself is at issue, Borremans makes mysterious and compelling paintings that combine both skill and intelligence. He has succeeded in creating, within a self-inflicted tight tonal range, a resinous and resonant art that demands a contemplative response. Many of his peers have opted for a strategy that belies or conceals the craftsmanship and labour of oil paint. John Curran plays for a perversion of subject, the distortions deflecting from the central issues of whether painting can carry meaning, and if so, how much and of what form. Another skilful handler of paint, Lisa Yuksavage, also American, incorporates pornographic grotesques as stand-ins for subjects but gets off some remarkable and memorable passages of paint as she does so. Luc Tuymans proposes the triumph of irony over probity and though a skilful painter has at times opted in favour of getting the image down and getting on with the next. Borremans' work epitomises time. Time in the making, a time encapsulated, and consequently, time for its reception. In an era when visual communication is getting faster, his paintings seem to be getting slower. In that, he is near to the artist Vija Celmins who also succeeds in making hard-earned paintings. But unlike Celmins who leaves her meaning dangling without a cause, Borremans has defined his themes, albeit obliquely. There is a ringmaster in charge here but his animals are not exotic, they are beasts of burden – the burden painting, the beast painting,

Hair(s)

On first coming across Michaël Borremans' paintings I was intrigued and suspicious. Intrigued by the virtuosity of the paint handling, a skill delighted in by the artist, to the extent that he can and does flaunt his talent. In *Rachel* (2002) an African girl is painted in a soft light and then again almost in the dark in *Rachel II (The Procession)* (2002). To play with the modulations of tone on such

Michaël Borremans, *Rachel II (The Procession)*. 2002. Canvas, 50 x 42 cm. Photo courtesy Zeno x Gallery, Antwerp.

Michaël Borremans. *Rachel*. 2002. Canvas, 50 x 42 cm. Photo courtesy Zeno x Gallery, Antwerp.

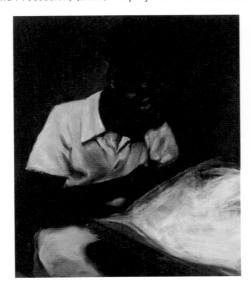

a narrow scale is an act of great skill and one that is rarely seen in painting today. A colder eye responded to the general imagery of the work. What were Borremans' themes, what was he getting at?

If fashion is a barometer of an era then Borremans challenges us to engage with a previous age and the gentle conventions that indicate it. Borremans locates his subjects in the past; it is the early twentieth century, somewhere in the 1930s.

In *The Hair* (2002), we are confronted with a three-quarters rear view of a French plait, the hair gathered to the centre of the back of the head, parted into itself and raised to the top. This quintessential evocation of the period is tilted by the appearance of three errant hairs protruding from the woman's cheek – style foiled by lack of grooming? Surveying other paintings, all the men sport the tight cut, short back and sides, a style that became popular during the First World War for the sake of military efficiency and hygiene. The women all have 'hairdos', coiffed, braided, pig-tailed; the artist doesn't like to send his girls out without having their hair done. Borremans points to the subtle variations that occur in arranging something as finite as hair into a style that itself so solidly situates them in a certain decade. And these paintings of hairstyles rendered

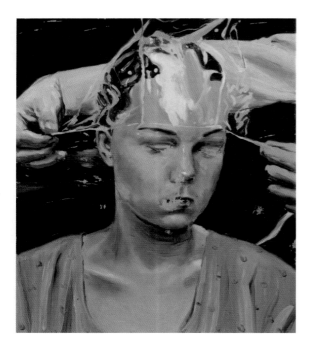

Michaël Borremans,
The Preservation, 2001,
Canvas, 70 x 60 cm.
Photo courtesy Zeno x
Gallery, Antwerp.

via the hairs of the painter's brush onto a canvas need to be protected from the ravages of the present for posterity's sake – which is cleverly commented on by the artist in *The Preservation* (2001).

The fashionability of painting

Precise attention is paid to clothes. *The Shirt* (2002), presents us with a striped waisted shirt with a pointed collar. Though fashionable and body-conscious it seems under-tailored, the cloth not fine enough to carry the design, again harking back to an age of shortage. His women and men often don the clothes of work – aprons, white coats, overalls.

In *The Marvel* (2001), a carefully modulated face is accompanied by a sketchy bow adorning the top of a dress. Painted in broad white strokes and a skipping red outline it is almost comic, but Borremans' humour is like a palette tightly held, preferring the wry smile to an open laugh.

Each aspect of Borremans' work is a reflection on painting, its practice, its cultural significance, its reception. In the past three decades painting has been intermittently heralded as being in a state of resurgence, which by deduction means that those making such claims feel that it has been in a state of decline. Depending on which side of the Atlantic these arguments emanate from the degree of decline or re-emergence differs, the Europeans having a lesser range of worry. But all commentaries reflect that painting is in some way on the edge of fashion, of what is relevant and reflective of our contemporary culture. Borremans' treatment of fashion is itself a rumination on the fashionability of painting. The work seems to suggest that painting is not of this era, and that is not in itself a concern, as its integrity, sensuality and poeticism has greater liberty outside of fashion and an increased expectation of a more discerning audience.

Michaël Borremans,
The Marvel. 2001.
Canvas, 65 x 50 cm.
Photo courtesy Zeno X
Gallery, Antwerp.

Busy people

Borremans sites his paintings in indistinct interiors. Architecture is not articulated; rather, space is defined by the ergonomics of the subjects and their activities. For the most part, whether singly or in groups, Borremans' subjects are
absorbed in an activity. From their clothing we discern that this is not in the
realm of the domestic but in the world of manufacture. Borremans' men and
women are dressed in white coats, overalls, suits. This is not the industrialised
world of machines and production lines but the realm of the laboratory where
cleanliness and precision are paramount. Their absorption is palpable as they
concentrate on adding their contribution to the process. In some cases we can
easily discern their work, as in the Trickland paintings where hunched suited
figures tend to the composing of a model landscape. The most obvious reference arising here is to the same type of preparation for conflict, the war room
where toy battalions and divisions can be moved to plot the progress or retreat

Michaël Borremans,
Add and Remove. 2002.
Canvas, 70 x 60 cm.
Photo courtesy Zeno x
Gallery, Antwerp.

Michaël Borremans,
Fisherman's Luck. 2003.
Canvas, 50 x 40 cm.
Photo courtesy Zeno x
Gallery, Antwerp.

of battle. Parallel to the Trickland paintings are *The Evening Walk* (2002) and *Add and Remove* (2002); here shelves of miniature trees wait to be chosen for inclusion in the creation of the landscape. In the latter, a hand holds a tree on the shelf, a choice, an act of decision to include or return.

Another form of work indicates the preparation of surfaces. *The Table* (2001), *The Saddening* (2001), *The Lucky Ones* (2002), each depicts a group of women attending to a flat surface. We cannot be sure of the nature of the work they are involved in, only that smoothed flat surfaces are the objects of their attention. In *One at a Time* (2003) a group of black attendants stands around a table stacked with three rectangular white flat objects.

If this indeed refers to the sizing of canvases it leads to another body of work on the performative nature of art-making. In *The Butter Sculptor* (2000) and *The Modification* (2001) we see the genesis of form from mass. The locating of this initial aesthetic act in the realm of handicraft points to the artist's self-effacing stance in the face of much pretension about the making of art. The paintings that deal directly with the act of painting insist again on the artisan ethos of the studio, as in *The Mill* (2003) and *The Shift* (2004). In *Fisherman's Luck* (2003) the artist is poised to make a stroke, the outcome of which we can speculate will either succeed or fail depending on the skill of the tutored hand.

A circus of comment and mystery

The decorative is an old chestnut surrounding painting. The term is mainly used as a pejorative. But in truth, painting probably always has had such a role as well. Within the hushed perception of Borremans' work there is a series of paintings that depict ornaments – those porcelain figurines that graced many a 'best' room in our parental houses. Borremans tends not to reproduce them

Michaël Borremans,
The Performance. 2004.
Canvas, 71 x 83 cm.
Photo courtesy Zeno x
Gallery, Antwerp.

fully but to paint a fragment, as if we cannot in this age appreciate the whole and conceive of how they were originally enjoyed. The fragment also avoids the argument of kitsch while admitting admiration of the ornament, the glint of light on the glaze, the delicacy of the modelling.

The artist directs his paintings to be self-aware, denying the fictional space of illusionistic painting. In works such as *Anna* (2003) and the *Four Fairies* (2003) the women subjects literally arise out of the oil of the paint. Anna whose arms are slicked with pigment and linseed ponders the medium of her creation.

Borremans is the ringmaster of his work, directing medium and subject through the hoops to create a circus of comment and mystery on the meaning of painting at the beginning of the twenty-first century. In *The Performance* (2004) a small square stage stands covered in drapery, reflected upon a polished floor; the painting is itself the drama, the actors and the theatre. ■

O body swayed to music, O brightening glance,
How can we know the dancer from the dance?

('Among School Children', W.B. Yeats)

7 March - 1 April 2006: *Horse Hunting* by Michaël Borremans at David Zwirner's Gallery (NY). See www.davidzwirner.com

A version of this article first appeared in *Michaël Borremans, The Performance* (Hatje Cantz, 2005).

Hit the Road

Bands in Search of an Audience Abroad

A reporter from the Dutch music magazine *Fret* is in the audience for Within Temptation at the Columbiahalle in Berlin. In the March (2005) issue, he writes: *'An evening when no fewer than 3000 Berliners have turned out to see a Dutch (Goth) band and every one of them has shelled out 28 euros. What a bizarre idea!'*

The idea that a group from the Low Countries might attract large crowds elsewhere has become less and less bizarre in recent years. The world's become smaller because of the spread of music via the internet, which means that fame is no longer just a question of being in the record shops and the magazines and appearing on the radio and television. Flights to popular destinations have become cheaper, so groups can go abroad under their own steam. But the explanation's not that simple. When bands go on the road, it's generally not something that they do on spec; there have to be destinations, contacts, invitations and agreements. The days are gone when, just after the Beatles split up, Paul McCartney could hop into a minibus with his new group Wings, drive to a student town and knock on the door of campuses, cafés and trendy galleries, offering to put on a surprise performance for an unsuspecting audience.

Within Temptation, who come from Waddinxveen, first appeared far from home when they played at a festival in Mexico City in 2001. That's great, of course, but at the same time it's too far away and it's in a country that's only on the fringes of the rock music world. Much more important for the band, therefore, was the Flemish Rock Werchter festival in 2002. Reputations made at Werchter quickly blow over the borders to music fans in neighbouring countries. The group broke into Germany in 2003, partly as the result of a lengthy tour. As well as a number of artistic prizes, they have twice won the Dutch Export Prize, as the band with the most success abroad in 2003 and 2004. It all comes down to cold hard sales figures, because in business that's the real 'success', no matter how exhausting, alienating and lonely it often is to work abroad. The ultimate accolade for a band will always be recognition in the form of applause from a real audience. Before that happens, though, an unbelievable amount of work is usually required. Success abroad does not remain the crowning achievement of a career for very long. In fact, it just results in more work.

A hit in your own country and in the countries where your music is distributed will signal the start of a tour for bands who are signed to big labels. But

how does it work for bands who haven't had any hits, for bands who have contracts with independent labels or groups working on a 'do-it-yourself' basis? What does 'success' abroad mean when a group has to manage without the traditional channels of the established music industry and media? What sort of adventure is a band of this kind, often independent of the prevailing tastes and trends in the music industry, embarking on when they attempt to find an audience in another country for their concerts and CDs?

Another town, another place / Another girl, another face...

It all used to be considerably easier. Golden Earring from The Hague, who first became successful in the sixties thanks to the support of Radio Veronica, the commercial pirate radio station on the North Sea, had a worldwide hit in 1973 with 'Radar Love'. However, in the early seventies Golden Earring found that success abroad came with a price attached. If you want to 'make it' in the States, you have to go and live there and be constantly available to concert promoters, tour organisers and the media. Life on the road is hard; there are all kinds of nasty types hanging around and an excess of dangerous substances is always on offer. You're surrounded by hangers-on, who all want something from you because you're a star. The guys from Golden Earring stayed put instead, but 'Radar Love' was still voted one of the best car songs of all time in America in 2005.

Large international music fairs have brought foreign countries closer over the past ten to fifteen years. Bands on the verge of success are sent off to big trade meetings, such as Midem in Cannes, Popkomm, which used to be in Cologne and

is now in Berlin, or to CMJ in New York and SXSW in Austin, Texas, to name just the largest fairs. Something similar also exists for the dance world, with Miami Winter Music and Amsterdam Dance Event. There is even government funding available for this kind of promotion, although the golden years have been and gone as far as that is concerned. Once they're within the system of the promotional organisations, success abroad is something that more and more pop groups are able to achieve. This has made it less special and spectacular.

Pop music journals regularly print diaries of trips abroad and accounts of exotic experiences. In the mid-nineties, *Fret* began a series in which bands at the start of their careers or more experienced bands who were not widely known could write about their experiences without the intervention of a music journalist. These diaries soon became rather predictable: another broken-down bus, the wrong food, having one too many again, running out of condoms again. When you're travelling in a car or a bus, you always encounter the same things on the way: customs officials, petrol prices, roadside cafes, police, hitch-hikers and breakdowns. The best thing about these stories is always the encounters with intriguing strangers, which usually happen because of the music; it's so good at breaking down barriers.

And so to the music... How to get it across, to describe it, to promote it to the right audience? What language should you sing in and how is that going to come across in foreign countries? Which countries are you aiming at and what relationship does your own country have with those countries? Then there's the audience. Can you reasonably expect a foreign market for your music? How can you reach that audience? That's what the media are for, but it's much more important for unknown bands to have friends and contacts abroad who can 'do something' for them. Do those friends have the time and the energy to help? And how good is their network? Financial resources are very important: who pays the bills? Are all the band members willing to accept any risks and, finally, do they have the time for this adventure? After all, most pop musicians have to do some other work for a living and end up sacrificing their holidays for the band.

Battle of the Bands

A group that doesn't come from the original centres of pop production (the United States, Great Britain) will always have the idiosyncrasies of their national and cultural origins and the creative struggle with the material they have adopted, including the language. There are only a very few bands from outside these centres whose origins cannot be heard. Anyone who can tell that dEUS are from Belgium without being told beforehand must be clairvoyant, for example. And then there's the question of 'competing nations'. When it comes to music, the Netherlands and Flanders have been hugely competitive for over twenty years. It began in 1983, when the first 'Noorderslag' (Battle of the North) was organised in Groningen, as a competition between the Netherlands and Belgium. That battle was won by the Netherlands, according to the Dutch media, while the Belgians also returned home victorious as far as their media were concerned. Since then, the two countries have been keeping a very close eye on each other's music industry and successes abroad. Academic research has been carried out into the image of Belgian bands in the Netherlands. It showed that in the nineties the 'Made in Belgium' label had become a guarantee of quality following the rise of English-language pop music from Antwerp and Ghent. For a Belgian group, success in the Netherlands means something different than success in Luxembourg. Neighbouring countries with the same language and a similar culture are each other's most critical audience. An Ethiopian group, for example, can count on a warm welcome in the Netherlands, and the reverse can also be true (The Ex, a Dutch post-punk band with a rich history and a cult following in the US, have good contacts with Ethiopia, for example), because they're not poaching on each other's territory. The bigger the difference in musical identity, the more 'world music' for local listeners; so there's no threat to local acts. The more similarity with leading international groups, the more competition there is.

Great Britain is the Mecca for pop groups from the Low Countries. When the Antwerp group dEUS performed at a famous London club in 1992, it didn't take long for them to be contacted by Island, the record company of Chris Blackwell, one of whose 'discoveries' was Bob Marley. That really is a fantastic start. Sometimes, though, even a fantastic start may never really result in anything. This is what happened to the Rotterdam R&B act Ké Shaw, who were signed in 1994 by Motown, the legendary black American label. There was great excitement throughout the Netherlands when the news got around. However, Motown was no longer the successful independent record company it had been in the sixties and seventies. International commercial events and decisions meant that Motown got a new management and the Ké Shaw project was dropped.

Not just any old foreign country

Singer-guitarist Tim Vanhamel of the Belgian rock group Millionaire, who released their second CD *Paradisiac* in 2005, has long enjoyed fame as one of the members of Evil Superstars and briefly as a guitar player for dEUS, where the binding force is creativity rather than musical taste, background or speciality. In these various roles, Vanhamel experienced the international breakthrough of Flemish rock groups in the nineties. Josh Homme, of the American post-stoner-rock-group Queens of the Stone Age 'discovered' Millionaire somewhere on the rock circuit. The group was invited to tour with QOTSA in America and Europe. After that, they also toured with Foo Fighters, the band formed by Dave Grohl, former-ly of Nirvana. As well as with Millionaire, Vanhamel also plays with Homme in Eagles of Death Metal. Homme worked in Los Angeles as a recording technician on *Paradisiac*. Millionaire are now a contemporary model of success precisely because their success abroad was not achieved in just any old foreign country.

The path to adventure and success abroad, in whatever form it comes and whatever experiences it brings, is one of the most attractive parts of a band's career, perhaps especially so for bands from the Netherlands and Belgium. In our small countries with their national club circuits that really don't take very long to get around, the home territory can be explored very quickly and then you have to start all over again. And to do that you preferably have to record a new CD first.

Creative bands with their own sound and an ambitious cast of mind will sel-dom hang around for very long on local stages. Truly independent musicians on the international music scene will keep on ploughing their own furrows without being seen by a wider audience. They'll go headbanging in the Balkans for sau-sages and beer, or play in a Moroccan village for a cup of strong tea and a bit of chat about life on the streets of Brussels or Amsterdam. And then there are the groups in between, who will try to gain experience abroad, perhaps with the help of subsidies or by taking part in special projects. Sometimes they're very successful in managing to connect with an audience and building up a fan base in a great location (like the Nits in Finland, for example). Many musicians under contract however have no choice but to go where their record companies send them to boost their CD sales and to broaden the market.

The pleasure of being a foreigner

Alamo Race Track (ART) from Amsterdam have their origins in Redivider, the 1998 winners of the Grote Prijs van Nederland (a kind of rock/pop grand prix), and they also briefly appeared under the name of Morningstar. This is a group that works very carefully and without compromise to create an original oeuvre. In 2005 they caused quite a stir when they went on tour in France. A question for bass guitarist David Corel: how do ART make their contacts abroad? Corel: *'In March 2004 we went to Austin, Texas, for the annual music fair South By South West (SXSW). Our manager and booker got talking to someone from Fargo Records, a French independent specialising in issuing existing releases, usually American ones, in Europe. He gave him a copy of Birds At Home, our first and, so far, only CD. In January 2005 he got in touch with our label Excelsior Recordings. After that, it all got sorted out pretty quickly: in April they brought out the record in France, and shortly afterwards in Germany and England.'*

Corel answers the question *'What role does the record company at home play in setting up the tour(s)?'* as follows: *'Well, actually, none at all. In France, there's another booking office working for us and they work with Fargo Records. First we decide when we want to go on tour and then the booker abroad gets to work. When everything's sorted out, Fargo enter the picture to see if there's any promotion and press to sort out.'*

ART certainly enjoy the fact that when they're abroad they're a foreign band. Corel: *'The very first time we went to France after the record came out there (at the end of May 2005), we noticed that we were treated differently than in the Netherlands, both by people from the record company and by journalists. Fargo really looked after us and made sure that we had everything we needed on our promo day, which was a whole day of interviews in various cafés in Paris. The journalists were well prepared. It was the first time we'd had proper conversations with journalists.'*

Language problems arise in countries where people don't speak any English or prefer not to. Corel: *'Even in France most people can manage to speak and understand English fairly well now, so it works out fine. And, apart from Germany, we had only performed in English-speaking countries. We went to Scotland, England and the United States.'*

The question of how you would describe your own 'success' is very tricky to answer if it's not in terms of the numbers of CDs that have been sold or the air time on TV. Corel: *'For me, the recognition is the most important. I don't want to come across as some tormented "rock star", but I've always thought that our debut album deserved more than we achieved with it in the Netherlands.'* Do you need to have a bit of luck? Corel: *'As far as France is concerned, we were lucky that a number of Belgian bands have just become popular there (including Ghinzu and Vive la Fête), and we're riding on their coattails. And then everyone suddenly starts talking about the "Benelux-wave" that's "flooding" France. They also associate us with the new-wave trend that's going on at the moment. A lot of reviewers mention Joy Division and The Strokes as comparisons. I can't hear it myself, but when they all started saying it, it worked to our advantage.'* So what did Corel get out of it? *'I'm certainly happy that we've reached a much larger audience with our album by touring abroad than by staying on the Dutch club circuit. And that we've played to crowded venues where you feel that people have certain expectations. It means you've often won them over as soon as you play the first notes. And as a foreigner you're treated differently, better.'*

In the longer term, the experience of life on the road is not only exhilarating and good for group solidarity, it's also usually positive in terms of creating and building up a reputation. Corel: *'The next album's coming out in spring 2006; we're planning to release it at the same time in England, Germany, the Netherlands, Switzerland and Scandinavia. With the French success under our belts it might be easier to make a name for ourselves in other countries, as well as our own. So we're hoping that this was a step up and that the next record will allow us to climb a step higher still.'* About the hierarchy of foreign countries, Corel says: *'If we'd had the same media attention in England, we'd immediately have been "well-known" in many more countries. Lots of other countries keep a very close eye on the English music press, so that they don't miss any new trends. At the same time, it's difficult for a band from the Netherlands to get a foot in the door there.'*

Missionaries of sound

Does the group know which French media were interested in Alamo Race Track's tour? Corel: *'Fargo gave me a press pack. There was a piece about us in "La Libération" on the evening we performed in Paris, and later there was a review of the show at La Route Du Rock in Saint-Malo. The French "Rolling Stone" published a review of the CD and an interview; in "Les Inrockuptibles" there was a CD review* and an interview (under the heading "Salvateur Alamo", a pun on the group's name – Salvatore Adamo is an Italo-Belgian crooner); a review and interview in "Rock Mag"; a review and a short article in "Rock Sound"; reviews in "Magic" and "Guitar Part", "Crossroads", "Velvet", "Atmosphere"; an interview at "Les Inrocks.com"; and another fourteen reviews in a variety of French webzines. We also did a live performance on Radio France and part of the show at La Route du Rock was broadcast on Arte.' A huge amount of publicity, then, for a band from Amsterdam with no more than a not very recent debut album to their name.

When asked for his favourite memory, David Corel says: 'The Route du Rock festival in summer 2005. We played on a large stage in an old fort in front of seven thousand people while the sun went down. People were crowd surfing and for the first time in France I saw people singing along to our songs.' The intense involvement of the audience with the music that you bring to them as a kind of missionary of sound is still the ultimate kick for a band on the road. It means that, even though you're far away, you feel as though you've come home. ■

Translated by Laura Watkinson

FURTHER INFORMATION

www.muziekcentrum.be
www.hollandrocks.com

Joost Swarte, Knight of the Clear Line

In April 2004 Joost Swarte (1947-) was knighted by Queen Beatrix of the Netherlands. Admittedly, he had to share the honour with, among others, the enormously popular singers Marco Borsato and Frans Bauer, but even so.... It is still an honour that was not accorded in his lifetime to, for example, Marten Toonder, the godfather of the Dutch comic strip who died in 2005. Once, but a very long time ago, Joost Swarte drew the underground comic *Jopo de Pojo*, that was full of sex and drugs and rock'n roll. Nowadays Swarte is a law-abiding citizen with an exceptional graphic talent, he enjoys an international reputation, and is an artist who can do whatever takes his fancy: create posters, stained-glass windows and postage stamps, or design bookcases, watches and buildings. There's a name for that: artistic Jack-of-all-trades.

Joost Swarte was never one to sit around doing nothing. Turn the computer on and surf to www.joostswarte.com and you will learn a lot. This is the site of an artist/entrepreneur, of an artist of international renown: the artist addresses you with a letter of welcome, his life and works can be consulted in five languages, and, provided they have the cash, anyone who feels like it can shop in the on-line shop. Not that there is anything wrong with that. But I'm a little disconcerted that on this gem of a web-site Joost Swarte has chosen to play down his own early years as a strip cartoonist and underground artist, as if this were something to be ashamed of. Surely it's all part of life's rich pageant?

Modern Papier, Tante Leny and the clear line

As a young man Joost Swarte studied Industrial Design in Eindhoven in the late sixties. It was there that he began drawing comic strips. In 1971 he abandoned his studies and began producing his own magazine, *Modern Papier*, which was to run to ten issues. *Modern Papier* was taken over by the underground magazine *Tante Leny Presenteert* (Aunt Leny Presents), probably the finest ever to be published in the Netherlands. For *Tante Leny Presenteert* Swarte drew, among other things, the strip referred to earlier, *Jopo de Pojo*, a randy, weed-smoking black man with a greased quiff. We are talking and writing Amsterdam, early

Jopo de Pojo.
© Joost Swarte.

seventies. The heyday of the city as the navel of the European underground scene is not yet over, but it is losing a good deal of its edge.

So Joost Swarte has something a lot of people will envy him: a style of his own. Whether he is drawing for *Tante Leny Presenteert* or for the children's paper *Okkie*, his work is clearly recognisable. In an inimitable manner Joost Swarte combines the famous clear line of the Belgian Hergé (of Tintin fame) with post-war modernism. How to explain this? The clear line is a style both of drawing and of narration; it stands for clarity, sharpness and functionality. From all the possible lines that could be drawn the only right one, the single appropriate one is chosen *and* not without significance emphasised. So as not to lose any time in telling the story all the ballast is thrown overboard, economy and succinctness are exercised. That's the clear line also, and Swarte is a master at it. He combines this style with cartoon figures and settings that reflect the modernism of the fifties and early sixties. This is no gimmick that will quickly lose its shine, quite the reverse. Swarte is still using the combination, and it still doesn't look outdated. At most it provides a breath of good quality nostalgia. His book *Modern Art* (that came out first in French and German and only then in Dutch from De Harmonie) is the best illustration of Joost Swarte's period as (strip) illustrator.

Joost Swarte is a professional, but he is also first and foremost a man of ideas. In 1981, in *de Volkskrant*, he described how he sets about drawing: *'The idea has become more and more important in the drawing, its execution is a second phase in the work. I'm dealing with a pictorial language and my job is to get a particular idea across. For instance, you ask yourself, to speak in film terms – how you'll place the camera, what should be in the foreground, what should catch the eye first. Are there certain lines in the drawing that'll take people's eyes to a second detail? That's how a story-line develops within a drawing. That's the craftsman's department of the work. There must be something in the drawing that people find attractive, and once you've got their attention, then you can begin to tell them something, but not before. Otherwise they pass over it much too quickly. They turn the page straightaway. Precisely because for me the idea is the most important thing , the drawing must actually be such that people forget it's a drawing. It has to come alive ....'*

It has to come alive, indeed: Joost Swarte is (and remains) the child who can spell out his dreams, his fantasy, his absurd hare-brained schemes in a style of drawing that is seemingly perfect.

If we were to compare Swarte with one single other cartoonist/illustrator, then it would be the Fleming Ever Meulen. They are of the same age, they were brothers-in-arms on *Tante Leny* and later the Flemish weekly *Humo*, they are both mad about flash American cars and art nouveau buildings, they both make their naïve figures take giant steps and wear sloppy suits, but above all their work has this much in common: it is deceptively simple. *Deceptively simple*: maybe at the end of the day that is also the best definition of the clear line.

Joost Swarte's style is of international quality, and even in the seventies it did not go unnoticed: he published in the French magazine *Charlie Hebdo*, where his compatriot Willem had been at home for a long time (but there is absolutely no connection between their respective work: Willem draws hard political strips and has elevated ugliness to a style).

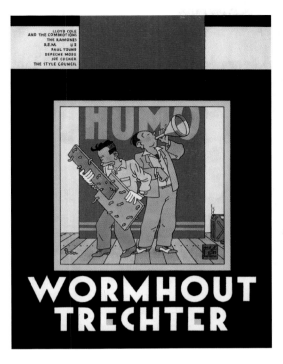

From strip cartoonist to illustrator

At the end of the seventies Joost Swarte gradually changed from drawing comic strips to illustration. He did his first cover for the book supplement to *Vrij Nederland*, at that time still a flourishing and leading weekly. For the same weekly, but this time for the children's paper, Swarte drew two further strip series: first *Dr. Ben Ciné & D*, later the unrivalled comic strip *Yes How! No How!* (Niet zo! Maar zo)

Humo also took on Joost Swarte and would have no regrets on that score. He drew a number of fine covers for the Flemish weekly that later found their way into large exhibitions of Swarte as posters. Naïve, absurd, funny, original, surprising, mischievous, boyish, dreamy: these are apt words for the covers of *Humo*. Never crude, or sharp, or wounding, or misplaced, and certainly never offensive. And always perfectly executed. In 1986 there was a fine exhibition of this work: *Humo Behind Glass*, that toured throughout Flanders.

From 1980 onwards the pace hotted up for Joost Swarte. He took part in the Great Comic Show in Angoulême in France, the dream of every aspiring European cartoonist. Swarte's work was published in *Raw*, the famous underground magazine of Art Spiegelman, the cartoonist of *Maus*, and to date the only comic strip artist to have received the Pulitzer Prize. By the way, Ever Meulen was also published in *Raw*. A few years later Swarte and Ever Meulen met up again in the literary periodical *The New Yorker*. Swarte was awarded the Prix St-Michel from the city of Brussels (for the best foreign artist!!!), and the international aspects of his career were reinforced with lectures in New York and exhibitions all over Europe. Indeed, in his work you can see that the importance of words, of text, is constantly diminishing, that only the drawing still speaks its international lan-

Yes How! No How!
(Niet zo! Maar zo;
De Harmonie/Het Raadsel,
Amsterdam, 1985).
© Joost Swarte.

Cover for *Humo*, 1985.
© Joost Swarte.

guage. Yet Joost Swarte remained the child who could spell out his dreams, his fantasy, his absurd hare-brained schemes in his seemingly perfect style.

In Holland itself Swarte drew a firm clear line under his bohemian years: he started to give guest lectures at the Rietveld Academy in Amsterdam. At that point he was – how shall we put it – accepted. In 1984 the Dutch Post Office asked him to design 4 comic-strip postage stamps. Swarte made funny and beautiful miniatures of them – like the drawings of medieval monks. In Italy they were so taken with the stamps that in 1985 they awarded them a prize (the Asiago Prize for philately as art!).

The Joost Swarte World Exhibition

Cover for
The New Yorker, 1998.
© Joost Swarte.

Swarte must have been thinking discretion was the better part of valour when he put together a retrospective exhibition of his own work in his home town of Haarlem and called it *Joost Swarte's World Exhibition*. He had been working for seventeen years as a cartoonist, illustrator and designer and had apparently effortlessly built up an impressive oeuvre: comics, comic strips and humorous illustrations (never cartoons in the true sense of the word), posters for rock festivals, jazz concerts etc, covers for periodicals, jackets for books, record sleeves (for Fay Lovsky among others), postage stamps, murals (in Lyons and elsewhere).

Joost Swarte's World Exhibition toured the whole world with success. I still recall how in Brussels – in the Beursschouwburg – I stood flabbergasted and dumbfounded by the sample of such a prolific talent displayed there. Joost Swarte was there, giving the journalists a friendly and patient hearing: a slouching overgrown teenager in a T-shirt that had seen better days and pants of indeterminate hue.

His work gained a place of honour at large comic festivals, he participated in the big exhibition of the underground magazine mentioned earlier *Raw* (under the well-known title *Images of the Grafix Magazine that overestimates the Taste of the American Public*), he gave lectures in New York, in short, Joost Swarte took his place in the Gallery of the Great.

From illustrator to designer

In fact, *Joost Swarte's World Exhibition* marked the end of a period in Swarte's life and work. He had already taken a number of sideways steps with the comic-strip postage stamps for the Dutch Post Office in 1984, with the design of a pictorial language course for Apeldoorn Museum and a reading table with stools for the Frans Hals Museum in Haarlem, both in 1987.

This evolution was to continue. I think we can consider 1989 as the pivotal year between illustration and design. While his world exhibition was still touring the world, Swarte designed the logo, the poster and the trophy for the Holland Animation Festival. For MTV New York he designed a *stationcall*, an animation between the clips and the various parts of the programme that shows which broadcaster you are watching.

And, not insignificantly, Swarte began to make his mark as a prominent citizen of his home town Haarlem (his birthplace, Heemstede, is close by). He was involved with the beginning of the Haarlem Comic Days, a show that quickly grew into the most important comics event in the Netherlands and pushed other organisations with a richer tradition into the background. The almost forty-year old *Stripschap* (Comic Art Show), for example. In the case of the *Stripschap* they made the best of a bad job and awarded Swarte the Medal for Exceptional Merit. And there was more to come: Joost Swarte became a member of the Comic Strip Foundation of the Netherlands (comparable to the Flemish Bronze Adhemar Foundation). He also designed a banner for the Prague *People to People* (music) festival and ventured into creating wine labels.

The trend continued: a wallet for phone cards for KPN Telecom, children's furniture for Apeldoorn Museum, the corporate logo for a gramophone record company, wristwatches, Swarte got his teeth into everything. *En passant* he established his own publishing house at Oog & Blik, (which would often cooperate with the publisher Harmonie, his regular publisher up until then). Yet more banners were to follow: for the city of Amsterdam, and with portraits of artists like Duchamps, Panamarenko and Beuys for the Lyons Biennial. And then a medal for the retiring Mayor of Haarlem.

In the nineties there was a torrent of prizes for book and jacket designs by Swarte. He designed party cakes for Fransen, the Haarlem bakery. In 1995 he started on the design of the new theatre building, the Toneelschuur, also in Haarlem. Two years later the design was ready. It was his first design for a building. His rough plan was then transformed into a useable building design in cooperation with a 'proper' architectural bureau (Mecanoo). In 2003 the Toneelschuur theatre was opened amid celebrations. Haarlem adored Joost Swarte. But what is it about that building that is typically Swarte? It's a difficult question to answer clearly. It's a beautiful building, true, modernistic on the exterior, a mixture of styles on the interior. It's the kind of building Swarte has often drawn as a setting in his comic strips and illustrations. But does that make it exceptional? No.

Booklet and CD for Fay Lovski, 1992. © Joost Swarte.

The Toneelschuur theatre in Haarlem, designed by Joos Swarte (in cooperation with Mecanoo). 2003. Photo by Henze Boekhout.

From the dozens of Joost Swarte projects from the nineties (music with Fay Lovsky, film animations, murals, furniture, you name it) I'll pick out two more: at the request of an Amsterdam housing company he designed stained-glass windows to brighten up and liven up 35 houses in boring working-class Marnix-straat. A very original approach and a very successful project: whoever would have thought that the old-fashioned stained-glass technique would still find an application in the comic strip? And in the betterment of the masses?

Leporello is Don Giovanni's manservant in Mozart's opera of the same name. And 'leporello' is also the Dutch word for an illustration folded like the bellows of a concertina. And it is the title of the catalogue of Swarte's most recent ret-

rospective. The exhibition began its travels in 2004 in Erlangen in Germany, moved in 2005 to the European capital of the comic strip, Angoulême, and could be marvelled at in Paris until the end of the Summer.

Leporello is a crash course in Swarte in 352 plates. The catalogue gives a clear and convincing picture of the immense talent of the Dutch cartoonist/illustrator/designer. Of his boundless imagination, his absurd humour. Of the Jack-of-all-trades he is. The only pity is that so little material from the seventies has been included. If you pay attention carefully, you can see how the drawing has evolved: it gets more angular all the time, more sparing. Swarte needs fewer and fewer lines to bring his idea alive. ∎

www.joostswarte.com

www.lambiek.nl

www.griffioen-grafiek.nl

www.deharmonie.nl

All illustrations courtesy of Joost Swarte and De Harmonie + Oog & Blik.

Translated by Sheila M. Dale

The Tao of Literature

Life as it is, according to Patricia de Martelaere

She herself is unwilling to provide any detailed explanation of her novels. She refuses to give interviews and declines TV appearances. Patricia de Martelaere (1957-) is first and foremost a professor of philosophy, as well as being a brilliant essayist who writes lucidly and inspiredly about the very essence of life itself, about love and death. At the end of 2004, she published *The Unexpected Answer* (Het onverwachte antwoord), a bizarre love story which no-one can quite make head or tail of. Six women are in love with the same man and talk incessantly about their feelings and thoughts. Transparent as De Martelaere's essays are, just as 'unexpectedly' obscure and sometimes even irritating is this literary tour de force, full of associations, philosophical plays on words and lyrical asides. And yet in a certain sense *The Unexpected Answer*, her fifth novel, is her ultimate book. Not just because it is twice as thick as her four previous novels. There is also a gap of twelve years between this symphony of ideas and *The Tail* (De staart), her penultimate novel from 1992. Why did she wait so long before embarking on a new novel? Anyone who browses through the essays and readings she produced on the literary sidelines will gradually discover the oriental ideas that lie behind the new De Martelaere. If prior to 1992 her writing was rational and Western, since then she has been oriental and inspired in equal measure. What does the path look like that this philosopher wielding a literary pen has followed until now?

De Martelaere is not only a trained philosopher; she also won a First Prize in Solfeggio at the Brussels Academy of Music. In 1971, when she was only four-teen, she had already published a book for young people, *King of the Wilderness* (Koning der wildernis), in which things went badly for the main character. Even as a teenager De Martelaere was alternating between philosophy and art, be-tween reflection and music or literature. In 1984, she gained her doctorate with a study of the philosophy of the eighteenth-century philosopher David Hume. Anyone wishing to understand De Martelaere's literary work will find a good starting-point in her fascination with Hume. *Hume's 'Moderate' Scepticism: Futile or Fatal?* was the title of her doctoral thesis. Since then De Martelaere has continued to publish on his work. In masterly fashion, Hume deconstructed the way in which we humans form our idea of reality. He warned us that the reality we perceive and call objective is in actual fact a highly personal construction. It happens to be part of the nature of things, according to Hume, that people be-lieve in the existence of an objective reality, but there is no real proof. Our pic-ture of reality, according to De Martelaere along with Hume, stands or falls by the 'vividness' of our perceptions. There is no philosophical basis that can trans-mute this 'vividness' into truth.

After this sober observation, De Martelaere certainly did not proceed cheer-fully to the order of the day. In the four novels she published between 1988 and 1992 the 'futile' cares and worries of the main character always prove more or less 'fatal'. In *Night Diary of an Insomniac* (Nachtboek van een slapeloze, 1988), her first novel, the protagonist finds a rather drastic means of overcoming the 'cold fire' of his despair. Unable to come to terms with himself and thus doomed to fret all night long, he finally commits suicide. In *The Painter and His Model* (De schilder en zijn model, 1989), De Martelaere has two lovers attract each other and, mainly, repel each other. This mini-novel could possibly be seen as a pre-liminary study for *The Unexpected Answer*. In *Scars* (Littekens, 1990), the most successful of her small novels, Eva, a medical student, is secretly in love with an older man. While occasionally making love with a fellow student, she thinks of the cold perfection of corpses on a dissecting table. *The Tail* (1992), her last small novel before the great (literary) silence, was yet another confirmation of the fact that De Martelaere's main characters are condemned to lifelong loneli-ness. Theo, a young man who has difficulties in dealing with the unfaithfulness of his friend, tries to console himself by means of an imaginary conversation with himself. The moral of De Martelaere's solipsistic story: we all happen to be imprisoned in our own self. So it is a question of fantasising ourselves out of that prison as 'vividly' as possible. The supreme fantasy is love. But it is also the most dangerous fantasy, as the fathers of the church knew long ago. Postcoital melancholy is the fate of the lover. De Martelaere attempts in these first novels to compose musical variations on this theme, with varying degrees of success.

To experience truth

After *The Tail*, silence falls on the house of the novelist De Martelaere. She ap-plies herself to writing essays – and does so with great virtuosity and success. In *A Longing for Inconsolability* (Een verlangen naar ontroostbaarheid, 1993), for which she received the Jan Greshoff Prize, she elaborates further on the huge question that preoccupied the heroes and heroines of her novels: How can I escape from my own head? And here again she stands up for drastic solutions, as in the essay 'The connoisseur of the art of living. Towards an aesthetics of suicide', where she comes to the conclusion that while there's life there's not hope but death. Four years later De Martelaere brings together new soundings about life, art and death in *Surprises* (Verrassingen, 1997), for which she received the Triennial State Prize for Essays and Criticism. Here too she explores the contradictory nature of loss and illness, of murder and incest. The positive attraction of what at first sight would seem to be negative phenomena becomes almost engagingly clear in De Martelaere's limpid prose. In her cerebral, unsentimental view, isolation and dying acquire a strange grandeur. But her insights in this last collection were no longer really 'surprising'. In a certain sense, she had landed up in a cul de sac. De Martelaere's philosophical imagination, however, proved versatile enough to find a way out of the impasse of Hume's philosophy of perception. If you cannot argue philosophically for the objectivity of reality, you can perhaps always experience it.

After all, Ludwig Wittgenstein had already announced that the inexpressible, the unnameable – in short, truth – will eventually show itself: *'What can not be put into words, makes itself manifest.'* Via Taoism, De Martelaere now gains a Pauline experience that has definitely set her on the path towards her new, emancipatory novel. Lao Tse, with his collection of sayings *Tao teh King*, forms a natural link to the rather cryptic way in which Wittgenstein 'shows' the 'right way' *(tao)* to truth. Taoism, just like Buddhism and other oriental techniques of meditation, does not immerse itself in human thought or the subject, as do Hume and traditional Western philosophers. On the contrary, in the oriental vision only at the point where thinking stops do life and reality start. Oriental philosophers, according to De Martelaere in *Unworldliness* (Wereldvreemdheid), seek via certain techniques of perception first to totally empty or depersonalise the human being. Then, from the emptiness that has been created, reality can flow into the purified human being as into an empty vessel. The individual who is able to reset his mind to zero gets the chance of plugging into the world around him: *'Creative writers and artists, just like magicians, are constantly and in the most intimate way aware of the immense, nameless force-field (...) that governs us and of which we are a part.'*

Stop thinking

De Martelaere, who sided with Hume and was thus unable to recognise any objective basis for subjective impressions and ideas, now sees the chance, thanks to oriental philosophy, of getting firm ground under her feet even so. The only condition is: to stop thinking. Plug into the cosmic force-field and you will discover the forces within yourself. The oriental techniques of perception call on the individual to open up to the other (person) by adopting a waiting attitude. Not by passively keeping one's hands in one's lap but by actively keeping a lookout, in the sense of concentrating on what is about to happen. Whenever the spark jumps across and contact with reality is made, according to De Martelaere in *Who's Afraid of Death?* (Wie is bang voor de dood), it is a question of having the faith and the nerve to let everything go, *'not for the sake of an external reward but for the sake of the force itself that is released in this letting go'*. Anyone learning to swim jumps confidently into the deep water and is rewarded by the buoyancy of the water.

After *Unworldliness* De Martelaere, who in her early work deploys characters who are looking in vain for a way out of the perplexities of life, chooses the tao of life and literature. She professes 'a cold art' in which the writer and the characters rid themselves of their sentimental, subjective humanity in order, in so doing, to be able to make contact with the impersonal, energy-filled force-field of full, natural life. Or, as De Martelaere herself says in *Unworldliness*: 'The *highest attainable form of involvement: not an involvement towards a person but towards the World (with a capital letter).*' That De Martelaere minimalises the position of the human being in the world is not solely due to her discovery of Taoism. The laconic way in which Arthur Schopenhauer and Friedrich Nietzsche relativised the human ego into a plaything of voluntaristic forces had always appealed to her. But what for these philosophers was the work of the anonymous will has in the work of Charles Darwin a more precise, analytical content. Through systematic study of the way in which Darwin perceived nature, De Martelaere felt keenly aware of humanity as merely one of the numerous products of natural selection, alongside all the other life-forms. Darwin convincingly demonstrated that man was not the measure of all things. On the contrary, it was the things and nature that constantly took the measure of man. Man only had one option – to adapt to the laws of Mother Nature or disappear.

The Unexpected Answer is a love story without the classic psychological or relational ups and downs. In her novel, De Martelaere shows how you can let women love without lapsing into melodramatic or emotional language. At first sight the layman cannot make head or tail of it. But the six women in search of cosmic love are six different ways of providing such a love with a shape or form. What is more, they sometimes speak with the same voice, as if we were dealing with the same woman. It is indeed striking how certain aphorisms constantly recur in some sort of mantra. It is intriguing to make a small anthology of these which reveals just how perceptually oriented De Martelaere's vision remains. Not thanks to Hume this time but thanks to Taoism. *'Listening is a form of looking'*, *'stroking is looking with the hands'*, *'drawing is stopping thinking'*, *'feelings do not exist'*, *'writing is (...) a matter of looking (...) it has to do with the whole world through my eyes'*. It is probably no coincidence that the character who paints and, in the Chinese tradition, draws with charcoal, supplies the female voice extremely frequently: *'Painting is a relation with reality, not with the onlooker. The onlooker is ridiculous – just as ridiculous and fatuous as the voyeur who peers through the keyhole while you and I are screwing.'* That is not how an average woman speaks in an average Dutch-language love novel. But then, *The Unexpected Answer* is an exceptional novel.

Professor of love

The object of this female longing is also completely out of the ordinary. Godfried H. is the man whom all the female protagonists are crazy about. He epitomises the wait-and-see manner used in Taoism by the individual in order to empty himself and let go of everything (*wu wei*) so as to be able to participate in a new total experience. In *Unworldliness* De Martelaere typifies mystical receptiveness as follows: '*It requires a great exertion to arrive at the letting go of all exertions; you have to do a great deal for it before you succeed in doing nothing more and become nothing more than an antenna, a focus of rays that converge and meet and are able on the spot and "of themselves" to catch fire.*' Godfried H. is in a certain sense De Martelaere's Taoist professor of love, the Lao Tse of longing. And, as is fitting for a mentor, he prefers to stay silent rather than offer explanations, unless in lines by Rainer Maria Rilke or T.S. Eliot. Godfried H. is De Martelaere's Pied Piper of Hamelin, the male siren who turns the heads of the female characters and thereby offers them the chance of being seized by authentic love.

The novel ends with a passage that gives a description of the concentrated energy of the enlightened person who is rewarded with an instantaneous life-fulfilment: '*And once more it is not clear from where one is standing looking, tense, almost breathless, at the formless shadow under the bushes. If it is the cat, or a form carved like the body of a cat – and if it is still alive and purring inside, or already completely dead, dissolved and discharged – but then it finally breaks through the door, and the answer is yes, no matter how, completely, utterly: yes.*' So De Martelaere grants her character a happy ending. She embraces the *tao* of life, the 'right path' that is also often hinted at as a 'formless form'. She endorses the pulsating energy of reality. In other words, this is a completely different De Martelaere from that of her earlier work. She allows her character to acknowledge the *amor fati*: be happy with what nature has to offer you. She accepts life as it is, also and above all in its negativity: '*Whatever may be, there is much more nothingness than what there actually is*'

East and West

Does that mean that De Martelaere has renounced her earlier rationalism and foresworn Hume's philosophy of perception? No, on the contrary, she has deepened her original philosophical position and saved the mentor. It is just that the Western philosophy of perception has been transformed into an oriental technique of perception and the associative 'vividness' of Hume's theory of perception has been turned 180 degrees into the animating link of a nature practice interpreted in a Taoist way. To watch keenly and alertly remains the point of departure for both Hume and the Taoist doctrine. Only the person who observes reality coolly and impersonally can ever dare make the leap into its unfathomable depths. In *Unworldliness*, De Martelaere allows herself to forget that East and West are fire and water to each other: '*To think, feel and act are the three great pillars of Western culture. To stop thinking is one of the great devices of the oriental search for wisdom. East and West are incompatible because it is simply impossible to think and not-think at the same time.*' To think and not-think at the same time: this is the new paradox that De Martelaere wishes to work on in this novel. So De Martelaere is actually trying to reconcile East and West with each other, although Rudyard Kipling once wrote that the two cultures would never manage to reach out to each other: '*For East is East and West is West, and never the twain shall meet.*' That also explains why this book is so difficult to understand. Maybe also for the writer, who after all is trying to sweat out an 'inhuman' work of art by transforming herself while writing and associating into the focus of the world. So she reveals as in a mirror what cosmic love can and cannot do, although this time the positive aspect gains the upper hand. Could it be that De Martelaere, after this experiment in 'cold art', will consider the novel as an art form as having been definitively examined? Most likely she will not be prepared to admit it. She can only go with the flow as she experiences it. Perhaps next time she will make a collection of quintessential sayings?

While De Martelaere was acquiring inspiration for a new, Taoist turn in her writing, she wrote a number of poems that she later collected under the title *Nothing that Says* (Niets dat zegt, 2002). In its colophon, she talks about a '*completely one-off collection of occasional poems*'. Not all the poems are equally successful, though some of them reveal well on a small scale what De Martelaere is trying to achieve in her latest novel on a large scale. How does the tao of literature work? 'In the Garden', the love poem quoted below, is by no means as solid as her ambitious love story, but it is certainly no less hungry for reality. It reads like an ecological plea for a life in harmony with nature. Could that be what the tao of literature is all about: an ethos that listens to the voice of everything that lives and has ever existed and modestly seeks its own place there?[1]

In the Garden

We in this great grass-patch, clover, dandelions
and what teems here, what gets

involved: the caterpillar, the grapevine. Us underneath,
all in a mess once more, a jumble once more. We're

similar. Completely. More tangled than ants, in
this presence of the garden, in which included:

this wilderness. What hesitates there, water falls
over it, plunges, gathers force. ∎

Translated by John Irons

NOTE

1. In March 2006 De Martelaere's *Taoism. The Road not to Follow* (Taoïsme. De weg om niet te volgen. Baarn: Ambo Publishers) came out.

Two Extracts from *The Unexpected Answer*
by Patricia de Martelaere

Doesn't the whole of life reside in a single instant? And doesn't it for that very reason not reside anywhere? Life holds no more secrets for me, he says when he's sixty-three. By that time she no longer sees him, no longer knows him, she hasn't kissed him for thirteen years. He fell asleep like the prince in Sleeping Beauty. Nothing surprises me any more, I've seen everything over and over, I have to force myself to get up, life bores me. But she, she would have liked to do it all again, not in order to repeat it all but so she could pause amid all that doing – it went so fast the first time round. Daddy, don't go so fast, I can't keep up, my legs are so short. Please walk a bit slower, I'm already so tired. The difficult thing about life is not that it's difficult, but that it goes so fast.

Or a key that fits everything.

It's the wrong one, he says. They are standing by her car. She is trying to open the door, she has put the key in the lock and is trying to turn it but cannot. She takes it out and tries again. It's the wrong one, he says. What do you mean the wrong one? she says. How on earth can it be the wrong key? The wrong car, he says. And he's the wrong man in the wrong life, the wrong God of the wrong creation. Everything stays firmly shut. When you've got the right one, it opens.

Don't worry, she says, I'll take care of it if that's what you want. Being buried in the green flowered Sunday dress doesn't need a falling star or a notary. If death was something I had to do, I wouldn't do it. But it happens all by itself, don't worry. Although it's not the king himself who lies buried at the appointed spot next to the château of Sans-Souci, but his Afghan hounds. Poor king whose friend and lover was beheaded. Sitting in the long corridors with paintings above his head and mirrors opposite in which he could see the paintings. And the room with the aviary in it where Voltaire spent the night. *I've decided to be happy since that is better for one's health.*

I decided to be unhappy, she says. It's not just a right, it's a science. All things are the same colour, black. Black as the habits of the sisters in the convent. Black as a room when the light's just been turned off. Black as the asphalt of a road on which in summer we can see a pool of water that we know isn't there. In the same way we know that everything isn't there. Only Geraldine's pink lace petticoat may perhaps be saved. She does it in order to be chosen by the bridegroom of them all. At night she lifts up her skirts high above the knees and dances the cancan for him with a spotless soul.

He is in my heart, she says with those feverishly shining eyes. But then what kind of place is a heart to have a man in.

It's not the absence of sound, but the absence of speech that is hardest. An absence that makes you hoarse and gives you a sore throat. That makes you thirsty at five in the morning, when what happened in your dream has to be swallowed unspoken, that lies heavily on your stomach after lunch and towards evening makes you drool like Pavlov's dog when you hear the bell. The kind that drives couples to madness or manslaughter, or makes you long for someone to be there in a different way from those who are there. They walk beside each other like puppets in a puppet show, like mimes not even allowed to pull faces at each other. The sound's gone dead. Power cut. Oh, if only absence of speech brought silence. But for every voice that is hushed in the outside world, ten strike up inside. O dear, Sybille, how did you wind up here? Ten times you forgot your lunchbox on the first day of term and no one noticed and offered you a sandwich, and you didn't dare say or ask anything.

Umpteen times you were excluded in the playground since no one wanted to hold your hand because you had warts on both hands. Umpteen times you found yourself with the microphone in your hand at the end-of-year school party and suddenly couldn't think of anything to say. And all these things are eternal, just because they happened, and pursue you the way normally only great sorrows are supposed to pursue you. Oh save me, let some one say: Down! Like a master to his dog, or like Jesus to the storm at sea. Stop the absence of speech around me, a word, a word, I'll sell my immortal soul for a word. Speak and I shall be whole. If there is a word that is the right one. The password is what fits in the fitting room: yes, it fits me, I'll take it. The password to the computer that no one can find: enter your password here. It doesn't fit, it's too tight. *All things hem me in.* I'm so wide. Cinderella's password is the prince's 'I do'. But it wasn't a glass slipper that Cinderella wore and lost, glass slippers break if you run down the steps to the palace, it was a fur slipper, that's what happens when words and fur start flying. The 'dancing worm' in French class on Friday afternoons, the last lesson, when they are all doubled up with laughter. *Le vers dansant de Baudelaire.* And *vert* meaning green, and *verre* meaning glass and *vair* meaning fur. If a word can mean all that, isn't there a word that can mean everything, a pass key for the whole world?

(…)

About getting married. Yes, I'd have done it like a shot, if, providing, and suppo-sing. But at the same time I'm also glad I can't (and don't have to). It's such a contradiction: on the one hand I'd like to be with you always, make love to you every day, get to know you in every situation, in other words wear you out completely – on the other hand, I want most of all to keep you as I have you now, don't have you, that is, separated from everything, making days special. (Actually, I sometimes think, you ought to be able to learn to want not to want to get what you want.) Actually it's a luxury: two hours a week, far too little, so that you never get enough of someone. The luxury of insufficiency – though of course you can't experience it like that. If I were with you always I would lose this – but I would still have liked to have it (that, I think, is the tragedy of desire) – and that's why I'm glad I can't, that it can't be wanted. (You can want something, and yet be frightened of getting it.)

On days when I feel calmer, I think of you in a completely detached, vague way, I think at the same time, while still enjoying the rest: I don't really want this to diminish, I want to stay like this, breathless, that is, I want to keep this unbearable feeling. But on days when it gets difficult, like now, since Tuesday, I think: clear off, go away, from my head, from my body, and I think, I want it to be bearable.

Sometimes, when I'm making love to you, like on Tuesday, or in the flat in B., I really don't want to go on, I feel like I'm at the end of my tether, another inch and I'll burst into tears. And yet I have to go on. The misery they bring, those sorts of things. And I just don't understand them. All my life I've tried to see those things as normal (the mating of animals: *birds do it, bees do it*), but I can't manage it, and certainly not with you. I need to be consoled, for once not for metaphysical reasons, but because of your hand on my skin. And to console me you'd have to put it back again, that's why.

From *The Unexpected Answer* (Het onverwachte antwoord).
Amsterdam: Meulenhoff, 2004, pp. 148-150 & 216-217
Translated by Paul Vincent

Mystery on the March

On Dirk Braeckman's Photos

[HANS AARSMAN]

V.H.-S.L.-00.
180 x 120 cm.
© Dirk Braeckman/
Sofam Belgium 2006.

There's a vagrant living in Dirk Braeckman's photos. No-one has ever seen him, but he does live there. He is the one operating the camera. He often hangs around in buildings where the gas and electricity have been cut off. Where it is pitch-dark and freezing cold. It may even be haunted. Our vagrant doesn't mind, as then at least he has something to kill time with. He sits in a corner, ears pricked for any suspicious sound, camera at the ready. As soon as he thinks he hears something he swings the camera towards it and presses the button. Then, in the light from his flash he descries the outlines of a sofa, a chair, a radiator, but never a ghost. That does not mean there are no ghosts. That is not a valid conclusion. They may just be keeping out of the picture. The films the vagrant puts in his camera have passed their expiry date. He once had the opportunity to pick up a few boxes at a bargain price. The disadvantage is that expired films are no longer so sensitive to light. That means the prints of the photos are extremely dark. The vagrant doesn't mind this at all; it is fitting that the prints are dark, for after all the world he lives in is dark too. The only light there is comes from the camera, from the flash. If you look carefully you can see the flash in his photos. It's the bright spot in the middle, reflecting the focus of the flash-light. Very occasionally someone comes along to keep the man company. It's always a woman. Bringing him a pan of soup and some bread. These women then end up in the photo, just like the chairs, sofas and radiators. In the darkness their skin lights up like alabaster. You don't understand why they feel like undressing in these cold, creepy, damp houses. In fact you don't understand why women undress in front of a camera at all. But the vagrant gets them to do it anyway. He must have an intriguing personality, this man in Dirk Braeckman's photos. Rather forceful too.

An artist's work need not necessarily correspond to his personality. I know a woman painter who is decidedly embittered. If one were to believe her, it would appear that life is nothing but trouble. It's not her fault, it's always someone else's. You can listen to her for fifteen minutes, but then you have had enough. Her paintings are nicer places to spend time. Not that I am mad about them, but at least they are not so gloomy. They are full of flowers of every colour, the sun is always shining and no one is blamed for anything. This painter is not belying her own nature with such cheerful paintings. An artist does not necessarily have to express his everyday frame of mind in his work; his painting might just as easily be a way of setting a counterpoint to these feelings, and may actually reveal the other side of his character. Van Gogh was like that. A mournful pessimist who painted jolly yellow sunflowers. The opposite is possible too. I once shook Dirk Braeckman's hand at an opening. I remember he was wearing a lumberjack shirt. He did not strike me as a particularly jovial type, but he was certainly not as introspective as his vagrant. On that occasion I did not ask him what sort of place he lived in, but it's quite possible that behind the vagrant in his photos there is a lively personality who lives in a bright house with central heating and pays his energy bills on time. With a spooky side to his character. Definitely. But then don't we all have a spooky side?

I still remember a dream I had a few weeks ago in which I was sitting in a posh restaurant and had to go to the toilet. When I got up from the table I was startled to find I had no trousers on. I was terribly shocked and immediately sat down again. How could I not have noticed this before? I had another good look under the table and saw that things were even worse: I didn't have any underwear on either. What now? I had to go to the toilet urgently and it was on the far side of the restaurant. I got up and shuffled as inconspicuously as possible to the toilet, while disapproving glances from everyone in the restaurant pierced my back like needles. And then I had to go through the same agony on the way back. Pay the bill quickly and go home. But before I could get safely home, a second ordeal awaited me: I discovered that the brakes of the car I was driving didn't work. However hard I pressed the pedal, the car refused to slow down. A hundred metres ahead a woman with a pram stepped onto a zebra crossing. I screamed and yelled , but she didn't hear me.

What on earth makes one dream of something like that? I don't even have a car. It must be the dark side of the character that thinks up dreams like this. The vagrant in me, who takes over the controls in some dreams. I don't worry about him too much, as long as he has gone by the time I open my eyes. As long as the brakes work during the day and I turn out to have trousers on in restaurants, my vagrant counts for nothing. But not Dirk Braeckman's. Braeckman takes his vagrant seriously. He speaks to him, and gives him a voice. He puts a camera in his hands and lets him immortalise his dark side.

How did all this come to me? Am I just making it all up? Can I make all these assertions simply on the basis of a few photos?

Z.P.-P.L.-95-01.
180 x 120 cm.
© Dirk Braeckman/
Sofam Belgium 2006.

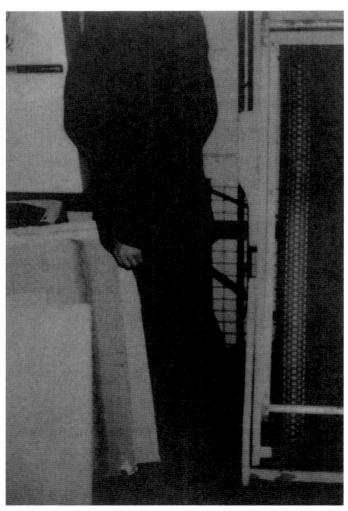

I have the two volumes of *z.Z.(t)* in front of me, published by Ludion. They are thin books packed full of ink. Do not look at them at home under a lamp. They have already been taken indoors in artificial light. It's better to take them outside and look at them in the sunlight. The greyness and blackness then suddenly open up and the photos assume more depth. Is the vagrant with his stock of expired films hiding somewhere in the depths or not? Dirk Braeckman himself certainly does not have a big stock of expired films. He achieves the darkness and elusiveness of his photos with a range of photographic techniques, a thin negative being just one.

Like many a self-respecting artist, Braeckman has a website: www.braeckman.be. Apart from a great many photos to look at there are also a couple of interviews with him, one in French and one in English. To look for an answer to my questions and to see if any of the vagrant theory makes sense, I read one of the interviews, the one by Erik Eelbode.

Eelbode wants to know about the edges of his pictures. Dirk Braeckman's answer is: *'That's where the image is made. The image is formed at the edges. When I'm photographing, I try to keep my movements to a minimum. What I do is make a sort of swaying movement. To extend my experiential moment – my "small format". And then I make a choice, a cut-out, from that image area. I never simply look straight ahead. I always look at the edges. I play with the edges. I always look in that way, even without my camera; it's a continuous urge to concentrate on what's just next to the image. Maybe it's a bit paranoid. As if I constantly want to monitor my field of vision.'*

Then the interviewer asks, *'A sort of mistrust of what escapes your field of vision? Can you call that paranoid?'* He's beginning to sense the ghosts, of course.

'That runs through the way I live, so it's also there in the way I photograph. My photos do certainly have a few paranoid facets. In the sense of a constant monitoring of my environment, my biotope. Monitoring that has to do with fear, always. And for me also with the boundless power of imagination. Whatever space I'm in.'

So the vagrant I encountered in Braeckman's photos is not entirely unfounded.

Yet Dirk Braeckman does not want to put too much emphasis on the psychological, narrative side of his work. That is only a distraction and detracts from the mystery. He has his motives and his way of seeing, and the people who look at his photos have their motives and their ways of seeing. The mystery of his work is to be found where the two coincide. And that is the way it should stay. An artist should not want to provide too much explanation of his work.

Braeckman's photos are undoubtedly mysterious. His photos still have an elusive feel even when they are not taken in buildings without heat and lighting. They form a world in themselves. Wherever he looks his gaze is always dark and that focus of light is somewhere to be found. I see the strength and quality of his work and I appreciate the fact he allows his dark side to express itself. Nevertheless I continue to view his photos from a distance. I can't feel them, I just keep on seeing underexposed images of dismal facets of human existence. I would prefer it to be otherwise. I would like to be able to become absorbed in Braeckman's work. In the same way as I would later like to be absorbed into the hereafter. It would make the idea of death a lot more cheerful. But I don't believe in the hereafter. When you are dead it's finished, done. I do not believe in ghosts either. Of course there is more in heaven and earth than a man might suspect. But not ghosts, paradises and suchlike. All conceived too much on a basis of human perceptions. I would think it's to be found more in things for which one cannot dream up a picture. Things that go beyond any human imagining. But surely the spirit has to go somewhere after death, doesn't it? That's what a lot of people ask themselves. I say the spirit does not have to go anywhere. The spirit belongs with the body and when the body is dead the spirit is dead too. We really are no more important than mice and whales. And there is no hereafter for them, is there?

Sometimes I think it's my Dutch blood. I am too down-to-earth. That might also explain why for a long time Braeckman's work didn't have much of a success in the Netherlands. The level-headed people who live there do not have much time for ghosts. But in the end he did get his first big exhibition there, at De Pont in Tilburg. It must be the spirit of the age; even the Dutch have had to give in. Mystery is on the march. Ghosts are reaching out on all sides. Harry Potter, The Lord of the Rings, the Axis of Evil.

I was glad about the big exhibition at De Pont. At last it gave me the opportunity to stand and look at his monumental prints. Until then I had only seen his work in books and magazines, and I imagine they do not do full justice to them. It may be that these big dark areas make it a lot more difficult to get away from the black side. I took my precautions: I did not go there by car and I did not eat in a restaurant. ∎

Translated by Gregory Ball

FURTHER READING

Dirk Braeckman, *z.Z(t)*. Ghent/Amsterdam, 1998, 88 pp.

Dirk Braeckman, *z.Z(t). volume II*. Ghent/Amsterdam, 2001, 88 pp.

Dirk Braeckman, *Chiaroscuro*. Ghent, 2003, 64 pp.

www.braeckman.be

Doing the Fosbury Flop

Gerrit Krol's Literary High-Jump

Anyone who knows Dutch literature only through translations will probably never have heard of Gerrit Krol. Unless, that is, they have read *La testa milli-metrata*, the Italian translation of his novel *The Cropped Head* (Het gemillime-terde hoofd, 1967), which in 1969 was awarded the *Il libro giovane* prize for the best translated novel by a young writer. Or the Russian translation, published around 1970, of his novella *Son of the Living City* (De zoon van de levende stad, 1966). Since then, so far as I know, none of Krol's work has been translated, with the exception of a few short fragments into English and German. Why? Well, they say that Krol is 'difficult'. And 'they' are right, he is. In the same way that Italo Calvino, W.G. Sebald, Michel Houellebecq, Lars Gustafsson, Milan Kundera – to name but a few – are difficult. Great writers for sure, and Krol certainly belongs among them.

Perhaps the difficulty lies in the fact that nothing he writes is contrived. Neither can his work be pigeonholed – the only possible 'categorisation' is that of a writer who constantly shies away from fixations, who takes the readers on a journey and leads them astray. Reading his work, one experiences the slightly uneasy feeling of not quite knowing whether to agree with him. But does that justify the label 'difficult'? No. I would prefer 'exciting', 'surprising', 're-freshing', 'dazzling'; the work of a playful and versatile mind. We do not feel a sense of identification, so much as a sense of having bathed in a sea of refreshing thoughts, images and formulations, as if our spirit has been thor-oughly cleansed.

Sandwich-construction

Some biographical details: Gerrit Krol was born in 1934 in Groningen. Throughout his working life, from 1957 to 1994, he worked for Shell as a computer specialist. He spent several years in Caracas, Venezuela, in the late 1960s and a couple of years in Lagos, Nigeria, during the 1980s. The rest of the time he worked in the Netherlands. Krol was one of his country's first computer programmers, and began his career at the Shell Laboratory in Amsterdam. In the 1970s he moved to NAM (a Shell subsidiary) in Assen, where his work concerned 'the world's largest gas field', as the natural-gas field at Slochteren in Groningen was known when it was discovered in around 1960.

During all those years Krol never stopped writing. Since his debut in 1962 he has published more than fifty novels and anthologies of essays and poems. His oeuvre has been honoured with the most sought-after literary prizes in the Netherlands, including the Constantijn Huygens Prize (1986) and the P.C. Hooft Prize (2001). In 2005 he was awarded an honorary doctorate by the Vrije Universiteit Amsterdam (VU) for the way in which his work brings together science and literature.

The Cropped Head, Krol's fifth book in six years, was a significant departure from his earlier, more traditional work – in the first place because it contained illustrations as well as text, but also because mathematics and computers play a central role in the novel, and for the trifling reason that the chapters are numbered from 00 to 99. Hence the idea that Krol is 'difficult'. The most striking thing about *The Cropped Head* is, however, that Krol appears to have invented a completely new type of novel, a novel in which narrative, contemplation, poetic principles and the need to formalise language hold each other in a tense equilibrium. The novel tells its story in an entertaining way, with spiritual reflections. It is often lyrical and quite humorous. It is compelling rather than difficult.

Since then, Krol has become the master of the fragmentary novel, structured on the poetic principle that blank lines are just as important as text. Krol later called this process 'sandwich construction', in which the writing alternates between concrete and abstract passages, narrative and debate. The 'sandwich construction' is just as original as the Fosbury Flop high-jump technique. In 1968, Dick Fosbury won a gold medal in the high-jump event at the Olympic Games. He did not use the standard 'straddle' technique, but his own new technique that involved turning his body as he jumped, arching his back and flinging himself backward over the bar. In the novels that Krol has written since 1967, he makes a similar quarter turn.

This has led scholars to label him as a post-modern writer, but he is certainly not a hardcore post-modern writer aiming to shatter the world view; on the contrary: there may be chinks in the armour of his stories, but he wants to create a sense of unity, of uniformity, for the reader. In *The Cropped Head* there is a passage about his views on writing: '*A book is read, but that takes no more than a couple of days. The rest of the time it's on the bookshelf, but a good story can survive that. Once the reader has finished the book, the story begins to open up. The reader goes to bed, but the next day, while he is sitting in the train gazing out of the misted windows, the story unfolds more and more in his mind. He sees the story as he could not see it while he was reading: as a whole. He also sees the flaws, and then the story disintegrates. A good story should have no flaws.*'

Industry and girls

Gerrit Krol, the Dick Fosbury of Dutch literature. If we confine ourselves to literature, whom can we compare him with? Sebald, Gustafsson, Calvino, Houellebecq or Kundera? Certainly, Krol writes philosophical novels too. His fascination with eroticism and sex links him with Kundera and Houellebecq, his imagination can be compared with that of Calvino. As a mathematical lyricist

Cerrit Krol (1934-).
Photo by Hans Vermeulen.

he is Gustafsson's equal, and the melancholic undertone in his writing reminds us of Sebald. But the differences are equally significant. Whereas Sebald's work expresses melancholy in meandering sentences, often without paragraph breaks, Krol uses short, clear sentences with a great deal of spacing. If Sebald's writing is 'round', Krol's is angular. But both achieve a similar effect.

Above all, Krol is a writer *in his own right* – a writer whose views evolved during the period of post-war reconstruction, and whose main characters can feel delirious with delight at a gleaming world of industrial renewal. The following passage from *The Driver is Bored* (De chauffeur verveelt zich, 1973) is typical of his writing: '*I wanted to make progress, and began to model myself on the mighty industries that were springing up everywhere during those years. The city was growing. Everyone was proud of that growth and welcomed it. How wonderful to see the fields, streams and willow trees being bulldozed to make way for a plain of sand, on which stood, only a year later, an oil-cracking plant edged with neat rose beds – a perfect world.*' Even more typically, a blank line separates this passage from the words that follow: '*I wanted so much. But I couldn't commit myself to anything. I saw lots of girls, but never went up to talk to them. I didn't think it was necessary.*' The fascination with industry and with girls, pride and desolation, are linked together here by an unmistakable sense of melancholy.

Krol's work is also characterised by its striking diversity of themes: where *The Cropped Head* focuses on the phenomenon of 'images' as a form of communication (hence the illustrations), other novels focus on the contradiction between hard and soft in various human contexts, or on issues of rights and justice. Apart from these abstract themes, his work is alive with real-life issues and his original views on them: the oil industry and automation, daily life, the relationship between city and countryside or between Africa and Europe, as well as pornography and adultery. Each of these subjects is addressed in a highly thought-provoking way.

A central element in his work is his characters' attempt to find their place in various life contexts: personal happiness (love, domesticity), environment (workplace, home), abstract contexts (time, eternity). At the same time, Krol is also fascinated by the mechanisms of reality and language that underlie these quests. Questions such as 'What formulation will allow me to ask who and what I am?' characterise his way of thinking on paper.

In his earlier work in particular, Krol's protagonists are searching for their niche in life. His novels contain quite a few autobiographical references, such as a main character who moves from Groningen to Amsterdam to work as a computer specialist at the Shell Laboratory. Equally important is the search for the ideal woman. In Krol's later work, autobiographical elements make way for imagination. Love and adultery remain important themes, but they are often intertwined with murder, guilt and justice – themes as old as literature itself. They add suspense to Krol's work, but they also lead us to contemplate the worth of the individual and the right to life. In this context it is not surprising that at the end of the 1980s Krol launched himself into the debate on capital punishment. Not necessarily, as many people claimed, to advocate the death penalty, but to break the taboo on discussing and thinking about its legitimacy.

A continual willingness to reassess

Despite its diversity of themes, Krol's oeuvre has a remarkable coherence. This impression is reinforced by the fact that he cannot resist making changes to his earlier work. A reprint always involves a face-lift, at the very least. However, his reworking of the novels *Middleton's Illness* (*De ziekte van Middleton*, 1969) and *The Road to Sacramento* (De weg naar Sacramento, 1977) into, respectively, *Middleton's Death* (Middletons dood, 1996) and *The Road to Tuktoyaktuk* (De weg naar Tuktoyaktuk, 1987) is more like a sex-change operation than a face-lift: Krol has taken 'old' novels and used them to create new ones.

This ever-present willingness to reassess reality and his own writing is fundamental to Krol's work and thought. This is evident to a modest extent in his most characteristic figure of speech: self-correction, which Krol refers to as '*semantic counter-rhyme*'. In his prose poems in particular, the words '*geen*' (no, none) and '*niet*' (not) – with which many passages begin – are a driving force. This figure of speech is to Krol what rhyme and metre are to a traditional poet. Its crucial importance for his vision of literature is apparent from what he writes in the anthology of essays *Beauty is Difficult* (Wat mooi is is moeilijk, 1991): '*All writers experience it when they scrutinise what they have written and start to tamper with it: the moment when they suddenly put a line through everything, thereby erasing it. The art of writing is to verbalise the line you draw through your work. It is the crossing-out of your writing, the slash, the wound – which itself is made up of words. Only then is your soul revealed, I would almost claim, but which soul? In your fit of recklessness you've just created a new soul for yourself. The old one, the one that led to your tampering, no longer exists. Every sentence you write is a line through what you were planning to write before you put pen to paper. It's a question of technique.'*

Murder, sex, science and eternity

As I have already said, very few of Krol's works have been translated. Non-Dutch-speaking readers therefore have a great deal to look forward to. A translation, for example, of the crime and confession novel *Maurits and the Facts* (Maurits en de feiten, 1986), in which the title character gives himself up to the police and confesses to murder, but is released because there is not enough evidence against him. But the unfettered world of the mind means so much more to Maurits than the restricted world of facts that he commits suicide, thereby carrying out his own death sentence , as it were. Or a translation of the spiritual science-fiction novel *The Man at the Window* (De man achter het raam, 1982): about a robot called Adam who becomes human, in mind and in body. The book is particularly challenging in the sense that the reader can never be certain whether the events in the story take place only within Adam's brain, or in the world created by the writer. There are several reasons for translating the more recent novels *The Vitalist* (De vitalist, 2000) and *Rondo Veneziano* (2004). The main reason is their literary quality. But they are also characteristic of Krol's work, as discussed above. If I had to write a promotional text for these two novels, it would contain the key words *murder*, *sex*, *science* and *eternity*. But I realise that these words alone reveal nothing; what makes Krol's novels so special is his style and the way in which he weaves these themes together.

Believing in the impossible

The graphic artist M.C. Escher became famous for 'impossible' objects such as his 'impossible cube', a three-dimensional image that only 'works' because it is projected onto a two-dimensional plane surface. Krol is Escher's literary counterpart; he uses language to portray human relationships and human endeavour, and he does so mainly by projecting one situation onto another: murder onto mathematics, daily life onto science, sex onto eternity, etc. In doing so he allows us to believe in the impossible. He is a great writer. And not yet lost in translation. ∎

Translated by Yvette Mead

Two Poems and an Extract
by Gerrit Krol

Over de bossen bij Hooghalen – dat is ook iets waar je
niet over schrijven kan,
tenminste niet als je er geweest bent.

(Over de kracht van weemoed)

About the woods near Hooghalen – that's something else you
can't write about,
at least not if you've been there.

(On the power of nostalgia)

From *Polaroid. Poems 1955-1976* (Polaroid. Gedichten 1955-1976).
Amsterdam: Em. Querido Uitgevers b.v., 1976, p. 95.

Delta

Where a river begins to flow and where it ends.

As small as anything can be and flow, fails to flow or even disappears again. So wide
and expansive does it end at the eternal shores,
at the sea.

Not the river but its freedom, striking out in loops to left and right
along the horizon and back again.
Not back, but around a town and on again .
Not a town, but a height and it is the low places it seeks.
Not seeks, but finds.

The weight of all the sand it transports . The current carries it along.

The places where it lies down, no longer that swiftness .

On its way to the sea, guided by dikes, a river raises itself, bed and all.
Higher than the houses it runs past, but it will not reach the sea unless the dikes are
raised once again. The Rhine at Katwijk, a quiet ditch.

A sluice.

No sluice, but the screw with which one turns on the water.

Turns off the tap, for no water.

The Rhine at Lobith. The ships career downstream.

The Rhine at Tiel, where it takes the bend. Turns around, deepens and quickens.

At Zaltbommel it lies still.

Not still. What lies still is the ship that, intelligent, plays the Rhine as
its element.

Watches how its long, soft body more and more – New! –reinforces
itself with a ribcage.

While the water's greatest enemy is man its greatest friend.

Not man, but the marker, the Normal Amsterdam Level.
Not the rivers, but the sea.

No dikes, but embankments strengthened with rye-straw protected the land from
the violence of the autumn gales.
Not an embankment, but a dike profile with a very gentle incline.

'Deep insight is shown by his observation that a very wide and slowly rising dike does
not so much break up the
advancing waves but rather exhausts them, depriving the water of all its energy by
forcing it upwards.'

The dike, covered in grass and sheep.
Not grass, but the red of young roofs.

The glass behind which the goldfish is safe.
For in his element where calmly he turns.
His back to us.

From *No Man, because no Woman* (Geen man, want geen vrouw). Amsterdam: Em. Querido
Uitgevers b.v., 2001, pp. 40-41.

Delta

Waar een rivier begint te stromen en waar ze eindigt.

Zo klein als iets stromen kan, niet stroomt of zelfs verdwijnt. Zo
wijd en breed eindigt zij aan de eeuwige stranden, aan zee.

Niet de rivier, maar haar vrijheid, uithalend in lussen naar links en naar
rechts langs de horizon en weer terug.
Niet terug, maar om een stad heen en verder.
Geen stad, maar een hoogte en het is de laagte die zij zoekt.
Niet zoekt, maar vindt.

De zwaarte van al het zand dat zij vervoert. De stroom neemt het mee.

De plaatsen waar ze gaat liggen, niet langer de snelheid.

Op weg naar de zee, door dijken geleid, verhoogt een rivier zichzelf, met
bedding en al.
Hoger dan de huizen stroomt zij voorbij, maar ze zal de zee niet halen
als niet opnieuw de dijken worden verhoogd. De Rijn bij Katwijk, een
kalme sloot.

Een sluis.

Geen sluis, maar de schroef waarmee men het water aandraait.

De kraan dichtdraait, want geen water.

De Rijn bij Lobith. De schepen jakkeren stroomafwaarts.

De Rijn bij Tiel, waar zij de bocht neemt. Zich omgooit, zich verdiept en versnelt.

Bij Zaltbommel ligt zij stil.

Niet stil. Wat stilligt is het schip dat, intelligent, de Rijn bespeelt als element.

Toeziet hoe haar lange, zachte lijf zich meer en meer – Nieuw! – met een
ribbenkast versterkt.

Terwijl de grootste vijand van het water is de mens zijn grootste vriend.

Niet de mens, maar de meter, het N.A.P.
Niet de rivieren, maar de zee.

Geen dijken, maar met roggestro versterkte kademuren beschermden
het land tegen het geweld der najaarsstormen.
Niet de kademuren, maar een dijkprofiel met zeer flauwe helling.

'Van diep inzicht getuigt zijn observatie dat een zeer brede en langzaam
oplopende dijk de aanrollende golven niet zozeer breekt als wel uitput,
het water van alle energie berooft door het omhoog te dwingen.'

De dijk, begroeid met gras en schapen.
Geen gras, maar het rood van jonge daken.

Het glas waarachter de goudvis veilig is.
Want in zijn element waar hij ons kalm.
De rug toekeert.

1.1

Modern man. Sits glued to the TV, and I don't mean evening TV but daytime. His work. His daily hassle and the picture he has of the world, which is: his own world.

For the first time in history, he is able to think about everyday occurrences as he does about his own affairs: (a) because the precision of his methods enables him to do so and (b) because he is alone. So man is no longer the masses, and all those speakers who need to hear a crowd cheer before they know they are right (for the mechanics of this, see page 53) – those people would do better to go home and take a retraining course.

What happens today happens in the mind of each one of us separately, and what has to be done I have explained on page 27 – especially how each of us can indicate the wish to do it by pressing a button. If that system is in place and this word can process longings, then everything becomes dead easy and hyper-just. It is just, for example, to remember how many times somebody's wish has not been fulfilled and to compensate him for it (Art. x, Code of Compensation, 21st century). That's how tomorrow's world operates.

I was thinking about all this at midday as I was walking along Badhuisweg, enjoying the sunshine – beside the stagnant water where hundreds of used condoms had congregated in a corner – happy simply because I was and apparently had the right to change myself, the chance to organise my life as I wanted, and the others too.

A little later I'm lying at an angle of forty-five degrees to the surface of the water: on a steep grassy slope, from where I look out over the working-class districts of Volewijck and dream. I'm talking here about the Noordhollands Kanaal, the place near the sluices, under which the IJ Tunnel now runs. A wonderful day, on which the world was in sharp focus.

Back to the gleaming laboratories again – it's never too late to feel like doing some work. The young trees lining the footpath to the new lunch-room, one afternoon in the distant past – these little trees have grown a lot since then, the footpath now lies buried under their masses of foliage; beneath it the 'promising young academics' hurry to their jobs, to their desks where they will spend yet another whole afternoon. Hands between the knees with outstretched fingers or clasped behind the neck, that is how the researcher sees the world: he is bombarded with questions and perhaps, once a year, one afternoon – the glimpse of an answer.

A glimpse of Marie's skirt while she is busy with the laundry. She is hanging out towels. But I'm not looking at that. I'm looking at something else. Fabric for kitchen curtains (red and white checks) – Marie has made a little skirt out of it. And as I look at it, I make a note: it's only the squares that show how round she is there.

And while she is hanging out the washing, I decide that it is unnecessary to work so hard. And when she comes in I caress her, take the spherical kitchen curtain on my lap and tell her that. I say, you don't need to work any more. She says that I'm out of my mind, that she still needs more money and that is why she... I say, and I mean it profoundly: that everything that needed doing has already been done.

The circle is closed. In in-house magazines as well as prospectuses one often finds the same sort of photograph: some piece of apparatus (a high-pressure meter, a spectrograph) with a man in front of it regarding it attentively – or operating it. A chemist removing his pipette from some liquid. Dedication.

Today listened to a lecture and looked at viewgraphs by a Mr Valentine, come all the way from the USA to show us how a visual display unit works and how you can steer the information that appears on its screen by pointing at it. You can tell the information system what it has to do by doing what it expects you to do – and the system does it for you.

When you flush the WC the cistern fills up again with water, automatically, but just as automatically the cistern does not overflow, for the ballcock floating on the water that has flowed in eventually ensures that no more water can flow in – an example of balance restored completely automatically. The disturber of this balance was back in his living room long ago – he doesn't need to bother about it.

This world which constantly restores itself, the automatic way in which it does it can be reassuring, especially when we consider what the image above depicts: a man who has sat down in front of the visual display unit, which tells him about everything that is not as it should be. This man, he just sits there and only has to point to indicate how order can be restored.

The image is also synonymous with that of the chemist withdrawing his pipette from the liquid, and because of this, whatever we are doing, in our activity we can all be presented as the man who, sitting at the monitor of his own enlight-ened reason, ensures that (a) nobody is any worse off than the day before and (b) nobody is any worse off than anybody else. And that sufficiently defines the function and the responsibility of each one of us.

Said as much to my boss, who asked me if he could take it that I was bored.

In the evening made my way quickly through the busy streets between the cars and the trams to my house, my home that was called Marie. Maria Schepers who loved me, took care of me, called me her 'learned spouse' and for the rest pinned all the hopes without which she could not live on other times.

From *The Driver is Bored* (De chauffeur verveelt zich).
Amsterdam: Em. Querido Uitgevers b.v., 1973, pp. 24-27.

Poems and extract translated by John Irons.

One Only Has Oneself

Fernand Khnopff, a Belgian Dandy in European Symbolism

[JOHAN DE SMET]

Fernand Khnopff (1858-1921) was more personally and artistically oriented towards contemporary British art and culture than any other Belgian modernist of his generation. As the Brussels correspondent for the authoritative journal *The Studio*, and an occasional writer for *The Magazine of Art*, he promoted Belgian art among the English-speaking public. He also wrote essays on British art that were highly regarded in Great Britain. His predilection for British *savoir vivre*, which incidentally he loved to flaunt, combined with a wide international reputation to give him access to the most important avant-garde circles in Europe.

Born in September 1858 in the family chateau at Grembergen, near Dendermonde in East Flanders, Fernand Khnopff grew up in a secluded middle class environment. His early childhood memories were primarily of Bruges, a city where the family had strong ties that went back to the eighteenth century. As

Fernand Khnopff, *Listening to Schumann*. 1883. Canvas, 101.5 x 116.5 cm. Koninklijke Musea voor Schone Kunsten, Brussels.

well as Bruges, the village of Fosset in the Ardennes, where the family spent their summers, was also to make a lasting impression upon him. Khnopff's family played a conspicuous role in his artistic career. His brother Georges brought him into contact with leading lights of the Belgian, French and German literary milieux, with Stéphane Mallarmé, Paul Verlaine, Emile Verhaeren, and the circle associated with the Brussels journal *La Jeune Belgique*. His sister Marguerite was and remained one of his favourite models.

From the early 1880s, Khnopff was a member of the youthful Brussels avant-garde who grouped together to form the artistic circle of Les XX. The leading figure among them at the time was James Ensor. However, Khnopff's painting *Listening to Schumann* led to the break-up of this group of friends when Ensor accused him of plagiarising his own painting *Russian Music*. In fact, *Listening to Schumann* employs neither the extrovert narrative momentum of Ensor's bourgeois salons nor his *tachiste* impressionism. Khnopff attempts rather to convey a higher reality in which emotional involvement is woven around a timeless conception of music. Technically, *Listening to Schumann* is very different from the hyper-refined ethereal and idealistic art that Khnopff was to perfect in later years. However, the painting stands as a beacon in the breakthrough of pictorial symbolism in Belgium.

Between French decadence and Anglophile purity

In an artistic and literary context where old dogmas of traditional religiosity were being questioned, where religion, mysticism and the esoteric crossed into one another, the female figures in Khnopff's work played an increasingly important role. His sphinxes, for instance, consistently operate on the borderline between seductive, animal-like sensuality and a higher spiritual idealism. In contemporary literature – as in Khnopff's own treatment of Joséphin Péladan's *Le Vice Suprême* of 1884 – the sphinx personifies the conflict between Christianity and heathendom. Influenced both by Péladan and by Félicien Rops, Khnopff's work acquired a decadent, satanist dimension which scandalised the Belgian

Fernand Khnopff,
I Lock My Door upon
Myself. 1891.
Canvas, 72 x 140 cm,
Bayerische Staatsgemälde-
sammlungen, Munich.

art world. Indeed, together with the Belgian symbolist Jean Delville, Khnopff was one of the major attractions at the first of Sâr Péladan's Rose+Croix Salons in 1892. However, Khnopff did not just subscribe automatically to the idealistic Rosicrucian movement. In the years that followed, his symbolist universe transcended Péladan's inflexible body of ideas. What is more, the free-thinking Khnopff signed up as a lecturer in the Arts section of the socialist *Maison du Peuple* in Brussels. And as an artist he was equally at home in the liberal milieu of the Belgian Art Nouveau.

Khnopff's formal language is clearly inspired by decadent and symbolist literature. The multi-religious world of classical antiquity, for instance, which had also intrigued Khnopff's great role model Gustave Moreau, was an important source of inspiration. Those characters from classical literature and mythology who fired his imagination appear repeatedly in his work: Medusa, Orpheus, Sappho, Venus. And mysticism, of course, whereby the use of images to point the way to a higher reality became Khnopff's *modus operandi*. It was this world of solitude and silence that created the bond between him and the British Pre-Raphaelites, especially Edward Burne-Jones. As he was to write in *The Magazine of Art* in 1898 on the Englishman's death, Khnopff considered the pre-Raphaelite desire to use imagination to escape from reality and create an ideal world as itself a mystical experience. His unbounded admiration for Burne-Jones was reflected not so much iconographically, but rather at an abstract level in the intellectual tension between dream and reality, between the external and internal, between life and death. This focus on the inner world reached a peak in 1891 with *I Lock My Door upon Myself*. Based on a similar phrase in Christina Rosetti's poem *Who Shall Deliver Me*, fragments of dream and reality, memory and reflection, meaning and symbolism are mounted on a geometrically divided surface. The painting also reveals Khnopff's interest in the cult of androgyny, which was considered to be the new ideal in these circles. His interest in Great Britain was mutual, and from the early 1890s Khnopff was in great demand for successive exhibitions in London and later on in Glasgow. In 1891 and 1893 he spent a prolonged period in Great Britain. In Brussels, Khnopff defended the work of the Pre-Raphaelites in numerous lectures, and with Georges Lemmen and Henry van de Velde he introduced Arts & Crafts influences into Belgian book design.

Brussels dreams

As well as in France and Great Britain, his work was widely known in Germany and Central Europe, from Berlin and Munich to Vienna. The high point was the first exhibition of the Vienna Secession in March 1898 where an entire room was reserved for Khnopff's work, reflecting chairman Gustav Klimt's admiration for the Belgian. The journal *Ver Sacrum*, the mouthpiece of the Secession-Modernists, devoted the whole of its December 1898 issue to him. For his part, Khnopff introduced Viennese modernist architecture into Belgium with the construction of his own studio-residence in Brussels. The house was conceived of as a temple, a shrine dedicated to himself and his oeuvre. At its centre, Khnopff dedicated an altar to Hypnos, the Greek god of sleep. This interest in the figure of Hypnos is a reminder of the ritual occultism that appealed to so many artists in the last quarter of the nineteenth century, from Dante Gabriel Rossetti and James Tissot to Jean Delville. Hypnotism was, after all, a key element in occult

Fernand Khnopff.
Incense. 1898.
Pastel and charcoal on
paper, 89 x 29,5 cm.
Museum voor Schone
Kunsten, Ghent.

séances and the dream world of *Incense* in 1898 makes reference to them. Set in the Church of Our Lady in Bruges, Marguerite Khnopff, who was the model, seems to play the role of a medium, standing in a haze of holy mist. Shrouded in expensive robes, her body language exudes a cerebral peace. Typologically the work is reminiscent of fifteenth-century Flemish panel painting in which expensive materials and realistic detail were similarly predominant. *Incense* calls to mind the medieval theme of the Madonna in the Church, or even as the Church.

Images and memory

Fernand Khnopff's obsession with the medieval city, its ossified memories and unfathomable religiosity, manifested itself in numerous works associated with ancient Bruges. Khnopff's emotional ties with the city as he remembered it – he confessed that he never returned after leaving it as a child – were something he had in common with his young Belgian literary friends. He wove images of the city into the frontispieces of two beacons of Belgian symbolism: *Mon coeur pleure d'autrefois* by Grégoire Le Roy (1889) and *Bruges-la-Morte* by Georges Rodenbach (1892). Between 1902 and 1905 this theme was vigorously resumed in Khnopff's pictorial work. It is striking that he mingled his instinctive recollections with photographs, some of which were taken from *Bruges-la-Morte*.

Fernand Khnopff.
Secret-Reflection. 1902.
Coloured pencil on paper.
49.5 cm (diameter) and
27.8 x 49 cm.
Groeningemuseum, Bruges.

Hans Memling,
*The Mystic Marriage of
S. Catherine* (Central panel
of the St. John Altar).
1474-1479. Panel.
Stedelijke Musea, Bruges.

In fact, photography played an important part in Khnopff's work, not only in the preparation of his compositions but also as compositions in their own right, frequently highlighted with coloured pencil or pastel. The water of the canals or 'reien', the city's symbol, regularly features prominently in these compositions in which the reflection of the water simultaneously mirrors the Ego or the soul. The *Secret-Reflection* of 1902, conceived by Khnopff as a vertical dip-

Fernand Khnopff.
Fosset/Under the Pines.
1894.
Canvas. 65.5 x 44 cm.
Koninklijke Musea voor
Schone Kunsten, Brussels.

tych, reveals how closely he identified the old city with his own work. Above, in an undefined space, a priestess looks stealthily at a mask, which seems to be her likeness. Softly she caresses the lips of the Psyche-character who has been condemned to silence and to the Mystery. The immobility and hyper-realism of photographic technique also played a primary role in the creation of the lower picture, *Reflection*. The upper picture was based on a photograph in which his sister posed in a staged scene in front of a mask. Furthermore, the woman's arm movement seems to make reference to an analogous gesture in Hans Memling's *Mystic Marriage of St Catherine*, that now hangs in the St John's hospital in Bruges. One can see part of this very same medieval hospital in *Reflection*, possibly inspired by a photograph of the hospital's facade in Rodenbach's *Bruges-la-Morte*. Just as the female figure is mirrored by her own likeness in the mask, so Khnopff applies the popular symbolism of the mirror to the oppressive, photographically framed *Reflection*.

The strong sense of spiritual affinity that one can observe in his paintings of Bruges and the canals which ran through the medieval city, also pervades his landscapes at Fosset. As with the enigmatic figures in the former, in the landscapes too order and structure predominate. Stripped of all anecdote, the landscapes mirror an emotional experience, a tranquil synthesis of inscrutable Nature. For instance, *In Fosset/Under the Pines*, painted in 1894, is no superficial impressionistic work but a refined, atmospheric composition. The perspective is resolved into successive horizontal lines and the atmosphere is dark, mysterious and oppressive.

Fernand Khnopff,
Portrait of Marie Monnom.
1887.
Canvas, 50 x 50 cm.
Musée d'Orsay, Paris.

Anti-bourgeois sophistication

Although Khnopff heightened the mystery surrounding his own person and allowed the outside world only a carefully staged glimpse of his life as an artist, he was happy to enter the sophisticated world of the Brussels aristocracy and upper middle classes. Until the mid-1880s he excelled in portraits of children. But the *Portrait of Marie Monnom* (1887) heralded a long series of adult portraits, usually of well-known figures in Brussels cultural life. Marie Monnom was the daughter of the Brussels publisher responsible for, among other things, the authoritative avant-garde journal *L'Art moderne* and the catalogues of Les XX. Two years later she was to marry Khnopff's good friend, the neo-Impressionist Théo van Rysselberghe. Typical of Khnopff's portraits is the distance that is maintained between the subject and the viewer. Somewhat unusually for this genre of painting, the sitters reveal little of themselves, enclosed as they are in their own world of ideas. Any indication of time and space is consciously avoided and the unusual framing adds to a sense of silence and immobility.

The golden circle to the left of the doorway in the portrait of Marie Monnom is a recurring theme in Khnopff's work. In the famous Blue Room at his house two golden rings encircled the names of his favourite artists, Edward Burne-Jones

Fernand Khnopff, *Brown Eyes and a Blue Flower*. 1905.
Pencil and gouache on paper, 18.5 cm (diameter). Museum voor Schone Kunsten, Ghent.

and Gustave Moreau. In the same room, his easel was placed within a golden circle. The circular form, which can symbolise intimacy, infinity or perfection, sometimes forms an integral part of his compositions and at other times borders the painting, as in his *Brown Eyes and a Blue Flower* of 1905. The mysterious face in this picture, surrounded by a transparent veil, gazes at the viewer. Her eyes are brown, the colour of spirituality. In the foreground, a flower and a pearl lie on a translucent dish. The blue colour of the flower, probably a (dyed?) cyclamen, symbolises the Ideal. A circular passepartout, cutting off part of the head, and the predominant, virtually unbroken monochrome, draw attention to

Fernand Khnopff, *Memories* or *Lawn Tennis*. 1889.
Pastel on paper, transferred to canvas, 127 x 200 cm. Koninklijke Musea voor Schone Kunsten, Brussels.

the woman's penetrating eyes. The unusual golden passepartout is like a halo and reinforces the sacred atmosphere of the composition.

We shall close with the intriguing *Memories*, a pastel of 1889 that seems to encapsulate Fernand Khnopff's artistic thinking. As in certain medieval representations of the Pleiades, the female figures make no contact with each other. Gazing into infinity they are situated in an unreal landscape, which is divided into four bands of colour devoid of any form of perspective. Technically the landscape is reminiscent of Khnopff's monochrome, schematic Fosset landscapes. The realistic detail of the female figures heightens the element of surprise in his treatment of space as Khnopff breaks the natural relationship of its proportions. In reality, the pastel is a collage of different photographs in which his sister Marguerite adopted the poses of each of the figures. Khnopff's use of photographs as an intermediate stage underlies the effect of light on each individual and also explains the stiff immobility of the tennis players. The lighting is also unrealistic in that there appear to be several light sources. The second title of the pastel, *Lawn Tennis*, refers to the then young sport that had become fashionable with the founding of the London Lawn Tennis Association in the previous year. Seizing on the newly fashionable game of tennis to emphasise the unfathomable nature of human memory, Fernand Khnopff at the same time placed the abstract world of ideas beyond time, space and action – a clear indication of his pictorial preference for the ineffable merging of spirit and soul. ∎

Translated by Chris Emery

FURTHER READING

Robert L. Delevoy, Catherine De Croës and Gisèle Ollinger-Zinque, *Fernand Khnopff*. Brussels, 1979 (1987).

Michel Draguet, *Fernand Khnopff 1858-1921*. Brussels/Ghent, 1995.

Frederik Leen, Dominique Maréchal and Gisèle Ollinger-Zinque (ed.), *Fernand Khnopff (1858-1921)*. Exhibition catalogue, Brussels / Salzburg / Boston, 2004.

A Beacon for Europe

Emile Verhaeren 1855-1916

'Tolerant but indifferent to so many of her distinguished visitors, England made no exception in the case of Emile Verhaeren, the fair-haired young Belgian poet', wrote Beatrice Worthing.[1] Though the poet came to Britain almost annually from the 1880s onwards, appreciation of his work did not extend beyond a small band of enthusiastic translators: Michael Sadleir, Arthur Symonds, Osman Edwards, Jethro Bithell, F.S. Flint, and Alma Strettell ... Consequently one will look in vain for any influence on English *fin-de-siècle* poetry. Only after 1900, when all Europe acclaimed Verhaeren as a leading poet and thinker, did the English public at large pay any attention to the author. Verhaeren was certainly an exceptional figure: first, as a French-speaking Belgian of Flemish origin, he had taken the literary world of late-nineteenth-century Paris by storm. Later, in the years 1900 to 1914, he became a guiding light for the European intelligentsia, fêted as far afield as St Petersburg and Moscow! Yet after World War I he disappeared virtually without trace from the literary firmament. What caused the meteoric rise of this Flemish poet who wrote in French? And what caused him subsequently to disappear into the mists of history?

Verhaeren's first collection, *The Flemish Women* (Les Flamandes, 1883) – a naturalistic tribute to the erotic, Rubensesque women of a mythical Flanders – enjoyed a *succès de scandale*. One critic did not pull his punches: *'Emile Verhaeren is doubly guilty: trying to be incisive, he has opened an abcess'*. But the avant-garde was enthusiastic: *'The volume as a whole nevertheless strikes a serious, powerful note, with a delectable vigour that evokes the lusty quintessence of the spirit and heart of Mother Flanders.'* Such disparate reactions are typical of the Belgian literary scene in the 1880s: the younger authors grouped around the journal *La Jeune Belgique* wanted to break free from the eulogies of the young state of Belgium that had hitherto been a literary imperative. Art, they believed, should no longer serve a political or moral ideal, but should be an end in itself. The young Verhaeren immediately became the champion of these subversive ideas.

Even today, an author who writes in French only really counts if he gains recognition in Paris. From the beginning Verhaeren sought and found contacts in the French capital. As early as the 1880s he acted as an intermediary be-tween the artistic worlds of Paris and Brussels. He was a welcome guest at

Stéphane Mallarmé's celebrated 'Tuesdays', at which the elite of the literary world congregated around the master of emergent symbolism. Down with the pedestrian naturalism that showed only the surface of things! Long live symbols, which subtly suggest the experiences and emotions evoked by the sensory world!

The *nouveau vers,* forged in the old smithy

Verhaeren was to apply this perspective very successfully in his 'black trilogy'. It has been often claimed that these collections – *The Evenings* (Les Soirs, 1888), *The Disasters* (Les Débâcles, 1888) and *The Black Torches* (Les Flambeaux noirs, 1891) – are the product of the severe nervous illness that afflicted the poet after the death of his parents. But the fact that in this same period Verhaeren launched on a period of hectic activity is a clear indication that the morbid nature of this poetry is largely a literary choice.[2] Decadent and symbolist authors like Barbey d'Aurevilly, Léon Bloy, Joris-Karl Huysmans – and also painters like Fernand Khnopff – took the view that only melancholy and despair were of any artistic value.

What makes Verhaeren the leading figure of his generation is the evocative power of his poetry. More than any other French symbolist, the Fleming is able to find images that imprint themselves on the mind. The mill at the centre of 'Le moulin' (from *The Evenings*), is not just an allegory of the despairing struggle of the impoverished rural population, it embodies that despair.

While the poet's main source of inspiration is the Flemish landscape with its endless plains and humble cottages, metropolises like London regularly loom up as a bleak backdrop to his mental torment:

Theo van Rysselberghe,
*The Reading by Emile
Verhaeren* (detail). 1903.
Canvas, 181 x 241 cm.
Museum voor Schone
Kunsten, Ghent.

And this London of cast iron and bronze, my soul,
Where sheets of steel clang in the workshops (...)
Where beasts of boredom yawn hugely at the
Mournful hour that strikes at Westminster.

And these endless embankments with fatal lampposts (...)
And all at once there's death, among these crowds
O my evening soul, black London lingers in me.

In the concluding poem of *The Black Torches* the poet seems to have lost all faith in the power of rational thought. Like a Shakespearian Ophelia the corpse of his reason drifts down the Thames:

In its robe of dead jewels, solemnised by
The purple hour on the horizon
The corpse of my reason
Floats lazily downstream (...)

Literary France was bowled over by this 'Northern exoticism', especially since Verhaeren was not only tapping into a new reservoir of imagery, he was also using a new verse form. He reworked classical French verse – hitherto inextricably linked to fixed patterns – and turned it into a supple instrument: short and long lines, with an even or odd number of syllables, alternate, depending of the demands of rhythm or the image.

Mallarmé himself paid tribute to this new form of poetry: '*You (the verse form) come from the ancient smithy new-forged in every respect, to the point where the line is extended beyond its obligatory length, and yet remains a line. On that especially I congratulate you.*' (letter of 11 January 1888)

Some have seen this 'free verse' as an attempt to impose on French poetry a Germanic verse form, with strong accents and much alliteration. But though as a child Verhaeren may have spoken the local Sint-Amands dialect, he was definitely not familiar with poetry in Dutch. What seems more likely is that his tempestuous temperament demanded a more flexible verse form. Moreover, he was not alone in his attempt to escape the straitjacket of French prosody: poets like Gustave Kahn and Vielé-Griffin were heading in the same direction. It is still striking, though, that it took three poets with a background that was not totally French to initiate this renewal.

On machines and marital bliss

In his following collection the poet seems to change course entirely. In the 'black trilogy' he had very much turned in on himself, but in his later work he focused on the social reality around him. He was fascinated by English philosophers and social thinkers like Ruskin. Though he himself knew no English, his friend, the socialist leader Emile Vandervelde – an acquaintance of Bernard Shaw's – told him how men like William Morris, Cobden-Sanderson and Walter Crane tried to make art easily accessible to the working class. It was partly this example that led the two Emiles to set up an Artistic Section in the socialist party's 'People's House' headquarters in Brussels.

Strange as it may seem, this new Verhaeren actually celebrates the triumph of the industrial revolution, mechanisation and the modern world that is fast approaching. The great cities – *The Many-Tentacled Cities* (Les villes tentaculaires, 1895) – appear to him as huge octopuses that stretch out their tentacles and swallow up the living strength of the countryside, yet do so in order to create the radiant city of the future! The villages are only shadows of their former selves: *Illusory Villages* (Villages illusoires, 1895).[3] These socially inspired collections established Verhaeren's reputation in France once and for all: the Paris publisher Vallette published three volumes containing the principal collections that had appeared up to then (*Poèmes*, 1895 and 1896).

A striking feature of this poet is his ability to draw on different sources of inspiration simultaneously. In the same year as *Illusory Villages* and *The Many-Tentacled Cities* he published a ravishing collection of love poems dedicated to his wife, the artist Marthe Massin: *The Limpid Hours* (Les heures claires, 1896). The herald of the roar of machinery could also celebrate the quiet happiness of a happy marriage.

The culture of enthusiasm

But there were still more sides to Verhaeren. Around the turn of the century he emerged as the prophet of the new age. Hoping to reach a wider public, he wrote *The Dawns* (Les Aubes, 1898), a play that exudes confidence in a glorious future in which fraternity and solidarity will reign supreme.[4] He professes the same belief in such collections as *Life's Faces* (Les Visages de la Vie, 1899), *The Tumultuous Powers* (Les Forces tumultueuses, 1902), *The Manifold Splendour* (La Multiple Splendeur, 1906), *The Sovereign Rhythms* (Les Rythmes souverains, 1910). Strikingly, there is a wholesale return to the alexandrine, the pre-eminent classical French verse form. Partly because of their more familiar form these more hopeful collections were a runaway success. The poet was invited to give lectures. One of his favourite themes was 'The Culture of Enthusiasm'. Today it would be almost inconceivable: a Flemish poet, speaking in French, attracting full, enthusiastic houses in Germany, Switzerland and as far away as Russia (St Petersburg and Moscow). Verhaeren found the perfect expression for the expectations of a society tired of *fin-de-siècle* pessimism. He preached belief in reason and science as the lever that would help create a new world. Modern technology would make work so much lighter and abolish so much inequality. All peoples would become brothers, the masses themselves would join forces. This idea was to be taken up by a number of younger writers – among them Jules Romains – under the name unanimism. Verhaeren's poetry acquired a prophetic ring: *'Admire each other'* (*The Manifold Splendour*), *'Future, you excite me as my God once did'* (*The Sovereign Rhythms*). The whole European intelligentsia regarded him as its guiding light, but for a long time England rather lagged behind: the English public found the tender, lyrical plays of Maurice Maeterlinck, the later Nobel Prize winner, more congenial.

Not until the outbreak of World War I did Verhaeren attract wide public notice. He and his wife fled to England, where they were hospitably received, first by Osman Edwards in Kensington, and later by Henry Webb MP in Cardiff. Deeply hurt by the German assault on his belief in universal brotherhood, the poet wrote a scathing indictment of the aggressor: 'La Belgique sanglante' (1915).

Michael Sadleir translated the work immediately as 'Belgium's Agony'. Many poems appeared in leading English dailies, intended to support the cause of the Allies. Verhaeren lectured in many English cities and on 15 November 1914 was awarded an honorary doctorate by the University of Leeds.

An urgent appeal from King Albert I took him back to the continent: here too he gave lecture after lecture to encourage the population in its struggle. The day after speaking in Rouen, on 27 November 1916, he fell from a crowded railway platform and was crushed by the train on which he was due to return to Paris.

There was great consternation: some wanted the celebrated poet to be interred in the Pantheon. But it was decided that this 'poète national' should be buried in the last patch of Belgian soil that was still free, in Alveringhem near De Panne. Not until 1927 was he reburied in his home village, on the banks of the Scheldt, as he had requested: *'le jour que m'abattra le sort ....'* ('the day when fate strikes me down...')

Today, almost a century after his death, if we look at what has survived, what do we find? Verhaeren's later collections – from *The Tumultuous Powers* onwards – were often excessively rhetorical and, in the light of history, rather naïve. World War I was gruesome proof that the nations of European were far from ready for universal brotherhood: the poet's influence evaporated overnight. But even today we can admire the tender poems of *The Hours* (Les Heures: Les heures claires, les heures d'après-midi, Les heures du soir). These are undisputed masterpieces: where else has married love been so delicately celebrated?

There is also general agreement that the 'black trilogy' contains some of the most powerful poems of French Symbolism, both in imagery and rhythm – free verse. What other French-speaking Belgian had such an impact on French *fin-de-siècle* literature? And finally, Verhaeren was able to cast his faith in a bright future in such an inspirational form that he became a beacon of hope for the European intelligentsia. What other poet could match this achievement? ■

Translated by Paul Vincent

NOTES

1. Beatrice Worthing, in *Adam International Review*, 250 (The Centenary of Emile Verhaeren), 1955, pp. 55-87.

2. In these 'sombre' years Verhaeren regularly reported on exhibitions by painters and sculptors in Brussels and Paris; he was active in the organisation of the salons of les XX; in a series of articles he described his journey to Spain with Dario de Regoyos (*Impressions d'artiste. A Dario de Regoyos*, 1888).

3. Two poems from this collection, 'The Rain' ('La pluie') and 'The Fishermen' ('Les pêcheurs') were translated by Alma Harrison. She published them under the name Alma Strettell in the *Yellow Book* (IX, April), the leading decadent journal in England. Osman Edwards translated 'The Ropemakers' ('Les Cordiers') and wrote an appreciative article in the *Daily Chronicle* (19 May 1895).

4. Verhaeren was to write three more plays: *The Cloister* (Le Cloître, 1899) and *Philip II* (Philippe II, 1901), both translated into English by Osman Edwards; *Helen of Sparta* ('Hélène de Sparte', publ. 1912, but previously translated into Russian in 1906 and into German in 1909 by Stefan Zweig).

www.emileverhaeren.be

The Mill

Deep in the evening slowly turns the mill
   Against a sky with melancholy pale;
   It turns and turns, its muddy-coloured sail
Is infinitely heavy, tired, and ill.

Its arms, complaining arms, in the dawn's pink
   Rose, rose and fell; and in this o'ercast eve,
   And deadend nature's silence, still they heave
Themselves aloft, and weary till they sink.

Winter's sick day lies on the fields to sleep;
   The clouds are tired of sombre journeyings;
   And past the wood that gathered shadow flings
The ruts towards a dead horizon creep.

Around a pale pond huts of beechwood built
   Despondently squat near the rusty reeds;
   A lamp of brass hung from the ceiling bleeds
Upon the wall and windows blots of gilt.

And in the vast plain, with their ragged eyes
   Of windows patched, the suffering hovels watch
   The worn-out mill the bleak horizon notch, –
The tired mill turning, turning till it dies.

I Bring to You as Offering To-Night

I bring to you as offering to-night
My body boisterous with the wind's delight;
In floods of sunlight I have bathed my skin;
My feet are clean as the grass they waded in;
Soft are my fingers as the flowers they held;
My eyes are brightened by the tears that welled
Within them, when they looked upon the earth
Strong without end and rich with festive mirth;
Space in its living arms has snatched me up,
And whirled me drunk as from the mad wine-cup;
And I have walked I know not where, with pent
Cries that would free my heart's wild wonderment;
I bring to you the life of meadow-lands;
Sweet marjoram and thyme have kissed my hands;
Breathe them upon my body, all the fresh
Air and its light and scents are in my flesh.

From *The Evenings* (Les Soirs, 1888)
Translated by Jethro Bithell

From *The Afternoon Hours* (Les heures d'après-midi, 1905)
Translated by Jethro Bithell

The Ferryman

The ferryman, a green reed 'twixt his teeth,
With hand on oar, against the current strong
Had rowed and rowed so long.

But she, alas! whose voice was hailing him
Across the far waves dim,
Still further o'er the far waves seemed to float,
Still further backward, 'mid the mists, remote.

The casements with their eyes,
The dial-faces of towers that rise
Upon the shore,
Watched, as he strove and laboured more and more,
With frantic bending of the back in two,
And start of savage muscles strained anew.

One oar was suddenly riven,
And by the current driven,
With lash of heavy breakers, out to sea.

But she, whose voice that hailed him he could hear
There 'mid the mist and wind, she seemed to wring
Her hands with gestures yet more maddening
Toward him who drew not near.

The ferryman with his surviving oar
Fell harder yet to work, and more and more
He strove, till every joint did crack and start,
And fevered terror shook his very heart.

The rudder broke
Beneath one sharp, rude stroke;
That, too, the current drove relentlessly,
A dreary shred of wreckage, out to sea.

The casements by the pier,
Like eyes immense and feverish open wide,
The dials of the towers – those windows drear
Upstanding straight from mile to mile beside
The banks of rivers – obstinately gaze

Upon this madman, in his headstrong craze
Prolonging his mad voyage 'gainst the tide.

But she, who yonder in the mist-clouds hailed
Him still so desperately, she wailed and wailed,
With head outstretched in fearful, straining haste
Toward the unknown of the outstretched waste.

Steady as one that had in bronze been cast,
Amid the blenched, grey tempest and the blast,
The ferryman his single oar yet plied,
And, spite of all, still lashed and bit the tide.
His old eyes, with hallucinated gaze,
Saw that far distance – an illumined haze –
Whence the voice sounded, coming toward him still,
Beneath the cold skies, lamentable, shrill.

The last oar broke –
And this the current hurried at one stroke,
Like a frail straw, toward the distant sea.

The ferryman with arms dropped helplessly,
Sank on his bench, forlorn,
His loins with vain efforts broken, torn.

Drifting, his barque struck somewhere, as by chance,
He turned a glance
Toward the bank behind him then – and saw
He had not left the shore.

The casements and the dials, one by one,
Their huge eyes gazing in a foolish stare,
Witnessed the ruin of his ardour there;
But still the old, tenacious ferryman
Firm in his teeth – for God knows when, indeed –
Held the green reed.

From *Illusory Villages* (Villages Illusoires, 1895)
Translated by Alma Strettell

The Factories

Watching each other through their windows' clouded panes
And reflected in the water full of pitch and saltpetre stains
Of a straight canal, shutting them off into infinity,
Face to face, along the shade- and night-cloaked quays
All through the ponderous suburbs
And the wretched tears of those suburbs,
Plants and factories give awesome roars.

Rectangles of granite and monuments of brick,
And long, black walls continuing for miles,
In massive suburban files;
And on the roofs, racked
By iron and lighting conductors,
The chimney stacks.

Watching each other with their black, symmetrical eyes,
Through suburbia, into infinity,
Day and night roaring ceaselessly,
Plants and factories.
Oh, the districts rusted by rain and each thoroughfare!
And the women and their rags who appear there
And the squares, where there blooms, in holes
Of white rubble and dead coals,
Flora decaying and pale.

At the crossroads, doors open, the bars:
Tin, copper, mirrors' gaunt scars,
Ebony dressers and bottles droll
From which the gleam of alcohol
Glows at the pavements.
And pints that suddenly shine down
On the bar, in pyramids of crowns;
And people drunk, on their feet,
Whose broad tongues lap, while no word is said,
Topaz-hued whisky and golden ales' head.

All through the ponderous suburbs
And the wretched tears of those suburbs
And the neighbourhoods murky and drear
And personal hate intertwining too

And from household to household here,
And theft among those who haven't a sou,
At the back of their yards forever more
The panting, dull throbbing sore
Of plants and symmetrical factories.

Here, under great roofs of sparkling glass,
Steam condenses, lets nothing pass:
Steel jaws smoke and clash;
Great, monumental hammers
On the anvils blocks of gold smash,
And in a corner, the pig-iron's flame
In braziers twisted and frantic that men tame.

Below, the looms' careful fingers deftly pick,
With minute gestures, a tiny click,
Weave sheets, with threads trembling in line,
Like strands of gossamer, so fine.
The leather transverse belts don't stop
And run the whole length of the shop
And the flywheels fierce and wide
Turn, like the sails of mad-eyed
Windmills a gale has caught up.
From the backyard, all pinched and shorn,
Through the panes, comes the morn,
Through a basement window, smeared with oil,
Brushing their toil.
Mechanical and clipped,
Workers, tight-lipped,
Control the natter
Of universal clatter
The seething fever and screech
That shreds, with its stubborn chatter,
All banished human speech.

Further on, a thunderous din of shocks
Rises from the shadows and builds up in blocks;
And suddenly, breaking the wave of violence,
The walls of noise seem to fall
And to hush in a pool of silence,

While the exacerbated call
Of the crude whistles and signs
At the lanterns suddenly whines,
Raising their wild lights
In gold bunches up to the heights.

And all around like a belt of light,
Below, the architecture of night,
See docks, ports, bridges and lighthouses there
And the stations with their frenzied blare;
And further still, more plant roofs rise
And tanks and forges mounting the skies,
Great vats of naphtha and resinous size,
From which hot packs of fire and magnified rays
Gnaw the sky now and then and bark and blaze.

Along the unending old canal,
Through the vast wretchedness
Of the black highways and cobbled distress,
The nights, the days, evermore,
The constant dull thuds roar,
In the wards of the poor,
Plants and symmetrical plants.

Dawn makes a serviette
Of their squares of sweat;
Noon and its gaunt dog
Like a blind man's, stray through their fog;
Alone, when at the week's end, at eve,
Night sinks in its shadow, takes leave,
The bitter effort breaks off, but remains in the air,
A hammer above an anvil, it seems,
And the shadow, distant, among the crossroads, hangs there
Like gold mist that gleams.

From *The Many-Tentacled Cities* (Les villes tentaculaires, 1895)
Translated by Paul Vincent

Loud Chords and Calm Moments

Louis Andriessen, Composer

[EMILE WENNEKES]

Louis Andriessen (1939-).
Photo by Klaas Koppe.

When can you describe a composer as 'setting the tone' for his contemporaries? When his work is regularly performed throughout the entire (Western) world and key works from his oeuvre are known to a relatively large audience? Perhaps. Another indication is the demand for the composer's music – for music on CD, for sheet music, but also for new works for eager musicians. A further sign is when the composer is stylistically influential and attracts pupils from near and far. Holding important positions in the music world is also part of the description of such a composer, as is the large number of publications about him.

All of which certainly applies to the Dutch composer Louis Andriessen. In the United States and London, festivals lasting several days have been devoted to his work, accompanied by a great deal of media attention – but that's something you get used to. Celebrated ensembles all over the world, such as Ice Breaker, Ensemble Intercontemporain and Ensemble Modern, include his work in their repertoire, and he has a portfolio of commissions that will keep him busy for years. One of the works that he's concentrating on at the moment is a new opera-in-the-making inspired by Dante's *Divina Commedia*, parts of which are already being tried out in occasional performances by various ensembles. And as for the positions that Andriessen holds: in the Netherlands he has been teaching composition at the Royal Conservatory in The Hague for decades. From time to time he also plays a professorial role elsewhere. In 1997, for example, he spent a year in an endowed chair at what was then the Catholic University of Nijmegen (now Radboud University). Since 2004 he has held a chair in the Arts Faculty of Leiden University, which has close ties with the conservatory in The Hague. Outside his own country, too, Louis Andriessen is a respected teacher. He has held visiting lectureships at the Californian Institute of Arts (Los Angeles), Princeton University and the Catholic University of Leuven, and has lectured on music theory and composition at Yale. It should also be mentioned that Andriessen was for a time artistic director of the Meltdown Festival at the South Bank Centre in London and the prestigious Tanglewood Festival in the wonderful American Berkshires.

Speaking volumes

Theses, dissertations, articles and books based on Andriessen's work are published at home and abroad as regularly as clockwork. In 1993 Frits van der Waa compiled a sizeable collection of essays under the title of *De slag van Andriessen*. A number of Andriessen's talks and lectures have been edited and published under the name of *Gestolen tijd* (2002, translated as *The Art of Stealing Time*, 2002, and also available in Russian since 2005). And when the University of Bristol began to publish a series with the highfalutin title of *Landmarks in Music since 1950*, Louis Andriessen's composition *The State* was given the honour of having an entire volume (written by Robert Adlington) devoted to it – something previously achieved only by Dmitri Shostakovich and György Kurtág.

The first two chapters of this book say a great deal about Andriessen's style and ideals: the first chapter has the brief title of 'Music and Politics' and the second is entitled 'Jazz, Minimalism and Stravinsky'. Stravinsky occupies a special place in Andriessen's work. He has played a role in Andriessen's music ever since the latter's first published composition (*Nocturnen*, 1959) and Andriessen frequently quotes him directly and indirectly. Andriessen also collaborated with the musicologist, writer and composer Elmer Schönberger on *Het apollinisch uurwerk. Over Stravinsky*. This book, which was published in 1983 (and translated into English in 1989 as *The Apollonian Clockwork. On Stravinsky* and also published in Russian in 2003), was described by the prominent musicologist Richard Taruskin as *'the one book about Stravinsky Stravinsky would have liked'*.

As far as international stature is concerned, Andriessen is placed on the same pedestal as Jan-Pieterszoon Sweelinck (1562–1621). A pretty coincidence, given the way Andriessen flirts with Sweelinck's music – for example, the quote from *Mein junges Leben hat ein End* in the opera *Writing to Vermeer*. Just as composition and the improvisational techniques of keyboard players changed somewhat because of Sweelinck, so Andriessen has influenced post-war composing with his stylistic interpretations.

The jury report from the prestigious 3M Prize, worth 100,000 guilders at the time, fully endorsed this: *'He has always been contrary and gone against the flow. He has never accepted existing traditional forms of expression, performance practice and the structure of the music world. He created his own.'* Not even his greatest enemy could refute this description.

A born artist

In short, no self-respecting music encyclopaedia nowadays can be without an entry on the life and work of Louis Andriessen. There's also a very good chance that he won't be the only 'Andriessen' listed in such a work of reference. After all, Louis was born in 1939 as the youngest son of the composer, organist and conservatory director Hendrik Andriessen (1892–1981) and the younger brother of Jurriaan (1925–1996), also a successful composer, to mention just two members of the dynasty. The Andriessens have been an artistic family for generations. Grandfather Nico (whom Louis never knew) was a respected musician in his day. One of his uncles was the pianist Willem Andriessen (1887–1964; also a conservatory director); another was the sculptor Mari Andriessen (1897–1979, known for his many memorial monuments, including the famous statue of the *Dockworker* in Amsterdam: see p. 138).

With a background like that, it's not surprising that the young Louis was destined for an artistic career. He initially studied composition with Kees van Baaren at the Royal Conservatory and was subsequently taken under Luciano Berio's wing. Andriessen gained national celebrity at the end of the sixties when he caused a stir as one of the so-called 'Notenkrakers' (Nutcrackers), a group who anchored their political and social attitudes in a rather exuberant artistic credo. The Nutcrackers, formed by a.o. Peter Schat, Misha Mengelberg, Reinbert de Leeuw, Willem Breuker and Louis Andriessen, acted as a catalyst in the modernisation and later the reorganisation of the musical infrastructure of the Netherlands. In 1969, they got together to perform a *Nutcracker Suite* with rattles and horns with which they disrupted a performance by the Concertgebouw Orchestra under its chief conductor Bernard Haitink.

This demonstration was aimed at the programming policy, which they regarded as conservative, and at the authoritarian structure of the most important orchestra in the Netherlands, which was seen as a symbol of the 'ruling classes'. More generally, the demonstration expressed their dissatisfaction with *'the cosy little ways of distributing funding and designing conditions for subsidies, which passed for cultural policy only because of a loose understanding of the term'*, as *De Tijd* put it shortly before the demonstration. However, the *Notenkrakersaktie* (Nutcrackers' demonstration) was primarily an expression of frustration at the way the younger generation could hardly get a toe in the door with the institutionalised artistic organisations.

A result of Andriessen's views on art and politics was his rejection of the symphony orchestra, which he saw as antiquated and authoritarian, and his subsequent establishment of alternative music ensembles with unorthodox instrumentation. Take, for example, Orkest De Volharding (initially a politically motivated street orchestra made up almost completely of wind instruments) and the instrumentally egalitarian Hoketus, both of which were named after compositions by Andriessen. The name of Hoketus very clearly illustrates the fact that Andriessen is a keen supporter of the time-honoured 'hoketus' or 'hocket' technique, where individual notes of a shared melody line are alternated between different players.

Music as a monolith

The opera *Reconstruction* (Reconstructie, 1969), devised together with Jan van Vlijmen, Misha Mengelberg, Peter Schat and Reinbert de Leeuw, made history. This work brings together many themes relating to the sense of cultural uneasiness prevailing at the time as well as a growing involvement in social issues: Vietnam and the colonialist policy of the United States, the Cuba crisis, the charismatic personality of Ché Guevara and so on. Its performance led to disturbances, even to parliamentary questions, because government money had supposedly been used to insult a friendly nation – the United States. The issue eventually fizzled out, but it firmly established the reputation of the young composers. Before long, however, they each went their own way once again.

Not long after this, Louis Andriessen would become the main representative of the so-called Hague School of composition. His crystal-clear idiom of crashing columns of chords amongst often slowly meandering minimalist movements soon won him international recognition. In addition to the loud percussive chords, the repetitive structures, the flirtation with jazz and the constantly recurring hocket technique, Andriessen also regularly prescribes plain, vibrato-free song lines in his work. The vocal element plays a crucial role in all of Andriessen's music. Not only in the large-scale music-theatre works, but also to pieces that were not designed for the theatre, such as *The State* or *Mausoleum*.

In Andriessen's instrumentation, the string instruments are expressly subordinate to the wind instruments. These are usually supported by a rhythm section of percussion, piano, synthesizer, electric bass and guitar – a typical line-up adopted from pop and jazz music. With such instrumental combinations, Andriessen is able to create an extremely fluid synthesis between the different worlds that even today are often thought of as very far apart. Even when Andriessen occasionally makes use of more traditional genres or instrumentation, he manages to treat them in such a way that the end result is still original. For example, in his first string quartet, *Facing Death* (1990), he treats the strings almost as wind instruments; hardly anything remains of the heavy emotional charge of the Romantic string sound because of the jazz riffs that are played in unison – a nod to the furious solos of the legendary jazz saxophonist Charlie Parker.

Andriessen creates mono-dimensional music with the components that have been mentioned above, in the sense that – at least on first hearing – he usually provides only one aspect of the overtone, with no complex layering of melodies. But this does not mean that his music is easy to perform. Quite the reverse, in fact, as may be illustrated by the dreadfully tricky *Facing Death*. Many of his more extensive pieces are rather monolithic in character, as is the case with philosophically high-aiming pieces such as *The State* (De Staat, 1976, based on texts by Plato), *Mausoleum* (1979/rev. 1981, based on texts by writers including Bakunin), *Time* (De Tijd, 1981, based on the work of St Augustine) or *Velocity* (De Snelheid, 1983/rev. 1984). And yet Andriessen's work can also be extremely so-phisticated. Examples of this are the subdued *Hadewijch* (1988), based on the texts of the medieval mystic of the same name, which forms part of the musical dramatic quadriptych *Matter* (De Materie, 1989), and *TAO,* the second piece of the *Trilogy of the Last Day* (Trilogie van de Laatste Dag, 1996/97), written for the Japanese-Dutch pianist Tomoko Mukaiyama.

Living paintings and cows on stage

The highlights of his oeuvre include the previously mentioned opera *Writing to Vermeer,* which he devised in 1999 with Peter Greenaway, the English writer, art-ist and director. This work has been staged in various cities, including New York. In the opera, the cinematographic signature that brought Greenaway worldwide fame via films such as *The Draughtman's Contract* and *The Cook, the Thief, his Wife and her Lover* is unmistakable. His visual concept brings paintings to life, a cow lumbers over the stage and impressive images breathe new life into facets of Dutch history. With its large-scale projections of the letters that various women write to Vermeer, *Writing to Vermeer* is visually similar to *Rosa, a Horse Drama*, the music-theatre production created by Greenaway and Andriessen in the mid-nineties for De Nederlandse Opera. In parts of *Writing to Vermeer*, Andriessen's musical style is more sober and at the same time more dramatically powerful than ever (the fact that he is currently working on a Vermeer suite with mate-rial from this opera reveals a lot about a new kind of development in Andriessen's composing.)

Andriessen's oeuvre now stands at around one hundred published works. Their unique and headstrong idiom, their instrumentation and their role in the history of music make some of the compositions that have been discussed key works of international composition from the last quarter of the twentieth cen-tury. Other works, however, have more of a one-off character. For that too is a side of Louis Andriessen: the artisan, the craftsman, the musician in heart and soul, who doesn't approach music like a cell biologist, but sees it as a living passion that is constantly being reinvented. What is always present, even in the shorter pieces, is his strong and recognisable musical personality. Generally you can tell after just one bar: this is Andriessen. Setting the tone... ■

Translated by Laura Watkinson

Leeuwarden: Triumph and tragedy

When it came to higher education, Leeuwarden was the place to be. At the end of the sixties, after having spent a few years in Amsterdam, I returned to Friesland badly infected with the artistic bug. I thought I might do something with language or the fine arts, but my talent was meagre. Evening classes in Dutch Language and Literature seemed promising. It wasn't my mother tongue that we spoke, and it wasn't Frisian either. We spoke something in between – city Frisian – a broad, agreeable little language that you only heard in Frisian cities and larger towns. It's doomed to disappear, though I speak it to this day.

That's Leeuwarden for you: not Dutch, not Frisian, but something in between.

In the early centuries of the first millennium, the people living near the confluence of three Frisian waterways – the Vliet, the Ee and the Potmarge – built a *terp*, or artificial mound, to protect themselves from the aggression of the sea. That *terp* was known as Oldehove. A couple of centuries later, some enterprising inhabitants constructed a second, two-part *terp* on both sides of the Ee a bit further to the east. It was much higher than the first and developed into a trade settlement: Nijehove. Also on the Ee, even further to the northeast, there was a high ridge along the mud flats that was also suitable for habitation: Hoek.

In around 1200, this region on the eastern shore of the Middelzee, which had become increasingly important in economic terms, was diked in. The course of that dike, which followed an angle of the Middelzee, can still be seen near Wirdumerdijk and behind the buildings on the north side of the Nieuwestad. After the construction of the dike, the old path that had connected Oldehove with the northern *terp* of Nijehove became the first inhabited street outside the *terpen*, today's Grote Kerkstraat. It became necessary to build outlet sluices in the waterways, which stimulated transhipment and trade. The sluices were located in today's Naauw and probably in the canal that is today's Herenwaltje. The former property owners became the bosses – the early Frisian nobility known as *hoofdelingen* – who exercised a primitive form of rule over the new migrants, artisans and merchants. The settlements gradually grew closer together, forming a varied community. By the end of the thirteenth century Leeuwarden was able to call itself a city, and a large monastery of Dominican friars, who only established their communities in solid urban centres, put down roots on the flank of the Nijehove-terp. At the end of the thirteenth century the Middelzee began silting up. Large pieces of land in the southwest could be diked in, resulting in the Nieuwestad with its broad market quays.

Turbulent centuries followed: the *hoofdelingen* and the new middle-class elite jockeyed for power, internally as well as in alliance with factions elsewhere in Friesland. When authority was centralised at the very end of the fifteenth century and Leeuwarden was quickly chosen as the capital of Friesland, a new period of prosperity began that lasted until after the Revolt of 1580. The city continued to serve as the administrative centre as well as the royal residence of the Frisian Nassau family, which began looking more and more like a dynasty and imparted the expected measure of propriety to the city.

Letters in the street

Dutch in Leeuwarden. I landed a part-time student job at the Municipal Archives, and that's how I learned the history of the city down to the finest details, including its literary history. Near the first bridge (the round brick bridges are called *'pijpen'* – pipes) over the long series of canals known as Kelders and Voorstreek – De Brol – Jan Jansz. Starter ran a bookshop called *In d'Engelsche Bybel* in the early seventeenth century. The founder of the chamber of rhetoric known as *Och mocht het rijzen*, and author of *Friesche Lusthof* (1621), was as restless as Jan Jacob Slauerhoff three centuries later. Two bridges further up, near Vismarktpijp, is the house where that *poète maudit* spent his youth. A Plexiglas plaque in the alcove of the facade of the distinguished furniture establishment that is still run by his family features his portrait as a ship's doctor and this quote: *'My only home is my poetry. / As long as I know I can find that shelter / In wilderness, steppe, city and forest / No trouble will harm me.'*

His poem 'The end' ('Het einde'), engraved in stone, was recently set into the pavement on the *pijp*. The last few lines read: *'Now I know: nowhere will I find peace, / Not on earth and not at sea, / Only in that final narrow port / Of wood anchored in sand.'*

On the bridge in between, the Korfmakerspijp, is a small statue of Mata Hari, the dancer who ended her life facing a firing squad in 1916 for spying on France. The provocative performer, who was born in Leeuwarden and given the name Margareta Zelle, is depicted in bronze as a silly little elf. But not a trace of Alexander Cohen, who lived nearby and wrote about his youth in Leeuwarden in his autobiographic picaresque novel *In Revolt* (In opstand, 1932). When I was privileged to sit on cultural committees a few years after coming to Leeuwarden, I proposed the idea of placing nicely made signs bearing quotes from the poets on the *'pijpen'* that crossed the canals. For further on again, near Dubbelepijp, is the birthplace of François HaverSchmidt, the melancholy poet known as Piet Paaltjens.

Nothing ever came of the series of signs, fortunately, since from 1993 on poetry in Leeuwarden seemed to start growing on trees. It all started as a goodbye gift for mayor John te Loo. One of his teachers at the gymnasium had been

Ida Gerhardt, who awakened in him a love of poetry. The initiative produced a growing number of street poems hacked out in Belgian slate, and in no time at all thirty-five poems had been placed in prominent locations around the city. There's nothing by Piet Paaltjens on the Dubbelepijp, but his bronze bust can be found on Vrouwenpoortsbrug, in an entirely different part of the city. Number XCVI from *Sobs and Snickers* (Snikken en Grimlachjes, 1867) has been placed near Prinsentuin: '*A prayerful person walking by / Fills my heart with joy. / It makes me think that soon enough / He'll also be praying for me.*'

When I first came to live in Leeuwarden there seemed to be an explosion of special events. Ben Webster was playing sax at a youth centre. Each season saw a new play by the Fleming Hugo Claus, which I soon had the honour of reviewing for the *Friesch Dagblad*. On stage at the Harmonie city theatre, Gerard Cornelis van het Reve and Simon Vinkenoog came to blows during a literary festival.

Earlier on, Reve had been taken to court for blasphemy by the editor-in-chief of my *Friesch Dagblad*. A good twenty years later, Reve's 'Penitential Psalm' ('Boetpsalm') would be memorialised in slate and placed near the Oldehove: '*Penitential Psalm / Full of alcohol, melancholy, and devotion to the Blessed Virgin, / I live in Friesland. / Not my but Thy will be done.*'

Poets writing in the Dutch or the Frisian language who were born in Leeuwarden, live or lived there, or are related to the city in some other way, were invited to contribute to the poetry tombstones: Eddy Evenhuis, Theun de Vries, Martin Veldman, Remco Ekkers, Gerrit Komrij, Douwe Tamminga, Obe Postma, Kees 't Hart, Simon Vestdijk, Remco Campert, Michaël Zeeman and many others. The last of these, Michaël Zeeman, gave me a tiny supporting role in his first collection of stories as a literary hack in a story about a beloved mutual friend.

Vismarktpijp over the Voorstreek Canal with the poem 'The End' ('Het Einde') by Jan Jacob Slauerhoff. Photo by Peter Karstkarel.

Slauerhoff display window on Voorstreek with plaque commemorating the poet. Photo by Peter Karstkarel.

Writer/poet/performer Anne Feddema even wrote a poem in my own language. Here it is in Liwwadders and English:

Selfportret	Self-portrait
Jou hewwe my in disse waereld stuurd	*You put me in this world*
As un nosse komyk	*As a surly comedian*
Met un soad poeha	*With a lot of brouhaha*
Met un soad publyk	*And a lot of admirers*
Nou idde saal leech en duuster	*Now the hall is empty and dim*
Nim ik noch un sluk	*I take another swig*
Maak myn jammeleke siel	*Make my miserable soul*
Wear wat	*A bit*
LENTEACHTECH!	*SPRINGLIKE again!*

The Stadholders' Court, still known as the Royal Palace in the 1970s and now an upmarket hotel. On the right the statue of Willem Lodewijk van Nassau Dietz, Stadholder of Friesland for many years around 1600. A brilliant strategist and administrator, which earned him the affectionate title of 'Ús Heit' (Our Father). Photo by Peter Karstkarel.

Even though this kind of poem strikes close to home, my interest had gradually shifted in the intervening years from literature to art and architecture. After about five years I took up a study of art history. That was all because of the Oldehove. In the beginning, my girlfriend and I only worked in Leeuwarden, she in a posh office on the ring canal just outside the downtown area and I in the mezzanine of the old City Hall. Before we came to live in Leeuwarden as well, we'd meet during our lunch breaks in or near my Citroën 2CV on a bumpy square paved with granite cobblestones at the edge of the city centre. Before us loomed the Oldehove. Loomed? The stubby tower was trying hard to stay vertical. I suddenly became interested in the stories that the buildings and the urban structure of my new city had to tell me.

The unfinished pride of Leeuwarden

The Oldehove is the pride of Leeuwarden – a remarkable fact, since the old pile of stones is unfinished, leaning *and* crooked. Yet the tower is unreservedly the symbol of the city. And not for want of candidates, mind – the Frisian capital has other monuments that are far more fascinating – but because it has always been the high point of the city's silhouette and because its dramatic history continues to strike a sympathetic chord.

In May 1529, during a period in which Frisian society had finally calmed down after a couple of turbulent centuries, the city council and the church wardens of St Vitus Church signed a contract with master builder Jacob van Aaken to construct the tower. The city had become involved because it wasn't only the interests of the parish that had to be served. The city had ambitions as well. Soon after the establishment of the central authority of the dukes of Saxony in 1498, Leeuwarden had become the capital of Friesland. At that time, it was difficult to see that position reflected in the city's rather long, drawn-out silhouette. It didn't have a proper tower. In its function as the centre of government, the city really could do with a good high tower to embellish it.

Although the economy was improving during those stable years, there wasn't any ready money yet available to pay for the construction of such a prestigious tower. Interested individuals began soliciting financial contributions and the gifts streamed in from all over Friesland. The city took different measures to cover the cost of the building. 'Brick penalties' were introduced: misdemeanours and minor crimes against ecclesiastical and civil authority were punished by requiring the culprit to pay a fine in the form of bricks, wood, mortar or other building material. A clever arrangement was devised for the leasing of a city brickworks: for every batch of about 40,000 bricks, the manufacturer was to deliver 7,000 bricks 'for the benefit of the church'.

Although extraordinary creativity went into financing the tower, the construction itself was a disaster. When the tower had risen to a height of no more than

View of the Achmea tower from the Emmakade, Leeuwarden.

The leaning, crooked Oldehove, the symbol of Leeuwarden. An underground car park is currently under construction, so that the area around the tower may remain unobstructed. Photo by Peter Karstkarel.

ten metres, those involved became aware that the monster had started leaning to the northwest. Something quite serious was going on underground. It must have been an old canal or ditch that was the causing the mischief. The base of the tower began to sink. The crew continued working, building straight up from the crooked, sinking base. And so little by little the Oldehove became a leaning, crooked tower. Not an encouraging sight for those involved and a personal tragedy for the master builder. Jacob van Aaken died in 1532 – of mortification, according to the records. Master builder Cornelis Frederiks picked up where Van Aaken left off, but after a year it became apparent that there was no point in continuing and construction was suspended, for good.

The Oldehove, in its unfinished state, marks a period of historical change. A few years after building was discontinued, the activities of religious reformer Menno Simons and his followers ushered in a new age, an age that took shape architecturally with the Renaissance. Exactly because it is unfinished, the Late Gothic Oldehove is a perfect metaphor for the end of the Middle Ages. The monument is also an expression of a fascinating contrast. The overall effect is strikingly massive, but the lump of stone itself is surprisingly fine in its detail. The colourful use of materials, sturdy but expressively decorated buttresses, gigantic niches with lovely contours and tracery, and even the dentils show how St Vitus must once have been.

Few towers in Europe have such a poignant history. Yet the Oldehove has not become an embarrassment. It's melancholy in stone. It's a memorial to brutally disrupted enthusiasm, a monumental symbol of the pursuit of ambition *and* modesty.

The loneliness of a building

But Leeuwarden also challenged me to broaden my cultural perspective. There was theatre in abundance and concerts, too, even in the churches – I saw and heard an unforgettable experimental *Carmina Burana* – contemporary art in active galleries and, gradually, in the museums as well. I was invited to write art reviews for the *Friesch Dagblad* and I began documenting buildings. But more than just documenting the city I set about smelling it, looking at it, feeling it. Many of the buildings turned out to be much more communicative than their descriptions suggested.

The fascinating Kanselarij already had a reputation as a Renaissance monument. The Municipal Archives had occasionally sent me on errands to the National Archives, which were housed in the Kanselarij on Turfmarkt on the eastern side of the downtown area. I would walk there in an arc along the series of covered canals from the Eewal and Wortelhaven – with houses that were still pretty seedy at the time – and through Koningsstraat. Around the corner from the City Hall was the Royal Palace on Hofplein, a large winged building done up in nineteenth-century attire but with a heart and interiors that still recalled the time when the Nassau Dietz family resided there as stadholders of Friesland. In the palace, which didn't look anything like a palace – a building whose appearance has nothing to report – it was always silent and dark. For generations the Frisian Royal Commissioners had lived in one of the wings, but that was no longer the case. Whenever Queen Juliana came to visit Friesland her accommodation was quickly given a bit of spit and polish. Her ancestors had lived

there with a full royal household. It must have been especially lively at the time of the ostentatious Albertina Agnes, daughter of the Dutch stadholder Frederik Hendrik and wife of his Frisian colleague Willem Frederik, with receptions, banquets and fireworks on Hofplein. In around 1970 the palace ceased to participate in the slow-moving life of the city. But Leeuwarden had been given a dash of gentility thanks to the stadholder's court, and it can still be felt today.

The real royal palace of Leeuwarden was the Kanselarij, and that building tells a remarkable story, the story of the great historical transition from the Middle Ages, with its centralised power structures, to the New Era, with its movement towards democracy. The majestic Kanselarij was built between 1566 and 1571 by order of King Philip II as an administrative palace. His master builder, Bartholomeus Jansz., was sent north to provide the legislative and judicial body of the Court of Friesland, Philip's principal regional administrative organ, with suitable premises once and for all after persistent complaints about dilapidated accommodation. The power of the king faltered, however; the first signs of the Revolt were making themselves known. The expressive building style ended up as fully Late Gothic, which, like royal authority, was very old-fashioned for the years around 1570. The lavish gable became a stairway for the personified virtues, and at the top even featured Philip's father, Emperor Charles V, wearing a tiara. It was a propaganda piece for the power of the throne, a palace that was meant to inspire awe. But the entrance gate, corbels and other carved details are in the new Renaissance style. The Renaissance made its way to Friesland quite early, starting in the early 1530s. A substantial number of excellent sculpture studios were active there, providing magnificent tombstones, among other things, to the entire North Sea littoral from Leiden to Bremen. These sculptors were called in to take care of the palace's refinements, and brought the new style with them. Thus the Kanselarij became an expression of this historical change: within ten years, the Revolt and the Reformation were a fact.

The building was abandoned a few years after I came to live in the city. The National Archives were housed in a new building in the shadow of the Oldehove, next to the Provincial Library where I borrowed books for my school courses. These institutes recently merged with the Frysk Letterkundich Museum en Dokumintaasjesintrum to form the Tresoar, Friesland's primary study and research centre. For a number of years the Kanselarij was used for all sorts of mostly unworthy functions, until about ten years ago it became part of a considerably enlarged Fries Museum, one of the richest regional museums in the country. In the not too distant future it will be abandoned again because of plans to erect a new museum on the great Zaailand square, thanks to a bequest from the architect Bonnema. My heart goes out to the Kanselarij.

Leeuwarden became a centre of trade, mainly agrarian, so the fact that it expressed its Renaissance style in a typical weigh-house and not in a city hall is quite revealing. Urban development again took place mainly in the southwest, where beyond the Herengracht, the city's old defence moat, the Zaailand was drawn into the city. Leeuwarden had already been equipped with ramparts and a moat years before, and after this later expansion modern fortified defences were built. But work on the defences was discontinued after the armed struggle moved to the Southern Netherlands. The bastions on the southeastern corner of the otherwise exemplary fortifications were never completed.

At the beginning of the nineteenth century Leeuwarden was one of the first cities in the country to espouse the ideals of the Enlightenment and do something about its shabby appearance. It underwent a complete facelift, paving its quays, streets and alleys, followed by the dismantling and then landscaping of its ramparts, making it the first city in the country, along with Haarlem and Utrecht, to do so. This meant that by as early as the mid-nineteenth century it was a clean and open Leeuwarden that entered the new era.

During the second half of the nineteenth century a number of canals were filled in for hygienic reasons, resulting in the broad streets with series of names: the Turfmarkt, Tweebaksmarkt, Druifstreek and the Eewal-Wortelhaven. By filling in the Herengracht, the badly deteriorated Zaailand could be turned into the spacious Wilhelminaplein. At the end of the century the Stationskwartier was created, the first urban development project since the end of the 1860s, followed by eastern expansion on both sides of the Nieuwe Kanaal. Urban development proceeded steadily during the twentieth century in a more or less radial pattern, drawing on past experience.

While the Kanselarij was erected in awe-inspiring splendour in sixteenth-century Leeuwarden and still makes a big impression on account of its sheer size, the building across the street at 48 Tweebaksmarkt strikes one at first as nothing but a little architectural trifle. The building's special character didn't really hit me until the mid-seventies, when it was in danger of being disfigured. A few like-minded individuals set up a foundation to defend Friesland's recent architecture, which at the time was still without legal protection. The building, a branch of De Utrecht insurance company, was erected in 1904. It had been designed by the then very young architects Kropholler and J.F. Staal in a style that, under the influence of Berlage, can be regarded as the Amsterdam variant of art nouveau. The building was saved and became the home of a good restoration workshop for fine painting and stained glass.

On the outside of the building, the carvings by Jozeph Mendes da Costa announce that this is something quite special. But the real splendour is mainly on the inside: decorated panelling on walls and ceilings, stained-glass windows, tile tableaux and a striking number of rhymed proverbs and catchphrases from the world of life insurance mounted on ceiling beams and doors. On the door panels leading to the large and small office is the great lie of the insurance trade: 'From the chrysalis of the insurance premium the golden butterfly of capital will surely grow'. The verse on the frame around the fireplace is the most bizarre: 'Lighting a fire in this hearth / Will shield you from the cold / Make sure the shield of insurance / Guards you from the scourge of fate'. On the beautifully carved and richly painted roof beams over the windows we read 'ziet in 't verschiet' ('look to the future') and 'ijl een wijl' ('keep up the pace'), above the door 'kom weerom' ('call again') and above the office window 'eisch naar prijs' ('demand value for money') and 'telt uw geld' ('count your money'). And there's a great deal more monetarily inspired doggerel to be enjoyed in this captivating little building.

De Utrecht branch office. One of the nine stained-glass windows with the arms of the cities where the company had branches. These include Amsterdam and Rotterdam, but also Copenhagen, Brussels (photo) and Lille. Photo by Peter Karstkarel.

De Utrecht branch office. Richly decorated coffered ceiling, walls with tiled friezes and stained-glass windows. Photo by Peter Karstkarel.

The money was mainly counted by the insurance companies. Thanks to mutual insurance arrangements by farmers in the past, Leeuwarden is one of the cities where the insurance system has put down deep roots. The city is one of the bases for a few giants, such as Aegon and Achmea. Their office buildings dominate the Leeuwarden skyline. When we first came to town the Stationskwartier still smelled of cows (the cattle market had just been moved to a covered market complex), but afterwards we witnessed the rise of the office-building landscape. I threw myself into the breach at one point to prevent the demolition of a powder-white villa that was to make room for a new Chamber of Commerce building. I also came to the assistance of another lovely nineteenth-century structure, with partial success.

But sometimes it was a case of tilting at windmills. The attempts were of no avail for the western part of the Stationskwartier, but in fact that was a good thing. For 35 years I watched as Langemarktstraat was transformed into a Manhattanised insurance mall with genuine skyscrapers designed by the Leeuwarden architect Abe Bonnema, he of the new Fries Museum bequest. Elsewhere Bonnema had built the tallest office tower in the Netherlands: the

The office towers of Leeuwarden's financial services industry. Photo by Peter Karstkarel.

Nationale Nederlanden building in Rotterdam's station district. So does my Leeuwarden count? I'm happy either way, but for Bonnema it was a matter of real importance. Shortly before his death, as we stood chatting beside his almost completed Achmea office tower rising well over 100 metres, he told me the following, in Liwwadders: *'Ja jong, Liwwadden ferdiend un nij silhouet, die sielege Oldehove krije we niet meer ou'* ('Yes, my young friend, Leeuwarden deserves a new silhouette. That miserable Oldehove is with us for good'). ■

Translated by Nancy Forest-Flier

Yes, But

Rembrandt as an Unstable Medium

[GARY SCHWARTZ]

Sand Sculpure Festival,
Thorn 2003.

Rembrandt studies are a nerve-racking field. It is nearly impossible to write a proper paragraph about the artist or his work without stepping on the toes – or kicking the shins, depending on your mood – of a colleague. Part of this is due to the argumentative nature of scholars and part to the equivocal personality of the artist. By the time he arrived on the scene at the age of eighteen or nineteen, the man had set in swing a dialectic that has never since come to rest. Students of Rembrandt never had a chance.

The very first words written about Rembrandt's art, jotted down in Leiden in 1628 by a visiting humanist from Utrecht, lay down the terms. *'The Leiden miller's son is highly praised, but before his time.'* How could he know? Was Arnoldus Buchelius such a genius of premonition that, while slighting the Leiden miller's son for not living up to his hype, he divined future greatness? I think not. My suspicion is that he was simply annoyed that his host, the Haarlem-Leiden humanist Theodorus Schrevelius, was touting in superlatives a young artist whose better qualities were indiscernible to him. From the word go, admiration for Rembrandt was offset by annoyances and uncertainties of various kinds.

An abrasive personality

Going beyond Buchelius's *'sed ante tempus'* – 'but before his time' – to more highly articulated complaints about Rembrandt, we come across five main kinds of shaky vibes:

- questionable taste
- personality issues
- financial unreliability
- sloppy craftsmanship
- attributional insecurity.

Objections to Rembrandt's taste have a certain unpleasant flavour of their own. They betray physical discomfort on the part of the critics, combined with snobbism and art-theoretical disdain. All of this is expressed in Andries Pels' disapproving remarks on the bodies and social class of Rembrandt's models:

If he came to paint a naked woman, as he sometimes did,
He took for a model not a Greek Venus
But rather a washerwoman or a turf stomper from a shed,
Calling his fallacy the imitation of Nature
And all the rest vain adornment. Hanging breasts,
Twisted hands, even the imprint of the bands
Of the corset on the belly, the garters on the legs
It all had to be followed, or nature would be dissatisfied.

To this Samuel van Hoogstraten adds censure of the coupling dogs in a Rembrandt painting of the preaching of St John the Baptist, while the defecating mutt in the foreground of the etched *Good Samaritan* was sufficient evidence for some later connoisseurs to remove the print entirely from Rembrandt's oeuvre. While I have no sympathy with this line of criticism, I cannot help but observe that there are a good number of art lovers who feel that Rembrandt invades their personal space and violates their code of propriety. In general they will not admit this, finding fault instead with the quality of the offending works. This introduces a false element into the discussion that is difficult – say impossible – to correct. In this it resembles the unhelpful discussion about the taste of Robert Mapplethorpe in relation to the merit of his art.

That Rembrandt had a (possibly related) personality problem speaks clearly from the documents. In preparation for a Rembrandt website, I inserted into

Rembrandt van Rijn,
The Good Samaritan. 1633.
Etching. 24.7 x 20.3 cm.
Museum Het Rembrandthuis,
Amsterdam.

a database the basic facts in the known documents referring to Rembrandt and his works. Of the 509 documents in the system at the time of writing, 157 relate to twenty-five different conflicts. The other parties, in alphabetical order, were agents, art dealers, artists, craftsmen, creditors, debtors, merchants, neighbours, nobility, officials, patrons, professionals, regents, relatives, servants and tradesmen. The many colleagues of mine who refuse to admit that Rembrandt had an abrasive personality do not care to look this record in the face. Personally, I am sufficiently impressed by it to offer a reward to anyone who can show a matching record in the biography of any other Dutch or Flemish artist.

Of his financial unreliability Rembrandt himself was a prime victim, but so were his son and friends who lent him money that they never saw again, not in cash nor in the form of frequently promised and never delivered works of art. Rembrandt's relationships with others were riddled with bad debt.

'*My X-year-old can do that*' is the present-day form of a complaint Rembrandt had to endure from ill-wishing critics. Especially his later works were attacked for fudging over difficulties. '*Great painters*,' Abraham Bruegel wrote to a Rembrandt patron, '*are not usually willing to lower themselves for a trifling draped half-length in which the light shows only the tip of the nose... this kind of painter does the contours so that one does not know what to make out of it...*'

For the art historian, the direst form of instability in the Rembrandt perplex is attributional insecurity. An early instance of this phenomenon is to be found in no less authoritative a source than the papers of Stadholder Frederik Hendrik.

Rembrandt van Rijn, *Simeon's Prophecy to Mary.* c.1628. Panel. 55.5 x 44 cm. Kunsthalle, Hamburg.

The well-informed clerk who in 1632 drew up the inventory of the prince's possessions entered a painting in the cabinet of His Excellency as *'A painting in which Simeon, being in the Temple, has Christ in his arms, done by rembrants or Jan Lievensz.'* This was an item that cannot have been acquired by the court longer than five years earlier. Let this example, dating from a time when Rembrandt was barely twenty-five years old, stand as a symbolic as well as concrete example of the problem. (The fact that we are not sure whether the painting concerned is the version in Hamburg, of 1629, or that in The Hague, of 1632, does not make matters any better.)

Lifetimes for the cause of art history

Like politicians and captains of industry, art historians have traditional ways of dealing with these issues.

1. No comment. If you do not *have* to deal with these impossible problems, don't.
2. Deny they exist. If you are forced to comment, try this one first. Denial is still the option of choice for historians unwilling to acknowledge Rembrandt's personality problems.
3. If they are proven to exist, shrug them off as being irrelevant. Say that Rembrandt's financial shenanigans took place in a completely different universe than his artistic production, which is marked by spotless integrity.
4. When the instability concerned is shown to impact massively on Rembrandt studies, say that you knew about it all along anyway and that it has been discounted by the field. This ploy is applicable in all cases.

Evasive tactics such as these actually have a certain point beyond sheer self-defence. To acknowledge the complete range of difficulties in arriving at a comprehensive and responsible image of Rembrandt and his art is to acknowledge the impossibility of succeeding at the task. Consider only the dilemma of the Rembrandt Research Project. Six top talents joined forces in the years following a large Rembrandt exhibition in 1956 to tackle only one of the five conundrums, and then only in part: attributional uncertainty regarding Rembrandt's paintings. Since the inception of the project some forty years have passed; more hours have been spent on it than the working life of any one mortal, perhaps two or more. Despite this monumental effort, as of the year 2006 the RRP has not got beyond about half the paintings that come into consideration. If one extrapolates on this record, one arrives at a total of some five lifetimes needed to answer the RRP's initial question : which paintings are by Rembrandt and which are not? Add a lifetime or two to answer the same question concerning drawings and etchings.

But even an attempt on that scale, if we go by the experience of the RRP, is doomed to failure. With the appearance of vol. 4 of the *Corpus of Rembrandt Paintings* in 2005, the project revamped its methodology drastically, diluting its original ambition, stirring in some new criteria for Rembrandtness and reversing several previous judgments. Because the RRP is not redoing vols. 1-3, even if it manages to cover all the relevant paintings in volumes to come it will not have solved the attributional dilemma but only exacerbated it.

The above remarks are limited to complications arising in Rembrandt's lifetime. The confusions that emerged after his death are so extreme that some art historians write of 'Rembrandt' for the legend in opposition to the historical personality Rembrandt van Rijn. If only they were that easy to keep apart.

Rembrandt van Rijn,
Self-Portrait in Oriental Attire. 1631.
Panel, 66.5 x 52 cm.
Musee du Petit Palais, Paris

Rembrandt van Rijn,
Self-Portrait as a Beggar.
1630. Etching, 11.6 x 6.9 cm.
Kunsthalle, Hamburg.

My own first entry into this battlefield was on the coattails of a past master, the late Horst Gerson (1907-1978). As assistant to Gerson in his contribution to the 350th anniversary of Rembrandt's death in 1969, a monumental book called *Rembrandt Paintings*, I arranged the catalogue section and wrote capsule texts for each double spread. Under the cover of Gerson's authority, I was able to launch a number of new ideas. For example, I broke up the category 'self-por-traits', which I mistrusted, inserting the self-portraits into the general rubric 'Portraits and studies'. My work under Gerson was a high-powered initiation into Rembrandt studies.

With the first Big Rembrandt Year since 1969 upon us, I find myself at a more advanced age than Gerson in 1969 out there on my own, without an assistant, writing a book in which I am trying to do justice to Rembrandt's drawings and etchings as well as his paintings, life and milieu. I find myself dependent on, and in competition with, not only the field at large but also myself of thirty-seven years ago. That isn't the worst of it. Halfway back, twenty-two years ago, I wrote a book on Rembrandt's life and paintings that leaned heavily in its at-tributions on the work of Gerson and the RRP while going far further in its treatment of Rembrandt's life. Leaving attributional uncertainty to these con-noisseurs, I set out to synthesise what we know about Rembrandt's life in com-bination with the accepted paintings. Given the uncertainties regarding the paintings as well as the doubts regarding the adequacy of the documentary coverage, this was like crossing a wild cold river with ice floes as snowshoes. I am convinced that I reached the opposite bank, but not everyone is.

Be that as it may, I am now dependent on and in competition with that book of 1984 as well. This compounds the instability attending Rembrandt studies with imbalances introduced by my own new interests and ideas. Who wants to simply repeat the ideas and examples of others, even if the other is your former self? So I step on my own toes and kick my own shins.

The problem with Rembrandt, once one is resigned to the impossibility of capturing him entire, is how to deal with the Yes and the But. In the biography, too much Yes leads to hero worship, too much But to a misanthropic image of the man that no one is willing to accept. In attributions, too much Yes creates an oeuvre lacking in critical definition, too much But a corpus that eliminates work of high quality for which no other candidate is available.

It is easy to repeat the cliché that the truth lies in the middle, but in this case that will not do. There is no middle-of-the-road consensus concerning attribu-tions, only the overblown, self-contradictory authority of the Rembrandt Research Project on the one hand and some fulminating, helpless critics on the other. Nor is there a biographical Rembrandt image one can fall back on, if only on account of wildly conflicting opinions concerning his role in the incarceration of his mis-tress Geertge Dircx.

Welcome, then, to the Rembrandt Year 2006. What will it bring us? Will the impossibility of dealing with Rembrandt/'Rembrandt' only increase? Or will the aggregate of contributions – more than 60 exhibitions and God knows how many books – finally turn the corner from Yes, But in the direction of But Yes! ■

www.codart.nl/rembrandt_2006

www.garyschwartzarthistorian.nl

'Nothing worthwhile ever happens, except maybe some acts of consolation'

Literature according to Herman Brusselmans

Herman Brusselmans, the self-proclaimed Handsome Young Jupiter of Flemish literature, is nothing if not prolific. Since his debut in 1982 he has published two books a year with clockwork regularity and his total production now exceeds thirty titles. His first effort, a collection of stories, was not an immediate hit, but in the novels that followed it Brusselmans (1957-) attracted an ever-growing band of readers with his humorous, semi-autobiographical accounts of the of-ten less than scintillating life of a young man afflicted with angst and melan-choly in the 1980s. Brusselmans brought sex, music and booze – in short, rock 'n roll – into Flemish literature, and the effect was all the more dramatic since at that moment the literary scene in Flanders was dominated by a 'quiet gen-eration' of writers, whose subdued, neo-romantically-inclined work was more redolent of lavender soap than of beer and cigarettes. Sex, music and alcoholic beverages always have a wide appeal, and magazine and TV producers soon realised they were on to a good thing. Brusselmans found himself writing col-umns for numerous publications in Flanders and Holland and working on many TV shows in the role of joker and provocateur to which he was ideally suited. Since that time, the early 1990s, Herman Brusselmans has been a genuine Flemish Celebrity. With the appearance of each new book he is interviewed in the major dailies and weeklies and invited to appear on all kinds of talk shows. As the son of a livestock dealer Brusselmans knows how to run a business. He made clever use of his newly acquired status and started to introduce all kinds of well-known models, TV presenters and other media figures into his books. Media attention is guaranteed, and many people prefer reading about someone they know from the TV rather than some fictional character. In 1999, however, Brusselmans came unstuck: in one of his books he called the celebrated Flemish fashion designer Ann Demeulemeester *a frog-eyed dwarf polyp* and she took him to court. He lost the case, the book was withdrawn from sale, and though Brusselmans was by now quite comfortably off, he had not reckoned with the financial headache this would give him. From then on he has taken a more cautious line, though the case of course attracted considerable media attention and confirmed his reputation as a provocateur. These days Brusselmans is if anything better known as a Flemish Celebrity than as a writer: when he married for the second time in 2005 there was wide coverage in newspapers, magazines and even gossip sheets. He sells more books than many Dutch-language authors could ever dream of: between 10,000 and 20,000 copies per book. But what sort of books are they?

I'm glad I've stopped doing autobiography

Stylistically Herman Brusselmans takes his cue mainly from his literary idols Gerard Reve and J.D. Salinger. From the former he has adopted the heavily archaic and ceremonial language, which when combined with banal events produces humorous effects, and the quasi-religious, prayer-like monologues. Echoes of Salinger's *The Catcher in the Rye* can be found in the streetwise slang in which every word is preceded by 'damn' and every sentence begins with 'I mean'. In fact, Brusselmans has written his own version of the latter book. *Gorgeous Eyes* (Prachtige ogen), from 1984, which chronicles the empty hours of Julius Cramp, a student of Germanic languages at Ghent University, echoes Salinger's classic in many respects. Mix the archaic language registers with the street talk, puncture the conventions of the traditional novel, pour on lavish amounts of absurd, Monty Python-style humour, add a few zany or sadistic sex scenes, a dash of rock music, a few politically incorrect pronouncements about women, homosexuals, the handicapped or blacks, combine with a main character suffering from a host of anxieties and depressions who can be consoled only by the women he loves, top with the occasional melancholy childhood memory, and there you have the standard recipe for a Brusselmans book. Brusselmans uses the same ingredients each time, but the result is always different. Because he writes (semi-)autobiographically, the content invariably depends on what he is experiencing at the moment of writing. In that respect one can see a watershed in his work, which comes with the book *Old News about These Times* (Het oude nieuws van deze tijden, 1994).

Brusselmans had his first success in the mid-1980s with *The Man who Found a Job* (De man die werk vond, 1985), a book that in more than one respect recalls Gerard Reve's *The Evenings* (De avonden, 1947) and deserves to become as great a classic. It tells the story of Louis Tinner, who works in the staff recreational library of the Department of Employment in Brussels, where Brusselmans himself was once employed. He spends his days in absolute idleness in his stuffy office. In *Today I'm Sober* (Heden ben ik nuchter, 1986) and *Are there Canals in Aalst?* (Zijn er kanalen in Aalst?, 1987) the main character is called Eduard Kronenburg. His job too is fairly uninspiring: Kronenburg has to phone pensioners on behalf of some government department to ask if they are still alive. Still, he experiences more than Tinner in the previous book: he is married to Gloria (in reality Brusselmans' first wife Gerda), spends his days joking and drinking with his colleagues and, besides his quite successful marriage to Gloria, becomes infatuated with a string of girls called Valium, Sunshine, Splendide, Pico or Mabiche. In a wonderful, moving chapter at the end of *Are there Canals in Aalst?* Kronenburg firmly resolves to become a writer: 'Later, as he got into his car, he was still thinking of Mabiche: you made me give up my job, my sweet bitch, and you made me mumble innumerable epilogues, and you made me feel that I can love two people more than I love myself... Perhaps you even turned me into a writer. But goddammit you're worth it. You're a symbol, Mabiche, a symbol of how it might have been. He got into the car, said to Gloria: "I love you,"* *and cursed all the words that were ever used to communicate.'*

In his following books, the first that Brusselmans wrote as a professional author, the protagonist is usually called simply Herman Brusselmans. Things are not going too well either for the writer or for the main character in his books, who is only able to keep his anxieties in check by drinking himself into a stupor every day and popping tranquillisers. He experiences turbulent times, filled with tempestuous love affairs, nervous crises, alcoholic excesses, para-lysing existential doubt, sentimentality and cynicism and deep depressions. The years 1990-1992 were a period of very real crisis for the author: his marriage to Gerda collapsed on 1 June 1991 and his mother, of whom he had written in *Gorgeous Eyes*: *'If there is one human being who deserves a monument, it's my mother,'* died on 16 June 1992. Those facts are simply reported in his books, which switch back and forth between fiction and reality. Beside dates, he also gives exact locations in Ghent, the city where he lives, and real people crop up in his stories. It is always difficult to tell what is 'real' and what invented. Brusselmans plays on this uncertainty.

His crisis years are described in the famous 'Ex' trilogy that comprises *Ex-Writer* (Ex-schrijver, 1991), *Ex-Lover* (Ex-minnaar, 1993) and *Ex-drummer* (1994). The loss of his wife and his mother regularly drive him to poignant elegiac re-flections, which then recur at regular intervals in his later books: *'I shatter into a thousand fragments; I burst out of my skin with desire when I think of Gloria; I flood the floor with tears when I think of Gloria.'* (*Ex-Writer*) His mother's death robs him of his belief in God: *'My hatred for the God who let my mother die, thus proving that He does not exist, goes so deep that I have never, and certainly not now at Christmas, wanted my mother to arise from her grave, and walk by my side, because that would only be possible through Divine Intervention, and I no longer grant God Divine Interventions after His last one, on 16 June 1992, when, breaking His promises, He took my mother's life.'* (*Ex-Lover*)

But then something changes. *Old News about These Times* represents a clean slate, a resurrection. Brusselmans has stopped drinking, has a new stable re-lationship with Phoebe (in reality Tania) and buys a dog, in the book called Speedy and in life Woody, *'a splendid little creature with intelligent eyes'.* Brusselmans' life becomes calmer, more settled , and consequently also duller. For readers of his books that is a regrettable development, but the writer feels differently: *'Occasionally, it occurred to me, one might conclude that I have an empty life. Nothing wrong with that, I've savoured the fullness of life in the past. It was a very exhausting time, when the peaks were too high and the troughs too low, and plateaus were quicksand. Now I do circuits in a solid, roomy cage and it's a lot more reliable. There's nothing more to look forward to, except death, and that will come in its own good time.'* (*Old News about These Times*). And: *'I'm glad I've stopped doing autobiography. You have to describe all that pain, all those wounds, all that desire, all that love, I couldn't face it any more.'* (*The Ghost of Toetegaai –* Het spook van Toetegaai, 2005)

Herman loves Tania

The consequence of this emptier life is that Brusselmans no longer experi-ences anything of note to fill a book with. In such a situation someone who writes for a living does two things: he writes down the few things he has to say, and repeats them ad infinitum. For example, that he loves Tania De Metsenaere. Apart from that he uses his imagination. He starts writing more fiction. And that is precisely not Brusselmans' strong point. He is not good at developing a believable story, and he has gallantly admitted as much in his books. Both in the Guggenheimer trilogy (*The Return of Bonanza* – De terugkeer van Bonanza, *Guggenheimer Washes Whiter* – Guggenheimer wast witter and *Guggenheimer Publishers* – Uitgeverij Guggenheimer) and in *Pitface* (2001) or *The Ghost of Toetegaai*, the characters are more or less caricatures and the story line is very thin. In order to fill the pages Brusselmans starts undermining fictional conventions too explicitly. Semi-sophisticated meta-passages like the following, about a rather flat character in his latest novel, abound in his later work, but make for pretty dull reading: *'You can't determine from my literature what Indra is like. What kind of character, what kind of personality is she? Your guess is as good as mine. There's nothing explicit about her. She's just a young archaeologist who snorts coke and muddles through and crops up in the life of someone like me, who will very likely soon get rid of her, painlessly.'* (*The Ghost of Toetegaai*).

But the author is not bothered by this criticism. Since his book of the same name Herman Brusselmans calls himself an 'ex-writer', although he only really became one in *Old News about These Times*. The books preceding it sprang from a certain belief in the consoling or therapeutic function of autobiographical prose. He lost that belief during his crisis years: *'All a writer must aim for (...) is to become an ex-writer, so that he finally realises the literature he has produced is worthless. Has never saved anyone from death. Has never shown anyone true love. Has never brought anyone to his own god, and never will.'* (*Ex-Writer*). More and more Brusselmans persuades the reader that literature is no match for reality. In his latest book Brusselmans is home alone, while his wife, who used to be called Phoebe in his books but is now simply called by her real name of Tania, has gone to Paris for her work. Together with the ashes of his dog Woody, who has just died, he waits for 336 pages for her return. The book's ending reads: *'We waited, my dead doggy and I. Tania came home. Reality finally took over again.'* 'Herman Brusselmans loves Tania De Metsenaere' is the only autobiographical fact Brusselmans now considers worth mentioning in his books.

Choose life

Since his personal crisis Herman Brusselmans no longer writes in order to realise some artistic or autobiographical project, he writes because that is how he earns money: *'I'm a true writer, because I write firstly for money and secondly to banish other people's boredom for an hour or two, with stories about how their lives might have been or, if necessary, how they are. A real writer has no other job.'* Elsewhere he states: *'Writing is adding words.'* Not the usual view of literature, but a defensible one: why shouldn't a novel be as much a consumer item as any other product on the market? Something you read for a moment's entertainment and then throw away. Something for an instant, and not for all eternity? Literature can't do anything radical – it couldn't even stop Brusselmans' first marriage from going on the rocks or his mother from dying. So you shouldn't take it seriously.

For any autobiographical writer there comes a moment when the tension between literature and life becomes unbearable. In order not to be destroyed by this Brusselmans ultimately chose life. But the paradox remains that he can only live the way he does by producing literature, and that he wrote his finest books at a time before he had yet made such a clear choice. Brusselmans is at his best in his prose from the late 1980s and early 1990s, imbued with existential angst and longing, pain, love and desire, in his two great trilogies: one a trilogy in all but name (*The Man who Found a Job*, *Today I'm Sober* and *Are there Canals*

Hermans Brusselmans,
Tania De Metsenaere
and Woody.
© Puch en Tomos Club
Vlaanderen.

in Aalst?), and the previously mentioned Ex-trilogy. Those six books are anything but throwaway literature. They are some of the best writing to come out of the Low Countries in that period.

Hence Brusselmans' later deprecation of his own craft creates resentment in many readers. They feel made fun of by Brusselmans' prose, partly because in most of his books not a great deal *happens*. But that, says Brusselmans, is *'because [I have] written the truth: nothing worthwhile ever happens, except perhaps some acts of consolation.'* (*Ex-Writer*). That is the core message of Brusselmans' work. That, and the awareness that there are more important things in the world than literature. Tania De Metsenaere, for example. And one's mother: *'If my mother could have been granted another five years of life in exchange for the complete works of Beckett, my dearest wish would have been that the bastard had never put one word down on paper.'* (*Ex-Lover*, p. 92). ∎

The work of Herman Brusselmans is published by Prometheus, Amsterdam.

Translated by Paul Vincent

Two Extracts

by Hermans Brusselmans

Hands over my ears

'Can I have another vodka and orange?' asked Carla.

'No,' I said.

'I'm off home then.'

'Fine.'

'Are you coming?'

'Maybe. I haven't finished my whisky and coke.'

'OK, I'll wait.' She waited while I took my time.

'I thumped someone tonight,' I said as I drank, 'for no reason, just some passer-by. Bang, fist in the face. Then I was off.'

'Yes,' she said, staring straight ahead in a daze, not understanding a word I'd said, 'I feel the same sometimes, especially when I'm alone.' She was already preparing for our intimate moment, unaware it was going to be a flop, at least on my side; she didn't know I would try to offend her, hurt her; that I would treat her like dirt and the next time we met would greet her with a 'Hi there, how are you doing, how's things?' and leave it at that. My glass was empty.

'Let's go,' I said.

We left. Outside there was still a slight commotion resulting from the routine collision between the two cars. Carla was nosy (wanted to look under the blanket and see who it was, that sort of thing), but I said we had to get moving.

I checked to see if some bastard (who I'd get even with some other time) had bent my mirrors, scratched my petrol tank, or snapped off the accelerator pedal. No, everything was fine.

'Hey,' said Carla, 'it's the motorbike from that photo in the paper!'

'Yes,' I said, 'but listen, I've only got one helmet. So you'll have to do without. If the cops catch us you'll pay the fine, OK?' She gave me a worried, almost anxious look.

'OK,' she said. If she'd had any sense, she'd have told me then and there: 'Leave me alone. I'll go home by myself. Beat it.' But horny women and sense just don't go together, and even before I'd started up she was on the pillion.

'Nice,' she said.

'Where do you live?' I asked. She told me her address. It was a bloody long way on the bike, almost on the other side of town. I took it slowly, being fairly pissed.

'Won't it go any faster?' the bitch asked.

'Of course it will,' I said. But I'm almost out of petrol so it's best to go as slow as possible.'

'That's true,' she said. Oh yes? I wondered, is it true? Best go as slowly as you can when you're almost out of petrol? And how come a bitch like her knows, and I don't? Who gives a fuck?

'This city,' I said suddenly, without taking my eyes off the road,' seems peaceful at first sight…'

'What?' yelled Carla.

'Nothing,' I roared, and went on: '… it's like an orphanage, an old folks' home, a mortuary – compared with psychiatric hospitals and abattoirs like Paris, or New York, or Antwerp. But that's just an illusion. Here too all kinds of incomprehensible things happen behind walls, in houses, above and below ground. Here too there are meetings of fascist groups. Here too children are sexually abused by their fathers, here too women are beaten up by their useless drunken husbands for no explicit reason, here too victims hang in cellars tied to sandbags shitting themselves, here too students and old people, mental defectives and addicts and ordinary pigeons and god knows who else die, of loneliness, or grief, or pent-up fury, or hopeless longing, or gas fumes. Or just of some disease. Here too it's seething with wounds oozing pus, backs torn open, badly set fractures, chronically runny noses, decaying glands, exploding hearts, wrecked livers, shrivelling kidneys, fermenting brains… Is this the street?'

'Is *this* the street?' I repeated loudly. We were nearly there, I thought. 'I said, is this the street?!' I screamed.

'Next on the right!' shouted Carla.

Number seventeen was quite a big house and not too run-down for this mostly deprived area. Who paid the damn rent? Mummy or Daddy I expect, but that was their problem. (Even if it was Santa Claus who paid the damn rent.)

'What were you going on about on the way here?' asked Carla. We got off.

'What?'

'I asked what you were going on about on the way here.'

'I was singing a couple of songs,' I said. She opened the door.

'Quiet,' she said, 'my neighbours are asleep. I'm on the second floor.' And I thought she had the whole place to herself.

I followed her upstairs. The house smelled of unshaved women's armpits and men who seldom changed their underpants. Carla opened the door of her room, and we went in. She switched on a dim light. It was an unpleasant room, crammed with all kinds of clutter that I would have thrown out long ago, or rather wouldn't have carted up here in the first place. On the wall there was a lousy, dated Jim Morrison poster, a stupid painting, an advert for a Lou Reed gig at Vorst Nationaal and a notice board with thousands of photos pinned to it, doubtless mainly of Carla herself (bloody summer snaps).

I sat down in a really expensive chair, designed by the Ghent seating guru Rafaël Verzeeveren. 'How did you come by a Verzeeveren chair like this?' I asked.

'I was given it,' she said, 'I sometimes baby-sit for Rafaël.'

'Christ, has he got kids?' I said. 'You know, I can't stand people who call themselves artists and still have kids.' She looked at me in surprise.

'What have the two things got to do with each other? Picasso had kids too.'

'Do you call Picasso an artist?' I said menacingly.

'Uh… I don't know…' said Carla, 'perhaps not, no…' She walked about awkwardly. Shifting ashtrays, moving her coat, and so on.

'Do you want a drink?' she asked. I was about to ask if she had any whisky, but bitches like her never have any whisky, and anyway I was drunk enough already, so I said: 'I'll just have a glass of tap water.' She rushed to her kitchenette like a madwoman to fetch me a glass of water.

'There you are,' she said. She was panting restlessly – she wanted sex. I was sorry for her (but not very).

'Is something wrong?' I asked. She dithered, hesitated, then could contain herself no longer and yelled: 'I'm getting horny! I want to go to bed with you!' There, she'd got if off her chest.

'No so loud,' I said, 'think of the neighbours.'

'But I want to go to bed with you. I want to be fucked.' She tore her clothes off. I lit a cigarette. Her clothes were nothing special. Boutique stuff. Pink lingerie, but not sexy. Peasant-style shorts and a peasant style blouse, as far as I could tell. Designer socks. In short, she could have done better. When she was naked and stood before me trembling fit to burst, I said: 'Let's take it nice and easy. Lie down on the bed.'

I drank some of the water. Hard. That's what you get in these parts of town: the water pipes are virtually never de-scaled. The council's reasoning is: 'Let the poor, the underprivileged and the lousy foreigners absorb plenty of calcium, it'll give them good strong bones and make them sturdier, which in the long run will actually save the health service money.' No, there are no flies on the town council.

The girl tossed about feverishly on the bed, rubbing her breasts back and forth over the fairly grubby sheets.

'Now what?' she asked, eagerly and already aroused and sweating, 'when are you coming?'

'I want you to masturbate first,' I said. She moaned with excitement. Just hearing the word 'masturbate' made her moan.

'Does it excite you when I masturbate?' she asked. Saliva was running over her lips and down her chin.

'Start slowly,' I said, 'and then speed up.' She had already started. She had two fingers of one hand in her cunt and with her other she squeezed her breasts and nipples. After a while she began biting the sheets and making noises like a sheep with compulsive bleating syndrome. She should be climaxing in less than a minute, I estimated.

I finished the hard water (doesn't taste too bad actually), stubbed out my cigarette and just before the screaming started, I said: 'My God, you're ugly.' I got up and left, hands over my ears.

From *Ex-Lover* (Ex-minnaar). Amsterdam: Prometheus, 1993, pp. 25-29

There's no way God exists

If I simply didn't turn up in the morning, thought Louis, no one would notice.

For a moment he was very taken with the idea and was already making plans for the next day.

There's no point, he reflected immediately afterwards, there's nowhere for me to go. This is a place like any other. Running away is not an option. I'm doing a life sentence. When I'm eighty I may suddenly be happy. I'll have four years of happiness ahead of me. That's plenty of time.

He ate a fourth sandwich and read the paper.

That soon bored him to tears.

He dropped by to see the photocopying girl. It was a good idea. He could see her stretching, an endearing morning gesture, especially in young girls – and so he spotted the tufts under her arms.

She did not use the appliance known as Ladyshave, thought Louis. I prefer naked female armpits, but this is nice too. It must be a turn-on in bed.

He walked around.

Although I'm reflecting on certain sexual situations, he said to himself, I'm still not getting an erection. That's a plus point. It must be terrible getting an erection the moment you have erotic thoughts. Not only is there a considerable risk that others will see it, there's also the danger of being terrified you've lost control. Constant fear of erection must be deeply tragic. Women don't have this fear. And if they do, that's even more tragic.

Louis tapped the ash from his cigarette onto the floor of the library, despite the presence of several ashtrays.

He was still strolling along the book-filled shelves.

This early morning isn't too bad, he admitted, I've known worse. The loneliness is bearable, not one book title is giving me a panic attack and at present I have no physical ailments. No one is knocking ominously at the door, outside the rain is nice and summery and this week is going to be warm and pleasant. I'm thinking of beads of sweat running from under armpits and across breasts, and still I'm getting no embarrassing, pointless erection. I'm just walking about a bit, smoking a really nice cigarette and there are no major threats. I'm a happy man.

Louis felt a longing for music welling up. He still hadn't brought in a portable radio. Mains radios were out, they cost the government money.

So, very briefly, he hummed a tune to himself, the refrain of a song called 'Home Thoughts from Abroad'.

Louis' humming wasn't a patch on the original. He sat down.

'What do I do now?' he said. These, he knew, were the difficult moments. You've been going along nicely for a while, but suddenly things change. Like suddenly falling into an abyss.

If I wanted to... thought Louis, I could write a book about it. He sniggered.

Write a book... he continued, a book about my work and ideas. I can't imagine anyone wanting to read it. Perhaps it's already been written and has been somewhere on these shelves for years gathering mildew.

He banished all thoughts of books and looked around, lazily smoking.

My predecessor in this building died, he thought. Cancer. It was a woman. It's a crying shame that women get cancer too. It's supposed to be a male thing. But women get it too.

He thought of a girl he'd known, at school.

She had leukaemia.

Lovely young girl's breasts, thought Louis, and long, slender legs… There's no way God exists…

There was a knock.

At last, thought Louis. It's like the blindfolded man who senses the firing squad is there and when he hears a bang knows the bullets are on their way. At last, thinks the man. 'Yes,' he said calmly.

It was a guided tour for new members of staff.

The guide, someone from Personnel, seemed quite new to the job himself. At any rate he was very nervous and told the fifteen or so recruits they were now in the staff recreational library.

'That's right,' said Louis, assuming a grotesquely cheerful mask. I must look ghastly, he thought, but no one seems to notice. The guide is a bundle of nerves, why should I be?

Although he had a horror of crowds, Louis felt no fear. 'Come in,' he said, 'it's not private, whatever it says on the door. You should never trust notices on doors.'

They stared at him.

They're being subjected to gobbledygook, thought Louis, and on their first day at work.

'Do come in,' he repeated, 'come closer. This is the recreational library. I'm in charge of it. I'm the librarian, Tinner's the name.'

The though flashed through his mind: I expect they'll think I'm really important.

Meanwhile he'd had a good look at them all, sorted them out in his mind, and so addressed his absurd explanation to a young woman, enigmatically beautiful, despite a scar above her left eyebrow.

Like Nadia, he thought, a fall in the skating rink. The ghosts keep coming back.

'The idea is,' he held forth, 'for you to avail yourself of the opportunity to borrow books, especially books to help you relax. This library is an integral part of the Social Services that the department you have just joined are committed to provide.' Bullshit, he thought, and ungrammatical. Yet some of them were listening intently.

The girl with the scar looked extremely uninterested. Just like Nadia too, thought Louis. Perhaps she is Nadia. He looked at her closely, but no, it wasn't Nadia. This woman was mixed-race, Nadia was white.

Strange, skin colours, thought Louis.

He'd once longed to be black, singing along with the cotton-pickers. It was one longing of his that had never been realised. 'Any questions?' he asked.

'If there are any questions…' stammered the guide.

What a drip, thought Louis. He's somebody's child, though. I no longer wish to have this person in my sight, nor any of the others.

The group finally left the library.

No one had asked a question, though one young man had seemed to have a momentary impulse.

Of course, Louis had thought, he wants to ask where the toilet is. He urgently needs a loo before he shits himself. He's all nerves. He'd imagined his first day at work would be completely different. But he pulls himself together, recalling the slogan Be Thankful You've *Got* a Job at All. These days, he reflected later, it's one's duty to be happy about having a job. Anyone who finds work must yodel and jump for joy, after the fathomless misery of unemployment. It's ridiculous. Man was not made to work. Man was made to die.

From *The Man Who Found a Job* (De man die werk vond, 1985).

Here taken from *New Collected Works 3* (Nieuw verzameld werk 3)

Amsterdam: Prometheus, 2004, pp. 40-44.

All extracts translated by Paul Vincent

'Cast off the names that others had applied'

On the Poet Gerrit Achterberg

[PETER DE BRUIJN]

The *'repulsive oeuvre of a dangerous psychopath'* or *'the Netherlands' greatest poet'*: Gerrit Achterberg (1905-1962) is undoubtedly the most controversial figure in twentieth-century poetry. A hundred years after his birth he is still either acclaimed or reviled, as was apparent once again in the responses to the new edition of his *Poems* (Alle Gedichten) that appeared in 2005. In the same newspaper the poet and critic Piet Gerbrandy mercilessly pilloried the *'clumsy artificiality'* of this introverted *'monomaniac'*, while critical elder statesman Kees Fens then defended *'the incomparable linguistic world'* of Achterberg's *'indestructible poetry'*. This was the latest controversy in a seemingly endless chain of disputes that flare up with increasing regularity. Meanwhile the repulsive oeuvre has found its way to at least a hundred thousand readers at home and abroad (it has been translated on numerous occasions into at least fourteen languages) and has been the subject of an estimated three thousand or more reviews and studies. Are all those readers and reviewers wrong?

The poet and the landlady

The huge interest is not confined to the poet's work. On the publication of Achterberg's *Collected Poems* (Verzamelde gedichten) a year after his death, Dutch television broadcast a film about his life and work. The film broke what had hitherto been the 'Achterberg taboo' and revealed – albeit in fairly veiled terms – a tragic event in the poet's life: on 15 December 1937 Gerrit Achterberg shot dead his landlady and lover Roel van Es, also wounding her sixteen-year-old daughter. Achterberg was confined to a secure psychiatric hospital, and until 1944 received treatment in various institutions. During the poet's lifetime, his close friends and family had tried as far as possible to keep this secret from the outside world. In the film the veil was lifted a fraction for the first time, and in the torrent of reaction that followed the missing facts and details were finally made public. It became clear that Achterberg's endlessly repeated theme – reunion with a lost or dead lover – was based on a personal drama.

Since then Achterberg's literary 'you' figure and the landlady have been inextricably linked in standard works and school textbooks. And with that bio-

Gerrit Achterberg
(1905-1962). Collection
Letterkundig Museum,
The Hague.

graphical knowledge at the back of one's mind the reader certainly finds that at first sight his work contains countless autobiographical references, in lines such as *'It's the very same December/ of your death./ You don't remember'* and *'This girl is in her sixteenth year./ Take these her breasts and have no fear,/ she says, your hands long to hold them near'*. No wonder that many 'ordinary' readers became fascinated, and that 'professional readers' like Gerbrandy and Fens have been arguing for decades about the perennial question whether the biographical background is or is not a factor in experiencing Achterberg's poetry and whether – this was the subject of a national debate three years ago – there was any justification for wanting to read the chilling creations of such a *'psychopathic necrophiliac'*. This placed Achterberg in a rich international line of flawed geniuses.

If one reads this poetry as poetry – as is clear from contemporary responses, long before all the revelations – one discovers that Achterberg's work *also* belongs to an ancient metaphysical tradition: the absent 'you' figure is not a clearly defined person, but a symbol of the elusive Other for which mankind has been searching since time immemorial. Seen in that light, Achterberg's attempts to restore the lost harmony constitute one of the many undertaken to heal the rift in existence. His search is universal, however much personal misery it is based on and possibly motivated by. Increasingly the striving for reunion coincides with finding the magic word, writing the perfect poem. And this also makes Achterberg a modern poet, searching for the linguistic potential of poetry. The receptive reader can see a development in Achterberg's 'monomania', which resulted in his constant reclassification within the literary tradition and finally brought him fame, however relative that fame subsequently proved to be.

The contrast with Achterberg's early life and poetry could not be greater. He was born on 20 May 1905 into a simple farming family in the hamlet of Neerlangbroek, a poor backwater in the province of Utrecht. It was a world of strict Protestant orthodoxy, where – as the poet was to put it in one of his later poems – 'religion hung heavily from the roofbeams'. Gerrit was the only member of the family not to go into farming and was allowed to train as a teacher. During this period he discovered Dutch literature, and together with a friend started writing poetry. In their youthful enthusiasm they found a local printer prepared to publish their efforts under the title *The Songs of Two Men in Their Twenties* (De zangen van twee twintigers, 1925). The two worked hard to sell the small edition of 250 copies in their village, celebrating each sale with a box of cigarillos (at present second-hand copies of the little volume fetch a cool 3,000 euros!).

Achterberg's enthusiasm about this debut was short-lived. He soon realised that the volume was 'worthless' and anxiously kept his youthful peccadillo secret: 'What is not good, was never written.' The poems in the collection certainly show very little resemblance to his later work: they are childishly clumsy, edifying and above all rural tableaux featuring a faraway heron, a distant tramp, a belated traveller, in which the emptiness of life fills the young poet with nostalgia: 'Oh, sweet life's melancholy, I weep with you, I weep!' Yet these inoffensive poems contain the germ of the fascination with absence and death that will dominate the later work – there is even mention of a 'lost lover' – although that fascination here assumes an exclusively one-dimensional and sometimes morbid form, as in the description of a dead 'rigid body' in a 'narrow box': 'there lies the corpse's carapace,/ the nails grab at the box's side, / a few sporadic twitches/ of the dear life that's died.' How different is the conciliatory tone in the poem 'Trinity' that Achterberg wrote three years later:

How sweet it is, the alliance we've made,
yourself and death and I.
To think that love has lost nothing at all
in achieving such peace at last.

In Achterberg's 'official' debut collection *Casting Off* (Afvaart, 1931), in which this poem was included, reunion with the absent beloved, in death or in a new life, is a prominent theme. From the very first poem it is clear that ruptured existence (the 'old wound') can be healed only in the poem itself ('in this place'):

Across this land alone
I roamed, but this land has no end
and now I stray inside of you;
our old wound that would not mend,
will you begin to heal in this place,
or sting us even fiercer?

Casting Off is a thoroughly romantic collection, partly also because of the atmosphere evoked: 'These overcast afternoon poems are full of rain, dusk, snow and sadness,' wrote the poet and critic Martinus Nijhoff, 'and in this atmosphere *a poet and his dead love wander like ghosts, together for one last time, through the vague infinity of country roads shrouded in fog'.* Still, the personal voice found by Achterberg in *Casting Off* was welcomed by most critics as a pleasant surprise. J.C. Bloem wrote that it was years since he had been so struck by a talented and original debut, and others too discerned an individual poetic voice: warm, profound, elegiac and natural. Roel Houwink, who wrote an introduction to the collection, talks of a still *'virgin primitive quality'*, which he associates with Achterberg's farming background: *'The imaginative realm of this young poet lies somewhere deep in the country in the basin of a still, clear watercourse; it adjoins the pigsty and the dunghill, and in winter it is advisable to wear clogs.'*

The poet of the sarcophagus

After the fateful events of 1937 those publishing Achterberg's work were sensitive to its possible repercussions on his personal situation. His literary friends hoped that the appearance of a new collection of poetry would accelerate his referral to care in the community, and the composition of the collection was subordinated to that hope. The compilers decided, for example, that the cycle 'Sixteen' – including the poem quoted above – should be omitted, given the circumstances of Achterberg's 'case', because of its over-direct sexual references to the sixteen-year-old daughter of the landlady. *Island of the Soul* (Eiland der ziel, 1939) does on the other land contain various 'neutral' poems, which are not, or only obliquely, connected to the central theme, but take their inspiration from the outside world: the visual arts (Jan Toorop, Henri Rousseau, Théophile Alexandre Steinlen), music (*Eine kleine Nachtmusik*, Ravel's *Bolero*) and the Bible (the journalistic 'Traveller "Does" Golgotha'). Other striking inclusions are the light-hearted 'The Poet is a Cow' (*'... I meet/ my shape in ditches when I drink,/ and looking at my head, I think:/ how come that cow is upside-down?'*), and the nostalgic 'Hulshorst', about a country station in the wooded Veluwe National Park (the regular rendezvous point for Achterberg and his first fiancée):

Hulshorst, your name is like
abandoned iron, amid the pines
and bitter conifers
your station rusts;
where the north-bound train
stops with desolate grating,
letting no one on
no one off, oh, minutes
when I hear a faint waft
like an ancient legend
from your woods: grim gang
of robbers, rank and rough
from Veluwe's white heart.

Even the critic with the deepest dislike of Achterberg's *'monotonous obscurity'* was forced to admit that this was *'a perfect poem'*, and also found the other 'breakthroughs' in the collection 'very striking'. Indeed, for the leading poet and critic Hendrik Marsman the diversity found in *Island of the Soul* was proof that Achterberg's work 'ranks among the most important modern Dutch poetry'.

So *Island of the Soul* was a literary success, but did not bring the hoped-for social changes for Achterberg. The struggle for rehabilitation continued, conducted by the poet with the only means at his disposal: his work. '*If my work is anything, it has been written solely in* hope, *first and foremost in the hope of getting out of here*.' Poetry is literally a matter of life and death. Between 1940 and 1946 Achterberg published no less than eleven new volumes of poetry, and in the three subsequent years a further five. The titles of the collections indicate that since *Island of the Soul* other worlds have penetrated Achterberg's poetry, namely the exact sciences (*Osmose, Limiet, Radar, Energie*), classical antiquity (*Thebe, Eurydice, Sphinx*) and fairy tales (*Doornroosje* – Sleeping Beauty and *Sneeuwwitje* – Snow White).

The volumes gained Achterberg the reputation of being a modern but obscure poet, a '*magician*', an '*alchemist*' or a '*stray medicine man*', to mention a few tags used by contemporary critics to pin down the Achterberg phenomenon. The endless variety of 'non-poetic' words and concepts especially give his work an encyclopaedic quality, as the autodidact Achterberg readily admits:

Eighteen amino acids gave shape
to the protein from which you grew,
this lexicon tells me it's true.
Out of the window in awe I gape.

But of course, via those scientific facts the trail inevitably leads back to the death of the 'you' figure:

Measure and potential comprise
the unit to value your demise.
Graphically I track you down.

'*He has been speaking for whole collections to an alabaster statue of the beloved beside him on the tomb*', wrote Bertus Aafjes in his essay 'The Poet of the Sarcophagus', and was the first to venture to call Achterberg's quest '*crazy*', since the poet is trying to reconcile the irreconcilable – life and death – which is possible only in the extra-rational world of the poem. '*Don Quixote in the Underworld*' is another significant tag given to the poet at this time, except that Achterberg is both more normal and crazier than Cervantes' hero: more normal because he *knows* that he is fighting windmills, crazier because he nevertheless continues the struggle. The more hopeless things appear to him, the more obsessively Achterberg clings to the resources of poetry:

I forge the word
called after you,
and I exist
by dint of this
busy and blind activity.

After his 'release' from eight years' detention in institutions and home care – though he remained under official supervision until 1955 – Gerrit Achterberg led a relatively peaceful existence. By doing simple administrative work from home, he was able to earn a living and apart from that devote all his energy to poetry. In 1946 he married his childhood sweetheart Cathrien van Baak, and the couple moved into a number of rooms in a farm complex in Neede, a locality near Hoonte in the Achterhoek on the German border. Hoonte gives its name to his first 'neutral' collection, containing poems that fall outside his central theme. The title poem 'Hoonte' breathes the paradisial calm that has descended on the poet:

I've never savoured nature so
as here in Hoonte in the Achterhoek.
'Mariahoeve' is the tall farm's device.

Here the moments can gain depth and grow
enough to be an ever-open book
in which I can imagine paradise.

Meanwhile the torrent of poetry of recent years had not gone unnoticed or been in vain. In 1950 Achterberg was the first Dutch poet to be awarded the P.C. Hooft Prize, the state prize for literature, as *'the most gifted representative of the metaphysical current in European poetry'*. This was the first official honour he received for his work, although it was not his whole oeuvre that was crowned, but only a very small part of it: the orthodox-Christian *And Jesus Wrote in the Sand* (En Jezus schreef in 't zand, 1947). Quite apart from this official recognition Achterberg was regarded as a very important poet, precisely because of the new poetic avenues that he opened up. While the poetry of the rest of his generation was ditched as old-fashioned by the experimentalist Young Turks of the 1950s, Achterberg was revered as the major living poet, the *'Prince of Poets'*.

Remarkably, at this very period Achterberg's poetry became more traditional in form. While the Dutch poetic landscape was undergoing a drastic renewal and Achterberg was singled out as its main precursor, he presented himself increasingly as a formalistic poet, the *'mathematician of poetry'* (Bert Voeten). His collections consisted almost exclusively of sonnets and were largely cyclical. The main theme does not essentially change, though it is qualified: *'Sometimes I think it's no longer about you/and find myself losing track of you in me'*. At the same time the personal problems are objectified by having someone else pursue the quest for the 'you' figure (*Ballad of the Gasman*), by locating it elsewhere (*Ode to The Hague*), or by presenting it as an illusory performance (*Game of the Wild Hunt*, which is constructed like a play). The poetry of these years can be characterised by Simon Vestdijk's description of the latter collection: *'Hermetic humour'*. Achterberg remains an unrelenting systematist, but qualifies an overly absolutist approach to his central theme through self-irony. He takes a 'holiday' from his work:

Vacationer, a stranger in the present,
I roam through Africa, enjoy my fling
say letters home; they don't suspect a thing.

[...]
the main thing is to lose myself while here;
[...]
to be another, occupy his skin,
with ID, purse, suit, watch, hat begin,
braces, pumps, underwear, necktie and pin,
bygones are bygones; in his shoes as it were,
I reach a white town, and without a stir
greet you in the lobby checking in.

Poet

Bygones are bygones. In 1959 Gerrit Achterberg received the prestigious Constantijn Huygens Prize for his whole oeuvre, as a token of appreciation for a poet who *'throughout his poetic lifetime'* had remained true to his *'high poetic calling'*. This apparently marked the end of the poet's life. His low visible productivity in these years was interpreted as a decline in creativity: it was thought that he regarded his poetry as complete. The critics detected mainly frustration, depression and resignation in his last collection *Oblivion* (Vergeetboek, 1961), and wondered whether Achterberg was capable of developing in a new direction.

However, the view that the poet was 'burnt out', had done what he had to do and was resting on his laurels, is contradicted by a statement of his own, in an interview also from 1959: *'If I have to go on trying to my dying day, I shall keep going.'* At this period Achterberg immersed himself in new developments in astronomy and nuclear physics. On his sudden death in 1962, drafts for that new cycle were found in his study: forty or so manuscripts containing poems in progress, and notes on his reading. There were also two finished poems: 'Critical Mass' and 'Anti-Matter'. According to his widow, he planned to strike out in a completely different direction in his work. It is impossible to say what that direction was, and what effect it might have had on his reputation. Nor does it matter at this point, as witness 'Epitaph', the poem that quite appropriately was to be inscribed on Achterberg's own tomb:

From death to death he went, until he died.
Cast off the names that others had applied.
Saving this stone, with its inscription:
The poet of the verse that will abide. ■

Translated by Paul Vincent

by Gerrit Achterberg

Charlady

She knows the underneath of wardrobe and of bed,
rough wooden floorboards and forgotten nooks,
and crawling forward on all fours she looks
less like a human than a quadruped.

Her life to lower surfaces is wed;
she toils away to beautify their looks
for feet of grocers, preachers, men of books,
since rank and station cannot be gainsaid.

God will one day find her on His floor
working towards His throne down golden lanes,
with brush and dustpan she comes banging on.

Symbols resound like cymbals at death's door
– and see, to make a mockery of her pains,
there await the parson, the baker and the don.

From *Hoonte* (1949)
Translated by Paul Vincent

Werkster

Zij kent de onderkant van kast en ledikant,
ruwhouten planken en vergeten kieren,
want zij behoort al kruipend tot de dieren,
die voortbewegen op hun voet en hand.

Zij heeft zichzelve aan de vloer verpand,
om deze voor de voeten te versieren
van dichters, predikanten, kruideniEren,
want er is onderscheid van rang en stand.

God zal haar eenmaal op Zijn bodem vinden,
gaande de gouden straten naar Zijn troon,
al slaande met de stoffer op het blik.

Symbolen worden tot cymbalen in de
ure des doods – en zie, haar lot ten hoon,
zijn daar de dominee, de bakker en de frik.

Ichthyology

They've found a coelacanthus in the sea,
the missing link between two kinds of fish.
The finder wept, at its discovery,
in wonderment. The age-long broken chain

lay for the first time close beneath his eyes.
And everyone who stood around the fish
felt at that moment quite consumed by all
the thousand thousand years that stretched behind.

Order from man down to the dinosaur
and from the dinosaur deep into dust,
further than all our instruments can reach.

Aware of this, we may pretend as though
the order upwards is the same, and so
be able to look in on God at lunch.

From *Cenotaph* (Cenotaaf, 1953)
Translated by James S Holmes

Ichthyologie

Er is in zee een coelacanth gevonden,
de missing link tussen twee vissen in.
De vinder weende van verwondering.
Onder zijn ogen lag voor 't eerst verbonden

de eeuwen onderbroken schakeling.
En allen die om deze vis heenstonden
voelden zich op dat ogenblik verslonden
door de millioenen jaren achter hen.

Rangorde tussen mens en hagedis
en van de hagedis diep in de stof,
verder dan onze instrumenten reiken.

Bij dit besef mogen wij doen alsof
de reeks naar boven toe hetzelfde is
en kunnen zo bij God op tafel kijken.

The Dutch texts of the poems are taken from: Gerrit Achterberg,
Alle Gedichten (Eds. Peter de Bruijn, Edwin Lucas and Fabian R.W. Stolk).
Amsterdam: Athenaeum – Polak & Van Gennep, 2005. Vol. 1, pp. 657 and 812.

Recently, translated poems by Achterberg have also appeared in the Winter 2005/6 issue of the
Poetry Review (www.poetrysociety.org.uk/review.htm)

The Unexpected Popularity of Antoni van Leeuwenhoek

When the election for the greatest Dutch person of all time was held in 2004, Antoni van Leeuwenhoek came fourth – after Pim Fortuyn, William of Orange and Willem Drees, but before Erasmus, Rembrandt and Vincent van Gogh. Van Leeuwenhoek's success was largely overlooked by the press; all the media attention went to the questionable methods that had put Fortuyn in first place. Yet it's surprising, to say the least, that of all the representatives of the world of culture and science it was Van Leeuwenhoek who managed to garner so many votes. If the question regarding the greatest Dutch person had been asked to practitioners of the natural sciences alone (to limit ourselves to that single category), then undoubtedly geniuses such as Huygens (now twelfth) and Lorentz (now number 49) would have scored much higher. But the fact that Van Leeuwenhoek is clearly a popular favourite demands an explanation. What does this say about Van Leeuwenhoek, and what does it say – perhaps – about the Netherlands today?

An average Dutchman, but with a long-term pension

One obvious reason for Van Leeuwenhoek's popularity may be that everyone in the country knows about the Antoni van Leeuwenhoek Hospital in Amsterdam, the centre for the treatment of cancer patients in the Netherlands. Cancer is quite a common disease and everyone is afraid of getting it, so no-one can say they've never heard of Antoni van Leeuwenhoek. And while there's also a Huygens Institute, and the Lorentz sluices are part of the Afsluitdijk, these are not nearly as well known.

Yet this cannot be the reason why so many thousands of Dutch people voted for Van Leeuwenhoek. The fact that microbiology appeals far more to the modern imagination that mathematics or physics may be one factor. Van Leeuwenhoek was the discoverer of bacteria and red blood cells, and thus of a world that can only be observed by means of a microscope, although it exercises a great influence on our daily lives. Van Leeuwenhoek knew nothing about the cholera bacterium or the influenza virus, let alone about how such afflictions might be dealt with, but in one way or another his name has clearly become con-

The Educational **FOCUS**

A MOST SIGNIFICANT EVENT WAS THE DISCOVERY OF BACTERIA IN 1675 BY ANTONI VAN LEEUWENHOEK WHO USED A PRIMITIVE MICROSCOPE OF HIS OWN MANUFACTURE

March 1932

nected with them. And on top of that, Van Leeuwenhoek is the prototype of the ordinary Dutchman. He came from a middle-class environment, ran a textile shop for a while and held a few modest positions in the Delft city hall. In other words, he was a man of the people, someone with little education who nevertheless managed to become a person of consequence, very different from Huygens the aristocrat or Lorentz the professor.

Antoni van Leeuwenhoek was born on 24 October 1632, the son of a fairly prosperous Delft basket-maker. His father died when the boy was seven years old, and because he did not get on very well with his mother's second husband, she sent her son to a boarding school in Warmond and later to an uncle in Benthuizen. Van Leeuwenhoek then served as an apprentice bookkeeper to a Scottish cloth merchant in Amsterdam until he returned to Delft in 1653 or 1654. There he bought a house, got married and opened a draper's shop. Apparently the business was not very successful because in 1660 Van Leeuwenhoek closed it down and was appointed chamberlain to the Lords Regents of Delft, a combination of porter and bailiff. After the death of his wife he remarried a clergyman's daughter (1666) and began to mix in more cultivated society consisting of clergymen and doctors. It was at that time that he also developed a certain interest in intellectual matters. He trained as a surveyor and in 1679 was appointed *wijnroeier*, gauger of casks, responsible for certifying the capacity of wine casks for the city. All his jobs together earned him 800 guilders a year, which was equal to the salary of the city secretary at that time. Remarkably, the city of Delft continued to pay him this sum until his death on 26 August 1723, when he was almost 91 years old. Very few public officials received such pensions, and the fact that the Delft regents continued to pay Van Leeuwenhoek shows how proud they were to have this international celebrity within their gates.

Small world, great fame

Until 1673 no one outside Delft had ever heard of Antoni van Leeuwenhoek, but in that year the Delft physician and naturalist Reinier de Graaf sent a report Van Leeuwenhoek had written on the observations he had made using home-made microscopes to the Royal Society in London. As a simple chamberlain from Delft, Van Leeuwenhoek had no access to England's scientific community; on top of that, his only language was Dutch. De Graaf could arrange for an introduction, however, and was more than happy to do so. He had known for some time that Van Leeuwenhoek had an extraordinary talent for making microscopes with powerful magnification, enabling him to see things that no one had ever seen before. In an age bursting with the desire for more and more new discoveries such a talent should not remain hidden, and a letter to the Royal Society was the best means of informing the scientific world. Not only was the letter – in translation – read out to a meeting of the London Society, an excerpt was also published in *Philosophical Transactions,* the journal published by the secretary of the Royal Society, Henri Oldenburg. And on top of that a French translation of the letter appeared shortly thereafter in a French scholarly journal, the *Journal des Scavans*. Van Leeuwenhoek's reputation was secured at a stroke.

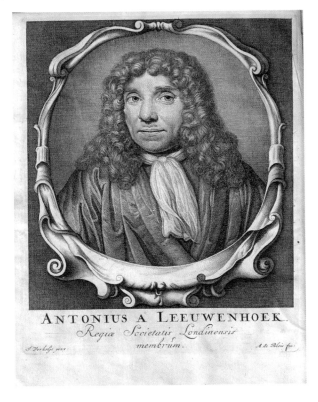

ANTONIUS A LEEUWENHOEK.
Regiæ Societatis Londinensis membrum.

After that Van Leeuwenhoek no longer needed special patronage to make his observations widely known. The first letter to the Royal Society was followed by more than a hundred others, and almost all of them, some in summary, were published in the *Philosophical Transactions*. His contribution was so highly valued that in 1680 the gentlemen in London named him a Fellow of the Royal Society. But Van Leeuwenhoek did not send his observations to the Royal Society alone or publish them only in the *Transactions*. Starting in 1684, he issued several books containing compilations of his 'epistles', which were eagerly snapped up by avid readers. From far and wide, too, people came to Delft to see with their own eyes what Van Leeuwenhoek was up to with his microscopes. Royal personages came as well, such as King James II of England, who honoured Van Leeuwenhoek with a visit to his office in 1687, and the Russian Czar Peter the Great, who visited Delft in 1698 and summoned Van Leeuwenhoek to demonstrate his microscopes. Van Leeuwenhoek was not always pleased with such visits (he suspected that some of his fellow-researchers wanted to steal his ideas), but he did feel honoured by the recognition that came to him from official quarters, as in 1716 when the University of Leuven awarded him a medal inscribed with the words *'In tenui labor, at tenuis non gloria'*, or: 'Small the work, but not the fame'.

The Columbus of a new reality

With the help of his microscopes Van Leeuwenhoek made the most marvellous discoveries. He not only studied the delicate structure of insects, he was also the first to describe red blood cells (1674) as well as an array of one-celled creatures that we now call infusoria and bacteria (1674 and 1676). He was especially proud of his discovery of capillaries (in 1688), the almost invisible vessels that connect arteries with veins, thus proving that Harvey's theory of blood circulation really was correct. In 1677 – with a certain diffidence, which was why it was reported in Latin – Van Leeuwenhoek also described the male sperm cell, which he believed was more responsible for the emergence of new life than the female egg-cell. Crystals, hair, the fin of an eel, 'toe jam' (his own) and dental plaque (also his own) – he looked at everything through his microscope and almost always discovered something new. When you read his letters and become a bit accustomed to his careless linguistic style, you experience the sensation of observing something for the first time and find yourself looking over the shoulder of a man who expects nothing, but for that very reason makes the most remarkable discoveries. Van Leeuwenhoek and his microscopes opened up a whole new reality, the world of the extremely small, which was just as extraordinary as the distant lands that his countrymen were opening up in America, Africa and Asia – a 'new world' on the other side of his lens. (Another good reason why Van Leeuwenhoek ended up scoring so high in the election of the greatest Dutch person: Van Leeuwenhoek is seen as the Columbus of the microscopically small.)

At least as remarkable as *what* he saw was *how* Van Leeuwenhoek made his observations – his working method and his instruments. In that first letter he said he had uncovered the structure and growth of mould, the sting and mouthparts of a bee and the limbs of a louse with an unsightly instrument, the simple microscope. Microscopes had existed since the beginning of the seventeenth century. Once the telescope was discovered (we hear of it for the first time in 1608, but the instrument must have been constructed in the late sixteenth century), it didn't take long before someone pulled the tube out a bit further and discovered that in this way nearby objects could be seen in magnified form. Modest observations began to be made with the microscope in Italy and later in the rest of Europe starting in the 1620s, and by around 1650 the instrument was making a triumphal progress through Europe's scientific community. The second half of the seventeenth century was the golden age of microscopic observation, involving the likes of Marcello Malpighi in Italy, Robert Hooke in England and Christiaan Huygens and Jan Swammerdam in the Dutch Republic. But in all these cases the instrument was a compound microscope, a microscope with two lenses in a tube that, when properly adjusted, could produce remarkable magnifications. Van Leeuwenhoek's microscopes had an entirely different appearance. The most common type consisted of two small metal plates clamped on to a small round glass ball, which functioned as the lens. Behind the two plates was mounted a pin on which the specimen could be secured and brought closer or higher by means of a screw thread. There was nothing simple about either making or operating this instrument. One had to have good, homogenous lenses at one's disposal as well as sharp vision. Because the focal length was very short (enabling strong magnification), the researcher had to keep his eye very close to the glass ball. So quite a bit of talent was needed to prepare and position the specimen in such a way that the researcher could see anything at all.

Van Leeuwenhoek had that talent. He had very sharp vision, and as a draper he was very skilled at handling and improving linen testers (a hand magnifier used to determine the quality of fabrics and the density of the weave). But exactly how he made his hundreds of little microscopes (he made a new instrument for each specimen!) was something he never revealed for fear of the competition. Such secrecy had its price, however, and brought its own problems. By being so secretive, Van Leeuwenhoek violated the unwritten rule that in principle research should be verifiable and reproducible. Because his microscopes were of superior quality, other researchers were at first unable to repeat his observations with their own equipment, and because the observations did not appear to be reproducible the obvious conclusion was that they had been invented.

That secrecy also gave colleagues who had a bone to pick with Van Leeuwenhoek the opportunity to claim that making little microscopes was the *only* talent he possessed. One rival, his countryman Nicolaas Hartsoeker, described Van Leeuwenhoek as a man with eyes, lenses and a great deal of patience but little or no power of reasoning. And while another, Leibniz, might say that he preferred someone who wrote what he saw (Van Leeuwenhoek) to someone who wrote what he thought (Descartes), there was a great temptation to portray Van Leeuwenhoek as a man who peered through his microscopes at random but was incapable of thinking systematically and therefore did not really advance scientific knowledge. Van Leeuwenhoek wrote as he spoke and rambled from one subject to the next, so that Hartsoeker could sneer that Van Leeuwenhoek needed five or six volumes to demonstrate what another could say in a few pages. That Van Leeuwenhoek had no academic education and could not read Latin — even in English books he was only able to pick up a few facts from the illustrations — could also easily be used against him. Jan Swammerdam, who clashed fiercely with Van Leeuwenhoek on a couple of occasions, complained in 1678 that it was almost impossible to discuss anything with Van Leeuwenhoek, *'because he is so prejudiced and his reasoning is barbaric, being without a university education'*.

The advantage of being unacademic

For his part, Van Leeuwenhoek also deliberately exaggerated the differences between himself and his academically-trained fellow researchers. His letters contain frequent expressions of an outspoken anti-intellectualism, as when he claims that the reason he can observe all those *'invisible created truths'* without prejudice is *because* he had no university education. Although his research was thoroughly grounded in a limited number of basic principles (such as that everything in the world consists of small mechanisms, and that spontaneous generation was impossible for theological reasons), he cultivated the image of the unlettered and unspoiled researcher who, unhampered by book-learning, observes the world as it really is. He also stressed that he was just a simple man from Delft and that for this reason his mistakes should not be held too much against him. But he still craved recognition from the official scientific community, however, which explains why he was so delighted with the medal from Leuven University. And when the Royal Society admitted him to their circle, Van Leeuwenhoek asked Constantijn Huygens in all seriousness whether he should still give way to a physician when walking in the street – which for Huygens was proof that Van Leeuwenhoek was really just an upstart.

Subsequent generations have done more to highlight Van Leeuwenhoek's alleged simplicity and modesty than he did himself. When the two hundredth anniversary of Van Leeuwenhoek's discovery of micro-organisms was celebrated in 1875 (erroneously, by the way), Pieter Jacob Haaxman wrote a biography of *'the man who, as a humble citizen of Delft, was not appreciated for his merits by his fellow townsmen or countrymen during his lifetime, but was mentioned with honour and glory and above all with great respect by the leading scholars of his day throughout the civilised world'*, referring to the many visitors who sought out the researcher *'in his humble dwelling'*. And in the twentieth century another biographer, A. Schierbeek, pointed out how unique it was *'that a simple city hall functionary using home-made equipment could make discoveries that would astonish the world, and that even centuries later scholars are compelled to honour him as one of the greatest among them'*. It would not surprise me at all if Van Leeuwenhoek's popularity at the beginning of the twenty-first century still had something to do with this admiration for an ordinary man from Delft, who just wrote what he saw and thereby astounded the world. ■

Translated by Nancy Forest-Flier

Such is our proud, though oft-diluted, Dutch heritage

An Extract from John Updike's *A Letter to My Grandsons*

The Updikes came to this continent in two installments. The first and more distinguished, the Wesel Updikes, arrived in New Amsterdam, in the person of Gysbert op den Dyck, before 1638. Gysbert – like Peter Minuit, the first governor of New Netherland – came from Wesel, a small city located on the lower Rhine, where it meets the Lippe. Wesel (which was all but demolished by air raids in World War II) is now part of Germany; in 1605, when Gysbert was born there, it was part of the duchy of Cleves, and though officially neutral in the Dutch-Spanish war, suffered incursions and hardship. A continuous line of Op den Dycks there went back to Henric, a Burgomaster and City Treasurer born late in the thirteenth century. Though no certain connection can be proved, the Wesel Op den Dycks are thought to be related to the family of the same name in Essen, which was of knightly rank, used armorial bearings (involving a pineapple, a star, and what seems to be a serrated tongs), and became extinct in the sixteenth century, 'leaving their name attached to an estate and to a castle.' For six generations after Henric, Op den Dycks occupied civic office in Wesel; in the seventh, Lodowick (b. 1565) became a brewer and an innkeeper. *The Op Dyck Genealogy* (compiled by Charles Wilson Opdyke, published in 1889) assures us, 'An explanation of his undertaking these somewhat humble occupations is to be found in the great decadence suffered by Wesel in his life-time.' The war and the confusion arising from the death of the Duke of Cleves without male issue had curtailed commerce and finally resulted in the siege and occupation of the town by a Spanish army in 1614. The Spanish stayed in Wesel for fifteen years, until 1629. After 1615, Lodowick disappears from the Wesel town records, and it seems probable that he and his son Gysbert, then aged ten, joined the many refugees seeking asylum in Holland, which had already thrown off the Spanish yoke.

Gysbert makes his first appearance in the records of the New World as an officer of the Dutch West India Company, and specifically as the Commander of Fort Hope, on the present site of Hartford. It was his ungrateful task to hold this fort while the English colonists from Massachusetts were overrunning the fertile Connecticut Valley. Failing to receive the reinforcements he needed, he resigned in late 1640 and 'returned to the Fatherland,' only to reappear in New Amsterdam in 1642 and, the following year, to marry Catherine Smith, the daughter of Richard Smith, the possessor of vast tracts on the West side of Narragansett Bay.

Wesel, Germany.

Land was easily laid hold of in the New World; Gysbert himself owned all of Coney Island – then three separate sandy masses, of which the easternmost was called 'Gysbert's Island' – as well as two farms on Long Island and a residence on Stone Street, in lower Manhattan. One's holdings were not always secure, however; the more numerous English brushed aside the Dutch claims to Connecticut, and the Indians were still a threat. Gysbert frequently sat on the Governor's Council and helped fashion Indian treaties; he advised against the petition, in 1643, of the Long Island settlers for permission to attack the Marreckawick Indians near Breucklen (Brooklyn); nevertheless, attacks and plunder occurred, and the Indian reprisals included the massacre of Anne Hutchinson and her family and the devastation of Richard Smith's extensive colony at Mespath. Both Hutchinson and Smith had sought refuge among the Dutch from religious persecution in the English colonies to the north; both New England and old England were jealous of the Dutch colonies. In 1664, Charles II awarded a patent for all New Netherland to his brother the Duke of York, and the Duke's ships plus Connecticut troops compelled the unpopular government of Peter Stuyvesant to surrender. Dutch rule on the North American continent ended. 'After the English capture, nothing further is found on the records concerning Gysbert… The tradition is doubtless correct that he went with his children to Narragansett, after the death of Richard Smith, Sr., in 1666, to take possession of the lands about Wickford bequeathed to the children of Gysbert's deceased wife Catharine.'

Thus began the notable, even glamorous line of Rhode Island Updikes. Gysbert, whose name became Anglicized to Gilbert Updike, was called 'Doctor,' though he was probably not a physician. 'He was well educated; his associations, official positions, reports, even his signature, show this. He must have spoken German from his birth, Dutch from his emigration, and English from his marriage.' The eldest son of that marriage, Lodowick (b. 1646), laid out the town of Wickford, once called 'Updike's New Town'; his son Daniel (b. 1694) was tutored at home, visited Barbados and mingled in 'the first circles of Society on the Island,' studied law, married the daughter of the Governor, and was repeatedly elected Attorney General of the colony. His son Lodowick (b. 1725) was 'regarded in his time as one of the most eminent citizens of Rhode Island. His qualifications were such as fitted him to shine either at the Bar, in political, or in military career. But he preferred the dignity and scholarly leisure of the private life of a large landed proprietor.' The thirty thousand acres of wilderness John Smith had purchased from the Narragansett Sachems in 1639 had become, augmented by marriage and subdued to cultivation, the basis of a plantation society akin to that of the South and like nothing else in the North. Wilkins Updike, Lodowick's grandson, wrote:

Their plantations were large, many containing thousands of acres, and noted for dairies and the production of cheese. The grass in the meadows was very thick and as high as the tops of the walls and fences; two acres were sufficient for the annual food of each cow. . . . Large flocks of sheep were kept, and clothing was manufactured for the household, which sometimes exceeded seventy persons in parlor and kitchen. Gramin was shipped to the West Indies. The labor was mostly performed by African slaves, or Narragansett Indians.

In this American Eden, roads and carriages scarcely existed, and the planter families rode horses back and forth through each other's fences in an incessant round of festivity and fox chase, entertainment and dance. The black slaves (among whom you, Anoff and Kwame, might have found distant relatives of your own – men and women speaking Twi like your African grandmother or Ga like your African grandfather, brought here in manacles from the Gold Coast) were allowed a reflection of such brilliancy:

In imitation of the whites, the negroes held a mock annual election of their Governor; when the slaves were numerous, their election was held in each town. . . . The slaves assumed the ranks of their masters, whose reputation was degraded if their negroes appeared in inferior apparel or with less money than those of masters of equal wealth. The horses of the wealthy landholders were on this day all surrendered to the use of the slaves, who with cues, real or false, head pomatumed and powdered, cocked hat, mounted on the best Narragansett pacers, sometimes with their master's sword, with their ladies on pillions, pranced to election at ten o'clock.

Gravesend, Long Island, NY

Lodowick – 'tall and fine-looking; always wore wig and small-clothes, and was said to resemble George III' – had eleven children, who lived to the average age of eighty years. The eldest, Daniel (b. 1761), became Attorney General of Rhode Island the same year, 1790, that the state ratified the Constitution; thus he served an independent commonwealth in the same office his grandfather had held in the King's colony. Lodowick's youngest child, Wilkins (b. 1784), served for many years in the General Assembly, which upon his death in 1867 passed a resolution saying: 'Resolved, that in the decease of Hon. Wilkins Updike, has passed away from earth almost the last of a generation of true Rhode Island men, worthy of our respect and imitation in the walks of private and of public life.' And indeed, in the nineteenth century the noble line of Rhode Island Updikes did rather suddenly shrivel and diminish, as if their Narragansett paradise, with its lush grass and powdered wigs, its abundance of cheese and sheep and slaves, had been something of a dream. The genealogy for the Wesel family sputters out in a chord of unmarried bachelors and men moved to Pittsburgh. When, a few years ago, I visited Wickford, or North Kingston as it can be called, the only Updike in the telephone book was an 'Updike Laundry' on Route One; the young woman behind the counter told me that 'Updike' was an old name for Wickford, and that nobody of that name worked in the laundry. Even before the turn of the century, when Charles Wilson Opdyke visited the vicinity of Richard Smith's fabulous holdings, he found the family all but vanished: 'A hundred years ago, Wickford contained so many of the name that it was often called 'Updike Town.' Very few of the blood and none of the name now reside there.'

Yet Wilkins, the youngest of eleven, himself had fathered twelve children. One of his sons was grandiosely named Caesar Augustus, and he 'was a fine

Narragansett Bay, RI

public speaker, inheriting much of his distinguished father's wit and humor, and like him was a thorough Rhode Islander.' Caesar practiced law in Providence, and became a member of the city Common Council, a member of the lower House of the General Assembly, and from 1860 to 1862 Speaker of the House. But at around the age of fifty he died suddenly, of heart disease, leaving his widow, who had been Elisabeth Bigelow Adams, and a teen-aged son. That son was Daniel Berkeley Updike, born in Providence in (like Hartley) 1860. Daniel's middle name commemorates the warm friendship between his great-grandfather – the colonial Daniel – and George Berkeley, the Anglo-Irish cleric-philosopher, in those years, 1728-31, during which the future bishop resided in Newport.[1]

Young D. B. Updike was frail and shy, with protruding ears and a religious disposition – the Rhode Island Updikes were keen Episcopalians. His father's premature death necessitated that he abjure higher education and go to work; he began as an errand boy for Houghton Mifflin in Boston in 1880 and showed a fine aptitude for the niceties of typography and printing. He set up as a free-lance designer in 1893, and founded the Merrymount Press in 1896. He under-took all sort of jobs but specialized in ecclesiastical work: the 1928 revision of the Book of Common Prayer was printed by him. A lifelong bachelor, he was meticulous, fastidious, and learned. He utilized and helped revive the historical roman and italic faces Caslon, Scotch, Janson, Bell, Poliphilus, Bodoni. From 1911 to 1916 he gave lectures on printing at the Harvard Business School, and these were the basis of his two-volume *Printing Types: Their History, Forms, and Use*, a work not only classic but still unsurpassed in its field. Daniel Berkeley Updike was, when I was a boy, the only famous Updike – the only one who could be found in the back of the dictionary.

Hartford, CT

Yet he, and all the Rhode Island Updikes, were not really my relations, or yours. No genealogical connection bas been established between the Wesel Updikes and our own ancestors, the Holland Updikes, who came, it is all but certain, from Elburg, in Gelderland, on the eastern shore of the Zuider Zee. Op den Dycks left their traces on records there since the fourteenth century, and the baptismal names Louris, Johan, and Albert recur in both the Elburg records and the first American generations.[2]

Louris Jansen Opdyck came to New Netherland before 1653, at which time he resided in Albany and bought land at Gravesend, Long Island. His Holland antecedents are indicated by written petition of 1653, in which he complains that the English inhabitants of Gravesend were determined 'that no Dutchmen should get into the Magistry there,' and by his widow's appealing, in 1660, to the 'law of Holland' in claiming half of his estate. Our genealogist takes Louris's Dutchness as reason to launch a patriotic rhapsody, as of the seventeenth century:

The cattle of Holland, grazing on the bottom of the sea, were the finest in Europe, its farm products the most valuable, its navigators the boldest, its mercantile marine the most powerful. Where of old were swamps and thickets, now dwelt three millions of people, the most industrious, the most prosperous, perhaps the most intelligent, under the sun; their love of liberty indomitable; their pugnacity proverbial; peaceful and phlegmatic, they were yet the most irascible and belligerent men of Europe.

Such is our proud, though oft-diluted, Dutch heritage.

Elburg, The Nettherlands

Louris participated in the fur trade with the Iroquois at Fort Orange, a Dutch fort dating from 1614, on the site of Albany, and was granted by Governor Stuyvesant a small lot there. But his main activity seems to have been at Gravesend, a farming colony dominated by the English. Gravesend was the only Long Island settlement to defend itself successfully in the Indian uprisings that destroyed Mespath; in 1655, another Indian war made Gravesend unsafe, and Louris resided with his family in New Amsterdam, on Pearl Street. The population of Manhattan was then one thousand people, of whom a quarter lived on Pearl Street. Money was so rare that purchases were made with beaver skins; the first brickyard and the first paved street had just come into existence, and cows were driven through the town gate at Wall Street to the public pasture at the present City Hall Park. The meadow for Gravesend was Coney Island, and one imagines that in this cozy wilderness community Louris and Gysbert must have sometimes met, and may have known each other well.

The lines diverged, however: one went northeast to Rhode Island, and the other southwest into New Jersey. Louris was dead by 1660, we know from a document whereby his widow, Christina (already engaged to marry again), divided his considerable estate of twenty-one hundred guilders among her three sons, Peter, Otto, and Johannes. The farm at Gravesend was sold and the family with its stepfather moved to Dutch Kills, in the jurisdiction of Newton, in what is now the Long Island City section of Queens. Peter disappears from the records after the English captured New York and may have returned to Holland; Otto

Hartford, CT

apparently never left Newton. It was Johannes, the youngest, a boy of nine when his father died, who in the early summer of 1697, by this time the father of seven and the grandfather of three, led his family into the fertile territory of West Jersey, where, a contemporary report had it, 'you meet with no inhabitants but a few friendly Indians, where there are stately oaks whose broad-branched tops have no other use but to keep off the sun's heat from the wild beasts of the wilderness, where is grass as high as a man's middle, that serves for no other end except to maintain the elks and deer.' It was, an early settler sent back word, 'as good a country as any man need to dwell in.'

In wagons and carts, with horses and oxen and farming utensils, the Opdyke party – which included Johannes's sisters Tryntie, Engeltie, and Annetie, who were all married to brothers called Anderson – made their way across the hills to Flatbush to a ferry at the narrows, across Staten Island, up the Raritan to the old Indian trail called 'the King's Highway,' which they followed across the future state to the two hundred fifty acres Johannes had bought that April, 'above the falls of the Delaware.' The land lay near the present town of Lawrenceville, just above Trenton, in an area then called Maidenhead. Here Johannes lived and farmed and bought and sold land for thirty years, until his death at seventy-eight in 1729; and here, in the vicinity of Trenton, Princeton, and Pennington, Updikes stayed for two more centuries, their name passing from the land only in my father's generation. The New Jerseyites were more tenacious of the Dutch spelling of the name than the Rhode Islanders; Johannes signed his name Johannes Lourense, using the patronymic in the Old World style, and his children were entered into the church and civic records as op Dyck, or Opdyck, unless an English clerk did the recording.

Louris Jansen op Dyck had begot Johannes Opdyck, who begat Lawrence Updick (1675-1748), who begat John Updike (1708-90), who begat Peter (1756-1818), who begat Aaron (1784-1861), who begat Peter (1812-66), who begat Archibald (1838-1912), who begat Hartley (1860-1923), who begat Wesley (1900-72), who begat me (b.1932), who begat Elizabeth (b. 1955), who begat you (b. 1985, 1987). On your mother's side, then, you are thirteenth-generation Americans, offspring of a favored white minority. The Dutch colony had lasted a mere forty years; after it surrendered in 1664, without a shot being fired, the English Governor was instructed to treat the several thousand Dutch inhabitants generously, letting them keep their lands, language, and religion. Soon they were intermarrying with the English and forgetting their Dutch. It was an easy assimilation.

And you, my grandsons, how will you fare here?

From *Self-Consciousness: Memoirs*. New York: Knopf, 1989. pp. 186-195
Reprinted by kind permission of the author

NOTES

1. He was there waiting for his proposed American University to be funded, a university he wished to see located in Bermuda and devoted largely to the education and coversion of American Indians. The vision was never realized, but in 1866 Berkeley's name descended upon a relocated California college and its town, which it continues to adorn. It was Berkeley who wrote the famous line "Westward the course of empire takes its way" and in his Principles of *Human Knowledge* set forth the arresting idea that 'All the choir of heaven and furniture of earth – in a word, all those bodies which compose the mighty frame of the world – have not any subsistence without a mind.'

2. Almost no Updikes survive in Europe. The genealogist in 1888 found two families called Oppedyk living in Friesland, one of which adopted the name under Napoleon; the other family had been living in Ylst since 1654. When I visited the Netherlands in 1977, the only Updike my publisher could turn up was my first cousin Jean, who had married a Dutchman called Kramer and listed herself with the double name Kramer-Updike.

Photo on p. 263
© Christophe Coppens, 2005.

A Sea of Models
The Second International Architecture Biennial in Rotterdam

As preparations for the second International Architecture Biennial in Rotterdam forged ahead under
the apocalyptic title *The Flood*, the surging waters of
the tsunami were wreaking havoc in Asia. This event
was a chilling reminder of the disastrous impact that
water can have on man and the landscape, a reminder reinforced later in the year by hurricane Katrina's
onslaught on the US and its impact on New Orleans
– wind and water allied against the land. Over the
past few years it has become increasingly clear that,
although it is unlikely that the Netherlands will be hit
in the same way as the countries affected by the tsunami, rising sea levels do pose a threat to the Dutch
landscape. Problems relating to water were the
theme for the biennial, which was organised by
Adriaan Geuze, landscape architect and director of
the West 8 firm of landscape architects. The Rotterdam Architecture Biennial is characterised by its the-
matic approach. It consisted of several exhibitions,
each presenting a different perspective on the theme
of water.

The main exhibition, *The Water City*, was held in
Las Palmas, a former warehouse in the Kop van Zuid
area of Rotterdam, at the foot of the Erasmus Bridge.
Themes such as early waterside settlements, commercial centres and garrison towns were used to illustrate the fact that most of the towns and cities in
the Netherlands have developed next to water, and
water has therefore defined the limiting conditions
for urban planning in those areas. The third storey of
the Las Palmas building was occupied by more than
one hundred scale models, enabling visitors to compare the different urban layouts. It was a visual feast,
for laymen and architecture buffs alike.

A large part of the exhibition was devoted to historical analysis, but two sub-categories presented
more future-oriented plans. In the *Utopias* category,
designs such as Constant's *New Babylon* and Van den
Broek & Bakema's *Pampus* clearly showed how unspoiled expanses of water have inspired architects to

design megastructures that extend over them. In recent years these two radical plans have attained cult
status, but are rarely regarded as serious options.
The plans presented in the *New Dutch Water City* section may have been less radical than *Pampus* and
New Babylon from the 1960s, but they do go rather
further than what has been considered possible until
now. Among others, the exhibition included a proposal by OMA (Office for Metropolitan Architecture),
the leading international firm of architects headed by
the Dutch architect Rem Koolhaas, for an extension
to Schiphol Airport built on an artificial island in
the sea, illustrated by a futuristic OMA-made scale
model. Students of the Academy of Architecture in

South Flevoland, 2000.
Photo by Peter van Bolhuis/
Pandion.

Amsterdam submitted designs that link the land and the water in locations that can be used for funeral ceremonies, and there was also a project for a catamaran city in the province of South Holland. The thirteen projects on display were commissioned for the biennial, and each plan was supported and funded by one of the parties involved (e.g. a local authority).

Mare Nostrum, the second exhibition in the Las Palmas building, was devoted to coastlines. This was the most internationally oriented element of the biennial, which otherwise focused on the Netherlands. Some twenty countries took part in *Mare Nostrum*, presenting themes relating to coastal development that are relevant to their part of the world. Since there was no clear brief for the exhibition, themes varied from the consequences of mass tourism for the Spanish coast to examples of creative self-build structures in Russia and ideas for reviving the beach paradise of Eilat in Israel. It was clear from the diversity of projects that the worldwide rise in tourism, while providing opportunities for the development of architecture and urban design, can have a destructive effect on native landscapes. Each country seems to be struggling to find its own balance between economic development and the resulting impact on the environment.

The latter aspect is also relevant for the development of historical polders in the Netherlands. The exhibition *Polders: A Scene of Land and Water*, organised by Linda Vlassenrood in the Netherlands Architecture Institute (NAi), presented an interesting selection of fifteen polders – out of a total of 3,000 in the Netherlands – using scale models specially made for the exhibition by students at the Delft University of Technology together with historical drawings from several Dutch museums. Historical maps of land plots for the peat polders and reclaimed polders were on display, including development plans for the Beemster Polder, which was added to UNESCO's World Heritage list in 1999, as well as plans for the polder cities of Almere and Lelystad. The newly reclaimed land inspired experiments in architecture and urban development. In some cases, the emphasis was on progressive, experimental architecture;

one example of this was the town of Nagele in the Northeast Polder. During the 1950s, a group of the finest Dutch architects, including Rietveld, Van Eyck and Mien Ruijs, were brought together to work on plans for the town.

But the *Polders* exhibition was more than a historical survey. The polder landscapes of the Netherlands, which are characterised by their vastness and their networks of dykes and ring canals, avenues and clumps of trees, are increasingly threatened by urbanisation. The question now facing us is whether these characteristic features should be sacrificed to economic development. With this in mind an interactive 'Polder Indicator' was being developed for the exhibition. By answering the questions in the indicator, visitors could see how their own opinions would affect the polders in the future. It was its combination of detailed historical analysis and a vision for the future that made this exhibition so interesting.

Unfortunately, this was precisely what the Las Palmas exhibitions lacked. Although solutions were presented for many topical issues, there was no overall vision for dealing with problems such as climate change and rising sea levels. Even Geuze, who in articles and interviews regularly voices his concern that there is no clear and decisive vision for spatial planning in the Netherlands, failed to make any real mark in this respect. Visitors were left with a series of impressions and interesting facts, but no clear statement. The key question is whether this biennial has attracted enough interest and support to persuade the Ministry of Education, Culture & Science to reverse its decision to withdraw funding for this new event. Or will the Rotterdam Architecture Biennial be allowed to slip quietly into oblivion after only two editions?

Marieke van Rooy
Translated by Yvette Mead

The second International Architecture Biennial was held in Rotterdam from 26 May to 26 June 2005.

www.biennalerotterdam.nl

Forever Curious
The Mondriaan Foundation

Is there an art-lover anywhere who has never heard of Rembrandt or Mondria(a)n? Probably not. Many people think of the Netherlands primarily as a land of visual artists, far more than of writers. But are today's Dutch artists also known abroad? Some people will immediately mention the photographer Rineke Dijkstra, or Marlene Dumas. But it is still difficult for painters, sculptors, photographers or designers working in the Netherlands to break through on to the international art scene. The Mondriaan Foundation, a trust for promoting the arts, wants to strengthen the position of contemporary art and design from the Netherlands. In fact, this is one of its two main aims. The other is to stimulate interest in, and demand for, contemporary art within the Netherlands itself.

The Mondriaan Foundation was established in 1994. It tries to achieve its objectives by means of a range of initiatives and supporting activities. To this end the foundation has two lofts in New York, which Dutch artists and designers can use to exhibit their work. The Mondriaan Foundation also maintains a presence in other top locations. For instance, it is responsible for the Dutch participation in the prestigious Biennale in Venice. International art fairs provide the main opportunity of arousing the interest of gallery owners, museum directors and art collectors. Therefore the Mondriaan Foundation supports stands from (Dutch) galleries at various important fairs. To name just a few where the Foundation has a presence of this kind: The Armory Show in New York, the Frieze Art Fair and Collect (both in London), the FIAC in Paris, Paris Photo and Art Cologne. Moreover, other foreign organisations that show the work of artists and designers working in the Nether-lands can call on the Mondriaan Foundation for support. And of course it also supports the publication of art books, catalogues and periodicals (in other languages) featuring one or more Dutch artists. Special attention is given to design, a branch of the arts in which the Netherlands has built up a whole tradition. The Mondriaan Foundation provides financial sup-

The Australian piano teacher and composer Paul Copeland's take on Mondrian's art…with blobs.

port to individual designers who present their work at important international design fairs such as the Salone del Mobile in Milan and the Paris fashion weeks.

The Mondriaan Foundation is also extremely active within the Netherlands. Every year it supports a number of presentations, purchases, school competitions, art events and publications as well as exhibitions. It organises its own symposia and debates and issues its own publications.[1] Two very interesting initiatives are the Art Purchase Scheme and the Prize for the Encouragement of Cultural Diversity. The Art Purchase Scheme enables less well-off people with an interest in art to purchase works of art. By means of this scheme individuals can buy works of art from some 150 galleries on credit. The Prize for the Encouragement of Cultural Diversity consists of a grant of 500,000 euros. The award is given to the museum of modern art that has come up with the best project on the theme of cultural diversity.

The Mondriaan Foundation works closely with other Dutch funds that promote Dutch art forms, in the broad sense of the term, in other countries. That is not an unnecessary luxury, for on more than one occasion the Netherlands' international cultural policy has been criticised for a lack of coherence and vision. Moreover, the context in which this policy has to operate is extremely complex. As Gitta Luiten, director of the Mondriaan Foundation, remarks in *All that Dutch*[2], in the Netherlands as elsewhere globalisation has led to an intensified drive for a sense of individual identity. But for Dutch art this has meant having to deal with increasing provincialism and running the risk of losing touch with international developments in art. So the need for international reflection has seldom been so great as now. This concealed paradox gives rise to fascinating discussions. For Gitta Luiten, one of the key words is curiosity. The Netherlands must be curious about what is going on beyond its frontiers and, as it were, enter into a permanent dialogue with foreign art. This is the only way in which Dutch developments can be set in the much-needed international context.

Hans Vanacker
Translated by Sheila M. Dale

1. Among other things detailed yearbooks. In 2004 it published *10 years of the Mondriaan Foundation* (10 jaar Mondriaan Stichting), a jubilee publication presenting a hundred projects supported by the foundation. At that time the Mondriaan Foundation had supported no less than 5,976 projects.

2. *All that Dutch* is a collection of some thirty contributions from people with important political responsibilities in the world of Dutch culture. Each gives his or her vision on the future development of international cultural policy in the Netherlands. *All that Dutch* is a joint publication with the Foundation for International Cultural Activities, the Foundation for Amateur and Stage Arts and the Foundation for the Production and Translation of Dutch Literature and is published in an English and a Dutch version. See below for a review of this publication.

Mondriaan Foundation: Jacob Obrechtstraat 56,
1071 KN Amsterdam, The Netherlands
Tel.: + 31 20 676 20 32 / Fax: + 31 20 676 20 36
www.mondriaanfoundation.nl

'We pay too much attention to ourselves'
The Netherlands and International Cultural Policy

All that Dutch is a varied collection of articles and opinions by those responsible for making and implementing international cultural policy in the Netherlands. The book does not make happy reading, because it gives the impression that complete chaos reigns. Charles Esche, director of the Van Abbe Museum in Eindhoven, neatly summarises the current crisis – because that's what it is: '*I see too much analysis and too much self-castigation in the Netherlands, which wasn't the case before. People want to map out the entire situation (this publication is an example) and then draw up a plan. We should forget about that, and say: Okay, we're in a bad way, what'll we do? And just follow our noses and concentrate on what we're doing, taking the risk that it will fail. It's only art.*'

The contemporary dogma of efficiency means that we may no longer permit ourselves any failures, even in the field of culture, but the idea of cheerfully rolling up your sleeves and using your common sense certainly has some appeal after you've wrestled your way through *All that Dutch*. Because what strikes you most is that the people responsible for supporting and propagating Dutch culture complain so much and are so completely lacking in pride in their own language and culture. The most flagrant case of contempt for one's own culture comes from sales agent (!) Sydney Neter from SNDfilms, who declares: *'Do people see me as a Dutch sales agent? No. Thank goodness my name doesn't sound particularly Dutch. I could advertise myself as a Dutchman, but I think it would be more of a handicap than an advantage. (..) Although Dutch documentaries do have a good reputation, there simply aren't enough quality products for the market abroad.'* Sydney Neter simply doesn't understand that you really need to exploit to the full the good reputation that the Netherlands has in the cultural arena and not wash your dirty linen in public. This is a failing of many of the authors in this book, and the tragic thing is that these are precisely the people who should be promoting Dutch art and culture abroad. Or, as Bas Heijne puts it in his excellent essay: *'If we scarcely believe in it ourselves, then how can we convince others?'* It is the disdain that these cultural ambassadors have for their own culture that often makes international cultural policy such a soggy mess. Jan Debbaut, who until February 2006 was Director of Collections at the Tate Gallery in London, names another *'typically Dutch trait: we overestimate ourselves'*. Once again, he's not referring so much to Dutch art(ists) (*'Dutch art is no better or worse than art anywhere else; as a matter of fact, sometimes it's very good'*), but to the cultural institutions and those who implement the policy. According to Debbaut, they just sit back smugly, fail to create international networks and invest far too little in arousing interest in Dutch art. His motto is *'Invest in interest'* and I completely agree with him. That's precisely what I and my team from the Foundation for the Production and Translation of Dutch Literature did for twelve years for the translation of Dutch literature all over the world. And with such success that the current director told the *NRC Handelsblad* newspaper that he was *'somewhat bewildered by all the interest'* – there's that lack of belief again! Other countries aren't just sitting around waiting for Dutch art and culture to come to them, and what you don't know you don't appreciate. Make personal contact with the people abroad who are important in your field (there are no more than ten of them in any country), provide them with good information, make sure that you're on foreign panels, invite foreign artists or institutions to the Netherlands and take really good care of them (international cultural policy could certainly make more money available for this purpose) and then they really will become interested in Dutch art and want to involve it in projects abroad. Or, to quote the very apt response of Ann Demeester, director of W139, when she was asked whether Dutch art had lost its international reputation: *'Might it be, for example, contrary to popular opinion on this issue, that the Netherlands actually does have an "international story", but lacks its own narrative, which, paradoxically, disqualifies it in the international arena?'*. And: *'We could perhaps say that the Dutch international paradox resides in the fact that in the field of arts this country is intrinsically international, yet does not perform well in an international context.'*

Gitta Luiten, the director of the Mondriaan Foundation, also reflects critically on the crisis in contemporary art: *'We pay too much attention to ourselves. It could well be that the key solution of our problems will only become visible when we learn to look at ourselves through the eyes of an outsider. (..) Artistic quality is valued in the international context. (...) That is why it is crucial that our connection with the international podium is maintained, even stimulated.'* Only, she says, that requires curiosity, and *'the Dutch art world does not shine in curiosity'*. She has a point there, to which I would like to add the loss of foreign-language skills in the Dutch art world. No longer having a command of French and German is an absolute barrier to getting through to policymakers in other countries, certainly in France.

What exactly *is* international cultural policy? Valentijn Bijvanck, director of the Zeeuws Museum in Middelburg, formulates it as follows: *'International cultural policy is a misleading term for an untidy collection of policy programmes devoted to government-supported promotion of the arts abroad.'* He means this negatively, but that's the way it is. In spite of this lack of organisation, there usually is some kind of thought behind the policy, and what's more, in my experience success abroad is often mainly a matter of chance. A translation happens to be on top of the reviewer's pile; the music critic happened to have had a good night's sleep and so gives an ecstatic verdict on a Dutch ensemble; the Italian designer happens for once not to be jealous and praises a fellow-designer from the Netherlands in the newspaper. You can indeed implement cultural policy, but it doesn't always have the effect that you would like. Aaron Betsky, the director of NAi, takes the same view: *'Precisely because there is no centralised control, an array of designers gets the chance to be promoted abroad.'* Of course there are also authors in this book who tell you what international cultural policy *should* be. Boris Dittrich, chairman of D66, puts it as follows: *'I think that it would be instead to our advantage to open wide to Europe and the rest of the world. Intensive contacts with other countries are indispensable to the creative, innovative society that I envisage,'* and: *'The ambition to put Dutch culture back on the world map must be a realisable goal of our cultural policy.'* Like a number of other authors in this book, he indicates that the European Union could take on more cultural responsibilities than is currently the case, such as promoting the mobility of artists and artworks, establishing programmes for travel grants and simplifying the rules for European cultural subsidies that currently resemble an impenetrable forest. President of the European Commission José Manuel Barroso has put it very nicely: *'Europe is not only about markets – it is also about values and cultures'.* So all we need now is the practical application of this idea.

The last essay in this volume was written by Thomas Michelon, cultural attaché at the French embassy in The Hague, and it's also one of the better pieces, perhaps because of yet another Dutch character trait, one from which this Frenchman does not suffer: *'the inability to see oneself and one's culture in perspective'* (Bas Heijne). Michelon sees the answer to the current crisis in the Dutch art world mainly in confrontation with other cultures: *'Holland has long enjoyed the reputation of thinking up new practices, and used to exert a strong attractive force on professionals from all over the world. This was, not impor-*

tantly, of considerable advantage to artists, designers and architects. It would be a sign of ambition to take this line of thought as the basis for reflection or policy.' As the director of the Institut Néerlandais in Paris I am happy to concur with the opinion of this Frenchman working in the Netherlands, my fellow cultural representative. Come on, Holland, enter into confrontation, devise new and clever methods, invest in interest, but above all: be proud of the quality of the work produced by Dutch artists, both now and in the past, and let the whole world see just how proud you are!

Rudi Wester
Translated by Laura Watkinson

Ben Hurkmans *et al.*, *All that Dutch. International Cultural Politics.* 2005, 118 pp. ISBN 90-5662-463-6. Published by NAi Publishers (Rotterdam) in association with the Fund for Amateur Art and Performing Arts (FAPK), the Mondriaan Foundation, the Foundation for the Production and Translation of Dutch Literature (NLPVF), and the Dutch Service Centre for International Cultural Activities (SICA).

Soundly Based, but not Set in Stone
In Search of a Canon to be Cherished

In 2005 the Dutch Minister of Education, Maria van der Hoeven, set up a commission of wise individuals to produce a canon for primary and secondary education. This canon, the 'Story of the Netherlands' in an international context, is to take account not only of history but also of other fields such as language and literature, art, science and technology. Its purpose is, among other things, to generate a shared knowledge of (cultural) history.

The establishment of this Canon Commission is due in the first place to a specific political-administrative process – a process sparked by a remarkably widespread popular feeling on the subject, with numerous calls for more attention to be paid to the canon. Now 'canon' can also mean a part-song, and as in a part-song many voices mixed and mingled.

Rembrandt van Rijn, *Moses
Smashing the Tables
of the Law*. 1659.
Canvas, 168.5 x 136.5 cm.
Gemäldegalerie, Berlin.

say that all these associations or desires are out of order, but for the commission they are certainly not at the heart of what we are trying to do and why we are doing it. Our actual motivation is, if I may put it that way, far less defensive or negative in its nature. We are not mounting guard on the nation's cultural dikes. The Commission sees the canon not as a remedy for all manner of calamities arriving from outside, but first and foremost as something that is itself of great intrinsic value. Better knowledge and awareness of what is particularly worth knowing in facts, figures and phenomena from our common history and culture – of the Netherlands initially, but then most emphatically in relation to the wide world outside – can be good for the whole country. And most certainly not aimed only at newcomers in the Netherlands, for concerns about the decline in general knowledge – for instance, about young people who think that Joan of Arc was Noah's wife – have been voiced for some considerable time. So the canon will be equally useful to Fouad Ajgou and Saskia de Vries, to Dutch citizens both 'new' and 'old'.

On top of that, paying extra attention to the canon also means deliberately selecting for quality. The canon is concerned with significant events, magnificent stories, outstanding people and splendid works of art. Of course there can and will be disagreements about the judgments on all these things, but the drastic selection processes that have been working on the canon for centuries mean that its component parts really cannot be changed at will for others, let alone for their opposites. One purpose of the canon is to dare to identify quality and lasting importance, and to keep impressing on us the difference between historic events and hype, and between art and kitsch.

But quality and differences in quality is something one has to learn to appreciate, Only a tiny minority is able to find its own way to what history and culture can offer by way of knowledge, beauty and inspiration. The vast majority needs the guidance of one or more middlemen. For those who happen to have been born into the right environment that guide may be a parent, an aunt or a neighbour; but history, in the

Some understood the canon as the need to dare show greater pride in their own past; others were mainly concerned with a possible way of encouraging newcomers to integrate in the Netherlands; others again see it as a natural consequence of increased awareness of Dutch identity, sometimes but not necessarily against the background of an expanding Europe.

As chairman of the Canon Commission I will not

Netherlands and elsewhere, teaches us that over the centuries it is the school that has fulfilled that role far more often than anyone or anything else. There are countless examples of great cultural figures whose brilliance was sparked at school, by inspired teachers who knew how to enthuse and guide their pupils and who saw their role in education, as the saying goes, not as filling a bucket but lighting a fire.

In these circles, that is among teachers in every type of school, there is currently a clear need for more back-up in teaching the canon, and for the commission that is perhaps the most important reason for gladly undertaking that task. We hope to be able to come up with something the educators in particular will be happy with, as regards both content and form. Discussion of the canon in recent months has focused mainly on the content; for instance, whether along with William of Orange the canon should also include korfball. No less important to the commission, though, will be the question of the ideal educational 'format' for the canon: which school subjects it should engage in, how the canon will fit into the legally prescribed final attainment levels, which means of delivery are most appropriate: a textbook, teaching packets, a TV series, wall posters, a website, courses for teachers, a multimedia approach, a collection of 'top tens', or a bit of everything.

In education, then, the canon is not just a matter of teaching material but also of presentation, of how it should be taught, and the Commission will also devote considerable attention to this.

So the Commission will begin its work with the educational aspect; but the canon must certainly not become merely something one gets tested on at school. Here if anywhere the saying that learning is not for school but for life holds true; and however pious it may sound, the quality of what the canon offers really should be able to make of it something that stays with one for a long time – until in later life one is able to look at it objectively, and if one prefers put one's own twist on it. Not the least of the canon's functions is to stimulate continuing talk, and argument too about it; it will prove its worth not so much by being there, but rather by being alive. The

Commission's remit also includes making proposals for future updating of the canon, and although I predict that much of it will be proof against the changing spirit of the times, the Commission certainly has no intention of creating a straitjacket. So do not expect from it a canon graven in tablets of stone.

Meanwhile, the Netherlands seems pleasingly curious as to what will happen about the canon. Even before the commission had started work it was already inundated with spontaneous suggestions and wishes. The commission sees this as an encouraging sign that the canon will fill a need, and will be happy to enter into an intensive discussion of its activities with all interested institutions and individuals. As a first step in this direction we have set up a website on which everyone can find information about the commission, its way of working and the running debate about the canon, and can also let the commission know their own views and suggestions, which we shall greatly value. The commission hopes that the site will develop into an effective and much-used instrument of communication.

All this is intended to give a first impression of the spirit in which the Commission hopes to operate and the method it envisages using. While the route we take is of genuine importance, what matters most is the goal – in our view, not so much a canon to be flaunted as a banner, or hammered into the ground like some massive pile, but first and foremost a canon to foster and to cherish.

Frits van Oostrom
Translated by Tanis Guest

This article is a version of the address by the Chairman of the Commission on the occasion of its presentation to the press.

www.canonvannederland.nl

Ben Benaouisse or the Art of Remembering

Critics love to take stock of an artist's development, sketching the broad outlines of his artistic evolution, roughing out a context for a creation that is always part of a bigger picture. And it becomes even more interesting and rewarding when the artist takes his own journey as the point of departure for his artistic output. Mohamed Ben Benaouisse, for example, sets about reconstructing and stage-managing the path he treads as an actor, choreographer and visual artist, and with each new production he invites the audience to accompany him and to reflect with him.

Mohamed Ben Benaouisse (1971-) hails from the Walloon village of Familleureux, near La Louvière. He grew up in a family where Moroccan and Belgian cultures coexisted quite happily. His father was authoritarian, but took a liberal approach to his Islamic faith. He would expertly slaughter a sheep for the Feast of the Sacrifice, while at the same time he shared his son's admiration for Enzo Scifo's footballing skills. These details have since become familiar pointers in Benaouisse's work.

When the Ghent production house Victoria chose Benaouisse for the dance project *Yes Wait!* (Ja Wacht!), staged as part of Antwerp's Cultural Capital of Europe festival in 1993, he took his first steps outside Familleureux. Coming second in the *Best Belgian Dance Solo* (1994), initiated by Alain Platel and Victoria, and above all his performance in *Mother and Child* (Moeder en Kind, 1995) by Alain Platel and Arne Sierens, made him decide to settle permanently in Ghent. He shortened his name to Ben Benaouisse and has since devoted his life to dance and the stage.

Still under Victoria's wing, Ben Benaouisse set to work on *Lifestyle* and *Club Astrid*. The production house also encouraged him to realise his own artistic ambitions. He began by setting up the dance trio Latrinité with Helmut van den Meersschaut and Noël van Kelst, which resulted in three dance productions between 1995 and 2000.

The urge to tell his own story led him to conclude that he had outgrown Victoria's improvisational style and approach. Benaouisse was not convinced that dance and theatre alone were adequate forms for expressing his own universe. Improvisation was replaced by a clear concept that combined several different artistic disciplines, which he pieced together like a jigsaw puzzle. He experimented with these ideas in the *Invasif I* (Lille, 2001) and *It is Lamb* (Het is lam, 2002) projects. After that the audience found it hard to pigeonhole Benaouisse's work. In a transitional area between theatre and visual art, poised between performance and installation, he sought the theatricality of visual art while at the same time testing the visual power of theatre. This is why Benaouisse sometimes presents his work in the theatre, but at other times believes it is shown to its best advantage in an exhibition space or even in the dunes.

Thus his *Invasif I* and *It is Lamb* are in fact exhibitions which play capriciously with the conventions of the theatre: at a set time the spectators are allowed into the exhibition, and although they are in a theatre they are not allocated seats. Neither are the spectators allowed to move round the exhibition at will; what they look at is strictly controlled and timed by Benaouisse. In *Invasif II* (2002) he reversed the procedure: he allowed the audience to visit an exhibition in the Caermers Cloister in Ghent in the normal way, but constantly confronted them with live performances. The conventions of an exhibition space were rearranged theatrically, even if the public was free to reconstruct its own story in the total installation that *Invasif II* is.

Wherever Ben Benaouisse shows his creations and however diverse the forms of expression he selects, you are always aware that he is searching for an artistic and cultural identity of his own, attempting to stage-manage his autobiography in successive phases. He begins with family photographs, prints, drawings, objects, frames, texts, sounds, music and videos – all material which he catalogues, inventorises and structures to create a personal stage set. Thus the set for *It is Lamb* is almost literally a flea market of objects that revive the memory of his deceased father: against the background of the Van Eyck brothers' *Mystic Lamb*, he shows for example

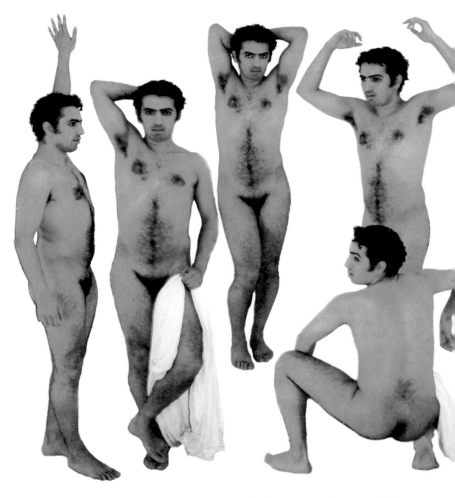

Ben Benaouisse, *It is Lamb*
(Het is lam, 2005; after
Picasso's *Les demoiselles
d'Avignon*).

a short family film in which his father slaughters a lamb – Benaouisse never tries to avoid the pathos of explicit symbolic images. Even stronger is the passion for collecting in *Invasif II*: he guides the visitor past a series of cupboards filled with memories representing his life, thereby making his memory visible and tangible to others.

Yet Benaouisse is careful to avoid the trap of laying himself open to the accusation of navel-gazing. The visitor does enter a strange universe, but at the same time he recognises elements that are typically Belgian. By interweaving the individual and the collective memory, subjective and objective documentation, Ben Benaouisse legitimises his autobiographical investigation. Perhaps it is a Messianic trait on the part of the artist that he first bares himself so as to become a metaphor for others, thereby illus-

trating his conviction that a person's memory is instrumental in forming his identity.

Invasif, which has since become the name of Benaouisse's own company, now consists of five stages which are related, though in different constellations (exhibition, performance, theatre, choreography): it is a multiplicity of vestiges of the past, as if Benaouisse is trying to arm himself against the future and to unravel the mystery of human existence.

The desire to embrace everything dominates a new version of *It is Lamb,* which had its première in January 2005. In this multidisciplinary production Benaouisse brings together his previous projects and makes the most of the abundance of material which alludes (among other things) to Christian iconography and Arab culture. Animals, texts, video, a light and colour show, requiem music, a naked female dancer, a paralysed man in a wheelchair... the spectator is assailed simultaneously and bombastically by all this. Again Benaouisse generates a number of powerful images, such as the ritual opening image in which a frail, naked dancer smears black paint over the upper part of her body, or the cockerels in a Moroccan setting, and he builds an extraordinary tension between hectic activity and motionlessness. You see a lot and a lot eludes you, yet almost nothing happens on the stage. Whilst you are bombarded by symbolism and philosophical and religious references, none of it engages you because there is no real explanation. Benaouisse tries to create an open theatrical space by inviting the audience to explore the stage after the show, but during the performance he chains his public to the fourth wall. It seems that in *It is Lamb* Ben Benaouisse has rather lost his way in his own universe. Evidently he was enticed into an all-embracing and extravagant approach by the sheer scale of the large stage, just as inexperienced writers have no qualms about packing all their concerns into one book.

In September 2005 Ben Benaouisse presented a new attempt to achieve solidarity between performers and spectators, by redefining the theatrical space in the performances *Taliban Evenings* (Les soirées talibanes) and *Pub(lic)-Theatre* (Open-ba(a)r-theater). In *Taliban Evenings* Benaouisse turned the stage of the Nieuwpoorttheater in Ghent into a café, thereby creating an area where the public could follow the work in progress openly and in a relaxed manner. Despite this scenographic manipulation, the spectators were still very much aware of the theatrical setting within which they were manoeuvred. For *Pub(lic)-Theatre*, on the other hand, Benaouisse kept the doors of the theatre closed and had the audience sit in the café throughout the performance. On a screen in the café they watched the artist at work in the auditorium. Both performances were preparations for *No Production*, the new show with which Benaouisse's company Invasif had its première in January 2006. So far at least, *Taliban Evenings* and *Pub(lic)-Theatre* have not managed to rid the performances of the sense of sterility and artificiality

which also characterised *It is Lamb*. Try as he may to achieve a new solidarity with his public, his efforts all too often founder in alienation and remoteness.

Koen van Kerrebroeck
Translated by Alison Mouthaan-Gwillim

Language

Of Rabbits and Queens
The Hardship and Bliss of Learning Dutch

When I moved to the Netherlands, I met a lot of people who said that there was no point in learning Dutch.

Some people claimed that it was too difficult. Why otherwise would the English language contain the expression 'double Dutch', signifying something that is baffling beyond belief, like – as I was to find out later – road signs in Flanders. Other people said that learning Dutch was a futile exercise, since everyone in the Low Countries speaks perfect English. A third line of argument was that Dutch is an ugly language, spoken only by uncivilised tribes who inhabited the damp marshes north of Paris. A final blow to the aspiring Dutch speaker was the claim that Dutch is a dying language, on its way out. Within fifty years, the cynics said, Dutch would be a tiny regional dialect. Within a hundred years, it would be as dead as Latin.

I decided, nevertheless, to sign up for a language class in Utrecht. It was taught in a draughty convent building by a charming woman called Mevrouw Posthumous and was, I have to say, one of the best decisions I ever made. Not that it was easy. While Mevrouw Posthumous did her best, I had some moments of deep despair in that chilly Utrecht convent. I should have realised it was going to be a struggle a few weeks earlier, when I arrived at the Dutch national airport, and had no idea whether the airport name was pronounced 'Ship Hole' or 'Skip Hall'.

It was several months before I had properly learned to distinguish *konijn* – rabbit – from *koningin* – queen –, which meant that the Dutch Koninginnedag became forever confused with small furry animals. And I have never really been confident enough to describe someone as *zalig* (delightful, blessed), in case the word I really want to use is *zielig* (pathetic). When speaking Dutch, it sometimes seemed enough of a triumph just to get the words out in the right order, holding on to the verb until the very end of the sentence, even though by then you have totally forgotten how the sentence started, several minutes before...

Whatever confidence I gained in the Netherlands was immediately lost in the move to Belgium. Here, I had to buy meat in a *beenhouwerij* and not a *slagerij* – though both are just butchers' shops. I had to realise that *koopjes* (sales) had become *solden*. And I had to get accustomed to the fact that a plain *tosti met kaas* had changed its identity entirely and become an unrecognisable *Krok Madammeke*.

So, yes, Dutch is a difficult language.

And, to make matters worse, everyone in the Low Countries speaks perfect English. This is very convenient if you are a tourist on a weekend break in Amsterdam, but it makes it very difficult for anyone to make any progress in spoken Dutch. The moment you hesitate, even if it is just for a millisecond while you decide whether that regal lady is to be referred to as *Konijn* Beatrix or *Koningin* Beatrix, the Dutch speaker will immediately switch the conversation into English, which leaves you feeling just a little *zielig*, if that is the right word.

So that makes two reasons for not talking Dutch. But I am not prepared to concede any ground to those who argue that Dutch is an ugly language. Spoken by the right people, it can be one of the most sensuous languages in the world. In fact, I am so fond of spoken Dutch that I occasionally phone up the Dutch tourist office in Brussels, and ask some unnecessary question about museum opening times, just to hear the receptionist's voice. And, sad as it sounds, I occasionally watch a certain reality show on Flemish television simply because it is presented by Roos van Acker, whose voice is pure bliss. Which is *zalig*.

So, no, Dutch is not ugly.

But is it, as cynics say, a dying language?

Wim Daniels' book, *Talking Dutch*[1], sets out to persuade us that it is very much alive and well. He shows us how embedded it is in the Northern European identity, borrowing words from French, Latin, German and English, and occasionally returning the favour by exporting a useful word of Dutch. Where would the French be without the word boulevard, derived from the Dutch *bolwerk*? Where would the English be without the word boss, taken from the Dutch word *baas*? And where would sailors be without the word yacht, derived from the word *jacht*?

It is, quite honestly, impossible to imagine living in the Low Countries without talking Dutch. Deprived of Mevrouw Posthumous' teaching, I would remain baffled by Dutch street names, like Beenhouwersstraat, Handschoenmarkt and Eerste Tuindwarsstraat. I would never have read Dutch-language writers like Adriaan van Dis, Jeroen Brouwers or Erik de Kuyper. Nor would I ever have discovered the gutsy lyrics of the Flemish folk group Lais. And I would probably still be wondering why so many signs in Flanders point to a town called *Omleiding* – which merely indicates a *diversion*.

And, of course, I would be expecting to see rabbits on Koninginnedag.

Derek Blyth

1. Wim Daniëls, *Talking Dutch* (Tr. Laura Watkinson). Rekkem: Ons Erfdeel vzw, 2005 (see p. 320 for further details)

'Good butter and good cheese is good English and good Frieze'
Frisian Language and Culture today

' *I am always sorry when any language is lost because languages are the pedigree of nations and they of course are irrepressible*'. So said Doctor Johnson almost two centuries ago, and not long after, similar ideas inspired Sir John Bowring' s *Frisian Literature* (1829), one of the first histories of the literature of the Frisians, the linguistic minority living in the northern Dutch province of Fryslân.

The Frisian language is the nearest relative of English on the European mainland, and for many centuries there has been extensive traffic between the two nations. In Suffolk one can still find traces of early medieval Frisian immigration in place names such as Friston and Fressington; and across the North Sea the continental dialect closest to English is the Frisian spoken in the ancient harbour town of Hindeloopen.

Today, as a result of almost four decades of innovative sociolinguistic research by scholars such as Durk Gorter of the Fryske Akademy in Leeuwarden, we are rather well-informed about the actual state of the Frisian language. While the 600,000 inhabitants of the province all know Dutch, some 55% have Frisian as their first language, and 74% are able to speak and understand it. In total this gives some 400,000 social users of the language, and given that this figure has been relatively stable over the past 25 years Gorter is positive about the future, predicting that Frisian '*will be here on the mainland, a hundred years from now, if in a different, diluted form*' (cf. Drysdale 2001:149).

But although it is stable, the situation of Frisian is not without problems. A worrying demographic trend is the increasing influx of Dutch speakers who often do not bother to learn Frisian, whereas at the same time Frisians are leaving the province in search of higher education and a career. The use of Frisian may also be contested at the national level. Place names, for example, can officially be in Frisian, but the Dutch national Post Office refuses to have anything to do with this. A few years ago, when it was proposed that railway personnel working in Fryslân should be able to speak Frisian, this made the front page of the national newspaper *De Telegraaf*, which saw it as an almost secessionist proposal. And then there are the internal divisions amongst the Frisians themselves. Recently, for example, the councils of Harlingen and Vlieland sent back documents from another council simply because they were in Frisian.

We have to note here that the position of Frisian is rather different from and not as strongly embedded as that of other European minority languages such as Basque, Catalan and Welsh. In railway stations in Wales, for example, travel announcements are made first in Welsh and then in English. And in the European capital, Brussels – which is the only other officially bilingual part of the Dutch-speaking Low Countries – there is a well-established regime of functional bilingualism, which obliges government offices to provide services in both Dutch and French.

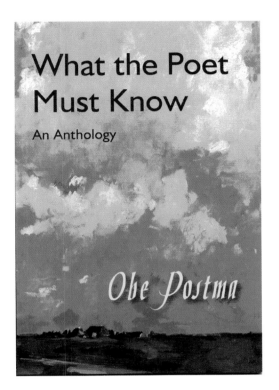

What the Poet Must Know

An Anthology

Obe Postma

In Fryslân, in contrast, room for manoeuvre in matters of language is much more limited. Even if Frisian has been officially recognised as the province's second language, language policy in Fryslân is a matter of small advances and the long haul. This has indeed been, from the 1930s onwards, the course towards increasing recognition of Frisian. Along the way, however, the political context has changed completely, from the monolithic Dutch nation-state of the 1930s to the increasingly globalised world of today. Today, the European Charter for Regional and Indigenous Minority Languages (1998) and the UNESCO Universal Declaration on Cultural Diversity (2001) present opportunities and challenges for minority languages that are being actively explored by the provincial authorities through a series of covenants with the national government.

As a result, we now have an interesting document on Frisian language policy, *The Natural Place of Frisian* (De natuurlijke plaats van het Fries), in which the provincial authorities have set out their vision and goals for the period 2003-2007. Their starting point is a recognition that in Fryslân bi- and multilingualism are an everyday social reality. And their central aim is to create a climate in which speaking Frisian is considered normal at all levels of communication, high and low, internally as well as externally. To achieve this, there is an ongoing campaign to stimulate the use of Frisian in government, in the schools, the media and at work, in culture, sports, the arts and sciences, and also of course in the home.

An issue of central importance in this respect is that of education. Here, the standard Dutch model is that of transitional bilingualism. That is, Frisian may be used in the early years of primary school, but after that the language of instruction will have to be Dutch. And, as national Education Minister Maria van der Hoeven has said, teachers from elsewhere in the Netherlands do not have to learn Frisian when they come to live and teach in Fryslân. But surely, more needs to be done if one wants to ensure that Frisian school leavers are fully qualified in each of their languages. Meanwhile, an interesting experiment has been running since 1997 with trilingual primary education in Frisian, Dutch and English. As Beetsma's Mercator-Education report of 2002 makes clear, this may well have a wider significance for other linguistic minorities across Europe. Furthermore, on a world scale we note that in India too many schools are offering trilingual education.

But first things first. What matters most is the vitality of Frisian culture in its homeland. A helpful insight is provided here by the Dutch historian Johan Huizinga, who described Frisian culture as *'volks'* ('popular'), in contradistinction to the dominant Dutch culture, which he saw as *'burgerlijk'* ('bourgeois').

It is certainly true that Frisian is first and foremost the spoken language of the people, and that Frisian culture is above all an oral culture. There is an active amateur scene in Frisian village theatre throughout the province. Storytelling is common, whether it is in summer time on the 'boasting benches' around the harbours, or during storytelling competitions in village pubs in winter. Frisian poets stand firmly in the bardic tradition: Tsjêbbe Hettinga's poems can of course be read as written texts printed on a page, but they are first of all spoken incantations. And this in fact is one of the great cultural strengths of the Frisians: Frisian literature is closely linked to this oral culture, and the distance between the spoken and the written language of literature is far smaller in Frisian than it is in Dutch.

There is a lively literary production in Frisian of about 100 titles per year, roughly divided amongst 30 titles in prose fiction, 15 in poetry, 30 in children's and young people's literature, and 25 in non-fiction. There are important and original writers of fiction, such as Tiny Mulder, Trinus Riemersma, Rink van der Velde and Reinder van der Leest. In the *Fryske Klassiken* series more than 25 titles have been published since 1992, and there is a regular flow of Frisian translations from world literature, ranging from Homer to Nietzsche and Walt Whitman. 2004 saw the publication of a bilingual anthology of one of Fryslân's greatest poets of the twentieth century, Obe Postma (1868-1963), and almost at the same time the trilingual volume *'Where Everything Becomes A Border: The Journey'* presented new work by some 20 young Fri-sian poets. Every year Frisian writers go out to sell their books in the countryside, and every year – as Teake Oppewal has reported – an estimated 60,000 people buy about 90,000 Frisian books, and some 300,000 Frisian library books are borrowed by 70,000 readers.

Beyond literature there are the other arts. In 2001, the Frisian film *Nynke* (2001) won the highest Dutch cinema award, The Golden Calf (Het gouden kalf), both for best film and for best actress. It is a portrait of the feminist writer Nynke van Hichtum (1860-1939). It is also an ode to Fryslân and Frisian culture; and in it one can hear the most beautiful spoken Frisian I have ever heard. In summer there are open air performances of Shakespeare's *A Midsummer Night's Dream* in Frisian, the island of Terschelling hosts the theatre festival *Oerol*, and the *Tryater* group performs its intercultural experiments. From the mid-eighties an attractive Frisian pop scene has been led by De Kast, whose *In Nije Dei* (A New Day) topped the charts in 1997.

However, Huizinga's distinction, while helpful, also has its limitations, for in a culture like the Dutch, which has been *burgerlijk* for centuries, the term *'volks'* is not without negative connotations, evoking as it does the unmannered, the uneducated and the lower class – which makes it easy to look down on Frisian as merely a dialect. One can still find this view in Holland, witness a recent piece by the columnist Ronald Plasterk in which he compared Frisian to his own rough city dialect of The Hague, noted that he could read it without much difficulty, and argued that it should be seen as just another dialect of Dutch, and not as a language in its own right.

Here, battle has been joined by a group of young Frisian language activists, the so-called Auwersk group, with a number of eye-catching proposals for symbolic action, such as having FRL bumper stickers on cars (instead of NL), and having Frisian ethnic identity and nationality written into their Dutch passports. These ideas have triggered a lively public debate on the website of the *Leeuwarder Courant*. What is striking, especially about the passport debate, is how some of the Dutch participants are contesting the use of Frisian: *'You are living in the Netherlands here, so you should speak Dutch instead of your dialect'*, and *'If you insist on your Frisian identity, you are either backward, provincial villagers, trying to turn Fryslân into a reservation, or extremists infringing upon Dutch people's rights'*. Statements such as these are not exactly overflowing with respect for linguistic and cultural diversity. They hark back to an earlier era, when the Netherlands was a much more monocultural and monolingual nation-state than it is today (see also my 'The Other Languages of the Netherlands' in TLC 8 (2000)).

This then, to my mind, is what makes the Frisian case so interesting and challenging today. If the quality of a society and culture can be measured by looking at how they deal with their minorities, then this holds true of the Dutch as well – and here they can point to their active support for the new European and UNESCO instruments for linguistic and cultural diversity. But the question is how these will be implemented in practice. Meanwhile, the Frisians, as a linguistic minority, have for many centuries had a language and a culture of their own, and today they too are having to find new ways forward in an increasingly Dutch-dominated context. It takes two to tango, and the first step here is to recognise the value of linguistic diversity and bilingualism, not as a social obstacle or a handicap, but as a substantial enrichment of the culture of the Frisians as much as of the Netherlands.

Reinier Salverda

REFERENCES

Bruinsma, Klaas et al. (eds.), *Gjin grinzen, de reis/Geen grenzen, de reis/No borders, the voyage*. Leeuwarden: The Cepher Foundation (including a CD with recitals), 2004.
Drysdale, Helena, *Mother Tongues. Travels through Tribal Europe*. London: Picador, 2001
Erkelens, Helma, *Language of the heart*. Leeuwarden: Province of Fryslân, 2004.
Gorter, Durk, 'Nederlands en Fries op gespannen voet? Over ontwikkelingen in de taalverhoudingen in Fryslân'. In: Jan Stroop (ed.), *Waar gaat het Nederlands naartoe? Panorama van een taal*. Amsterdam: Bert Bakker, pp. 84-94, 2003.
Gorter, Durk, Alex Riemersma & Jehannes Ytsma, 'Frisian in the Netherlands'. In: Guus Extra & Durk Gorter (eds.), *The Other languages of Europe*. Clevedon: Multilingual Matters, pp. 103-118, 2001.
Hettinga, Tsjêbbe, *Strange Shores, Frjemde kusten* (Tr. James Brockway). Leeuwarden: Frysk en Frij, 1999.
Oppewal, Teake, 'The Frisian Literary Industry in 13 Paragraphs'. In: *Literatuur uit Friesland/Literatuer út Fryslân/ Literature from Friesland*. Amsterdam: Foundation for the Production and Translation of Dutch Literature, 2001, 63 pp.
Postma, Obe, *What the Poet Must Know. An Anthology* (Tr. Anthony Paul; selection and introduction by Jabik Veenbaas). Leeuwarden: Tresoar, 2004.
Salverda, Reinier, 'Frisian'. In: Glanville Price (ed.), *Encyclopedia of the Languages of Europe*. Oxford: Blackwell, 1998.
Salverda, Reinier, 'The Other Languages of the Netherlands'. In: *The Low Countries* vol. 8. Rekkem: Ons Erfdeel vzw, pp. 245-252, 2000.

Fryslân: www.fryslan.nl – Fryske Akademy: www.fa.knaw.nl – Leeuwarder Courant: www.leeuwardercourant.nl (see under 'Frysk') – Tresoar: www.tresoar.nl

The Dutch Reformation Revisited

In January 2005, publishers De Bezige Bij brought out *Kneeling on a Bed of Violets* (Knielen op een bed violen) by Jan Siebelink. For thirty years now Siebelink has been writing well-received stories, novels and essays on subjects varying from cycle racing to French literature; yet his work has certainly never been part of the canon of Dutch literature. His latest book, in which he returns – not for the first time, as it happens – to the world of his youth, is widely seen as the most important Dutch novel of the past year. The book has gone through twenty-five reprints so far and 175,000 copies have been sold in twelve months. In October 2005, Siebelink won the prestigious AKO literature prize for *Kneeling on a Bed of Violets*. In this book Siebelink describes how his father, a Calvinist flower grower, has a vision and is touched by God. Completely focused on the hereafter, and more specifically on his life after death, the father then loses all contact with earthly reality. And consequently ruins his business and his family. But unlike Jan Wolkers and Maarten 't Hart, the neovitalist and neo-realist authors of the 1960s and 1970s, Siebelink does not put the faith of his fathers behind him. He wants to understand.

Judging from Siebelink's success, he's not the only Dutch person who wants to do that. The widespread secularisation of recent decades led to speculation that God would disappear from the Netherlands. This prediction did not come true. The terrorist attacks in New York (2001), the murders of Pim Fortuyn (2002) and Theo van Gogh (2004) and the fire in a detention centre for illegal immigrants on the edge of Amsterdam's Schiphol airport (2005) threw the nation into total confusion. How could it ever have come to this? Has that famous Dutch tolerance proved capable of dealing with these crises? And what exactly does that tolerance consist of? Can a democratic society restrict freedom of expression and worship in order to protect itself? Should it do so? These are all questions that the Dutch are fiercely debating in parliament, on television and radio, in newspapers and magazines, and also in living rooms, student bars

and village halls. This debate is accompanied by a quest for the identity of the Netherlands. What is it that makes the Dutch people who they are?

Siebelink has cast this question in a literary guise. But sociologists and historians of all kinds are chiming in with their own answers. History, or more precisely Dutch history, is at the centre of public attention. Last spring the country's past was even made the central theme of the national book week. A comparatively large amount of attention is devoted to the first phase of the Eighty Years' War, the period from the 1560s to the 1590s when the Netherlands gradually took shape as an independent nation. Unlike their predecessors, historians now see this uprising more as a civil war. Whilst the vast majority of the population had still not made a definite choice for the old church or for those preaching a new message of salvation but wanted only to be spared the violence of war, a small, radical group of Protestants attempted to seize power.

The Low Countries has always been one of the most urbanised parts of Europe. The successive reformational movements of Lutherans, Baptists and Calvinists quickly took root in those urban areas, which were meeting points for people, goods and ideas. On the orders of the Habsburg rulers Charles V and Philip II, however, the secular authorities subjected religious innovators to extreme persecution. Between 1523 and 1566 no fewer than thirteen hundred of them were executed.[1]

This early phase of the Reformation is Ghent historian Johan Decavele's special field of research. His book *The First Protestants in the Low Countries* (De eerste protestanten in de Lage Landen) brings together fourteen articles previously published in journals or *Festschriften* that were often difficult to get hold of. He has reworked his texts for a more general public and provided an introductory section. Some chapters go back to articles first published in the 1960s, whilst the most recent ones were published in around 2000. This book has made Decavele's academic oeuvre accessible.

After the recapture of the Southern Netherlands by Spanish troops under the command of Alessandro

The Dutch Reformed Church on Bergen Avenue in Jersey City, NJ.

Farnese, Duke of Parma, these territories formed an outpost of the Roman Catholic church and of the Spanish-Habsburg empire. The counter-reformation wiped out almost every memory of the Protestant past. Decavele's greatest achievement is to draw the attention of a more general public to this forgotten aspect of Flemish history.

Marked as it was by the persecutions, Flemish Calvinism was exceptionally radical in character. This radical Calvinism found particularly fertile ground in Ghent, a city with a long revolutionary tradition which had been broken by Charles V a generation earlier. The seizure of power by the Calvinists in 1578 was backed by the craftsmen's guilds, the traditional representatives of the ordinary people. Quite correctly, Decavele pays a great deal of attention to this interplay of religious and social factors.

The situation was very different in Holland, where the urban aristocracy was in charge almost everywhere and the guilds were represented only on the town council of Dordrecht. Just like the Flemish and Brabant mayors and aldermen, the Dutch city fathers made a stand against the advancing power of Philip II and his officials. But they did not envisage any reversal of the social status quo. They had not freed themselves from Mother Church to be patronised by ministers and members of the church council. In the Republic of the United Netherlands, the Reformed church was indeed given preference and recognised as the 'public' church, but that public church did not have any monopoly. Unlike in Scotland or in England, the authorities did not exert any pressure on the faithful to convert to the Reformed church, certainly not in Holland. In large areas of the Republic in around 1600 the church's membership may not have exceeded a quarter of the population, although it undoubtedly reached more people than that.[2] This figure was boosted by approximately one hundred thousand exiles who had fled the Southern Netherlands after the fall of the Calvinist city republics of Ghent, Brussels and Antwerp in 1584-85. So the public church would always be something of a shambles: independent of the authorities, but not in a position to enforce its influence on society. As a consequence, religious pluriformity was one of the characteristics of the Dutch Republic right from the beginning, making it unique amongst the states of early-modern Europe. In their recent surveys, Phil Benedict (*Christ's Churches Purely Reformed*) and Diarmaid MacCulloch (*Reformation*) rightly emphasise the unique character of the early-modern Dutch religious landscape.

The fracture lines that were drawn upon the religious map of the Low Countries at that time still continue to make themselves felt today, as Jan Siebelink's novel, with which I began this article, shows us. The only area of the Dutch Republic where the authorities allowed no religious pluriformity ran in a broad band from the islands of Zeeland in the south-west, via the river area of Zuid-Holland, across the province of Utrecht, to the top of Overijssel. This zone lay just behind the stable frontline that separated the Republic from the Habsburg Netherlands for the greater part of the Eighty Years' War. Later, in the seventeenth, eighteenth and nineteenth centuries, the 'frontline Protestants' who lived there would prove unusually receptive to the variety of reformational pietistic tendencies known collectively as the *'nadere reformatie'* or 'further reformation'. The movements that originated in this *'nadere reformatie'* form a stable, important undercurrent in Dutch Protestantism. The number of *'bevindelijk gereformeerden'*, who subscribe to a pietistic form of Protestantism, has for decades remained constant at around 300,000 people, regardless of all tendencies towards secularisation. This is the group that produced Siebelink's father.

Hans Cools
Translated by Laura Watkinson

FURTHER READING

Phil Benedict, *Christ's Churches Purely Reformed. A Social History of Calvinism*. New Haven / London: Yale University Press, 2002.

Johan Decavele, *De eerste protestanten in de Lage Landen. Geloof en heldenmoed*. Leuven/Zwolle: Davidsfonds / Waanders, 2004.

Arie van Deursen, *De last van veel geluk. De geschiedenis van Nederland, 1555-1702*. Amsterdam: Bert Bakker, 2004.

Joris van Eijnatten & Fred van Lieburg, *Nederlandse religiegeschiedenis*. Hilversum: Verloren, 2005.

Diarmaid MacCulloch, *Reformation. Europe's House Divided. 1490-1700*. London etc.: Allen Lane, 2003.

Andrew Pettegree, *Reformation and the Culture of Persuasion*. Cambridge etc.: Cambridge University Press, 2005.

Ronnie Po-Chia Hsia and Henk van Nierop, *Calvinism and Religious Toleration in the Dutch Golden Age*. Cambridge etc.: Cambridge University Press, 2002.

Peter van Rooden, *Religieuze regimes. Over godsdienst en maatschappij in Nederland*, 1570-1990. Amsterdam: Bert Bakker, 1996.

Jan Siebelink, *Knielen op een bed violen*. Amsterdam: De Bezige Bij, 2005.

FOOTNOTES

1. P. Benedict, *Christ's Churches Purely Reformed. A Social History of Calvinism* (Yale University Press: New Haven and London, 2002), p. 177.

2. Idem, p. 199.

One Foot in America
Antwerp and the Emigrants of the Red Star Line

The Belgian shipping company the Red Star Line was established in 1872 with rich industrialists from Pennsylvania as its principal shareholders. The company worked exclusively with steamships (some of which still had auxiliary sails) sailing between Philadelphia and Antwerp. Within a year it added another line, to New York. Its first steamship, the *Vaderland*

Eugeen van Mieghem,
Departure of the 'Belgenland',
c.1925.
Panel, 39 x 49 cm.
Private collection
© Eugeen van Mieghem Stichting.

sailed from Antwerp for her maiden voyage on 20 January 1873. In the first year alone the Red Star Line carried almost 25,000 passengers from Antwerp to America. The *Vaderland* was joined by the *Nederland* (1873) and the *Switserland* (1874). There was fierce competition between the European departure ports for emigrants: Hamburg (the Hamburg-America Line), Rotterdam (the Holland-America Line), Liverpool (the White Star Line) and, of course, Antwerp, as each sought to attract as many passengers and as much cargo as possible. In 1881 the Red Star Line carried 1,521 first and second class passengers and 24,694 third class passengers on 47 weekly sailings. In 1901 this had already grown to 6,241 and 32,793 respectively on 52 sailings between Antwerp and New York.

In the late nineteenth and early twentieth century thousands of Belgian emigrants left their native land to seek their fortune overseas. The majority went to the United States and settled mainly in states such as Michigan, Iowa, Ohio and Texas. Most of them came from the Belgian countryside, where small plots of land and poor harvests sometimes resulted in extreme poverty and famine. This was true particularly in 1847-1848, with the potato blight and the failure of the grain harvest. Another possible reason for emigration was compulsory military service (from

1909 on). It is estimated that during the period of the Red Star Line's existence a total of some 150,000 Belgians took the plunge (about 5% of the total number of Red Star passengers).

The Red Star Line had a very efficient network of agents throughout Eastern Europe who tried to attract the emigrants to Antwerp by offering competitive fares. Thus over the course of its lifetime the company managed to carry almost three million people. After a long journey, which could sometimes take several weeks, the emigrants finally reached Antwerp. On arrival at the station they proceeded to the Rijnkaai where the ships were tied up. Before departing, however, they had to have a medical examination. So, in 1893, the first Red Star Line warehouse was built on the corner of Rijnkaai and Montevideostraat, for the medical examination of emigrants and the fumigation of their clothing and luggage. Most of the emigrants spent the final days before their departure in wretched hotels. For the third-class passengers the entire voyage was an ordeal and a truly horrifying experience. The food was poor, they were confined in a space far too small for them, without fresh air, and the drinking water on board was often brackish. During the voyage many people also fell sick, which made conditions on board even worse. Emigrants had various reasons for taking the plunge.

RED STAR LINE.
Dinner Menu.
«S. S. Vaderland»
17th April 1905

Oysters on half Shell

Celery   Anchovies   Olives

Crême Lavallière   Consommé Spring

Turbot, Normande
Pommes Windsor

Capon Braisé, Toulouse
Celery au Jus

Sweetbreads a l'Ecarlate
Petits Pois, Francaise

Saddle of Mutton, Sévigné
Asparagus Polonaise

Sorbet Mocha

Suprême of Golden Plover

Salade Doucette

Gateau Leopold   Omelette Soufflé
Nesselrode Pudding
Tartines Russes

Camembert & Cheddar Cheese
Dessert   ---   Coffee

Menu card
(s.s. Vaderland, 17 April 1905).
Van Mieghem Museum, Antwerp/
© Eugeen van Mieghem Stichting.

Mostly it was from economic necessity, occasionally it was a desire for political or religious freedom, and sometimes it was just out of a sense of adventure. In Antwerp's case the majority were Jews from Eastern Europe. Refugees from the pogroms and the intolerance, they were in addition impoverished and unemployed and the hopelessness of their existence led them to dream of a new future. About a third of the Jewish population of Eastern Europe and Russia, around two million people, left for America between 1881 and 1914. Some who became famous Americans sailed from Antwerp to New York on Red Star ships, among them Irving Berlin, Albert Einstein and the Yiddish writers Sholom Aleichem and Yuri Suhl.

By the time the emigrants finally reached their ports of departure they were already reduced to a passive mass of human suffering, no longer in any fit state to withstand what they were about to undergo. Travelling third class, down in the bowels of the ship, meant being obliged to share a misery that was the same for everyone, educated and uneducated alike. Fortunately, from 1900 onwards, under pressure from public opinion and government, conditions did improve somewhat. To deal with the enormous influx of immigrants and ships impressive buildings were constructed on Ellis Island in New York where the registration and medical examination of the third class passengers could take place. When the complex opened on 1 January 1892 it dealt with over 2,000 people on the very first day. In the period between 1892 and 1924 thousands passed through it every day. Each was given a number on arrival, grouped according to the ship's manifest. Before they could finally set foot on American soil the third-class passengers had to go through yet another fairly complicated and time-consuming system of checks, which resulted in 2% of the passengers being sent back. The reason was usually some kind of incurable disease, a mental abnormality or suspected criminal behaviour.

The largest ship in the Red Star fleet, the *Belgenland II*, was launched on 31 December 1914 at the Harland & Wolff shipyard in Belfast. However, owing to the outbreak of war, it had to be converted into a troop transport. At the time it was the largest commercial vessel in the world. In the Spring of 1921 the ship was refitted all over again by Harland & Wolff and taken back into service by the Red Star Line. On 4 April 1923 it was given a rousing reception in Antwerp as the flagship of the Red Star Line; it was then the eighth largest passenger ship in the world, with a capacity of some 500 passengers in first class, some 600 in second class and some 1,500 in third class. The interior of the ship was almost the same as that of its two sister ships, one of which was the famous *Titanic*!

Throughout 1920 and 1921 there was still massive emigration from Eastern Europe to America. Shortly after that, however, emigration fell back by almost half, because in May 1921 the American Congress voted in a new immigration law which introduced a quota system by country of origin. The worldwide economic recession led to a crisis in world trade and a great many shipping companies went bankrupt. Red Star Line personnel in Antwerp were dismissed on 31 December 1934. On 29 November 1954 the American federal authorities closed Ellis Island. The buildings were neglected and left to fall into ruin. But after a long period of restoration the Ellis Island Immigration Museum was able to open its doors. Today Ellis Island is extolled as the 'golden gateway' to America that 12 million immigrants passed through. It is estimated that 90% of those who came were of European origin. Thus the building also holds a piece of European history. Today it is estimated that 40% of the population of the United States can trace its 'roots' to an ancestor who landed on this island.

In January 2008 the MAS (Museum aan de Stroom) Museum in Antwerp will open its doors. Aldermen Heylen and Van Campenhout of Antwerp want the old Red Star Line buildings to be a permanent part of the historical heritage of the old dockland area. In and around the complex American tourists will be told the intriguing story of the long journey of their forefathers who found, when they reached Antwerp in about 1900, that they already had one foot in America...

Erwin Joos
Translated by Sheila M. Dale

See also: Erwin Joos, *Eugeen Van Mieghem. Antwerp-New York: Emigrants of the Red Star Line, 1875-1930.* Leuven: Exhibitions International, 2006 (This exhibition takes place at the South Street Seaport Museum (New York) April-October 2006: see www.southstseaport.org).

Clio Offside?
University of Groningen Opens Biographical Institute

For centuries Apollo's muse, Clio, has looked after biography. Under her tutelage generations of biographers told tales of other people's doings. Under her patronage thousands of readers have experienced the fascination of past lives. Under her protection the genre developed into a symbiosis of art and science. It was long believed that these two would work to each other's advantage, but in the late nineteenth century that belief was shattered: the natural science methodology of the day was elevated to the norm and set new criteria for the study of literature and history – and so also for biography. It was thought that by giving an exhaustive description of the behaviour of one's subject, and then explaining it in objective terms, the biographer could reconstruct historical truth. The ultimate aim of this was to gain insight into the factors that defined an individual and his work.

Early in the twentieth century, however, biographers had to concede with disappointment that the laws of creativity and character were not capable of definition. People accepted that it was impossible to purge biography of subjectivity; it seemed quite simply to be inherent in the genre. Biographers were no longer obliged to deconstruct their subject into identifying factors, no longer did they search for explanations, no longer did they accept causality as a principle. From that time on biographers were expected mainly to try to understand someone's life and work. They were expected to attempt to locate their subject in the spirit of the times, to immerse themselves in his or her personality – but prove? No, biographers could not prove their hypotheses. At most they could make their assumptions plausible.

In the course of the twentieth century there was a heated debate over the ideal balance between art and science. Some were afraid that the disciplines of art and history would lose their status, and maybe even their right to exist, unless the subjective and literary aspects in biography were repressed as far as possible. Yet the other 'side' in the battle felt that literature could be an important stimulus for scholarly biography.

At the beginning of the twenty-first century this debate is still going on. 'The decisive factor', so M.B. van Buuren writes of the present situation in *Philosophy of General Literary Theory* (Filosofie van de algemene literatuurwetenschap), '*is not that the theoretical problems have been solved, but that the approach is supported by sufficient academics, and biography is thereby legitimised as theory. In this situation academics choose pragmatic solutions for the problems confronting them.*' Of course biographers choose pragmatic solutions, but they do that because they have no other choice. The never-ending battle between disciplines leads inevitably to theoretical relativism: there is no such thing as a generally applicable 'theory of biography' – because thinking with regard to biography is profoundly influenced by developments in, for example, psychology, society, and the study of literature and history. For this reason there will always be discussion about the genre; and for this reason, by definition, that discussion can never be brought to a satisfactory close.

None the less, people at the University of Groningen are going to have a stab at it. The Faculty of Arts there recently offered a home to an Institute of Biography, headed by Hans Renders, the biographer of the Dutch writers Jan Hanlo and Jan Campert. The Institute website states: '*The plan to attach an Institute of Biography to the University of Groningen is in line with the long-held view in Groningen that the study of culture is an intrinsic part of historical research as a whole. Biography accords with this view and has therefore been accepted into the university as a full academic genre, a development which has been going on for some time in other countries.*'

The Institute of Biography is financed by the Foundation for Democracy and Media, whose aim is '*the encouragement of media reflecting pluriform opinions within a democratic regime*'. That probably explains why the Institute rules the muse Clio offside when it sets out the history of biography: '*Paradoxical as it may seem, it is from biography as a journalistic genre*

that academic biography has increasingly developed', says the website, with good intentions but scant regard for the truth. Maybe the nature of its funding body explains why the Institute's area of research is rather strictly delimited, at least according to its own declaration of principle: the emphasis is more on people related to the media, whose life stories can shed new light on the history of newspapers and publishers. On this point the site states, cryptically: '*The specialism of biography involves a clear choice in favour of the discipline of cultural history. The press represents a particular culture. Both need further investigation, but it is very clear that research is needed not just into analysis of language, style and genre but also into the "biographical connection" between journalistic and cultural institutions.*'

But it would be foolish to judge Hans Renders by his words alone and not his deeds. We can warmly welcome the first initiatives he has come up with as director of the Institute of Biography. From November 2005 on, in co-operation with the publishing house De Bezige Bij, he has brought out a series of reasonably-priced reprints of biographies, under the title of *Second Life* (Tweede leven). '*The first two volumes in the series are the massive, brilliant biography of Sigmund Freud by Peter Gay, and the revealing biography of Hans Andreus by Jan van der Vegt*', states a press release from De Bezige Bij.

In addition Renders is organising symposia aimed at stimulating biographical research. At the opening of the Institute of Biography, in March 2005, writers, historians and journalists discussed the influence of journalism on biography, under the title *Necrology and Biography*. At the end of May there was another symposium on the relationship between psychology and biography, in which there was a discussion on the extent to which biographers play the psychologist and, vice versa, the extent to which psychologists draw on works of literature and biographies.

The Institute of Biography is providing opportunities for young academics: part of the budget is reserved for doctoral studentships. At the moment Renders is looking for a doctoral student to write the biography of the recently deceased historian Loe de

Jong (who was also Director of the State Institute for War Documentation from 1945-1979). In all probability the result will be a thesis that has little to do with *'the encouragement of media reflecting pluriform opinions in a democratic regime'*, and even less with the *'analysis of language, style and genre'* that must investigate *'the biographical connection between journalistic and cultural institutions.'* And thank goodness for that.

Annette Portegies
Translated by Sheila M. Dale

Institute of Biography: Faculty of Arts, P.O. Box 716, 9700 AS Groningen, The Netherlands
Tel. +31 50 363.58.16 / biografie.instituut@let.rug.nl
www.rug.nl/let/biografieinstituut

Fate Decided Otherwise
Henk van Woerden (1947-2005)

In October 2005 I interviewed the Dutch writer Henk van Woerden for the Dutch daily *NRC Handelsblad*. There in the Amsterdam art gallery Espace, where his novel *Ultramarine* (Ultramarijn) was being launched and there was an exhibition of his drawings and photos, he told me that he was *'dog-tired'*. He attributed his fatigue to jetlag. He had arrived only a few hours earlier from Ann Arbor, where he was teaching as writer in residence at the University of Michigan. The subject of death did not arise, he did not appear to be ill, and as he lit one cigarette after another with gay abandon had apparently had no 'warning'.

On 16 November, at the age of 57, Van Woerden died in his sleep in Ann Arbor as the result of cardiac arrest. When he did not turn up for his class, students alerted the campus police. It seems typical of the cosmopolitan perpetual wanderer this writer-painter had become that he should draw his last breath in another country, far from his birthplace of Leiden.

Together with his parents and brother, Henk van Woerden had moved to Cape Town at the age of nine.

Blind in one eye, he ascribed *'a special way of looking'* to this handicap. After high school he studied at the Cape Town Academy of Fine Art and developed into a gifted painter and photographer. The assassination of Prime Minister Verwoerd made the situation unbearable for ANC supporters like Van Woerden. In 1968 he settled in the Netherlands where Protestant stuffiness and the still prevailing 1950s atmosphere *'drove him nuts'*. He went to Italy on an art pilgrimage and subsequently spent two years on Crete in the house of the South African writer Jan Rabie.

His first book, the autobiographical novel *Mustn't Look* (Moenie kyk nie) published in 1993, was awarded the coveted Geertjan Lubberhuizen Prize. It was followed by *Tikoes* in 1996 and *A Mouthful of Glass* (Een mond vol glas) in 1998. Together these novels make up a unique triptych of South Africa.

A Mouthful of Glass especially, which is about Prime Minister Verwoerd's murderer (whom Van Woerden visited in prison), made a strong impression both nationally and internationally. In 2001 it received the Sunday Times Alan Paton Award. Van Woerden went on to script and co-direct a television documentary on the life of the South African poet Ingrid Jonker that received the Silver Rose at the Montreux Documentary Festival. A year later his travel novel *Notes of an Airborne Cyclist* (Notities van een luchtfietser) was less well received.

287

In *Ultramarine*, Van Woerden's first novel to be set not in South Africa but in the Mediterranean region he loved so well, he once again displayed his great talent. In this colourful mythical tale his gift as a writer who paints with language comes into its own. His journalistic flair also stands him in good stead. The principle character in *Ultramarine* is partly inspired by the Greek bouzouki player Iordánis Tsomídis, whom Van Woerden had interviewed for *NRC Handelsblad* in 1998.

Henk van Woerden was delighted with all the enthusiastic reviews of *Ultramarine*, a novel that if one reads between the lines is also his political testament. With his considerable experience of migration he felt compassion for migrants and was indignant about the impossible demands made of newcomers in the Netherlands. '*An immigrant's life has been ripped apart, he has as it were to transform his whole personality,*' is what he said in his last interview. '*The demand for total uncompromising assimilation, the insistence that immigrants should dissociate themselves entirely from their roots, shows no understanding of what is being asked of them.*'

In Ann Arbor Van Woerden had begun on a new novel in English. In mid-December this congenial globetrotter was due to finish his stint as writer in residence in Michigan and return to Amsterdam. He wasn't sure he'd be able to settle down in the Netherlands, he said to me in parting. He might have to try his luck in an English-speaking country. Fate, which plays a dominant role in his last novel, decided otherwise.

Elsbeth Etty (© NRC Handelsblad, Rotterdam)
Translated by Elizabeth Mollison-Meijer

An English translation of *Een mond vol glas* has been widely published: – *A Mouthful of Glass: the Man who Killed the Father of Apartheid* (Tr. Dan Jacobson). London: Granta Books, 2001 – *The Assassin: a Story of Race and Rage in the Land of Apartheid* (Tr. Dan Jacobson). New York: Picador, 2002.

www.henkvanwoerden.nl

Never Sell Out
More than 25 Years of The Ex

On anniversaries and other special occasions it is usual to talk about one's personal memories of the person or persons in question. My first memory of The Ex was a completely chaotic 'concert' in a squat in Utrecht, the number-one punk city in the Netherlands – or so the 'U-punks' believed. When The Ex – a shifting entity with a permanent nucleus: Terrie Hessels and Jos Kley – were 'formed' in 1979, the world of amateur amplified music was a turbulent one. The new DIY punk genre offered exciting new prospects such as performing in squats and in front of critical audiences, and developing a recognisably unique style; a feeling of 'this is *ours*' and 'us against the rest of the world' – all washed down with copious quantities of beer. Moreover, in left-wing circles in particular, punk provided opportunities for girls who wanted to play in rock bands. Before punk, this was one of the most frustrating ambitions a girl could have. In 1979, a couple of girlfriends asked me to play in a serious band with a basic repertoire that required regular rehearsal and an affinity with music, otherwise it sounded terrible. We soon became reasonably successful with our 'old' repertoire (uninspired cover bands were heavily criticised at that time, so we gave everything a musical 'makeover'). Once we were part of the much more exciting punk scene, we ventured into the world of ska, an improbably alternative but commercially successful English genre. So we changed our name and from then on performed with the same four girls as two completely different groups. Sometimes we performed in two different guises on the same evening at the same location. This was noticed by Terrie of The Ex. He wrote me a long letter advising me to choose between the two if I wanted to establish and retain my credibility as a musician and a person – in his view these two 'roles' were inseparable. After half a lifetime of packing and unpacking, lugging around and throwing away, I have lost Terrie's letter, but that does nothing to lessen the lasting impression it has made on me. This politically engaged punk musician is so ideo-

logically driven, so uncompromising when it comes to life choices – even when it comes to something as enjoyable as making music – that lesser mortals have given up hope of ever achieving that level of constancy. The ska band split up because ska went out of fashion, and the other band became very successful in entirely different circumstances. But Terrie's letter, which I'd read hundreds of times, gnawed away at my conscience. Sooner or later, every musician is confronted with the institutional-ised sexism of the music industry, its 'grabbing' mentality and lack of respect for creativity and groundbreaking musical innovation, but Terrie didn't need to experience this to be certain of it. He was familiar with the works of Marx, and perhaps already with Adorno (who was only later discovered by pop-

The Ex in Ethiopia, 2003.

studies circles as the first critic of the culture indus-try with a devastating view of the industrial approach to music production). These were the last years of the Golden Age in which the prefix 'anti-' could en-noble any cause, convincing people that they and their 'brothers' could actually make a difference in the world. The principled independence and interna-tional success of The Ex have everything to do with the 'never sell out' philosophy that Terrie introduced me to in his letter. That letter meant more to me than the most passionate declaration of love (so bour-geois!) ever could: I was sold. I didn't have the nerve to reply.

A quarter of a century on, The Ex are much the same. Bill Meyer wrote in *Ink Blot Magazine*: '*As a rule, there's nothing more pathetic than an aging punk rock band, but the Ex have never followed anyone else's rules.*' Terrie and Jos remain the nucleus of the group. Their independence manifests itself in a steady stream of surprising music that often conveys an extra-musical homage. Their highly individual commemoration of the fiftieth anniversary of the Spanish Civil War is a potent reminder of their philosophy. Antifascism, compassion, mobilising support from all quarters (it was a long time before the 'Weapons for El Salvador' campaign was forgotten) for a cause about which they had no misgivings. The Ex have never wavered from that path, even when they took their music in new directions and surrounded themselves with musicians from other musical genres and other parts of the world. Like-mindedness is the greatest unifier.

This was noticeable at their concerts. Visually and audibly, they always managed to communicate that message. You felt safe with all the decibels and windmill-armed musicians, surrounded by fireworks of emotions and the strangest sounds from the stage. In my view, there was – and is – something remarkable about The Ex. They travel all round the world, win awards everywhere, and have guested three times with John Peel at the BBC (the greatest possible achievement in alternative music circles). Is there *anything* they can't or won't do? Yes. They won't rest on their laurels, stroll into the room like arrivistes, jump on the subsidy bandwagon or forge strategic relationships because they want to be seen with the big names. Such opportunism is alien to The Ex. And in spite of that – or perhaps because of it – they do work with the really big names, from legendary fellow idealists such as the more-punk-than-thou recording engineer Steve Albini (Nirvana, among many others) and international stars in the world of jazz improvisation such as Han Bennink, to Tsehaytu Beraki, the mother of Eritrean political soul music who lives in Rotterdam. And early April 2006 The Ex will go into the studio to record an album with the Ethiopian saxophone-giant Getatchew Mekurya.

Everywhere they go, The Ex make the impossible possible by following the age-old adage 'do it yourself' ('...because no-one else will do it for you'). An American reviewer once described their sounds as '*a beautiful frenzy*', a phrase from the first number on their CD *Starters Alternators*. And you'll never find one of their songs on a karaoke machine.

Lutgard Mutsaers
Translated by Yvette Mead

www.theex.nl

The Listener's Contribution
Composing according to Joachim Brackx

Although experimental music only arrived in Flanders half a century after the successes of Charles Ives and Erik Satie, it has since then achieved an impressive record of accomplishments. This is to no small extent thanks to the Stichting Logos from Ghent, which, under the inspiring direction of Godfried-Willem Raes, has spurred on many young composers to respond critically to the traditional organisation of concerts. One of these young people is Joachim Brackx (1975-), who, in spite of his age, has already attracted attention as an original and sensitive composer.

The *dernier cri* in musicology is the so-called New Musicology, in which music is approached not from the point of view of the composer and the score, but from the point of view of the listener. By analogy, Brackx could be called the embodiment of a New Music, in which the composer mainly asks questions about the activity of the listener. To be perfectly clear and to avoid misunderstandings: in no way is this about commodification, or providing auditory pulp for the masses, thereby lining the pockets of the producer and dumbing down material for the listener. The discussion about comprehension, complexity or physical and psychological borders of perception that often occurs in contemporary music is not so much part of the debate. Rather, Brackx is interested in the creative contribution made by the listener during the

Joachim Brackx (1975-).
Photo by Klaas Koppe.

perception of the music. The listener is not a passive consumer, but during the listening he takes an active part in the creative process of the music. In this way, he becomes, as it were, a partner to the composer. Before he started doing this, Brackx first experienced the emancipation of composer and performer. Like John Cage, he liberated himself in his early works from the compelling duty to pin down a composition in its entirety and down to the last detail. This increases the responsibility of the musicians, who no longer merely 'perform', but also take decisions about the form and content of a work. A nice example

of this is *Indiscrete Sounds* (1996), where the adjective in the title refers to the indefiniteness and concreteness of the sounds. The form (the order of the five segments is not fixed), the duration and the pitch are not determined, only suggested in this score by graphic curves (instead of being recorded with conventional musical notation). In *Orchid Pavilion* (1998), based on a poem by Wang Hsi-chih, the pitch is also unfixed and the performer is free to put together his own version, by analogy with the nuances of meaning that are contained in different English translations of this poem.

With *Quiet Beings* (1998) and *Silent Forms* (1998) Brackx indirectly arrives at the emancipation of the act of listening. In the first instance, these works are a search for the essence of sound through its extreme reduction. Expression is the aim, with as few means as possible (less is more). As the titles of these works indicate, the noise level is kept very low, a quality also possessed by most of Morton Feldman's works. In contrast to Feldman, however, Brackx composes a perceptible process, which in *Quiet Beings* is very simple, but much more complicated in *Silent Forms* because of the superposition of two different processes (one in the string trio and one in the other instruments). In the programme notes for this last work, the composer writes: '*I also made a very conscious decision to use the soft end of the dynamic spectrum in order to oblige the listener to be involved and to listen actively, which I feel is also a point of interest in contemporary art in general: interaction with the audience, the investigation of the relationship between performers and listeners.*'

This investigation is continued with other means in works such as *{G}rayns* (2000), *metaforme* (2003) and *Pieci Pieces* (2003). What these three compositions have in common is the activation of memory: how does that which is observed influence the observation, how does the known influence the new? The first part of *{G}rayns* is recorded during the concert and fragments of that recording are reproduced during the second part of this work, which is performed later in the concert. Brackx is fascinated by the 'composition' of concert programmes for the same reasons. The musical context in which a work is performed cannot help but have an impact on its interpretation. A piano sonata by Beethoven gets another 'meaning' when it is surrounded by piano music by Mozart and Schubert than when it is placed amongst tape-compositions by Cage and Stockhausen. The individual compositions also grow together in the consciousness of the listener to create a meta-form. In *Pieci Pieces*, Brackx simulates this situation by writing short, individual pieces, which in the final section are placed on top of each other to create such a meta-form. In addition to this poetic game of ob-servation and memory, Brackx also activates the listening event by more direct intervention, such as shifts in the space of the audience (*Shifting Fields*, 1999) or performers (*Pieci Pieces*), or the discreet addition of tape-recorded sounds that cannot be reproduced in terms of register nor in timbre by the ensemble sitting on the podium (*metaforme*).

Mark Delaere
Translated by Laura Watkinson

www.brackx.info

This article was taken from *Contemporary Music in the Low Countries*, a new book written by Mark Delaere and Emile Wennekes and published by Ons Erfdeel vzw (see p. 320 for further details)

A Coffee-Cup Full of Helium
Heike Kamerlingh Onnes (1853-1926)

On 10 July 1908, Heike Kamerlingh Onnes became the first person to bring helium under control. In room E' of his Natuurkundig Laboratorium, opposite Van der Werff Park in the heart of Leiden, at the end of a long and exhausting day, he succeeded in liquefying the last of the 'permanent' gases. In so doing, he achieved a temperature of a few degrees above absolute zero (-273 °C), making Leiden the coldest place in the world.

This attack on helium was a huge and carefully planned operation. In the morning, before the crack of dawn, Kamerlingh Onnes was driven by carriage to the Steenschuur from Huize ter Wetering, his home on the Galgewater. On reaching the laboratory he immediately pulled on his white coat and went to join his technicians. They were already busy making the liquid hydrogen that served as a coolant for the helium. As the Burckhardt compressors in room Aa raced away, Kamerlingh Onnes and his assistants were rapidly turning taps, connecting and disconnecting gas cylinders and paying very close attention to manometers and thermometers. They did not stop for food. By half past one twenty litres of liquid hydrogen had been drained into vacuum flasks, enough to launch the attack on helium.

At twenty past four – his concerned wife Betsy had in the meantime come to check up on the situation, feeding pieces of bread to her Heike as he laboured away – the compressor got to work on circulating the helium. The method consisted of first compressing the helium to 100 atmospheres and then allowing it to expand in a vacuum, thermally insulated in double-walled vessels with liquid air and liquid hydrogen. This meant that the inert gas cooled every time it went around the system and the hope was that the drop in temperature would be sufficiently intense to condense the helium.

Initially the attack seemed to be unsuccessful. One thermometer had given up the ghost and the other showed hardly any signs of dropping. To Onnes' relief, the temperature eventually began to drop and by half past six in the evening the temperature was lower than that of liquid hydrogen. The temperature fluctuated its way down to six degrees above absolute zero. Kamerlingh Onnes had by then attached the last flask of the stock of liquid hydrogen to the apparatus, but still there was little more to see than a few wisps of vapour.

Then, at -269 °C, four degrees above absolute zero, the temperature suddenly began to stabilise. That was at half past seven. Shining a light on the apparatus revealed that the thermometer was suspended in liquid helium. Electric wires could clearly be seen sticking through the surface of the liquid. *'Once we had seen the surface,'* wrote Kamerlingh Onnes in his report to the Academy of Sciences, *'we did not lose sight of it. It was razor-sharp against the wall of the glass vessel.'*

The experiment had produced sixty millilitres of liquid helium, just short of a coffee-cupful. After carrying out a number of investigative experiments on his new liquid – an attempt to freeze it by vacuum suction failed – Kamerlingh Onnes decided to call it a day at twenty to ten. *'It was not only the equipment that had been pushed to the limits by this experiment and the preparations for it,'* he wrote in his report to the Academy, *'the utmost was also demanded of my assistants.'*

The liquefaction of helium was a milestone in Dutch (and international) physics. It was also the culmination of a programme that Kamerlingh Onnes had outlined when he took up his position in Leiden in 1882 and which he had carried out with a sure hand, organisational talent, guts, vision, dogged patience and tremendous perseverance. In his inaugural lecture, when he coined the maxim *'Door meten tot weten'* ('through measurement to knowledge'), Kamerlingh Onnes had announced that he wanted to put the molecular theories of his colleague and friend Johannes Diderik van der Waals to the test. The logical consequence of this decision was the construction of a cryogenics laboratory, a factory for the manufacture of cold.

Heike Kamerlingh Onnes was a product of the HBS (*hogere burgerschool*) high-school system. These

Heike Kamerlingh Onnes (l.) and
Gerrit Jan Flim (his chief instrument-
maker who was also in charge of
the cryogenics laboratory) in front of
the 'helium liquefier', c.1920.

Kirchhoff. Heike learned from Kirchhoff to value the unity of theory and experiment, which was of crucial importance in his career as a physicist.

Onnes' scientific mission was to test the theories of Johannes Diderik van der Waals. As a student in Groningen he had become acquainted with Van der Waals' celebrated thesis with its notion of the 'equation of state', which implied continuity between liquid and gaseous states. This was at a time when the notion of molecules was far from being generally accepted, let alone the thought that those molecules remain the same after phase transitions (such as evaporation). Molecular physics was a hot topic that appealed to Heike with his talent for both theory and experimentation.

Onnes' approach was based on two key principles: precision and cold. Precision was necessary because the equation of states was only valid approximately, so it was determining *deviations* from those laws that would advance physics. This required precision measurement, an area close to Heike's heart. Cold was required because it made sense to begin testing Van der Waals' theory by experimenting on simple substances and these only become liquid at low temperature. The construction of a cryogenics laboratory demanded almost all of Onnes' energy during the initial period of his professorship. Onnes expanded his empire step by step. Within a quarter of a century he had transformed the dusty physics lab left behind at the Steenschuur by his predecessor P.L. Rijke in 1882 into a cryogenics institute of world renown.

The focus in Leiden was not on sudden brainwaves, but on programmes of measurement. This emphasis on planned physics can be explained by circumstances in the field of cryogenics. In the early years, liquid oxygen was not always available and any scientist who managed to decant the blue liquid into his cryostat had to know what he was going to do with it. With helium this situation never really changed: in the academic year 1922-1923 there were still only eighteen 'helium days'. Just as Heike's weak physical constitution had taught him to conserve his energy, so he would not contemplate wasting a drop of helium just so he could have a quick shot at some-

new schools, introduced by Thorbecke in 1863, were remarkable for the great attention they paid to the exact sciences and their very well equipped laboratories, which many university laboratories were unable to compete with. At school his favourite subjects were chemistry and history. Heike was not converted to physics until his *Wanderjahre* in Heidelberg, where he was disappointed by the approach that chemist and dedicated experimenter Robert Bunsen (the man behind the Bunsen burner) took when supervising his independent research and began work on Foucault's pendulum (which can still be admired in the Panthéon in Paris) as an assistant to Gustav thing. The result: firmly fixed measurement days with no room for sudden brainwaves or other such mischief. There was little room for a more relaxed, qualitative approach, which is also necessary in physics. Even so, it was by chance that when working with frozen mercury in 1911 Kamerlingh Onnes discovered superconductivity, the phenomenon whereby electrical resistance suddenly completely disappears below a certain (extremely low) temperature. This achievement, together with the liquefaction of helium, earned him the Nobel Prize in 1913.

Following the advent of liquid hydrogen in 1905, Leiden developed into an international facility for physicists who wanted to carry out research at lower temperatures than were available at their home institutions. The Paris cryogenics conference of 1908, where Heike stole the show with his liquid helium, prompted a whole stream of researchers (and other visitors) to make their way to Leiden. Onnes leant over backwards to please these foreign guests and hospitably accommodated the visitors at his home Huize ter Wetering, thereby achieving his ideal of gaining international acclaim for Dutch physics. At the same time, though, this invasion led to distractions and sometimes hampered authentic Leiden research, as happened to Willem Keesom (Onnes' successor in 1924). Keesom needed liquid hydrogen for his work, but always had to let foreign scientists go first.

Heike devoted all of his energy to his laboratory and its unique apprenticeship system for instrument-makers. Other than that, his family was all that mattered. Huize ter Wetering was home to an artistically minded family, a place that was also pervaded by a cosmopolitan atmosphere because of the numerous foreign academics who stayed there, including Niels Bohr, Albert Einstein, Madame Curie and William Ramsay.

Heike Kamerlingh Onnes pushed his people onwards as the wind does the clouds, said Pieter Zeeman, one of his students. The miracle is that this frail individual, who as a boy had spent a year ill at home reading Plutarch and had to visit the Alps every summer of his life to take the air, still managed to find the energy to set up such a large-scale enterprise as a cryogenics laboratory – and to bring it to maturity with such great success. With the help of his wife Betsy, Heike was able to concentrate his limited energies on that one thing. Just giving something a quick shot was certainly not part of the Leiden programme. But you don't make liquid helium by messing around.

Dirk van Delft
Translated by Laura Watkinson

Dirk van Delft, *Heike Kamerlingh Onnes. De man van het absolute nulpunt.* Amsterdam: Bert Bakker, 2005, 667 pp. ISBN 90-351-2739-0.

A Truck Every Three Seconds
Antwerp and the Deurganckdok

Ten years ago the decision was taken, and in the Summer of 2005 it was officially opened in the port of Antwerp: the largest tidal dock in the world, the Deurganckdok. Thanks to this dock, large container ships putting into Antwerp no longer have to pass through time-consuming locks. Moreover, the Deurganckdok doubles Antwerp's container-handling capacity. It turns Antwerp into one of the few West European ports which can provide spare capacity for container transhipment for some years to come. The cost of the Deurganckdok: 643 million euros, almost double the original estimate. A beautiful polder village was wiped from the map to make room for it. But that hasn't stopped specialists from making plans for an even larger dock in the port of Antwerp.

Antwerp's port lies deep inland. By sending the ever larger container ships to a port like Antwerp you save many kilometres of container transport by road. That is a trump card the port of Antwerp makes good use of to persuade container shipping companies to come there. Until recently, the disadvantage was that the container ships had to pass through locks. Since the construction of the Deurganckdok you can sail directly from the North Sea to the port of Antwerp, with no locks. The water in the dock is influenced by the tides, and that is why it is called a 'tidal dock'. Once the largest tidal dock in the world is fully operational trucks will be able to leave the dock at a rate of one every three seconds, on average. The dock is providing 5000 new jobs.

The plans to expand Antwerp's port date back to 1995. Research had shown that there would be exponential growth in container traffic. If Antwerp wished to remain one of the most important container ports in Europe, extra transhipment capacity was needed. And Antwerp's port is vitally important, not just to Antwerp but also to Flanders and Belgium.

In 1998 the decision was taken to build the Deurganckdok on the left bank in Antwerp, to the south of the polder village of Doel. The Flemish government said from the start that it could no longer guarantee that Doel would be 'habitable'. In September 1999 work on the Deurganckdok began. Environmental organisations and the inhabitants of Doel took legal action to resist expansion of the port and to protest against their village being declared 'uninhabitable'. In March 2001 work was halted for a year.

Because the new dock was too important for the port of Antwerp and because the stoppage was costing vast sums of money, at the end of 2001 the Flemish government made an emergency decree, something unique in its history. The decree approved a series of new planning permissions and environmental compensation regulations so that work could recommence.

What was more important was that no further appeal against the planning permissions was possible. All further protests by the people of Doel to the Court of Arbitration, the European Commission and the European Court of Human Rights fell foul of that emergency decree. Work was resumed in April 2002. A plan for compulsory purchase, advice and support was devised for the nine hundred inhabitants of Doel.

In 2004 Antwerp was struggling with a shortage of capacity. It regularly had to turn ships away. The Dutch port of Rotterdam in particular profited from this. Thanks to the Deurganckdok, with a quay length of 5.3 kilometres, Antwerp can now increase its capacity to 7 million containers a year. Up until 2012 there will be no shortage of space. This means that – with the exception of the smaller Le Havre – Antwerp is the only container port in Europe with spare capacity.

Construction costs for the Deurganckdok were originally estimated at 430 million euros. The stoppage of work, the compulsory purchase of Doel and the environmental compensation costs raised the cost platform to 643 million euros. Once the dock is fully in use 2 million cubic metres of sludge will have to be dredged out annually to keep the dock navigable, at a cost of 25 million euros per year.

The Deurganckdok threatens to saddle Antwerp with a gigantic mobility problem. The extra 3.7 million twenty- and forty-foot containers that will be involved will have to be transported to and fro. It is expected that 20 percent will be carried by rail. To facilitate this there is an urgent need for a rail tunnel between the left and right banks. The 'Liefkenshoeks Rail Tunnel', as it will be known, will not be ready before 2012 at the earliest. The cost is estimated at 600 million euros.

Inland waterways would take 40 percent of the container traffic. But here too there is an urgent need for the authorities to carry out 180 million euros' worth of modernisation work along the Albert Canal.

On top of which extra locks will have to be built, at a cost of at least 250 million euros.

Road transport would take care of 40 percent of the container traffic. But trucks already make up 45 percent of traffic on the Antwerp ring road and traffic jams are the rule rather than the exception. Many road users are bracing themselves for the time when the Deurganckdok is operating at full capacity.

According to the prognoses the Deurganckdok will have run out of space by 2012. So plans are already being drawn up for the construction of a sec-

The Deurganckdok.
Photo courtesy of Gemeentelijk
Haven-bedrijf, Antwerp.

ond, even larger container dock. There are enough container customers to justify it, but whether there is sufficient community and political support for the project is at present extremely doubtful.

Ewald Pironet
Translated by Sheila M. Dale

www.deurganckdok.be

Citizenship is the Highest Office
Job Cohen, 'European Hero'

Talking on *Buitenhof* (a political discussion programme on Dutch television) on Sunday 27 November 2005, Frits Bolkestein stated that he is against the introduction of directly elected mayors. Because, as the former leader of the Liberal party in the Netherlands and until recently EU Commissioner, let slip: that could well mean that Amsterdam would soon have a Muslim as its first citizen and that – here he hesitated – '*could involve certain risks*'.

Bolkestein's outburst was so unexpected that the presenter completely failed to question him further. Not so the mayor of Amsterdam, Job Cohen (1947-). When Cohen took part in the ensuing discussion, the first thing he did was to haul Bolkestein over the coals. One of Cohen's aldermen, the Muslim Abouta-leb, had conducted himself admirably in the tense period following the shocking murder of writer and filmmaker Theo van Gogh, and Cohen wanted to make it quite clear that he would be proud to see Aboutaleb elected as the first Muslim mayor of Amsterdam.

That is typical of Job Cohen. He quietly waits his turn. He is polite. He is engaging. But he never hesitates to say whatever needs to be said, and is always prepared to step into the breach for groups or individuals who, for whatever reason, are in danger of being 'overruled'. Amsterdam's mayor has an unerring instinct for preserving good relations. He adds his weight to the scales whenever they seem likely to be tipped out of balance.

These qualities have not gone unnoticed. *TIME Magazine* recently named him one of the European Heroes of 2005 for the unique way in which he defused the racial tension that surfaced after the murder of Theo van Gogh. At the beginning of November 2005 he was awarded the Citizenship Prize by the Flemish P&V Foundation. This was the first time the prize had been awarded, and the theme for 2005 was 'diversity'. Cohen shared the prize with Fadéla Amara, president of the French movement Ni Putes, Ni Soumises (Neither Whore Nor Submissive). Amara, who is Algerian by birth, has campaigned since 1980 for emancipation, gender equality, and diversity in society.

Job Cohen's father was a professor of history. Job himself studied law. He continued his studies after graduating and, in 1993, was appointed to the Chair of Legal Methods and Techniques at the University of Maastricht. However, Cohen was more of an administrator than an academic. In the Netherlands he is most widely known as the rector magnificus of the University of Maastricht, as parliamentary leader of the social-democratic PvdA (Labour Party) in the Upper House, and as Deputy Minister first for Higher Education, later for Justice. In the latter capacity he was responsible for the difficult Alien Affairs portfolio, which, during the second Kok cabinet (1998-2002), included the challenging task of drastically tightening up asylum legislation. In all these positions Cohen proved himself an exemplary and steadfast administrator.

Two things give us a sharper impression of Cohen's personality: his views on citizenship and his stance on minorities. It is no exaggeration to say that he regards citizenship as the highest office. For Cohen, being a *good citizen* is the most important thing to which an individual can aspire. In this sense, he is following in the rich Dutch tradition of government by regents. The Netherlands was – and still is, to a certain extent – governed by a pragmatic ruling class. Historically, the regents were merchants who were aware that their interests would be best served by a society in which citizens were not after each other's blood, but were tolerant of each other: live and let

live. In terms of today's multicultural society, this means that we must also accept Muslims.

Job Cohen's approach to minorities is the most defining aspect of his character. Cohen himself has stated that he is not an adherent of any religion, but his name clearly points to his Jewish background. He knows what it is to live as part of a minority in a country of minorities. That is the essence of the Netherlands, a country in which Catholics, Jews, and Protestants of many persuasions consider their beliefs important, but are also aware that they must never impose those beliefs on others. It is a society in which the ability to integrate with others while retaining one's own identity is held up as an ideal.

This tolerance has been challenged by the arrival of Muslim immigrants. Autochtonous groups tend to impose their culture on newcomers as the *Leitcultur*. Cohen fights this tooth and nail. Those who want to force Muslims to become closely integrated – or even completely assimilated – into Dutch society therefore see him as a 'softie' and he has become the target of vicious ridicule. But those who are in favour of a pluriform society see him as an ally.

Willem Breedveld
Translated by Yvette Mead

The Passion of Creating
Christophe Coppens, Designer Artist

The *Sinterklaas* figures all took the stage together, their arms hidden protectively in their cassocks. Suddenly it became clear that each of them was holding a doll in his hand – a rag doll, specially made for the occasion out of scraps of material. Christophe Coppens had created the unique dolls for *Second Hand, Second Life*, an event organised by the Spullenhulp charity organisation in which twenty Belgian designers were asked to create something from second-hand clothes from the Spullenhulp collection centres in Sint-Pieters-Leeuw. Coppens also did well with his two dolls at the Sotheby's auction after the show.

The fact that Christophe Coppens chose not to exhibit hats at the show, when hats are after all the hallmark of this Belgian designer, is significant. Although Coppens gained fame in Belgium with his hats, he is at home in many fields, as is evident from his recent range of men's accessories, his various exhibitions in Belgium and elsewhere and a range of decorative items he produced a couple of years ago, which among other things included a candle in the shape of a baby's face and a *condomière* (a box for holding condoms), all of which had nothing to do with his more usual line in hats.

Christophe Coppens studied drama at the *Conservatorium* in Brussels, but later burst onto the fashion scene as a hatmaker. But this milliner was not content with simply producing a new hat collection every

© Christophe Coppens, 2005.

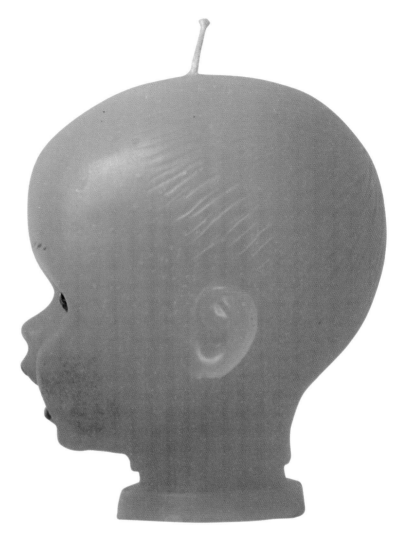

six months; on each occasion Coppens came up with an individual presentation which plunged the viewer into an idiosyncratic and highly personal universe. One of the high points of his early years was undoubtedly *The House of the Dying Mermaid*, a total spectacle in which music, video and fashion were combined. There was something typically Coppens-like about the show, in which a woman acted out her own death. The main character wanted everything to be perfect, including the objects around her and the entourage in which she moved. She hired a theatre auditorium and invited 500 people to witness her demise at close quarters. A somewhat lugubrious theme, or so it appeared, but Coppens imbued the whole performance with a great deal of emotion. The woman was fixated on mermaids and love; a universal theme.

Even at the *Première Classe* fashion fair in Paris (a fringe event during the Paris fashion week in which Coppens participated during the early years of his career), he was drawn to the extreme. He once filled the few square metres of his stand in Paris with golden chairs upholstered with red velvet cushions. Anyone wanting to see the hat collection from close by simply had to pluck a hat from a chair. On another occasion he placed his hats and accessories on light boxes. 'Ultimate lightness' was the theme, and as a result the feathers and plumes and pastel tints of his hats were imbued with a mysterious glow. On yet another occasion the cube in which he had exhibited all his designs was filled with stuffed animals. That he had managed to get them across the French-Belgian border was a miracle. Perhaps all these displays were a gesture to his theatrical studies.

In the mid-1990s he found a house in Zwedenstraat in Brussels which suited his purposes perfectly. Initially he turned the ground floor into a shop-cum-showroom, but that didn't work: too many people found their way to the open doors. Besides, he really did not have the time to sell his hats himself. By now he had already opened a shop in Bruges, his home base, followed fairly soon afterwards by Antwerp and Brussels. But this, too, changed, and today Coppens concentrates on the Belgian capital, where he has his shop and also his studio, Atelier Coppens, which can be visited by appointment. On entering, visitors see the numerous workers sitting at their work benches. There they are making hats, one by one. It is a sort of performance, again betraying his links to the theatre.

Is Coppens then not a designer pure and simple? Does he seek to be more? An artist perhaps? He himself does not use the word, but the question is not inappropriate, because in the last few years Coppens has taken on a new role as the organiser and curator of several exhibitions in Belgium and abroad, and he also thinks like a conceptual artist. During an exhibition at the Brakke Grond in Amsterdam, he went in search of the underlying inspiration of Belgian fashion designers. In *What Lies Beneath* he tried to penetrate the imaginations of designers such as Marina Yee, Anna Heylen and Walter van Beirendonck. He also added his own opinion: in one room everything was hung literally upside down, while a post-it sticker on the wall contained the significant words: 'Wanted: money'. That is what every designer desires most, of course: money with which to launch yet another collection.

The universe of Christophe Coppens does not revolve around money, however, but around the passion of creating. Precisely what should be created is not spelled out. Naturally, hats remain an essential part

of his work today, but they have now been joined by any number of accessories, including some for men. His decorative objects are also here to stay. A motley assortment, to be sure, the highlights of which are a set of caviar spoons, a vase with a fish on top and a condom-box. Coppens was frequently asked for other objects by his customers, and why should he make them wait? Moreover, this was an opportunity for him to join forces with craftsmen who, like Coppens himself, had their skills at their finger-tips: ebony-workers, candle makers and even glass-blowers.

The most remarkable feature of his work is of course the exhibitions: his *Dollhouse Project* came in three instalments, and certainly in the Netherlands it was seen as a highly artistic expression of creativity. It's a fact that at the time Coppens had to explain the exhibition to the *art critics* of leading Dutch newspapers, not to the fashion writers. This resulted in very different interviews, and in the label 'artist'. Is he happy about this? Well, Coppens is a creative millipede, an all-round designer who is never short of an idea – and who recently has even ventured into the world of 'actual' fashion design with skirts and shirts etc. And he is not to be pushed into any particular pigeonhole.

Veerle Windels
Translated by Julian Ross

www.christophecoppens.com.

Harmony
The Conciliatory Figurativeness of Matthijs Röling

Artists who choose painting as their medium have a hard time of it with the art critics. When they work figuratively in the tradition of the "old masters", their work is seen as almost deliberately perverse. For years the realistic figurative movement has been virtually ignored by museums and critics alike. The public, though, has never gone along with this. There seems always to be a demand for painted images of reality. One of the most important representatives of this movement in the Netherlands is Matthijs Röling (1943-). In 2005 there was a major retrospective of his work in the Drents Museum in Assen and later in the Frisia Museum in Spanbroek. Monumental works by him were also exhibited in Museum De Buitenplaats in Eelde.

In figurative art, rooted in ancient traditions, two trends are distinguishable in today's Netherlands and each has its protagonist: Henk Helmantel is the more precise and Matthijs Röling the more flexible. Both live and work in the far north of the country, in the province of Groningen. This is no coincidence. The city of Groningen is home to the Minerva Academy, for years *the* academy where the techniques of the old masters are taught – Röling has been teaching there since 1973. The tranquillity of the Northern landscape has always had tremendous appeal for painters wishing to work in this tradition. Helmantel's paintings are characterised by a certain austerity. Perhaps rather more coarsely painted when seen close up than one had first thought, they have a sober appearance which is partly due to a somewhat subdued palette, Röling's approach is in comparison 'abandoned'. Helmantel once said in an interview: '*I am not a natural talent, like Matthijs Röling for example, I have had to work at it more. You have the virtuosos such as Rubens, Leonardo, Vélazquez, but you also have really good painters, such as Vermeer and perhaps Mankes or Ket, who were not. In my opinion the nature of their talent was different.*' And where Helmantel places himself in the second category, Röling then automatically belongs with the virtuosos. This is not a bad assessment. Matthijs Röling can in fact do anything with paint and his paintings appear to have been produced very quickly and with little effort. In the publication that accompanied the exhibition the painter/critic Diederik Kraaijpoel calls '*the secret of Matthijs (...) the combination of spontaneity and concentration, such as you find in the great masters like Vélazquez or Rubens*'. Matthijs Röling distinguishes himself from his great predecessors by his feel for freedom of composition, his choice of subject matter, his blond tonality – many of his works are

bathed in light – and his personal signature. Röling lives in the *here* and *now*, and his paintings radiate this.

In the sense that figurative art is presently more and more museum-oriented – the exhibition of Röling's work in the Drents Museum in Assen was the seventh in a series and the private Frisia Museum in Spanbroek focused entirely on this movement – things were very different 25 years ago. Quite against the trend, when the ING bank set up its own collection it began collecting figurative art. The person responsible for this was Sacha Tanja, who put this school on the map with her acquisition policy. In December 2004, shortly after leaving her position as chief curator of the art collection, Sacha Tanja died. It had previously been decided to create a medal bearing her name, to be awarded to a Dutch figurative artist. She was able to present the first medal to Matthijs Röling, using the occasion to emphasise his importance: '*He held fast even when all the academies wanted to change in favour of the so-called avant-garde. He has gathered followers and inspired others. He taught his pupils to look at art with open minds and without prejudice. Without Röling, artists such as Pieter Pander or Peter Hartwig would not exist.*'

Matthijs Röling is a productive individual. And while there are stylistic developments in abundance, one cannot say that these form a chronological sequence. The exhibition too was not arranged chronologically, but grouped by themes and motifs. So one could see hanging side by side paintings that were separated from each other by perhaps thirty years. Röling's earliest paintings are characterised by rather free brushwork; but almost simultaneously he produced a painting with a much smoother surface. And in fact this typifies his entire oeuvre. Röling lays paint on thickly where he thinks it necessary, while elsewhere in that same work he may paint with the utmost delicacy. His backgrounds too are often applied more boldly. More often than not with a palette knife rather than a coarse paintbrush. His paintings are not, however, just a collection of tricks. You notice that he is looking for something, and finding it.

The choice of subject matter is just as varied as

Matthijs Röling, *Spring*. 1975.
Canvas, 90.5 x 80.5 cm.
ING kunstcollectie.

the technical treatment. A great many intimate nude portraits, but he has also mastered the still life. A superbly beautiful little panel is no more than a small piece of wood covered with a shard of pottery and a gleaming beetle against a worn white background. Contrasting with this are the typical cupboards with which Röling created an entire sub-genre of his own in the late 1960s and early 1970s. The principle remains the same. It is as if you are looking into a cupboard. In such a cupboard he paints everything that can redound to the credit of a still life painter. Vases of flowers, posters and letters (paper!), glasses, dolls, draped (tea) towels, eggs, Escher-like puzzles hanging on strings and (dead) animals inhabit the cramped accommodation. Here the still life painter can literally and figuratively display his handling of textures. A striking example is the four companion pieces illustrating the four seasons in the ING collection. Not only do the contents of the cupboards match the season they represent, so also do the col-

ours. In recent years Röling has drawn his inspiration mainly from his own garden in Ezinge (Groningen). The variation in garden views is immense, with constantly new vistas and as in his entire oeuvre the all-pervasive light.

A special place in Röling's oeuvre is occupied by the wall paintings. At first he painted only the walls of his atelier, but soon the commissions began to come in. One of the largest projects is the Nijsinghuis in Eelde. In 1983 Matthijs Röling was commissioned to decorate the walls. With gay abandon he set to work together with a few colleagues such as Wout Muller. Work still continues intermittently on this project. As well as the Nijsinghuis there is Museum De Buitenplaats. Here there were not only more paintings by Röling to be seen. There were a couple which are of a monumental size; these immovable works were shown as projected images.

Röling's monumental work can best be described as the crowning achievement of his painting. Even

Matthijs Röling, *Garden in Ezinge,
October*. 2002. Panel, 21 x 40 cm.
Private collection/
© Art Revisited.

blonder, even more loosely handled, and with a strong preference for ultramarine blue. This profusion can only be compared to the wall paintings of Pompeï.

So is there nothing at all to comment on, nothing to find fault with? You could say that social involvement is entirely missing. When it comes to talent, compared with such diverse colleagues as Ronald Ophuis or the Fleming Luc Tuymans Röling is the master. But whereas these two painters are increasingly attracting attention precisely because of their social commitment, Röling's work can be dismissed as coquettish. Röling armed himself against such a view in 1979 with his essay *About Art: a Sermon and a Parable* (Over kunst: een preek en parabel). When *About Art* came up in an interview with Laurens Balkema Röling added the following: '*Harmony, that's the key concept. The human creation must be in harmony with nature, and that does not work, I think, without a belief in an almighty authority. [...] Within the* *painting we have the power to honour nature as God or the gods intended. Nature is in reality a theatre of conflict. [...] Intervention by man only makes things worse. But in art we can transcend nature. That is the lesson of the Renaissance: to use elements from reality, but unite them in a higher harmony, in which all misery is conquered. To make paradise visible. That is reconciliation.*' That is also a vision and a legitimation of the art of painting.

Frank van der Ploeg
Translated by Joy Kearney

H.R. Tupan, *Matthijs Röling. Mimesis. Schilderijen en tekeningen*, Assen/Spanbroek/Zwolle: Drents Museum / Frisia Museum Waanders Publishers, 2005.
Jos van Groeningen, *Het Nijsinghuis te Eelde*. Eelde: Museum De Buitenplaats, 2004.

After Rogier van der Weyden,
*St Luke Drawing a Portrait
of the Virgin*. Late 15th-early
16th century.
Panel, 133 x 107 cm.
Groeningemuseum, Bruges.

Three Museums Working in Harmony
The Vlaamsekunstcollectie Project

Vlaamsekunstcollectie, written as one word and meaning literally 'Flemish art collection', is a new name for a collaborative project involving the three most important art history museums in Flanders: those of Antwerp, Bruges and Ghent. The project, which was set up in 2001 by the museum managements, covers all areas of the museums' activity: collection logging and cataloguing, restoration, exhibitions, academic research, merchandising, security, publicity, communication, etc.

The collaboration is in fact a logical step: the collections of the three museums go together very well in terms of content, and together offer a fine overview of the visual arts in the Southern Netherlands from the fifteenth to the twentieth century. Each of the three museums has its own area of specialisation: the Groeningemuseum in Bruges specialises in fifteenth and early sixteenth-century art, the Royal

Museum of Fine Arts in Antwerp in works from the late sixteenth and early seventeenth century, and the Museum of Fine Arts in Ghent in works from the nineteenth century. Together they can boast a world-class art collection. The collaboration means the three museums will no longer be competing with each other, but will regard each other as partners. The focus will no longer be on the institutions, but on their collections. The Heritage Decree of May 2004 removed the last major legal obstacles to their collaboration.

Vlaamsekunstcollectie organised its first major exhibition from 15 June to 11 September 2005 at the Palais des Beaux-Arts in Brussels. Using works from his own museum's collection together with a number of works on loan, curator Till-Holger Borchert, who is attached to the Groeningemuseum, presented an overview of the riches of these collections. The primary aim of the exhibition was to show how the collections were created. While not all the works exhibited were of top quality, those selected did reflect the taste of the medieval nobility and the collectors of the seventeenth, eighteenth and nineteenth centuries, as well as illustrating the importance of the French period, the Academies, etc. It was an interesting if somewhat technical exhibition, which could only be properly understood using the audio guide. Luckily there was also the catalogue which, with its lavish colour illustrations, recounted the story of the origins and development of the three major museums of Flemish art history in Flanders.

When did the collecting of works of art begin in Flanders? When did the appreciation of individual works by individual creators begin? In Flanders, there are no more than a few indirect indications of a growing appreciation of individual artists in the fifteenth century; this contrasts with Italy, for example, where in the same period a great many writings testify to the growing self-awareness of the artist. Such an indirect reference is found for example in the painting *St Luke Drawing a Portrait of the Virgin* by Rogier van der Weyden. Here St Luke, patron saint of artists, is no longer depicted as a painter, but as a splendidly robed scholar working in a dazzling interior. The diary entries of Albrecht Dürer, who visited Flanders in 1521, reveal the great esteem in which artists in Bruges were held at the time. The St Luke guilds played a prominent role in the growing self-awareness of artists in the Low Countries, helping to create a *milieu* which was conducive to the early establishment of art collections. The ruling classes also built up considerable collections. That of Margaret of Austria was the most notable, but after her death it was divided among several heirs, most of them in Spain and Austria. It was in this way that the famous Arnolfini Portrait by Van Eyck found its way to Spain before later, in the nineteenth century, moving to London. Commissions by municipal authorities were therefore of greater importance for the later museum collections than the rulers of the Southern Netherlands. The first art markets in Flanders appeared during the fifteenth century, but the religious problems in the sixteenth century led to their collapse, prompting many dealers and professional artists to abandon Flanders. This was a real blood-letting, though the 'fugitives' frequently kept in touch with the families and business contacts they

Théodore Géricault,
Portrait of a Kleptomaniac. c.1820.
Canvas, 61.2 x 50.1 cm.
Museum voor Schone Kunsten,
Ghent.

had left behind, enabling the Antwerp network, in particular, to grow in importance. The art trade was, not illogically, concentrated in those places where major collectors were located.

The increasing prosperity in the Low Countries from the fifteenth century onwards meant that more citizens and associations could afford to commission works of art: sixteenth-century inventories increasingly list works owned by private individuals. In the seventeenth century having an art collection not only brought social prestige, but was also regarded as an investment. One important collection which demonstrates these trends was that of the Bishop of Ghent, Antonius Triest, though studies have shown that in fact the majority of households in Ghent also possessed paintings.

Until the end of the eighteenth century the artist was a craftsman, who seldom escaped from the regulations imposed by the guilds. In 1773, however, Empress Maria Theresa issued an edict enabling all artists to pursue their profession without restriction. Artists began looking for an alternative to the guild system, and from the end of the seventeenth century onwards academies modelled on those in Rome and Paris began to appear in the Low Countries. The Academy of Antwerp was founded as early as 1664, the Bruges Academy in 1720 and the Academy in Ghent in 1751. Initially artists were highly enthusiastic about these new institutions and donated works to the Schilderskamer (Art Room). Former students of these academies often donated works to their old school; one such is Joseph-Benoit Suvée, a Bruges artist who received his early training in the town of his birth and who later went on to study at the Academy in Paris. Whilst there, he won the Prix de Rome, quite a rare accolade for a foreigner. Suvée donated several works to the Bruges Academy and his paintings, like those of many of his contemporaries, can today be found in the collections of the museums of Ghent, Antwerp and Bruges.

The *Ensor to Bosch* exhibition included a print by Benjamin Zix depicting Napoleon strolling through one of the galleries of the Louvre accompanied by his new bride, Marie-Louise. Anthony van Dyck's painting *The Mourning of Christ* hangs on the wall. This work had been removed by the French occupiers from the Church of the Friars Minor in Antwerp on 28 July 1794 and, together with a whole series of masterpieces, taken from the Southern Netherlands to Paris. They were to remain there until the defeat of Napoleon in 1815, after which most of the works were brought back in triumph to Flanders. Depictions of this joyous return were also to be seen at the *Ensor to Bosch* exhibition and in the exhibition catalogue. It was also during the French period that the first museums appeared, and confiscated church property ended up in art repositories. The repositories in Brussels, Antwerp and Ghent formed the core of the later museums of fine arts.

The public interest enjoyed by Flemish art works in Paris also boosted interest in old Flemish art in Flanders itself and internationally. This led to the creation of public and private collections in Flanders, which to this day shape the character of the Flemish art museums. In the nineteenth century the newly founded museums built up their collections further. They acquired older works more or less by chance, through bequests and gifts. The Antwerp Museum, for example, owns a fair number of Flemish Primitives which it inherited from the Mayor of Antwerp, Florent van Ertborn. His bequest included works by Jan van Eyck, Hans Memling, Rogier van der Weyden, Lucas Cranach and Quinten Massijs. Ghent and Bruges also received sizeable bequests and gifts. Contemporary art was purchased mainly at art fairs and auctions. The Ghent Museum, for example, purchased *Kingfishers* by Emile Claus, and *The Lecture by Emile Verhaeren* by Théo van Rysselberghe. And of course there was the famous *Portrait of a Kleptomaniac* by Théodore Géricault, bought by the Friends of the Museum for 1,155 francs, which lifted the Museum's collection of French art above the average.

In the late nineteenth and early twentieth century the museums acquired their own premises, starting with Antwerp in 1890, followed by Ghent (1902) and finally Bruges (1930). The museums became true academic institutions, publishing catalogues and organising exhibitions of international calibre. From then on their acquisition policy was also guided by principles of academic importance.

The *Vlaamsekunstcollectie* project marks a new step in the history of these three museums, which it is hoped will raise their international profile still further. The *Ensor to Bosch* exhibition was the first opportunity for the *Vlaamsekunstcollectie* to introduce itself to the public at large. Work has been going on for some time to develop an image bank providing access to the entire collections of the three museums. This image bank can be consulted at www.vlaamsebeeldenbank.be. By the end of 2005 it should be possible to view the majority of the art collections spanning the period from the fifteenth to the eighteenth century online.

The Antwerp, Bruges and Ghent collections mainly comprise works from the fifteenth to the first half of the twentieth century. The post-war twentieth century collections in Flanders are divided between the S.M.A.K. Museum of Contemporary Art in Ghent, the MuHKA Museum of Contemporary Art in Antwerp and the PMMK Museum of Modern Art in Ostend. Perhaps these institutions too should consider a similar collaborative venture.

Dirk van Assche
Translated by Julian Ross

Vlaamsekunstcollectie: Bijlokekaai 1b, 9000 Ghent, Belgium
Tel. +32 9 225 49 24 / Fax +32 9 225 49 55
www.vlaamsekunstcollectie.be

Short Takes

Trouble in Academy Award Paradise. In October 2005 Hany Abu-Assad's film *Paradise Now* was awarded the Golden Calf for the best *Dutch* film. After all, the producer is Dutch and the director holds both Israeli and Dutch passports (and qualified as an engineer in aircraft construction in the Netherlands). In January 2006 this film about the last days of two Palestinians preparing a suicide bombing in Israel won a Golden Globe. And soon after that *Paradise Now* was nominated for the Oscar for best foreign-language film. Just one problem: the film was submitted by the Ministry of Culture of the Palestinian Authority and accepted by the Academy as a film from 'Palestine'. But a number of Israelis and American Jews demanded that during the Oscar ceremony it should be announced as a film from 'the Palestinian territories'. Because Palestine is not a country.

It seems like some 'Dutch' films are as controversial as Danish cartoons. In 2004 Theo van Gogh made the short film *Submission 1* together with Ayaan Hirsi Ali. Naked women in transparent veils complain to Allah about violence towards women. On their bodies in fine calligraphy are controversial women-unfriendly verses from the Koran. Van Gogh, cheeky as always, announced that he was sending the film to

Al-Jazeera: '*They broadcast films of Bin Laden, so they certainly won't have any problem with this*'. Be that as it may, the Dutch Moslem Mohammed B. did have a problem with it, as Van Gogh would find to his cost.

On the last day of Van Gogh's life Pieter van Os was ready at his desk in Washington DC, remote control within reach and four Word files open on his laptop. It was a great day for the brand new correspondent of *De Groene Amsterdammer*, the big question being 'Kerry or Bush?'. But suddenly Theo van Gogh lay dead on the Amsterdam cobbles and nobody was interested in the American presidential election any more. The murder reverberated far beyond the Dutch borders. Astonished and intrigued, Van Os read in the local papers about the events in his homeland. And so he came on the idea of putting together a book of articles about the Netherlands by foreign journalists and scholars.

The Netherlands on the Edge (Nederland op scherp) turned into an anthology of '*foreign perspectives on a rudderless country*'. These are pieces written about the Netherlands in the past four years, and according to the back flap they provide '*clear wine, unclouded by insiders' detailed knowledge or the internecine quarrels of Dutch authors*'. And to a certain extent this is so. We see the historian Jonathan Israel, for instance, trying to find out what the national characteristic of tolerance means today. He demonstrates that for some time now there have been claims that the Dutch have lost their familiar friendly image. According to Israel it was notions such as tolerance, freedom of expression and personal freedom that Spinoza and Pierre Bayle brooded over for years and eventually worked into a number of solidly-constructed social, cultural and political doctrines. But when they talk about those values today the Dutch are totally lacking in any historical or cultural perspective. Israel condemns the present education system which, as a result of the Dutch government's Thatcherian obsession with what is 'useful' and 'cost-effective', has made noble unknowns of the above-mentioned Golden Age philosophers and eroded the nation's history in general until all that remains is a black hole. Tolerance has become official indifference. And so the worship of market forces and the obsession with a policy of efficiency have become the prime causes of a new narrow-mindedness and the end of society as we know it. And Israel is not the only one to take such a view. Where he speaks of *'cultural suicide'*, Magdi Allam, the Egyptian deputy editor-in-chief of the Italian *Corriere della Sera*, entitles his article 'Political Suicide'. *'Farewell multicultural society'*, sighs Allam. It is no longer sufficient to provide freedom to all nationalities and religions to make that freedom a common heritage. That kind of cultural relativism has proved no more than a fantasy. Ian Buruma describes the post-1960s Netherlands as a kind of Berkeley where everyone was free to do his own thing. *'Finally freed from the shackles of religion and strict social control, the Dutch cavorted (...) merrily in their perfect polder democracy, assuming that the rest of the world would leave them in peace.'* But now the turbulent world has rudely broken in on that idyll and the Netherlands looks like a Paradise Lost.

So that's all crystal clear. But *The Netherlands on the Edge* can also be razor sharp. Van Os quotes *The Providence Journal* of 10 November 2004 as saying that *'Van Gogh's murder has blown away the fog of marijuana from the heads of liberal-minded people who thought that a little friendliness would cool the hotheads down'*. And talking about those liberal-minded people: the American political analyst Bob Barr calls the Netherlands the land of Josef Mengele. As he sees it, a couple of years ago the country pushed its way with head held high to the forefront of modern decadence by passing the world's most liberal legislation on assisted suicide. Luckily, though, there is hope for the former Guide-land. Daniël Pipes writes an article in the *New York Post* entitled 'Murder by Education' and suggests that the gruesome murder of Van Gogh may well have done more for the Dutch than 11 September did for the Americans.

http://wip.warnerbros.com/paradisenow

Pieter Bots (ed.), *Nederland op scherp. Buitenlandse beschouwingen over een stuurloos land.*
Amsterdam: Bert Bakker, 2005. 252 pp. ISBN 90-3512-7994.

Reading all this, one gets the impression that the Netherlands isn't a good place to live any more. In all these foreign reports there is an overwhelming sense of loss and national crisis. As in the first British interview that Ayaan Hirsi Ali gave after Van Gogh's murder. In May 2005 Alexander Linklater met her, surrounded by expressionless bodyguards, on the 23rd floor somewhere in Amsterdam. *'She still marvels at the canal-chequered view below, an image of orderliness and freedom which she found amazing on first arriving at the borders of this country 13 years ago, and which is no longer available to her.'* On 13 February 2005 *The Guardian* ran the headline: *'Fading liberal dream tears Dutch apart'*. *Luctor et non emergo*: the guide-land has sunk and will not surface again, to turn the motto of Zeeland upside down.

In fact, to some extent it's all a matter of too great expectations. Let us go back a little in time. The book *John Adams in Holland. 1780-2005* looks at the relationship between the first US ambassador in the Netherlands and the people of Holland. Adams had travelled to the Netherlands on his own initiative, convinced that there he would readily find allies in the American war of independence against the English. Soon after he arrived he enthusiastically described the Netherlands as *'the greatest curiosity in the world'*. The cleanliness, neatness and orderliness of the country were particularly attractive to him: *'I am very much pleased with Holland. It is a singular country. It is like no other. It is all the effect of industry, and the work of art. The frugality, industry, cleanliness etc. here deserve the imitation of my countrymen.'*. But things went rather less smoothly than expected and after while a feeling of disappointment and discouragement crept into Adams' correspondence. The Dutch are worshippers of Mammon and the American complains: *'This country is indeed a melancholy situation; sunk in ease, devoted to the pursuit of gain (...), divided among themselves in interest and sentiment, they seem afraid of everything.'* The Dutchman as timid rabbit rather than model democrat.

In the same way as Adams expected too much of *'the greatest curiosity in the world'*, so perhaps foreign observers now expect too much of the 'guide-land'.

But quite often the average Dutchman too goes around with an exaggerated image of himself and so turns into a whining drama queen as soon as something happens to disturb his *'gemoedelijkheid'*, that stubborn cliché for Dutch conviviality, freedom and cheerfulness. Alexander Linklater points to Geert Mak's *Doomed to be Vulnerable* (Gedoemd tot kwetsbaarheid): *'The popular left-wing historian (...) views the response as a gross overreaction to a one-off event'.* The stiff Northerner responding like a passionate Southerner: one man is killed and everyone promptly loses his head. Mak warns the Netherlands that this national navel-gazing has to stop: *'Those who want to transform the Netherlands into a cultural fortress are reducing the complex time in which we live to one great domestic fantasy of terror.'* Idealism turns into cynicism, and tolerance is reduced to indifference and indecision. But where Mak sees the Netherlands as a small, rather blinkered land incapable of enduring the worldwide reality of our globalised society, in Linklater's view the problems are no fantasies. In a kind of inverted mental exercise he even notes: *'In many ways, the Netherlands is a crucible case within Europe, because the issues surrounding immigration are so stark'.* Not unlike Jessica Stern, the American expert on terrorism, who regards the Netherlands as *'a sort of laboratory where you can study how such fears develop'.* And so the Netherlands, with a twist, has again, in a very small way, become something of a guide-land for other countries.

Jan Willem Schulte Nordholt *et al.*, *John Adams in Holland 1780-2005*. Amsterdam: John Adams Institute / Cossee, 2005. 126 pp. ISBN 90-5936-0710.

Geert Mak, *Gedoemd tot kwetsbaarheid*. Amsterdam: Atlas, 2004. 95 pp. ISBN 90-450-1382-7.

So the Netherlands may or may not be a guide-land, but it's still very much the question whether Belgium is really a land at all (though Belgium is allowed to submit films for the Academy Awards). 'Is there a Belgium' is the title of a piece by Tony Judt that originaly appeared in *The New York Review of Books* in 1999. This *'brief initiation to Belgian life and to this country's history'* now also opens the volume *How Can One NOT Be Interested in Belgian History*, which is the tangible result of the symposium *Belgium Revealed* held in April 2005 at Trinity College, Dublin.

Judd's piece raised a little dust at the time, but let us summarise it briefly here anyway. For Judd the country whose existence he is questioning is more than a place where waffles, pralines and chips grow on the trees and the gutters run with beer. He talks among other things about the scandals (Marc Dutroux and a great many others), the Belgian's uncertainty about his national identity, the rapid progress of federalisation, the penchant for nepotism and the country's bad reputation in the international press. But it is the language problem and the resultant complex and confusing political structure that he is most concerned with. According to Judd Belgium is not one or two nations, but *'an uneven quilt of overlapping and duplicating authorities'.* A country whose national frontiers are purely formal, but which has very real internal frontiers. A country where corruption and white-collar crime are rampant (here Judd quotes Baudelaire: '*La Belgique est sans vie, mais non sans corruption*'). A country held together only by a funny king and a national debt. And look at this: as early as 1999 Judd was writing something about Belgium that is remarkably similar to what Mak is now saying about the Netherlands. For Judd sees Belgium as '*the first advanced country truly at the mercy of globalisation in all its forms*'. In an age in which employment, public safety and the cultural heart of nations are exposed to previously unheard-of pressure from outside, Judd sees salvation only in governments which are able to give their populations a sense of cohesion and a common interest, without threatening personal and political freedom in the process. And that makes Belgium important, and not only to the Belgians themselves: '*Far from being a model, it may be a warning: after the twentieth century we all know that you can have too much state. But Belgium may also be a useful reminder that you can have too little*'. A sort of inverse guide-land, then.

The same volume also contains, among others, articles about the First World War, when in foreign eyes Belgium was still a brave little fighter (Sophie de Schaepdrijver's 'Champion or Stillbirth? The Symbolic Uses of Belgium in the Great War') and about Brussels as a possible capital of a future multilingual, open and humane Europe (and not of the European Union, as Geert van Istendael stresses in 'In Brussels the Word Language Has No Singular'). In 'Belgium's Culture: A Dutchman's View' Benno Barnard argues for a Belgium above and beyond Flanders: '*Modern Flemish nationalism, nagging for a Flemish army and Flemish stamps, seems to be a good way to ruin a nice country.*'

The book's final contributor is Marc Reynebeau; in 'Belgian Quixotry: Historiography and Society in the Quest for Consensus', for the benefit of foreign readers he seeks out a number of topics which have been wilfully disregarded in Belgian historiography – topics such as colonisation in Central Africa and collaboration in World War II. It is noticeable that the common factor in all these issues is the royal family.

And Belgium is above all a divided country which buries its fault-lines under a thin layer of consensus so as to achieve an atmosphere of serenity.

In this context Reynebeau also writes about the *Made in Belgium* exhibition organised as part of the '175-25' celebrations in 2005. He describes it as a '*feel-good fancy-fair*', a colourful display of all the splendid, delightful and wonderful things that Birthday-land Belgium has contributed to this world of ours, from bright little Tintin via strong steel to delicious chocolate. But however well and professionally the exhibition was put together, it is and remains a travesty of modern critical historiography. It is no more than an assemblage of myths, blatant lies and propaganda. For anything else might have put a dampener on the festivities.

Just like the other great birthday exhibition (*Visionary Belgium*), *Made in Belgium* portrays the country as a dream. Here the dream is a populist fantasy-history, in *Visionary Belgium* a form of artistic utopia. Reynebeau calls it an anarchistic approach to history. It is indeed '*petit-bourgeois anarchism, in which mockery is more important than the urge for fundamental change*', but perhaps it is precisely that attitude that helps to ensure Belgium's (continued) existence?

Benno Barnard *et al.*, *How Can One NOT Be Interested in Belgian History. War, Language and Consensus in Belgium since 1830.* Ghent/Dublin: Academia Press/Trinity College, 2005. 151 pp. ISBN 90-382-0816-2.

Be that as it may, Brussels resident Richard Hill still finds Belgium well worth the trouble, for following his well-known *We Europeans* he has now published *The Art of Being Belgian*. Hill is very fond of his host country. He thinks that history has already dealt Belgium enough shrewd blows, and the often chilly and sometimes downright hostile attitude to the country of the foreign press is unjust. Like some gallant knight in the service of Belgitude Hill takes up his sword in defence of the scorned and ignored Belgians. Lifestyles and value-systems, Flemings and Walloons, qualities and faults: all have their place in this book. According to its press-release it is a documented and sympathetic account of an often underrated, but always essential part of the patchwork quilt that is Europe.

We see Hill move to Belgium and wonder at the surrealism he encounters everywhere, like the notice *'No admittance for children under 14'* in a Brussels maternity clinic. People drink beer and eat chips. He cites, and refutes, ten mocking reasons to be Belgian (no.1: *'You get to speak three languages, but none of them intelligibly'* and no.9: *'All your famous countrymen are imaginary'*). And of course Hill devotes a separate chapter to *'what others know about Belgium and the Belgians'*. The prime example here comes from Carolyn Mordecai's *Wedding, Dating and Love Customs of Cultures Worldwide* (1999): *'Belgium, a country with close traditional family ties, has a high Catholic population. According to Christian religious beliefs, women are expected to be virgins and their marriages are monogamous. Although Belgium is a highly modern country with international businesses, cars are not used for dating as much as in most industrialised countries. Single people can still walk down cobblestone streets to cafés and shops where they can easily become acquainted with members of the opposite sex. Being picked up at one these spots is normal and is not considered in bad taste. Otherwise, families and close friends introduce couples.'* Virgins, cobblestones and no heavy petting on the back seat. Truly, Belgium can become a guide-land for romantic souls.

Richard Hill, *The Art of Being Belgian*. Brussels: Europublications, 2005. 208 pp. ISBN 90-744-7-4001-50.

Any foreigner who is moving to the Netherlands and wants to learn something about the society in which he will be living before he gets there will find himself amply catered for in the *Holland Handbook*. The 2005-2006 edition advertises itself as *'the indispensable reference book for the expatriate'*. And that probably makes sense, for it really does cover all aspects of living and working in the Netherlands: housing,

schools, health care, insurance, childcare, and so on... The reader can also find information on Dutch habits and customs, the language, everyday life and tips on museums and events. Each chapter is neatly rounded off with an overview of relevant websites and telephone numbers.

Of course in this case the end justifies the means and the intention is certainly not to welcome the reader to Bob Barr's *'land of Josef Mengele'*. And so we read: *'If you take a stroll after sunset, you get a chance to admire family life, Dutch style. Grandma and Grandpa are sitting behind a steaming cup of coffee, savoring their evening ration of one cookie.'* or again: *'Pets have a position in Dutch households that is very similar to that of children. Some are served the best cut of the rarest beef, others are given the best chair, with the best view of the TV.'*

So here again at last is the Netherlands of uncurtained windows, of freedom and equality. The place where the smell of boiled cabbage and broadmindedness go together in a quite unique way. The open Netherlands where for example there was room for Spinoza's radical ideas. Though we have to take that with a pinch of salt, for when he labelled the ancient Torah texts 'inventions of the human imagination', within a couple of years he was expelled from Amsterdam's Sephardic community.

The young Macedonian writer Goce Smilevski brings the hologram of Dutch tolerance to life in his novel *Conversations with Spinoza*. Baruch Spinoza was a man of (usually too superficially understood) ideas, but he has left us few personal details. So here Smilevski has the man of the inner life converse with the external, real facts of his life and time: not only his philosophical contrivances, but also his sultry feelings for his very youthful Latin teacher Clara Maria van den Enden and later for his disciple Johannes Caesarius. So out of this 'conversation' grows a complex portrait of the life of an idea and of a man of flesh and blood who tries to live in accordance with that idea.

Another great advocate of tolerance is Pierre Bayle, dead for exactly 300 years in 2006. In 1681 this French Huguenot found himself forced into exile. He accepted a relatively modest position at a Rotterdam school and founded the Netherlands' first popular-scholarly journal, *Les nouvelles de la république des lettres* (1684-1687). His greatest work is considered to be the *Dictionnaire historique et critique* (1697), an early example of radical enlightened thought. It goes without saying, then, that the Dutch foundation named after him aims to foster and stimulate *'tolerance, critical sense and broadmindedness'*. The foundation seeks not only to draw attention to the life and work of the man himself, but also, through the Pierre Bayle Prizes for cultural criticism and art criticism and the Pierre Bayle Lecture (past speakers include Michael Ignatieff and Jonathan Israel) to promote cultural-philosphical reflection and stimulate the intellectual climate in the Netherlands.

Holland Handbook 2005-2006. The Hague: Xpat Media, 2005. 255 pp. ISBN 90-5594-406-8.

Goce Smilovski, *Conversation with Spinoza: A Cobweb Novel.* Evanston, IL: Northwestern University Press, 2006. 112 pp. ISBN 0-810123574.

Pierre Bayle Foundation: www.pierrebayle.nl

'This is a very free society, a free country,' says the Spaniard Mercelo Bendahan in *Holland Handbook*. 'People trust in their own opinion here, they want to be themselves, master of their own destiny'. Possibly that same stubborn self-reliance also lies at the root of the Dutch entrepreneurial spirit. And there the Dutch East India Company (Vereenigde Oostindische Compagnie, VOC) provides an outstanding example of the Dutchman as trader. In the seventeenth and eighteenth century this private organisation was granted a monopoly on trade with Asia by the Dutch government. The VOC thus became the world's first true multinational and the first company to issue shares.

On 8 January 1740 the VOC ship *Rooswijk* put to sea. It didn't get far. Just one day into its voyage to Batavia the *Rooswijk* sank with all hands on the Goodwin Sands off the south-east coast of England. A few days later English fishermen found a chest containing letters that came from the ship. After that: nothing. Until 2004, when the wreck was discovered by chance by a carpenter and an amateur diver. Between May and September 2005 part of the vessel's cargo was recovered by a British professional salvage expert. Silver ingots, coins, sabres, cannon, muskets and items in everyday use (including cooking utensils, a candle-snuffer, a pair of spectacles and a mustard-pot with the spoon still in it) were brought ashore.

But the greatest VOC find of the past 25 years was kept secret for a long time to protect it from illegal treasure-hunters. And there's the rub. On board a frigate in early December 2005 the Dutch Secretary of State for Finance officially took possession of the silver bullion. One quarter of the value of the cargo goes to the Dutch state, the rest to the salvager. But many Dutch archeologists are questioning the archeological necessity of excavating the ship in this way. They are unhappy with the contract agreed between Finance Ministry and a commercial salvage company. Since not one Dutch underwater archeologist was involved in the recovery operation, they fear that an important piece of Dutch maritime heritage will be lost. As the archeologists see it, the contract is *'actually a kind of licence to plunder a ship'*.

Treaty of Waitangi
(reproduction of 1939)

Perhaps not so different from the letters of marque which the English government issued to shipowners in times of war, and which made privateering a legitimate form of warfare at sea. These letters of marque specified precisely which enemy could be boarded, in what area and within what period. And once that enemy ship had been captured, the privateer was free to sell ship and cargo in his home port. In this way a great many Dutch ships fell into British hands. And this recently led to a discovery of the greatest importance for Dutch overseas and maritime history and the history of attitudes and ideas. In the National Archives in London more than 38,000 letters were found, dating from between 1650 and 1815. Letters written from Holland to places overseas and vice versa which were never delivered because the ships carrying them had been taken by privateers. At the behest of the Royal Library in The Hague a start has now been made on cataloguing this treasure trove and laying bare its secrets. Many of the letters were written by ordinary people who set down their everyday worries and hopes in much the same language as they spoke for their friends, lovers and kinfolk. But well-known names crop up too, such as the eighteenth-century writers Betje Wolff and Aagje Deken who wish an adventurous cousin fortitude in his *difficult journeys and most grievous disappointments*. But things aren't perfect at home either, for *we are getting old and ailing*.

www.kb.nl/sailingletters

Letters need stamps, and the Fleming Patrick Maselis has produced a fascinating book on the subject. In *From the Azores to the South Pole* (Van de Azoren tot de Zuidpool) this manager and impassioned philatelist uses documents and letters to tell the story of every Belgian colony in the world. Here philately is used as a source for historiography. In his introduction the author makes a heartfelt plea for 'post-history', by which he means not what happens *after* history, but the study of communication. And up until 1850, according to Maselis, that communication was limited to the post.

Maselis takes 'colony' in a very broad sense. It is not simply an overseas territory which is politically completely dependent another country. So-called 'settlements' too are colonies: *A group of compatriots who settle somewhere outside the territory of their own nation for purposes of trade, or to farm uncultivated land.* And closely connected with this is the third meaning of the word: the collective term for all foreigners of the same origin in a city or country.

So this book neither begins nor ends with 'The Congo'. *Our colonial history begins on 1 January 1451,* says Maselis. He is talking about the Azores. *But actually until 1700 people usually spoke of the Flemish islands, not the Azores. After all, the islands had been*

315

colonised by Flemings. It all started in Burgundian times in Bruges, when Isabella of Portugal married Philip the Good. Her brother, Henry the Navigator, asked whether she couldn't find some colonists to populate the Azores.' And so it goes on, from Nova Belgica (the forerunner of New York was not a Dutch but a Belgian colony) to Ruanda-Urundi and many more besides. Many of the stories are remarkable, like that of the Belgian baron Charles Philippe Hippolyte de Thierry. This megalomaniac aristocrat, who regarded himself as at one and the same time a Frenchman, a Belgian and a Dutchman, went to study in Cambridge in 1820. There he met a couple of Maori chiefs and bought from them 16,000 hectares of land near Hokianga, with the explicit intention of founding the independent state of Thierryan Territory there. He even checked with the British Colonial Minister and was told that Great Britain made no claim to the area. So his claim of sovereignty was not in danger. Later, though, the British did become rather more nervous and less well-intentioned when he maintained that all New Zealand belonged to him and had himself proclaimed everywhere as king of Thierryan Territory. So they bought the land back from the Maoris behind the baron's back, which they were able to do because the Treaty of Waitangi rendered all previous contracts invalid.

And the last Belgian 'colony'? That is Villaguay in Northern Argentina. A group of Flemings were granted free farmland in the area at the end of the nineteenth century; they earned a lot of money there and organised their own education and religious life. Their descendants still have their own postcode, 3244-Colonia Belga, and Belgian nationality. Though if the Argentine economy continues to perform so poorly many of them are seriously considering emigrating to ... Belgium.

Patrick Maselis, *Van de Azoren tot de Zuidpool*. Roeselare: Uitgeverij Roularta, 2005. 419 pp. ISBN 90-5466-951-9.

In March 1606 the *Duyfken*, a small ship belonging to the Dutch East India Company was ordered to ex-plore the unknown waters south of New Guinea and happened upon a hitherto unknown land. The continent that Captain Willem Jansz had unintentionally discovered was Australia. So 2006 is the 400th anniversary of the first Dutch contact with Australia, and this year numerous events both in Australia and in the Netherlands will celebrate these four centuries of bilateral relations.

Dutch Dare is a contemporary cultural programme which supports Dutch cultural activities taking place in 2006 in connection with existing festivals and institutions in Australia. Dutch artists wil take part in the Sydney Biennale, the ICP orchestra will play at the Wangaratta Festival of Jazz and Dutch writers will take the stage at the Age Melbourne Writers' Festival.

In addition there will be exhibitions of all kinds in both countries. For example, in Zoetermeer's Municipal Museum there is the exhibition *Zoetermeer Down Under* on 'living in two worlds'. The starting-point is Australia's Stolen Generations, the eight generations of Aborigines who between 1870 and 1974 were taken from their families as children and placed with white families or in state boarding schools. The exhibition also focuses on Newcomers in Zoetermeer and on local people who emigrated to Australia between 1950 and 1960. The exhibition *First Sight: the Dutch Mapping of Australia* in the State Library of New South Wales (Sydney) deals with the mapping of the Australian north, west and south coasts and Tasmania by the Dutch in the seventeenth century. And *Allies in Adversity* (Australian War Memorial, Canberra) spotlights the contribution of the Dutch armed forces to the defence of Australia in the Second World War.

www.nederland-australie2006.nl
www.sica.nl

'Infiltrating' existing festivals and institutions is a tactic that is being used more and more to promote Dutch-language culture abroad. In early 2006 the Foundation for the Production and Translation of

Dutch Literature and the Flemish Literary Fund collaborated with, among others, the South Bank Centre and the Poetry Society to put Dutch authors on the platform alongside those of other nationalities (there was, for instance, the *Stop the Clock* festival about writers and the perception of time, with a.o. Miriam Van hee, Cees Nooteboom and Harry Mulisch). And in 2007 it will be New York's turn. Efforts will be made to programme Flemish and Dutch literature in as many events as possible in that city.

2005 saw the first award of the Brockway Prize, a new biennial prize for translators of poetry from Dutch set up by the same Foundation for the Production and Translation of Dutch Literature. The prize money comes from the bequest of the poet and translator James Brockway (1916-2000), whose translator's hand has now given us *From Now On* (collected translations of work by the Flemish poet Marc Tritsmans) and *What Water Left Behind* (poems by Rutger Kopland, half of them translated by Brockway), both published in 2005.

Francis R. Jones received the first Brockway Prize for his whole oeuvre as a translator from Dutch. This expert in translation from Newcastle translates poetry from various European countries, has already received a number of translation prizes, and as regards Dutch poetry his *Against the Forgetting*, a selection from the work of Hans Faverey, made him a strong contender for the prize. Jones also translated some of the poems in *The Last to Leave*, a recently published volume of selected work by the Flemish poet Dirk van Bastelaere.

And those who want to know which literary works have been translated from Dutch are well catered for by the Foundation for the Production and Translation of Dutch Literature. On www.nlpvf.nl/translations you can search through some 9,700 translations since 1990. Details are kept of fiction, literary non-fiction, poetry and children's and young people's literature written in Dutch by authors from the Netherlands, Frisland, Flanders and Suriname. Publications still in preparation are also included in the record. The Foundation's aim is completeness: it is not only translations subsidised by itself that are

mentioned, it also gives details of translations of Dutch literature published or about to be published which it receives from foreign and Dutch publishers, agents, translators and authors. And also from the Flemish Literary Fund, for the Flemish fund keeps its Duch colleague informed about the translations it subsidises. And in this way the Bibliography of Dutch-Language Books in Translation (Royal Library, The Hague), which is no longer able to provide the bibliographic list which appeared in this yearbook in the past, has found a worthy successor.

Marc Tritsmans, *From Now On* (tr. James Brockway). Tielt: Lannoo Publishers, 2005. 55 pp. ISBN 90-209-6384-8.

Rutger Kopland,*What Water Left Behind (*tr. James Brockway & Willem Groenewegen). Waxwing Books. ISBN 0-9549771-3.

Dirk van Bastelaere, *The Last to Leave* (tr. John Irons, Francis R. Jones & Willem Groenewegen. Exeter: Shearsman Books, 2005. 118 pp. ISBN 0-907562-70-1.

www.nlpvf.nl

www.fondsvoordeletteren.be

An elegantly-written and well-composed survey of recent Dutch literature can be found in Kris Steyaert's contribution to *The Year's Work in Modern Language Studies* (ed. Stephen Parkinson. London: Maney Publishing, 2006; pp. 735-758).

Filip Matthijs
Translated by Tanis Guest

Contributors

Hans Aarsman
Photographer
c/o Ons Erfdeel vzw
Murissonstraat 260,
8930 Rekkem, Belgium

Dirk van Assche
Deputy editor
'Ons Erfdeel vzw'
Murissonstraat 260,
8930 Rekkem, Belgium

Klaas van Berkel
Professor of the History of
Natural Sciences
(University of Groningen)
Oude Kijk in 't Jatstr 26,
9712 EK Groningen,
The Netherlands

Derek Blyth
Journalist
Lange Haagstraat 18,
1050 Brussels,
Belgium

Willem Breedveld
Journalist *Trouw*/ Lecturer
in Mass Communication and
Politics (University of Leiden)
Waardsedijk 102,
3421 NH Oudewater,
The Netherlands

Peter de Bruijn
Staff member of the
Huygens Institute
P.O. Box 90754,
2509 LT The Hague,
The Netherlands

Raf de Bruyn
Staff member of
Toerisme Vlaanderen
Grasmarkt 63,
1000 Brussels, Belgium

Piet Chielens
Coordinator of the
In Flanders Fields
Museum
Grote Markt 34,
8900 Ypres, Belgium

Hans Cools
Staff member of the
Netherlands Institute in Rome
Via Omero 10/12,
00197 Rome, Italy

Mark Delaere
Professor of Musicology
(Catholic University of
Leuven)
Sint-Annastraat 30,
3050 Oud-Heverlee,
Belgium

Dirk van Delft
Science editor *NRC Handelsblad*
P.O. Box 8987,
3009 TH Rotterdam,
The Netherlands

Luc Devoldere
Chief Editor
'Ons Erfdeel vzw'
Murissonstraat 260,
8930 Rekkem, Belgium

Carl Devos
Professor of
Political Sciences
(University of Ghent)
Universiteitstraat 8,
9000 Ghent, Belgium

Louis van Dievel
Journalist/Critic
Heidestatiestraat 25,
2920 Kalmthout, Belgium

Elsbeth Etty
Editor *NRC Handelsblad*
Prinsengracht 4,
1015 DV Amsterdam,
The Netherlands

Michiel van Groesen
Research Assistant
Centre for Golden Age Studies
University of Amsterdam
Spuistraat 134,
1012 VB Amsterdam,
The Netherlands

Frank Hellemans
Lecturer in Communication
History
(Katholieke Hogeschool
Mechelen)/
Literary critic (*Knack Magazine*)
Keldermansvest 23,
2800 Mechelen, Belgium

Erwin Joos
Curator of the
Van Mieghem Museum
Beatrijslaan 8,
2050 Antwerp, Belgium

Peter Karstkarel
Writer/Journalist
Gysbert Japickxstraat 9,
8933 AZ Leeuwarden,
The Netherlands

Koen van Kerrebroeck
Theatre critic
Scheldestraat 55,
9040 Ghent, Belgium

Anton Korteweg
Director of the Netherlands
Literature Museum
(The Hague)/Poet
Wasstraat 23,
2313 JG Leiden,
The Netherlands

Filip Luyckx
Art critic
Estafetteweg 8,
9000 Ghent, Belgium

Filip Matthijs
Editorial secretary *The Low
Countries*
Murissonstraat 260,
8930 Rekkem, Belgium

Patrick T. Murphy
Director of the
Royal Hibernian Academy
15 Ely Place, Dublin 2, Ireland

Lutgard Mutsaers
Lecturer in popular music
studies/Researcher(Utrecht
University)
Frederikastraat 16,
3572 CS Utrecht,
The Netherlands

Vic Nachtergaele
Emeritus Professor
of French Literature (KULAK)
Karel van Manderstraat 1,
8510 Marke, Belgium

Frits van Oostrom
Professor of Dutch Medieval
Literature (University of
Utrecht)
Muntstraat 2a, 3512 EV Utrecht,
The Netherlands

Ewald Pironet

Journalist *FET*

Sint-Hubertusdreef 11,

3250 Wakkerzeel,

Belgium

Frank van der Ploeg

Art historian / editor *kM*

Weeshuisland 54,

1541 MD Koog aan de Zaan,

The Netherlands

Annette Portegies

Publisher

Em. Querido's Uitgeverij B.V.

Singel 262, 1016 AC Amsterdam,

The Netherlands

Jellichje Reijnders

Art critic / Curator

Westerdoksdijk 48 I,

1013 AE Amsterdam,

The Netherlands

Marieke van Rooy

Art critic

Sandvikweg 2D,

1013 BA Amsterdam,

The Netherlands

Reinier Salverda

Professor of Dutch Language

and Literature

(University College London)

UCL Dept.of Dutch, Room 324

Foster Court, Gower Street,

London WC1E 6BT,

United Kingdom

Gary Schwartz

Art historian

P.O. Box 162,

3600 AD Maarssen,

The Netherlands

Manfred Sellink

Curator-in-Chief

Municipal Museums of Bruges

Dijver 12,

8000 Bruges, Belgium

Johan de Smet

Staff member of

The Royal Museum

of Fine Arts (Ghent)

Zeswegenstraat 46

8790 Waregem,

Belgium

Bart van der Straeten

Editorial secretary *Ons Erfdeel*

Murissonstraat 260,

8930 Rekkem,

Belgium

Hans Vanacker

Editorial secretary *Septentrion*

Murissonstraat 260,

8930 Rekkem, Belgium

Ingeborg Walinga

Art critic

Bernoulliplein 24 A,

9714 BV Groningen,

The Netherlands

Emile Wennekes

Professor of Dutch music

after 1600

(University of Utrecht)

Smeesteeg 4,

8081 EN Elburg,

The Netherlands

Rudi Wester

Director Institut Néerlandais

121 rue de Lille,

75007 Paris,

France

Gerard van Westerloo

Journalist

Zacharias Jansestraat 39-b,

1097 CK Amsterdam,

The Netherlands

Veerle Windels

Fashion critic

Westhoekstraat 16,

8700 Aarsele,

Belgium

Ad Zuiderent

Professor of Dutch Literature

Free University of Amsterdam

Zacharias Jansestraat 52 hs,

1097 CN Amsterdam,

The Netherlands

Translators

Frans Andersson

Gregory Ball

A.J. Barnouw

Jethro Bithell

David Colmer

Sheila M. Dale

Lindsay Edwards

Chris Emery

Nancy Forest-Flier

Sam Garrett

Tanis Guest

James S Holmes

John Irons

Joy R. Kearney

Yvette Mead

Elizabeth Mollison

Alison Mouthaan-Gwillim

Julian Ross

Alma Strettell

Paul Vincent

Laura Watkinson

ADVISOR ON ENGLISH USAGE

Tanis Guest (UK)

As well as the yearbook The Low Countries,
the Flemish Netherlands Association 'Ons Erfdeel vzw'
publishes a number of books covering various aspects of the culture of
Flanders and the Netherlands.

Wim Daniëls
Talking Dutch.
Illustrated; 80 pp.

J.A. Kossmann-Putto &
E.H. Kossmann
The Low Countries.
History of the Northern
and Southern Netherlands.
Illustrated; 64 pp.

Hugo Brems &
Ad Zuiderent
Contemporary Poetry of
the Low Countries.
With 52 translated poems;
112 pp.

Jaap Goedegebuure &
Anne Marie Musschoot
Contemporary Fiction of
the Low Countries.
Illustrated and with
translated extracts from
15 novels; 128 pp.

NEW

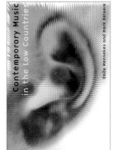

Hans Ibelings &
Francis Strauven
Contemporary Architects
of the Low Countries.
Illustrated; 128 pp.

Isabella Lanz &
Katie Verstockt,
Contemporary Dance
in the Low Countries.
Illustrated; 128 pp.

Mark Delaere &
Emile Wennekes,
Contemporary Music in
the Low Countries.
Illustrated; 128 pp.
(September 2006)

Between 1993 and 2005
the first thirteen issues
of the yearbook *The Low*
Countries were published.